Saving the Soil

Saving the Soil

The New American Farmer

Jerry Mader

Tolt River Press
Carnation,
Washington

Tolt River Press
PO Box 1075
Carnation, Washington 98014

Copyright © 2011 by Jerry Mader
All rights reserved
Printed in China
First edition 2012
Photographs copyright © 2009 by Jerry Mader
All rights reserved
Library of Congress Control Number: 2011921098
ISBN 978-0-9820246-1-4

This book was designed and assembled by Jerry Mader
All photographs are by Jerry Mader
Maps are from King County IMAP
Author photographs by David Casey (author on tractor)
and an unidentified worker at The Root Connection
Farm (author standing in field)

"Among School Children", W.B. Yeats, reprinted with the permission of Scribner, a Division of Simon & Schuster, Inc., from THE COLLECTED WORKS OF W.B. YEATS, VOLUME I, THE POEMS, REVISED by W.B. Yeats, edited by Richard J. Finneran. Copyright © 1928 by the Macmillan Company, renewed 1956 by George Yeats. All rights reserved.
"NOX" (excerpt of 8 lines), by Anne Carson © 2009 by Anne Carson. Reprinted by permission of New Directions Publishing Corp.
"Note" (excerpt of 6 lines), from COLLECTED POEMS, copyright © 1952 by Dylan Thomas. Reprinted by permission of New Directions Publishing Corp.
"The Woman Speaks" (excerpt of 14 lines), by Dylan Thomas from THE POEMS OF DYLAN THOMAS, copyright © 1953 by Dylan Thomas. Reprinted by permission of New Directions Publishing Corp.
I–SIX NONLECTURES by E. E. Cummings.Copyright 1953, © 1981 by the Trustees for the E.E. Cummings Trust. Used by permission of Liveright Publishing Corporation.
"O sweet spontaneous", copyright 1923, 1951, © 1991 by the Trustees for the E. E. Cummings Trust. Copyright © by George James Firmage, from COMPLETE POEMS: 1904–1962 by E. E. Cummings, edited by George J. Firmage. Used by permission of Liveright Publishing Corporation.
THE UNSETTLING OF AMERICA by Wendell Berry, copyright © 1977 by Wendell Berry. Excerpts reprinted by permission of Sierra Club Books.
FOOD REBELLIONS, by Holt-Gimenez and Patel, copyright © Food First Books, Oakland, CA, 2009. Excerpts used by permission of Food First Books.
DIRT: THE EROSION OF CIVILIZATIONS, copyright © 2007 by David R. Montgomery. Excerpts reprinted by permission of University of California Press.

for Stephanie, who promised to love me even more if I made this book.....

Acknowledgements

There are many people to thank and I will no doubt leave some out. Of course, I have undying gratitude to each of the farmers who generously gave of their time and patience as I pestered them with my camera and audio recorder through the growing season of 2009 and the winter of 2010. Their candor and clarity of thought made this project a delight for me. Thanks to all the folks at King County 4Culture Heritage, particularly Jim Kelly, executive director, and Eric Taylor, director of Heritage Special Projects. 4Culture Heritage not only helped financially with this project but continues to provide support for several Heritage organizations and many independent historians in King County. 4Culture Heritage has been the instrumental force in preserving the rich and varied history of the area and has ensured that its legacy will be maintained. Special thanks must go to my transcriptionist, Barbara (Barb) Jardee of Jardee Transcription, Tucson, Arizona for her professionalism and speed of delivery. Her work on this project as well as the previous one, "Carnation Verbatim," made everything happen without a hitch. Profound thanks to Andie Metzger, my proof reader/copy editor, who heroically dispatched all the typos, unintelligible fragments and oddities from this text. She is a master of her craft. Finally, my deepest gratitude to Roger Thorson, owner, Carnation Tree Farm, whose friendship and support for this work have made all the difference.

Mea Culpa

When I began this work in April, 2009, I had no idea what I was getting into. I could not have imagined the richness and the scope of what was happening to agriculture in the Valley or Western Washington generally. Nor could I have anticipated the amount of work involved in any attempt to represent all the farms in the Snoqualmie Valley alone. Initially, choosing which farms to document and which to exclude was a nightmare since each has so much to offer and each farmer has a unique story to tell. The present volume is absent many but in the interest of "getting the word out" the several exclusions were unavoidable and those included do not reflect any particular hierarchy. Rather, they were chosen to present as broad a spectrum as possible; large/small, new/old, and diversity of operation. I feel no small measure of guilt over these omissions since I've come to know most all of them personally and admire their efforts. Therefore, my sincere apologies to Engustment Farm, Fall City Farm, Farm Girl Collective, Full Circle Farms, Marigold and Mint, Misty Mountain Honey, Dog Mountain Farm, Ms. Cindy's Damn Fine Poultry, River Valley Cheese, Rocky Prairie Herb Garden, Soil to Seed Farm, Summer Run Farm, Nature's Last Stand Farm, and Clean Greens Farm. All the farms can be contacted through the Sno-Valley Tilth, Carnation, Washington and are more than pleased to have visitors (see the resources section). Finally my apologies to the volunteer at The Root Connection Farm who took the picture of me used in this book; somehow I neglected to get your name.

Contents

Preface—To The Reader..9
Of Time and The River—A Brief Snoqualmie Watershed History 12
Sunrise in an Eden of Gardens..17

Part One—Farmers

The Root Connection Farm..23
    Claire Thomas...25
Jubilee Farm...37
    Erick Haakensen..39
    Wendy Haakensen...53
Local Roots Farm..63
    Siri Erickson-Brown...65
    Jason Salvo...75
    Dan Beyers..83
Changing Seasons Farm..91
    Laura Casey..93
    David Casey..103
Two Sisters Dairy..113
    Lena Magnochi..115
    George Magnochi..123
Game Haven Farm..133
    Susan Schmoll...135
Growing Things Farm..143
    Michaele Blakely...145
Oxbow Farm...153
    Luke Woodward..155
    Adam McCurdy...167
    Sarah Cassidy...179
Blue Dog Farm..187
    Scott Turner..189
    Amy Turner...201

Part Two—Workers

Abe Stebbing, Oxbow Farm..214
Emma Frantz, Growing Things Farm...220
Everett Patterson, Local Roots Farm...224
Luke Yodel, Growing Things Farm..228
Rand Rasheed, Local Roots Farm...234
Shauna Frantz, Growing Things Farm...238

Thomas Arnold, Local Roots Farm..242
Ryan Lichtenegger, Jubilee Farm...248

Part Three—Tendrils

Heidi Bohan, Sno-Valley Tilth, Carnation Farmers' Market...257
William Aal, Community Alliance for Global Justice...267
Heather Day, Director, Community Alliance for Global Justice.......................................275
Barry Lia, Sustainable Agriculture Advocacy, Biodynamics..281
Don Stuart, PNW Director, American Farmland Trust...291
Douglas Hanson, Natl. Sales Manager, Organic Prairie..303
Judy Neldham, Owner, Grange Café, Duvall...312
David Montgomery, Professor, Geomorphology, University of Washington........................321

Epilogue
Somewhere Northeast of Eden...330

Maps...344
Bibliography...347
Resources..348
Postscript/Addendum...350

To the Reader:

This is a book about farmers. It is also a book about food. Specifically, it is a book about the people who grow your food; my food—our food. And, though it seems absurdly self-evident, it is a book about the fact that people, human beings like you and me, grow food for you and me and our communities. It is also about the equally absurd reminder that food is indeed "grown", it comes from somewhere other than the supermarket and is the product of personal effort and commitment by people who choose to be farmers in a world where they could choose to be almost anything else.

The text that follows is a set of oral histories; life stories of people who, through a variety of experiences, made their way to the Snoqualmie Valley of Western Washington and became farmers. One, however, Claire Thomas, has her farm in the Sammamish Valley but is included here because she is to many of these 'New Farmers' a 'Maven' in the recent history of organic farming in Western Washington.

As you will learn, these sixteen individuals are not among our usual conceptions of what a "farmer" is. Although each is a unique individual, they all share a common vocation. Most of them have turned away from corporate careers to grow vegetables using organic, soil-sustaining practices to provide healthy food for their local King County community. They are uncommon in their farming vocation because most do not have farming in their family history; indeed, most have Master's degrees in fields other than agriculture. And, as farmers, most grow food on no more than fourteen acres of land and therefore demonstrate the viability of the small organic farm as a practical alternative to current "Factory Farm" large scale agribusiness. Through their stories you will learn how each has confronted and continues to respond to the array of environmental and socio-economic crises we all face on planet Earth, not the least being our shrinking global food and soil resources. Finally, in contrast to the spate of books about the disasters humans have wreaked upon the world and the perils of our means of food production and consumption, these sixteen farmers offer you, as much as is possible in a book, the other side of human nature; the one that is committed to living in ways that regenerate the environment, the soil and the communities which sustain us all.

Coupled to the farmer narratives are the stories of eight of their workers. Each of them is either fresh out of college or about to matriculate. Each of them is at the first stage of their personal odyssey, in search of a path to a life worth living. Each of them, to some degree, has come to farming with the hope that it will provide a way to a life free of what they regard as the typical corporate prison most college graduates are offered. Each of them presents an intimate look into the consciousness of a growing segment of American youth.

Extending out from these two groups is a third set of narratives. These are from individuals in the wider community of King County, Washington who have devoted their lives and careers to professions connected to food production, distribution, land and water resources, food consumption, political action and soil management organizations. As with the others, these nine individuals present their personal histories and how it was each individually came to be a biologist-biodynamic farming advocate, a restaurateur, a sales representative for an organic food co-op, a Farmer's Market Manager, the director of a land trust organization, a leader in a political action group promoting food justice and a geomorphologist.

My contribution to the oral history theme appears throughout in the form of selected entries from my "Farm Journal" which I kept over the more than a year of work documenting the daily activities of these farmers. It is an account of my own journey into a world I'd scarcely known yet was easily accessible within a 15-mile radius of my home in Carnation, Washington. I've included the journal because it demonstrates (documentary work not withstanding) that it is possible for us—including you—to seek and find the origins of the food you eat and enter the web of connections binding individuals and their environment to each other. More personally, the journal is a record of my discoveries and transformations as my views about our status and future as citizens of the earth were challenged and reframed daily as each of these farmers opened themselves to me.

As journal entries, the excerpts are unedited and dated, thereby offering a certain spontaneity and chronology of response within the license usually extended to journal writing. And, as further coupling, I have included the date each interview was recorded to amplify the spontaneity of these as well; e.g. this is how this person thought on this particular day in this particular month and year. Although I gave each person a set of questions to consider, these were not necessarily followed in the interview. Rather, the unique stream of consciousness peculiar to each situation dictated what was recorded. And, from my point of view, a more accurate representation emerged as each person's effort to "self-edit" fell away.

The journal entries will also, I hope, serve minimally as an invitation, perhaps verification, that you too can meet and get to know your farmer; vicariously here and, who knows?—in your neighborhood as well. You might even be tempted to plant a garden.

As a preamble to all the histories, I've included a brief survey of Snoqualmie Valley Watershed history whose geological and human stories continue to define and direct land use and agriculture for present and future generations. The geomorphology of the Valley, which proceeds within a time scale beyond human consciousness, is, finally, the process we most need to understand and thereby inform our environmental behavior.

As complements to all of the above, I have interspersed various data in the form of citations from the research of others, quotes from various agricultural and individual experts in fields directly involved with climate, environment and economics as well as literature and poetry. These are listed in the bibliography and are placed in the text as support for some references made in each of the narratives and as components of the wider metaphor that forms the context of this account.

Finally, it needs to be noted that "Oral History" as a method and artifact has attributes which necessarily set it apart from standard scholastic history. Oral History begins as a spoken, not written, record, now preserved through the medium of audio recording as well as in the memory of the storyteller. As such it presents a view from the "front lines"; it presents the recent experiences of individuals who are, in fact, living the history they recall. Therefore, the story presents data unavailable from any other source and is, no doubt, within the history of histories, the primary root of the activity itself. The tale of the hunter told to the tribe after the long and fruitful (or fruitless) hunt. The saga of battle, the elegy sung in remembrance of an exemplary life.

As the poet/scholar Ann Carson notes:
> "We want other people to have a center, a history, an account that makes <u>sense</u>. We want to be able to say this is what he did, and here's why. It forms a lock against oblivion."

Ann Carson, "Nox", 2010

Herodotus, our first modern historian, said of history:
> "This is the 'showing forth', so that deeds done by men not go extinct nor great and astonishing works by Greeks and barbarians vanish....."

The personal narrative as oral history is, in the end, as much about the "voice" that tells the tale as the events it recalls. The personal and idiosyncratic manner of speech, unvarnished, groping for the essence of the story; these are the distinctions between the participant and the scholar. The "truth" of the account is the sum of all its details and the context of the moment it describes.

The stories here, therefore, are unedited beyond my efforts to ensure continuity and conform to the demands of publication. Neither grammar nor syntax has been altered from the original audio recordings. The hope is that you, the reader, will get a sense of the personality and presence of each storyteller.

Come with me then, dear reader, and follow my journey into the Snoqualmie Valley and meet the people who, over the course of this two year adventure, have become my farmers.

> Nature and human life are as various as our several constitutions. Who shall say what prospect life offers to another? Could a greater miracle take place than for us to look through each other's eyes for an instant? We should live in all the ages of the world in an hour; ay, in all the worlds of the ages. History, Poetry, Mythology!—I know of no reading of another's experience so startling and informing as this would be.
> Henry David Thoreau, "Walden", 1854

Of Time and The River
A Brief Snoqualmie Watershed History

This is a tale of two histories—one geologic, the other anthropological. These two, as they pertain to the Snoqualmie Valley Watershed, have been engaged in a complex co-evolutionary dance for the last five to nine thousand years. Geology, of course, mutates at rates for the most part out of human awareness. Nonetheless, that morphology has, in the end, the most significant impact on the evolution of human societies. The shape and movement of the earth's geology and climate determine where, how and for how long any culture may survive in any locale on the globe. As human populations have grown, however, their impact on the geomorphology of the planet has also grown to the extent that significant changes are now well within human purview. What follows is a sketch of one such co-evolutionary story and the challenges it currently presents.

The topography of the earth as we know it was fully formed at the start of the Pleistocene Era; roughly 2.5 million years Before the Present (BP). By 12,000 years BP the modern continents had arrived at their present position having moved no more than 100 km relative to each other since the beginning of the period. Also within that time frame, most of the known flora and fauna had emerged. These, in turn, suffered evolutionary change over the course of the era with the emergence and extinction of subsequent species in response to a succession of glaciations, the last ending roughly 10,000 years BP. The Puget Sound Basin is the product of that last glacial retreat after the Cordilleran ice sheet had extended as far south as present day Olympia, Washington.

Glacial drag and melt constructed the two basic forms of watershed in the region: Holocene (post-glacial) and Pleistocene (glacial). Pleistocene neo-glacial runoff and drag essentially created the pattern of the various river valleys. The rivers in Pleistocene valleys are the product of glacial runoff whereas those in Holocene valleys are the product of fluvial runoff. The Snoqualmie River is an example of Pleistocene sub-glacial runoff. As a low gradient, meandering river below Snoqualmie Falls, it has a meander belt several meters higher than the surrounding flood plain. The belt, i.e. the banks on both sides of the channel, is the product of annual flooding. Given its low gradient, the river can only move disposition material the size of coarse sand, hence the disposition of silt during floods.

By contrast, the Tolt River, one of the major tributaries to the Snoqualmie, is typical of the steeper valleys created by post-glacial (Holocene) incision into glacial deposits: bedrock, large boulders and gravel. Its channel has a fairly straight, steep gradient with the lower Tolt having a branching, multiple channel pattern. The branching is primarily the product of log jams caused by river under-cutting the banks and the subsequent undermining of tree root systems. At its convergence with the Snoqualmie, the Tolt deposits heavy gravel as well as logs and other dispositions which force the Snoqualmie channel to reconfigure generally into a broad bend at the mouth. The heavy dispositions remain there since they are beyond the carrying capacity of the Snoqualmie gradient.

These two opposite morphological flow patterns; fast/branching versus slow/meandering, have been constant for the last 10,000 years. Also, the Snoqualmie itself contains both principles; its upland reach above the falls defines the Holocene incision and the lower valley the Pleistocene meander. Separating the two, the 268 ft. Snoqualmie Falls is like a geologic knife edge dividing the two types of alluvial dynamics.

The other major contributors to the watershed morphology are climate fluctuations and human action. Climate change is generally caused by multiple factors, most being cyclical, i.e. those acting at the earth's surface; ocean currents, wind currents, temperature, periodic variation in solar radiation and orbital position. All of these are then mirrored in the longer cycles of glaciation and inter-glacial periods.

Human action has a more easily accountable record as a major contributor to changes in watershed morphology and, with the parallel developments of industrialization and population increase, changes in climate as well. The increase in CO_2 levels in the atmosphere has been accelerating since the advent of the industrial revolution in the 19th century raising the overall temperature of the earth proportionately. The global consequences have been glacial melt, more chaotic weather events, an increase in rainfall, combined rain/snow events leading to massive flooding and a rise in frequency and number of severe hurricanes and tornados. These, coupled with the increased erosion potential in the Snoqualmie Watershed due to the effects of logging, agriculture and urban development have profoundly affected the severity of flood events in the lower valley; each flood season, on average, more severe than the last.

Human impact on the Snoqualmie Watershed is well within historical access. Compared to geologic prehistory, humans are a recent intrusion. Although they have been present in the Puget Sound Basin since the last ice recession (human archaeological records date from roughly 9000 years BP), their population has only reached numbers with environmental significance in the last 150 years.

Beginning around 1840, settlers converged on the various watersheds in the basin and began the processes of resource extraction, industrialization, agriculture and urban development. Timber and, to a lesser degree, minerals (coal) were the most abundant. In order to facilitate removal, watersheds had to be cleared of deadfall, dredged and sometimes straightened to allow river transport of workers and products. As timber was cleared, settlements and towns developed with agriculture increasing as deforestation opened land for cultivation. Industrialization in the form of railroads, lumber mills and ferry boat fleets promoted the urbanization of many sites along the major rivers. The combination of logging, agriculture and urban development remain as the major contributors to geomorphological change in the watershed.

Limited Euro-American agricultural practice began in the Snoqualmie River Valley in the 1850s and 1860s with the first permanent settlements above Snoqualmie Falls where the native Snoqualmie people had harvested berries and root crops for centuries. These were subsistence farms established under the Donation Land Law, the Homestead Act and later by railroad land grant sales. A handful of pioneers settled in the Lower Valley in the 1860s but the heavily forested bottom land mainly attracted loggers; logging camps were located along the river which provided a ready means for floating logs to market. It was not until the late 1870s that a significant cash crop was developed in the Valley. In response to a general surge in hops growing in Western Washington, hops farms proliferated, beginning in the vicinity of Fall City. Many Valley famers became rich overnight. James Entwistle, the founder of the township of Tolt (later named Carnation) was among the new hops barons.

Hops brought prosperity to the Valley for twelve years. In the early 1890s, however, hops crops were devastated by the influx of the Hops Aphid. Simultaneously, prices for hops worldwide plummeted due to the Panic of 1893 caused by over leveraged bank investments in railroad building and railroad financing. James Entwistle, like all the rest, lost everything.

With the advent of the 20th Century, interest in cattle and pig farming gradually led to the beginnings of dairy farming. The rich river bottom was ideal for grass, providing at least two cuttings per season for silage. As improvements in transportation made food distribution easier and economical, dairy farms proliferated throughout the Valley. Carnation Milk Products Company began manufacturing condensed milk in Kent, Washington and the product quickly became their most successful item. Carnation Milk Products flourished during WWI as the major supplier of canned milk for US armed forces in Europe. Carnation Farms, a subsidiary of Carnation Milk Products, was established in 1912 in the Snoqualmie Valley north of the town of Tolt (later renamed Carnation at the request of the company) and by 1920 the farm was a major economic force in the Valley.

A statistical study by the Agricultural Extension Service of 21 dairy farms published in 1940 showed gross receipts per farm averaged between $4000 and $5000 per year. Most farmsteads had a comfortable house, a large hay barn raised above flood water level with a concrete floor and one or more silos. The average farm size was 110 acres but most were smaller. A typical farm was about 40 acres, and supported 17 dairy cows, with 14 acres of clover and grass hay, 7 acres of silage and 18 acres of tillable pasture. In 1940, there were 23 fully operational dairy farms between Duvall and Carnation on the east side of the Valley alone. Several local creameries received milk from valley dairies and Dairygold picked up milk at several Valley farms twice a day.

Although "row cropping" was not a primary cash crop business for valley farms, all farms had some vegetables in production year to year. By the mid-1930s there were three canneries in Carnation alone, one in Fall City and several north of Duvall in Monroe and Snohomish. Additionally, households within the various towns all maintained family garden plots; some even leased small portions on neighboring farms. The harvests from these were brought to the canneries where families had their corn, beans, peas, and other summer crops canned for winter use. Remlinger Farms in Carnation was a major supplier for people who didn't have gardens or needed more produce; they came to the farm at harvest and picked for a fee or bought at the farm stand and then headed for the cannery.

Dairying remained central to Valley economics until the late 1950s when several factors converged to bring it gradually to a close. Primarily, the post WWII growth of agribusiness spurred by production standards set during the war and the continuing general use of fossil fuel based nitrogen fertilizers began to shift the American population away from rural life as small farms were displaced by large corporate driven mono crop farms, large scale feed lots for meat and poultry and massive dairy product companies.

Government regulations on farm milk production accompanied all of these corporate inclusions, auspiciously in the name of food safety. These and the pressure from suburban property developers which grew as the once rural population (near 60% prior to WWII) moved off the farms to the cities after the war and the 1950's parents of the "Baby Boomers" needed housing and found more and more non-farm employment. By the 1970s, dairying was an historical artifact. Carnation Farms was sold to the Nestle Company in 1985 and the corporate headquarters for Carnation Milk Products moved to California in 1975.

The Valley experienced a 20-year lull in agricultural production from 1970 to the early 1990s, the nadir occurring around 1980. By then, only 7 fully operating dairy farms existed between Fall City and Monroe. Oddly, the rebirth of farming grew from the gradual influx of refugees from Southeast Asia paired with the beginnings of the "organic, back to the land, environmental preservation movement" spurred in the early 1970s by the "Whole Earth Catalogue" and the rise of interest in alternative social behavior in reaction to the Vietnam War and the corporate "Establishment". This "counter-culture" was born on University campuses and soon led to a surge of interest in "organics" as a healthy antidote to the perceived ills of society. The refugees from Vietnam and Laos, the Hmong people, who had been the core of the CIA's "Secret Army" in the US "Secret War" in Laos during the Vietnam War were among those displaced after the communist take-over in the region at the end of the War. Several hundred thousand refugees arrived in California, Washington, Montana, and the Midwest between 1978 and 1990. Many came to the Snoqualmie Valley and continued their traditional practice of "row cropping" vegetables and notably, flowers. The earliest organic farmers in the Valley credit the Hmong with leading the way to the current resurgence of row cropping vegetables as the primary agricultural practice in the region.

The real surge in the growth of organic farms in the Valley began in the mid-1990s with the steady emergence of small growers whose numbers have risen exponentially since; currently there are 20 organic farms between Fall City and Monroe that are members of the Sno-Valley Tilth. The Tilth is one of several farmer organizations in the State and region serving as advocates and organizing groups in support of small farms and local food production. Additionally, there has been an explosion of Farmers Markets in the Pacific Northwest, Washington State and the Nation. Currently there are 106 registered members in the Washington State Farmers Market Association. There are 17 CSA (Community Supported Agriculture) outlets in Seattle alone and most of the farms in the Snoqualmie Valley have CSA memberships which constitute the major outlet for their produce.

These New American Farmers, specifically those presented in this book, are the direct inheritors of the two historical progressions outlined above; the geomorphology of the Snoqualmie Watershed and the combined consequences of human history. Nationally, those making the effort to revive the small farm and organic farming bear the legacy as well, each facing the environmental challenges peculiar to their regions. Their primary challenge is embedded in the broader question, "Can renewable agricultural and environmental practices reasonably accommodate and respond to the cumulative history of the area and its natural dynamics sufficiently to secure food production and prevent further degradation of the Watershed? Moreover, can such practices reasonably assure a stable agricultural future for the Valley and a habitable environment for its citizens?"

Our citizens, farmers and all, need to face the relentlessness of watershed dynamics. Continued growth in urban development only exacerbates the natural geomorphology of the river systems outlined here; water runs down and without root systems, trees and buffer zones at its banks, river flow rates and volumes increase, floods increase in the lower valley and silt rises. Long term, without careful attention to soil replenishment and watershed preservation, farming in the Valley will be difficult, if not impossible. Globally, loss of topsoil will diminish food supply at ever accelerating rates. The earth turns and gravity is indeed a "cruel mistress".

It takes roughly 1000 years for microbes and natural erosion processes (breaking down rock into dirt) to create one inch of topsoil. Darwin, in his study of earthworms in Britain, thought English worms could make an inch in a century or two. Organic soil management, on the other hand, can do it in ten years, perhaps less. Currently, we are losing 1 percent of our topsoil per year and we have but three feet of topsoil covering the earth which is our singular life sustaining element. We can't eat without good dirt. Nonetheless, preventative measures can still be taken. Buffer zones at river banks can be reinstated, runoff from forestry and development can be abated, carbon emissions can be controlled and, with effort, watershed dynamics can be learned and accommodated in useful ways.

The questions remain; can we shift our 'way of life' significantly enough to move it toward a 'steady state' economy which keeps resource depletion for all living systems at tolerable levels of low entropy to create an acceptable way of life for all citizens? Can we learn to live better on less?

> Plato thought nature but a spume that plays
> Upon a ghostly paradigm of things;
> Aristotle played the taws
> Upon the bottom of a king of kings;
> World-famous golden-thighed Pythagoras
> Fingered upon a fiddle stick or strings
> What a star sang and careless Muses heard:
> Old clothes upon old sticks to scare a bird.
> ....
> Labour is blossoming or dancing where
> The body is not bruised to pleasure soul,
> Nor beauty born out of its own despair,
> Nor blear-eyed wisdom out of midnight oil.
> O chestnut tree, great rooted blossomer,
> Are you the leaf, the blossom or the bole?
> O body swayed to music, O brightening glance,
> How can we know the dancer from the dance?
>
> W.B. Yeats, "Among School Children", 1928

Much of the success of industrial agriculture lies in its labor efficiency: far less human work is required to produce a given amount of food today than was the case decades ago (the actual fraction, comparing the year 2000 with 1900, is about one-seventh). But that very success implies a growing vulnerability. We don't need as many farmers as a percentage of the population as we used to; thus, throughout the past century most farming families—including hundreds of thousands and perhaps millions who would have preferred to maintain their rural, self-sufficient way of life—were economically forced to move to cities and find jobs there. Today so few people farm that vital knowledge of how to farm is disappearing. The average age of farmers in the United States is over fifty-five and approaching sixty. The proportion of principal farm operators younger than thirty-five has dropped from 15.9 percent in 1982 to 5.8 percent in 2002. Of all the dismal statistics I know, these are surely among the most frightening. Who will be growing our food twenty years from now?

Richard Heinberg, "Fifty Million Farmers"

Farm Journal—May 14, 2010

Sunrise in an Eden of Gardens

I have a new daughter-in-law and recently, at a little pre-nuptial dinner party, she asked, since she knew I was working on this project, if I would explain why the mega-mono culture, corporate food structure was bad—or rather, she wanted to gain some understanding about the whole affair—organics and all.

There were a lot of guests at that table in a Chinese restaurant in the Seattle International district. It was noisy and talking about the politics of food over the turntable server loaded with pork, noodles, vegetables and sauces was awkward and shouting through the din proved impossible. We tabled the topic. It stuck, however, because I suddenly realized I would have difficulty with the answer. More so with its companion—how do I answer this for the reader at large who wants to know and hopes my organic farmer book will provide an answer s/he can understand?

Why should we buy local—support small farms, eat organic food? What's wrong with agribusiness? Aren't they solving the food crisis, feeding the starving "third world" masses and protecting food products from pests and contaminants? Isn't the science which supports these practices good science? How do we know so-called "organic" food is safe? This last may not be valid—although our general health/safety paranoia is rooted in our uneasy trust in scientific experts and—this certainly applies to food—food as a product that is supposed to be protected by the FDA, the USDA and sanctioned by the AMA.

The typical answers to my daughter-in-law's question all come from doomsday scenarios; environmental catastrophe, food shortage, famine and the general litany of bad news. Most appeal to moral sensibility and sympathy for our maligned planet whose resources are being stressed beyond our ability to control, resulting in environmental collapse, global warming and the rest. We are destroying Gaia or God's creation and we need a revival of environmental conscience. I generally wince at religious/moral exhortations and/or the plea for "spirituality" as an applied religion of the soil. Each of them celebrates those insidious simplicities, "good," and "bad," and their paranoid twin offspring, heresy and orthodoxy whose chief function is to define and condemn behavior that violates the "sacredness" of the earth. And with that, the notion that right, "moral" conduct assumes the position of "at-oneness" with natural systems and that the Corporate Empire is a heretical response to the sacredness of living things. Therefore, organics are the good, moral response to the politics of producing and eating food and, consequently agribusiness food is bad and immoral. In contrast, scientific prognostications and data build the case from "reason" as opposed to faith but it too, as much as I prefer it, seems to fall on deaf ears. Neither seems to promote much change in behavior.

Lately, I've had this image floating in my mind as I drift off to sleep of Moses standing in the desert, confronting two mountains. One has Paradise at its pinnacle and each level up to the summit confirms the abundance and unlimited bounty of God's Creation which exists for the faithful—to sustain them as they ascend toward eternity and the immortal grace of God.

The second mountain has at its peak a void—confirmation of entropic dissipation. The brutal fact that all life including the mountain itself are destined for ultimate collapse and beyond that final chaos there is nothing—nothing but the ceaseless silence of the universe. Nonetheless, each level upward to that summit offers the ways and means to delay or slow the rate of collapse—low entropy and prolonged steady state economics of resources, but no ultimate escape from the dynamics of a limited and finite system.

Moses' dilemma is this in my dream: "Which mountain do I tell my people I have climbed and received at its peak the universal truth and laws they must observe and sustain for all time? Which mountain shall be the foundation of our beliefs and ethical conduct in the world? Can we live morally responsible lives without the promise of a paradise in the afterlife?" The questions revolve around our beliefs about the nature of the planet. Is it a limitless source of life or is it a limited finite system with regenerative capabilities which also have limits? Can we really run out of food, water and fuel?

Today, after a year of wandering up and down the Valley, going farm to farm, I have all the pieces of a book—some 300 photographs (edited down from 1500 or so), 33 interviews, piles of research data, all of it. I have that mess but no clue as to how to assemble it and worse, I find myself standing next to my imagined Moses, facing his dilemma—transformed, in daylight into this Valley.

The Valley, the farmers and their farms present an idyllic garden whose beauty denies all the socio/economic issues typically coupled to discussions about organic farms, food, agriculture, and global climate change. To visit any of these farms is to visit a vision of natural abundance; fields with lush rows of vegetables tended by (dare I say) "happy" farmers. Here one has to strain to hold the image in one's mind of a world struggling with environmental crisis. The smell of rich, damp earth, fruit trees, row crops, the delicate vapor of cottonwood and the deep flow of the river combine to defeat any semblance of catastrophe. And, if that weren't enough, the health, clarity of eye and welcoming faces of each of these farmers at last walls off and silences the noise from a distressed and often terrified world.

Idyllic Edens notwithstanding, these are farmers, no matter how they came to be so, and they are committed to the process and so their stance relative to world crisis is filtered through the daily work of farming. As one of the senior members of the group told me recently, "If I wake up in the morning alive, that's a good day. It's a perfect day if I wake up alive and the tractor starts." As for the threats that surround the Valley from the world beyond, they are placed in line with those other elements in the process that require a "watchful eye"; the weather, the condition of the soil this year, pests, the ongoing harvest, getting it to market.

The "watchful eye" is, in the end, an antidote to denial. It sees the unrelenting presence and demands of our economic reality concerning food, food production/distribution, the factory farm, the steady loss of farmland to developers, the exponential growth of food corporations and their ongoing efforts to control the entire food system from seed to consumer and, finally, the entrenched denial by governments and citizens who willingly support the very agencies that threaten their lives and future.

I don't know how well each of these farmers sleeps at night (I doubt they dream about Moses and the two mountains); whether the list of concerns tallied at the end of the day contains details from our global crisis and if it does, where on that list of farm necessities global warming, the slow destruction of farmland worldwide and all the rest of it are placed. I suspect that beyond the wake-up tasks awaiting them the next day, the weight of their work as row croppers (90% handwork), with bodies bent over rows of vegetables, has accumulated enough fatigue to usher sleep quickly; a final act of self-defense and psychic restoration. At the end of an 18-hour day in the field there is little energy of any kind left for the crisis looming beyond the Valley. The "watchful eye" at last turns inward and is absorbed into the dream exchange that promises only sleep's deep silence.

To awaken here, of course, is to re-enter the dream that is the Valley and its unique Eden of Gardens. And that, in the end is the problem; rather, it is my problem as a writer—indeed, our problem as participants in a world ultimately dependent on the soil which feeds us all. The problem is that the beauty and the promise offered in this Valley will lull us back into that crisis free waking sleep and the dream we daily walk wherein the resources of the earth are immortal after all. An opulence further confirmed beyond the farm at every supermarket in America overflowing with food year round.

Forecasts of doom, however, seem to bring despair rather than action. Denial of bad news and resistance to change are our typical responses. Acceptance of bad news is more likely to generate feelings of helplessness and powerlessness—change is impossible. Finally, we hate being put in the wrong and being put there makes us feel bad and little else. Only sudden terror and/or disaster seem to spur motivation and action.

Paradoxically, we despise being told there is "hope" when there is none, calling this masking of the truth "false hope" which is itself an oxymoron. There is no such thing as "false hope"; hope is hope and as such defies both truth and lie.

Nonetheless and in spite of it all, these new American farmers in the Snoqualmie Valley demonstrate that it is possible to live a life worth living; a life whose wealth, like the soil and the food they grow, is regenerative and extends, therefore, beyond their existence and can be a vital part of ours. At the center of that life is their refusal to yield to despair and to act in those ways which are, finally, the solutions to our various socio/economic problems and our environmental crises.

By saying "No!" to the established corporate agricultural model and arranging their lives so that truly "sustainable" farming practices can continue, they do not deny the reality of the various forecasts of catastrophe and doom. Rather, they demonstrate what is, to my mind, the only sane response to a failed global economic system. They are behaving the solution.

Revelation for the day.............my problem cannot be resolved here in this Journal or in my as yet non-existent book that wants to become itself. I can only present the pictures and stories and their implications as they are; in the ways my camera and their voices reveal. Their stories and their faces speak for themselves. Maybe they will speak to my daughter-in-law as well.

We are an exceptional model of the human race. We no longer know how to produce food. We no longer can heal ourselves. We no longer really raise our young. We have forgotten the names of the stars, fail to notice the phases of the moon. We do not know the plants and they no longer protect us. We tell ourselves we are the most powerful specimens of our kind who have ever lived. But when the lights are off we are helpless. We cannot move without traffic signals. We must attend classes to learn by rote numbered steps toward love or how to breast feed our baby. We justify anything, anything at all, by the need to maintain our way of life. And then we go to the doctor and tell the professionals we have no life. We have a simple reality we live with each and every day: our way of life is killing us...................

Still, we could be free. We could walk out the door. We still can walk a little or at least crawl.
We can, actually, do anything. Anything at all.
Except, as we constantly tell ourselves, we know better. We tell ourselves that we live in a global village. But then why do we have no neighbors?

Charles Bowden, "Blood Orchid", 1995

'For in the immediate world, everything is to be discerned, for him who can discern it, and centrally and simply, wihout either dissection into science, or digestion into art, but with the whole of consciousness, seeking to perceive it as it stands: so that the aspect of a street in sunlight can roar in the heart of itself as a symphony, perhaps as no symphony can: and all of consciousness is shifted from the imagined, the revisive, to the effort to perceive simply the cruel radiance of what is.

This is why the camera seems to me, next to unassisted and weaponless consciousness, the central instrument of our time; and is why in turn I feel such rage at its misuse: which has spread so nearly universal a corruption of sight that I know of less than a dozen alive whose eyes I can trust even so much as my own.'

James Agee, *"LET US NOW PRAISE FAMOUS MEN"*, 1936

Farmers

Farm Journal

20 May 2009

The Root Connection is on the main road (Hwy 202) connecting Redmond and Woodinville but once out of my car and onto the property, the road sound fades and I'm confronted by long fields of the blackest earth I've ever seen flanked by eight or ten greenhouses. The front displays a market stand and building.

I'm here at the suggestion of Erick Haakensen who, at our first meeting, urged me to include her in my project even though her farm is in the Sammamish Valley and I intend to limit the work to the Snoqualmie Valley. Erick said she was the first organic grower in the general area and had been a real "Maven" for him. I'm here to meet her—I'm curious.

We meet in the little office attached to the open market. When she comes in, I know what the outcome will be. Claire is a widow in her early sixties who has farmed this ground for 23 years. She is slender, back slightly hunched from labor and the weight of her own private and often public war with the county and developers. She has won all challenges or worn down all challengers. Her outward demeanor is calm and self-effacing but her black eyes betray a steely core and a passion for the land and food production that is indomitable.

She is more than willing to contribute to my project but notes that she is, like all farmers, busy. She employs a dozen workers who earn between $15 and $22 per hour—more than any other farm workers in the area. Most of them have been with her for over ten years.

We talked generally about the food "crisis" in America (obesity, diabetes, etc.) and her efforts, mostly futile, to awaken the public to the problems and ultimate consequences. Her farm, with ten acres in cultivation, produces 80 tons of food per growing season. She notes that if all the agricultural land in King County was put into food production enough food would be grown to feed the entire county population. In addition to crops grown for sale in her roadside market and to vendors, she has U-pick gardens and CSA memberships.

....

On the other side of the hill, less than four miles away, lies the town of Redmond, WA; a sprawling Strip-Mall, housing project mess that houses an IGA, Bed, Bath and Beyond, The Home Depot, half a dozen or so supermarkets, fast food vendors and, of course, Whole Foods. Truly a marketing collision of world views which more than points to the dilemma—suburban wasteland meets rural "Green"—and there is no transition—an "Either/Or" which may indeed be the ultimate choice for the future; sustainable community or urban collapse.

....

Claire is a "must have" for the book; for her historical value as well as her vision and ongoing dedicated work.

The Root Connection Farm

Claire Thomas

30 November 2009

My name is Claire Thomas, and I was born on January 26, 1946, in Seattle, so I'm a native. My mother was from Minot, North Dakota, and my father was from Billings, Montana. They both came out here before World War II, and met at Boeing, like a lot of other people, and both of them decided to stay here.

I was just pretty much a typical city kid, liked horses, had a horse. Other than that, nothing remarkable. I graduated from high school; didn't go to college. As far as I know, nobody in my family was farming. Even my grandfather in North Dakota was a banker. It's hard to know what people *would* have done if circumstances were different. There's gotta be somethin' back there in my gene pool, I think.

I think when I was a kid I always liked to be out working in the yard—even though my mother didn't have any vegetable garden. I was the one that was doing all the weeding and doing all the yard work, and stuff like that. And then got married, had children, ended up with five children, two of them that weren't ours, that we were taking care of. And pretty much switched to vegetable gardening out of necessity. And I just really loved it. So whatever house we would be in, I'd have a big vegetable garden. But it was always in the back of my mind that it'd be nice to grow these things and sell them. So somebody told me about this place out here, McMurtry Tree Farm, where he rented spots to people—not like a pea patch, but bigger, you know, like a quarter of an acre or whatever. So I came out here to the Sammamish River Valley and looked the situation over, and really loved the soil, how beautiful the soil was, and just rented a quarter of an acre, and it just kind of took off from there.

And then, every year it seems like I was doubling it. He didn't make it with his tree farm on this piece of property. The ground actually was too rich for Christmas trees, because they grow too fast, there's too much space between the branches and things. So we basically ended up starting to pull out the trees, and then I gradually took over the whole property. And then he sold it to me later. I was selling to grocery stores, and it was really tough to do that.

This was in '84 and '85. And then I read about the CSA concept. Somebody had one they started back in Massachusetts, so I thought it was really a good idea. CSA stands for Community Supported Agriculture. People buy. They pay in advance for their share of the farm's output. So it was a new concept, nobody'd ever heard of it really. I think the first year we had twenty members. I was still doing this all by myself. I say "we," but there wasn't anybody else. And then my son started working for me, because he needed a job. He had a family already. And we got a little bigger, and then more people needed jobs, so we got a little bigger. And it just kind of grew that way.

The way I gardened at home, that's the way it was. It just never occurred to me to spray some poison on anything. And I read the "*Organic Gardening*" magazine, and they'd tell you what to do about whatever, if there was issues and problems and stuff. But everything always grew real well, so.... I learned about row cover and beneficial insects and things of that nature. By the time we were really farming in earnest here, I noticed that there was less insect damage on things, because the soil was getting healthier. And so then the plants were getting healthier, and the bad bugs don't like the healthy plants, they go for ones that are in distress. And that's what happens when you use chemical fertilizer and stuff on things, because the cell walls are really weaker, and they don't have the sweetness to 'em. Bugs kind of tend to go towards the more bitter plants. So the normal problems we have were kept in check pretty well. Eventually we got up to about 500 members. We went from half an acre to fourteen.

The agricultural history of the Sammamish Valley goes way, way back. I don't know a lot about it, but I do know that before they straightened out the Sammamish River, it was real curvy. And I believe that most of the people here were German. And then when they straightened the Sammamish River and opened up more farmland, a lot of Japanese people came in and farmed. And this was one of the first areas that shipped lettuce by railroad car back to the East Coast, and it was kind of famous for lettuce and carrots, this Valley. And then when World War II came, most of the Japanese people unfortunately lost their land. And then I think the majority of the farmers here were Italian. And after that, I think farming kind of stopped a little bit. I'm not sure why, but anyway, when I was farming here, there really wasn't any other farmers actively growing in this Valley at all.

It's amazing how that could just kind of go away. But since then, since 1986, it's just kind of—there's been a resurgence of interest in farming. Well, also, when we had the influx of Laotian immigrants, the Hmong people especially, they were really interested in farming. And so there's a few places here in this Valley where they farm. Now it's just kind of a mix of people that are doing it. So the Farmland Preservation Program in the early seventies helped a lot to save the farmland in King County. Just had to stay here long enough for more people to get interested in doing it. I was so single-minded about what I was doing. It didn't occur to me that it wasn't gonna work.

But it was kind of funny, because there was nothing here on the property, no buildings or anything, and my garden was kind of way out in the middle. So I'd be out there by myself, and get visitors, you know. Some guy would come along and he'd tell me a story about everybody he knew that tried to grow something here, and why it didn't work. I think I was somewhat of a novelty. Plus, I didn't live in the area, so nobody knew me. And then the local people would come over and kind of give me their opinion about things. I was always referred to for *years* after this, "Oh, the lady that has the herb garden," because they assumed that's the only thing I was capable of doing, was grow herbs. You know, that's what women did. Or the flower garden. So even now people don't really realize that we actually produce a lot, over ninety tons of food here, in a year. How many people that feeds is such a variable thing. I can eat basically almost a whole share myself.

A share works out to be about $30 a week, so we say it feeds two to six people, depending on their eating habits. And a lot of people actually don't sign up again, because they say it's too much food, and they don't want to just throw it away—even though it's cheaper. But it's the idea, it doesn't fit into their lifestyle. You have to actually cook it and use it. It doesn't come in a little plastic container already cut up salad kind of thing. But most of the people that stay year after year are people that they want it to be fresher, because it's healthier, the enzymes are still alive, it's just picked, and the taste is incredible. People that never have liked certain things, like beets, for example, is the number one I think, are really surprised at how things taste. And then we do a lot of U-pick greens. A lot of people, especially white people, they don't know what greens are. You know, I mean, they don't! I never did. My husband was African American, so he introduced me to growing greens, and I liked 'em. And so that was kind of a staple in our diet—*the* easiest thing to grow in our climate, of *anything*.

I used to grow 'em to put in the shares, and then after doing a few surveys—

this was in the early years—after doing a few surveys, people would say, "Oh, I don't eat the greens." So that's where the concept of part of the farm being U-pick came from. I thought, "Well, I'm not going to grow greens for everybody, but I'll just grow a little bit for the ones that want, and they can just come out and pick what they want. And as the farm grew, and I think people became more health conscious, especially as far as green leafy things go, eating them, we now grow about half an acre, and that's a lot of greens. And people pick 'em and they come out even in the wintertime and pick 'em. So that's all free. They get their regular share that we pick for them, and then they can go out there and do that. And then we started adding herbs and basil that they could pick themselves. Then we added flowers. So the objective, really, is to get people to get out of the car and actually go out there. And the people that do that are the ones that stick. The people that rush in and throw their stuff in a bag and head back to a car, or they come in after hours and grab the bags that we put out there for people that come late, they don't typically stay, because they're just too stressed. And there's kind of a thing where if you would eat right, you'd be less stressed. You're too stressed to eat right!

The level of knowledge about eating I've encountered is just really all over the map. And it's a wonder to me sometimes why people even sign up. It's interesting, too, because people that don't know anything about how to fix anything, they're kind of strangers to fresh vegetables. And they'll ask questions like, "How do I microwave the beets?" And I say, "Number one, you don't microwave your vegetables, because that kills all the enzymes," etc. etc. Don't know how to cook. Everything they want a recipe for. And I say, "Okay, first, taste it raw." And their eyes get big. "I'm supposed to do that?!" "Yeah, see if you like it." Like kohlrabi, for example, or little white Asian turnips or something. Then I say, "Just good old steaming it, sautéing it in olive oil, buy a few flavored oils. And then if you want a recipe, go to the store, and there's *tons* of cookbooks out there, that'll make your life really complicated." If you really want to spend lots of time cooking, it can be fun, it can be great, but if you don't, you just need to learn simple ways of doing things. I think the reason that people that aren't experienced in that, sign up, is because psychologically they're hoping it will—they're getting this picture in their mind about being healthy, all these healthy vegetables on their table, their family smiling as they're eating them; and then reality hits, the husband doesn't like anything, the kids don't like anything, "I don't have time to fix it, nobody will help me, I put it in the refrigerator when I get home, and don't separate it out, don't clean 'em up, don't package 'em, and it's kind of a nasty mess after four or five days." And that's the reality, unfortunately, for a lot of people. But probably 80 percent of our people are really into it: whether they're making complicated recipes, or whether they're just sitting down to greens, or just cook 'em in a little water, put some garlic salt in there, and put 'em in a bowl—eat 'em! You know? That's it! Yeah, everybody's different.

In the beginning all my customers were Seattle people, and probably 80 percent of our produce we went to drop sites in Seattle. PCC had started a few years before that, and kind of the northeast part of Seattle seemed to be where the people were that were interested in organic.... And there also wasn't too much on the market. Even at, like, PCC things looked pretty eaten up and not too good. So it took a lot of years to switch over to where people that are actually in the community.... And yet it amazed me. I was really surprised by it. Because at that time, too, when we built the store building, we started selling retail as well, because we were shipping all the CSA boxes to Seattle. So I thought, "We'll just start selling our produce. Put it on the counter and start selling it." We had big signs up, and an article in the paper, all this stuff, and nobody showed up. Just nobody showed up! And it took probably three years to get people to come in. In fact, I ended up asking the neighbors, whoever had a spare car, to park it over here, so that it would look like somebody was *here*. It just took a *long* time. People were very suspicious of organic, which surprised me, because this area was a little more affluent, generally speaking. You know, most people around here, a lot of Microsoft folks. And you'd think people like that would know, and want to do this stuff. But they weren't sold on it. Took a long time.

I just think people don't—and I'm like that too—we don't like to be told what's good for us, we really don't. And we've gotten so divorced from the soil. And that's where I got the name The Root Connection, trying to connect people with the soil. We've gotten so much away from that. We're just used to going in the store, and everything's in plastic, and the illusion that it's somehow cleaner, better ... I don't know. And the idea of coming and actually buying from a farmer, it's like they don't trust you or something. And we had the manure phobia. You know, "Do you use manure from those cows next door? And doesn't that come over here?" You know, just a lot of stuff like that. You can't tell them, "You have no idea where that stuff's been that you're buying at the grocery store." You can come out here and you can walk around and you can see what we do. So it just took a while. And then it sort of became "in" all of a sudden. It was kind of probably 1993 to '95, it just took off. Then everybody wanted it. And buying from your local farmer was in fashion. That was a good thing all of a sudden. But we still have trouble keeping our membership full. And now I don't think it's a matter of people not knowing about organic or not wanting to support local agriculture. It's time, their time. Their lifestyles are *so* complicated, *so* full, with all these gadgets and all this stuff, that nobody has time to relax and live. And you watch people pull up here, they've got a cell phone.... I even saw a woman come in the other day, and she had *two* of those things, one on each ear! I mean, she's monitoring two telephones at the same time! You know?! And she came in, bagged up her stuff and starts out the door, and I'm calling her, because she forgot this whole other bag of stuff, and she's not hearing me, because she's got these things going on in her ear. I had to chase after her with her things. But I wondered, what does she really have time to *do* with it when she gets home? I don't know.

We've tried to do educational things. But we just can't get people to sit down for an hour. We tried to do a movie thing, because we have a TV right there. You know, they can sit here. We could get fifteen people in here, you know. I wanted to show that movie, the one about engineered food, that came out. And I scheduled times, we had the VCR all set up, so all somebody had to do was start it up. Out of 500 member families, we didn't get one person to come out and watch that movie. They showed it at the grange—I think there was three or four people that came. People wanted to borrow it, to take home, and I said no. I told them where they could buy it. But I just thought every American should watch that movie, "The Future of Food".

So that didn't go over. Doesn't mean a lot of people don't know about it. We've tried having farm potlucks. Used to have garden tours in the spring. Finally I just quit doin' 'em, because nobody would come. I think the farms that are further out in the country have better participation in stuff like that.

We basically don't have any turnover with our workers. Maybe one person a year I might have to replace. At the most, we employ seventeen. And then for the winter, about six. And they've all come back, year after year. So that's pretty great. We pay a lot more than normal, which can be a bad thing, because it's hard on the budget. We pay about $16 an hour, plus they get food. That's worth another $2 an hour. But on the other hand, I get a crew that is experienced. I've had crews from other farms come over, and watched them, and how we organized out there in the field with our planting and harvesting and all that. And they tell me, it works like a well-oiled machine, and these guys just.... You look at 'em, and you don't really see it maybe, to the untrained eye, because they're talkin' and workin'. Nobody's just racin' around or yellin' at each other or anything. But it's amazing how much we get done. So that's good.

CSA shares vary in terms of pounds per share. In June it's pretty skimpy, lots of green stuff. We always have the big celebration and then we just put little cartoons in there saying "the first time there's not somethin' green in the share bags...." But July, August, September, October, they're probably weighin' about thirty pounds. It's just a lot of food every week. Yeah, we have records that we keep and stuff, and I actually should really have that information, but I don't. It'd be interesting to do that sometime.

But we don't really weigh things. I mean, I know what it feels like when you put everything in one bag, but we haven't tried to keep track of that. It's always kept track of, "bunches of this," or.... But our bunches tend to be bigger than what you find in the store. You get a bunch of carrots, you're gettin' two pounds of carrots, or more. Sometimes I have to scold the crew, because they're all big eaters of vegetables, and they think a bunch of carrots should be *big*. I'll say, "Now, come on, we're gonna run out next week on this crop if you don't cut 'em down a little bit."

And there's always the danger, too, if you give people too much food, it's just too much food. But on the other hand, it amazes me when people say, "Well, we just can't eat it all." I think, "Okay, what's in a share? You get a bunch of carrots every week, you get two or three bunches of something else. You get one or two lettuces. Granted, our lettuce heads are generally pretty big. Two people can't eat that?! I mean, what's twelve carrots? You eat a carrot a day, it's gone, don't even have to cook it! You make a salad. I can go through three or four heads of lettuce a week myself. So it kind of surprises me.

This is farm preservation property, we don't have an issue with developers. Well, I shouldn't really say that. There was a little thing that happened—I'm not sure what year that was, it was in the nineties, I think, late nineties, when the Lake Washington Soccer Association bought 110 acres of farm preservation property, and they were told they couldn't put soccer fields on it, because that's not an allowed use. And so they bought it anyway, and then they challenged the county in court, tried to get the farm preservation rules overturned. And the problem with that is it wouldn't have applied to just their land. It would have been the whole county. And the county really—their grounds that they used was that farming wasn't viable in this Valley anymore. And it's true, at that time, there wasn't anything too much goin' on. And so if it wasn't a viable use for the land, then the county didn't have any right to keep it from being developed, used for something else. And the Root Connection was basically the stalwart. They didn't need twenty farms, they only needed one, to disprove. And fortunately we weren't nonprofit; we weren't like a research thing, and being subsidized with money. I mean, we were a for-profit corporation, and we were making a profit. I was small, but we were making it.

They actually took the county to court two times, and it went all the way to the Supreme Court. It was just really amazing. And there was all this angst in the local paper. You know, soccer association people.... They had their own play on it that they were feeding their members about the situation, most of which was not correct. And so all these people were up in arms, we're keepin' their kids from playin' soccer. Anyway, after a few years, the truth kind of came out about everything, and it's my understanding that whoever was at the forefront of trying to get this done, is now in disrepute by the parents, because it kind of came out as to what the real story was, and stuff like that. So yeah, development can be an issue.

And I always counsel people about that, that you can't just say, "Well, because it's farm preservation property, it's protected." Because people can come in, and if they have enough money, they can try to change the law.

We also face the problem of property use for horses with the ranch next door, which actually *was* a horse ranch. But they sold out, and even though it's farm preservation property—it has a home site on it—then it's very attractive to someone with a lot of money, because they can build a huge house. And the taxes are subsidized by this bond issue. Taxes are a fraction of what they would be. And so basically someone could build a McMansion on a place, and have all this private land. It doesn't say you *have* to farm it. It tells you what you can't do, but it doesn't say you have to. So there was that piece of property that came up for sale. And then at the same time, the thirty-seven acres down on the corner came up for sale, and it *wasn't* deed restricted yet. So a guy from the county came out and wanted to know could I buy these two pieces of property. And I said, "You're kidding me!" They wanted $1.2 million for the forty-seven acres down there, I think. And this place over here was something like $450,000 or something. So a bunch of our members got together and formed an LLC and bought both the properties. And then after we bought the forty-seven acres, then the county came along—because we knew they would. I mean, this is what they told us they would do. Here we paid $1.2 million for it, but then the county paid $100,000 for the development rights. So it only cost us $300,000. But that's what they were trying to avoid. The county would have bought it themselves, just to keep it from just getting sold. They wanted to get that piece of property in the program. If they did that, they would have had to auction it, because it had a home site on it, and they were pretty sure that someone would come along that wanted to have their big spread. And so they wanted to find a buyer for it first.

I think it all gets back to what is the land made for? I mean, the topography of an area, if you look at it, anybody in the third grade can tell you where the farmland's supposed to be. If you know anything about geology or how the drain fields work, and how the hills drain into the valleys and the valleys drain into the river. The farmland, actually the valleys, filter the land from everywhere, and if you're not pouring chemicals on it, then it's actually cleaning the water that goes into the rivers. Also, providing a local food base. I did do a study on our production here, and multiplied it out by the amount of acres left in the Farm Preservation Program in King County, and then figured out how many people that would feed.

One acre of Sammamish Valley farmland can produce 130,500 heads of lettuce—one acre—or 62,250 bunches of carrots, or 4,500 pounds of potatoes, or 160,800 bunches of greens per year. Figures are based on yearly production averages of a local farm—meaning us—using sustainable chemical-free growing methods. One acre alone can produce ten tons of mixed vegetables, enough to feed approximately 250 people annually, at 80 pounds per person. King County has designated approximately 1,100 acres of farmland that is in the Farm Preservation Program. Using top production methods, each year these acres could produce 22 million pounds of fresh wholesome food. The combined population of the Woodinville-Redmond area is about 100,000 people. So the King County farm preservation land could feed almost three times that many. And we're not talkin' about *just* this Valley. We're talking about the whole county. Twenty-two million pounds of food. Now, what is that worth in terms of transportation issues and health issues? You know, filtering the soil, being good for the environment. I mean, all those things come into play. And agri-business does none of those things—just the opposite. Even agri-organic-business can be very harmful, because it doesn't use good sustainable methods. But we have to be patient. I mean, obviously not all these 1,100 acres are being farmed intensively—but they will.

Farmland in California is under stress. The water crisis in the Southwest is very real. The aquifers are getting pumped out, sea water's coming in underground. And that happens whether it's organic production or not. We're using the deserts to feed the people that are living on the land that should have been used to feed us. And that's the problem. So just the idea that King County could be almost self-sustainable—I mean, the most populace county in the state, we can actually feed ourselves as far as fresh produce. And if we had storage facilities—you know, had enough people that were growing crops that could be stored for the winter—we could do it. So that's amazing. If we get eastern Washington involved too, where the climate is more suitable for a lot of things. That's kind of a whole oasis there. You know, organic farming's growing there too, but.... Goodness sakes, we have an amazing state for agricultural production.

I just think we'll see more and more health problems as a consequence of genetically modified foods. We're already seeing it in non-organic foods and additives and all these things. I think at some point our love affair with having to have houses that are too big and cars that are too expensive, and people that have to work two and a half jobs—you know, families—I think that's going to gradually kind of change over again. Like King Solomon said, "There's nothing new under the sun." Always comes back. People are going to have to be more self-reliant.

We're growing corn to put in our vehicles?! C'mon! Please! I mean, you know, who thought that was a good idea? There's a difference between some small company running around and collecting all the waste product from restaurants and various places—oils and things—and making bio-fuel for tractors, for people in their community's cars and all that. When we get agri-business involved in it, then all of a sudden the whole world food supply is in jeopardy because we're putting it in our vehicles.

So I think we're just kind of at the tip right now, because all of a sudden other foodstuffs have been taken out of production, and increased reliance on GM [genetically modified] stuff. And unfortunately the type of crops they grow for bio-fuels are all GM now. The rate of herbicide that this was supposed to do away with, that they have to use on GM crops, is about one-third more than what they used to have to use. But now they're stuck, because they're licensed, they can't ever grow anything else there again, because somebody owns their life now—the chemical company. It's just bad. I mean, we're insulated now, because we still get California stuff, and Florida stuff. Mexico has been a great producer and really gotten into organic, and has tried to keep those companies out of their country, but they've snuck in, and so now some of the traditional corn and things that the native people rely on for sustainability is being contaminated. Whenever things like that happen, I mean, basically who are you gonna turn to? The guy down the street that's got a few acres that's growin' vegetables. Do you now want those vegetables? Yes you do. So it's just can they survive long enough to produce them? Keep producing them. Yeah, that's the thing.

Basically, we're not changing our strategy going forward. I think we're going to get more involved in the nonprofit, because I'm just tired of playing the game, tired of trying to sell a product that's so superior, but we don't really have enough support for it at this point in time. But there's people that need that, people that are in substance abuse facilities they're trying to train to survive, and they're getting fed refined carbohydrates, and their bodies are making alcohol, and they're trying to stay off alcohol. And the obesity and the diabetes problems, and all that stuff. The leaky gut problems now, which are increasing in children. We have a lot of our members have those health issues, and say it's the only produce they can eat, that their body will actually assimilate.

It'll be a 501(c)(3) corporation and the nonprofit would be independent. We can go to certain farms and say, "Would you be interested in selling us a certain amount of your product?" trying to work them into the program of what to grow, what do these agencies need. Then we provide the coordination. And then the nonprofit would pay relatively retail price for that. So in other words, our mission statement says that we're supporting farmers, saving farmland, and providing food for people in transition; and education as far as how to use those products. Distribution would be through the agency that they're staying at. In other words, we would be working with the agency, not individually with the people. They get it for free. That's the funding of the nonprofit. In other words, they're paying the farmer for the goods. The nonprofit will get funding from the general public, grants, things like that. We actually have a meeting at Microsoft on the sixteenth.

I would like to talk to Bill. He looks a little pasty to me. I don't know what he's eatin', but I bet it's not mustard greens. Yeah, really, he needs to get on the ball. But anyway, it's just kind of now gettin' started. We just got our incorporation. Now we have to start applying to the feds.

I'm not sure what to do for people in poverty. I think we need a niche. We need to do something well. So we'll start there. That, and women's shelters, and substance abuse facilities, youth shelters, those kinds of things. I'm particularly interested in families or something that's related to families and addictions. Because I think if mothers can learn and our educational program would be really simple. You know, go in there and you have twenty dollars worth of stuff, what the typical diet is, the Pop Tarts and the frozen waffles and the box cereal and all that, and you just have what this costs, and how many meals do you get out of that, but have some kind of translation as to what really is a meal as far as your body is concerned. And then you go with some vegetables and a bag of brown rice, and whatever, and you do the same thing. And people are amazed that it's actually cheaper to buy the good stuff. But then you have to say, "How can you utilize this?" and show 'em the easy way to cook 'em, and how to do that, and give 'em some hints about what to do when the rebellion starts at home. Duh! Don't buy anything else! They'll eat it! I can guarantee they will not starve.

The African-American community generally, I think they do—well, at least the older ones try to eat well. I don't know about the younger generation. But they eat a lot of vegetables. The problem is what you put it in. If they can get away from that pork stuff, and cooking them to death. Yeah, there was an old joke—I don't know if it's true, it could have been—the guy that told me swore it's true, worked with my husband. He was on the police force somewhere in Georgia or something, and he said they got this call, some little ol' town in Georgia, a neighbor was sure there were some bodies in a house, or a body, or something, because she's smelling this smell. She'd been smelling it for several days, wanted the police to go out an investigate. So he walks up there, knocks on the door. This lady opens the door, this horrible smell just rolls out of the house. Well, he knew what it was right away. She was puttin' up her collard greens for the winter, and she'd been doin' it for several days, and those things, especially when you cook 'em to death, they just smell foul. But every time we'd go for a family dinner and walk into my husband's relatives' houses, that's what you'd smell, because Thanksgiving you had collard greens, and they'd been cookin' *all morning*. I'd look at them and say, "Oh, just give me some nice steamed ones with some sesame oil on 'em or somethin'. But I'd always bring something raw—salads or whatever. And they all loved it, but it just didn't occur to them to change the way they were doing something, because that's the way it'd *always* been done. And so most of them are overweight, and kids and diabetes and health problems. Interesting, though, although my husband was from the same gene pool, he didn't have any of those problems. You look at people in Africa.... I mean, now it's changed, but in the olden days, how lean and physically fit they were, with the diet they were eating then. Now it's different.

I sold the farm to our members—some of our members. We formed another corporation just for that purpose, to speed the owner, and The Root Connection is actually a dba of that, called Roots of our Times, ROOT for short. There's another one. We wanted to get "root" into the name of the new nonprofit, and we finally all decided, you know, that's just too much. So it's going to be called Farms For Life, which I think is good. So, you know, it's kind of hard to say. My son is the foreman here, and he would have owned the farm but unfortunately he's better off with this arrangement because he's better off earning a salary, than trying to figure out how to pass it on and stuff. I own the ranch next door, personally, and he lives there. So he'll have that.

I'm hoping the nonprofit will expand a little bit into land acquisition, and possibly have a branch of some kind of a land trust or something, because we need to actually buy this land at some point. So we'll see. I don't know.

The more than three hundred billion dollars in global agricultural subsidies amounts to more than six times the world's annual development assistance budget. Oddly, we are paying industrial farmers to practice unsustainable agriculture that undercuts the ability of the poor to feed themselves—the only possible solution to global hunger. Political systems perpetually focused on the crisis du jour rarely address chronic problems like soil erosion; yet, if our society is to survive for the long haul, our political institutions need to focus on land stewardship as a mainstream—and critical—issue.

Over the course of history, economics and absentee ownership have encouraged soil degradation—on ancient Rome's estates, nineteenth-century southern plantations, and twentieth-century industrialized farms. In all three cases, politics and economics shaped land-use patterns that favored mining soil fertility and the soil itself. The overexploitation of both renewable and nonrenewable resources is at once well known and almost impossible to address in a system that rewards individuals for maximizing the instantaneous rate of return, even if it depletes resources critical for the long term. The worldwide decimation of forests and fisheries provide obvious examples, but the ongoing loss of the soil that supplies more than 95 percent of our food is far more crucial. Other, nonmarket mechanisms—whether cultural, religious or legal—must rise to the challenge of maintaining an industrial society with postindustrial agriculture. Counterintuitively.........this challenge requires more people on the land, practicing intensive, organic agriculture on smaller farms, using technology but not capitalization.

David R. Montgomery, "Dirt, The Erosion of Civilizations", University of California Press, 2007

Farm Journal

17 May 2009

Met Erick Haakensen in the field at Jubilee. He is supervising 4 female workers and one male volunteer (I'm not really sure about their employment status). They were dropping flats of seedlings in long rows—one plant at a time. The girls range in age from mid-twenties to one (from Germany) in her late forties. They are here to learn about "row cropping" and the agriculture movement in the Valley.

Erick is riding the tractor, loosening the soil—they follow, drop the seedlings from the flats then set them in the rows. He goads them along chiding them good heartedly to "stop communing with the plant—put it in the ground and move on!" He is operating on two hours sleep and has little to say. As they break for lunch, his neighbor, Dave Casey shows up to ask for dumpster privileges; has some garbage he needs to be rid of.

He asks Erick if he's sold his development rights yet for the farm which brings a proper rebuke from Erick whose "No!" contains everything he's going to say. His response to the "Why not?" from Dave is "Because it's immoral and unethical, but other than that it's fine!' They go around a bit and end it with Erick introducing me as a reporter from the Seattle Times who's going to make Dave look really bad for what he's said. Farm development rights are somehow saleable and provide protection to small farmers who want their land to remain agricultural. I will need to find out the structure of this arrangement; who buys rights, etc. Dave invites me to his place just down the road—Changing Seasons Farm.

Erick's enterprise is large—don't know how many acres, but a lot under cultivation. He owns the land—has built a new house—raised above flood height—has several workers—is steadily expanding. He is passionate and deeply committed to preserving agricultural land in the Valley—complicated personality; explosive enthusiasm—easily depressed but dogged—he's been growing organically for twenty years. They break for lunch at 12:30. He tries to be cordial with me but has to excuse himself to head for a nap—a half hour respite before the next batch of volunteers arrive.

Jubilee Farm

Erick Haakensen

12 December 2009

Erick Haakensen is my name. I was born on November 20, 1951, right here in Seattle. I'll tell you about something that I did when I was a little boy that was to have an impact on my whole life. My parents were busy getting a divorce when I was pretty young, kind of about from the age of first grade through third grade—some really unhappy times at home, lots of arguing, lots of fighting. Us kids, the three of us, were very naïve but very fearful, and we'd have little kid meetings when our parents were fighting, and talk about how we were gonna get dragged off to homes and stuff like that.

In the summertime, I could do a lot of things on my own. And I used to start going down to the Puget Sound. I lived about five miles from the beach, and I'd walk down there and spend the day. And then my parents, one of them, would pick me up. And I became very fascinated with fishing. Of course I never was provided with very much. I didn't have a fishing pole, I didn't have fishing line, I didn't have hooks, but I learned that if I went down around the pilings at low tide, I could find lines that had got tangled there, and hooks. Eventually I learned how to catch sea perch, which would come in with the incoming tides, and I was really a pretty good fisherman. I'd go down there with absolutely nothing and come back with all these fish. There's something about it that just really excited me.

The other thing that I did is, I figured out that the fish came in to feed off the barnacles, and when the tide was out, I could wade out there and break barnacles off the pilings right below where I was gonna fish. Then when the fish came in, there'd be all these half-broken barnacles that would attract just schools of fish there, and I'd be sittin' there, just pullin' up fish after fish after fish.

I don't know why that little story comes to mind, but it's indicative, I guess, of the fact that I always enjoyed the sea, and I always enjoyed nature, and early on I realized I was just an outdoors kind of person. I never got over it, I always wanted to be outside. And a lot of my activities were outside activities, even later in high school when I got into sports and athletics: I was a long-distance runner. I loved going out and running five-mile courses, ten-mile courses, sometimes fifteen-mile courses. I was living with my dad in those days. My parents had separated and my dad and I lived together. And I guess I just kind of sensed that whatever I ended up doing would be something to do with the great outdoors.

I was interested, as a young person, in gardening, although I didn't have hardly any exposure, except for one thing: and I'm sure this was very important. I say "my grandfather"—he really wasn't my grandfather. He was about four-foot-nine, and very Italian; there were a lot of Italian immigrants in South Seattle back in those days. And he had a garden, and the garden was absolutely wonderful. He grew *so* much food. And I remember him composting and saying, "You gotta compost, you gotta build compost." I was fascinated by that.

I went to college for a couple of years, and that was in, what was it, 1969 and 1970. But I just couldn't focus on school and so I dropped out. As you know, the streets were full of protestors in those days and it was not a good time. I mean, the year that I dropped out of college at the U. Dub (University of Washington) was the spring that we had the massive assault on Seattle, 50,000 people marched right up over the ship canal freeway, just shut it down. I happened to be in a group that started throwing rocks, which was kind of shocking to me. It was a big mob, is what it was.

Anyway, I was penniless—absolutely penniless—penniless to the point of selling my blood cells twice a week for gas money. Gas didn't cost much then, and I had a motorcycle, and it was pretty easy to get by. One day I went down to Fisherman's Terminal and ran into a kid that I'd known from high school. He kind of showed me what he was doing, and I thought, "This is the life for me!" Outdoors, adventurous. I kind of got hooked into the fishing thing. Some fisherman saw me and talked to me a little bit, and saw a big, strong, dumb, Norwegian kid. I thought it was such a break for me. I look back and know it was a big break for him, because he just worked me to death! But I did learn to fish in Alaska, and I liked it a lot, and I actually fished there for twenty-five years, so that the fishing definitely overlapped with my farming career.

"What is it exactly that made me love the land?" The short answer is I just don't know. I don't know, there's just something that appealed to me about growing. I don't think that's unusual. I don't know if one could look at it metaphysically—"We came from the earth" and all that sort of stuff. But the long and short of it is, I just have an interest. And I had an interest especially in being able to somehow make a living off the land. That's a very romantic notion. In practice, it's not nearly so romantic. But I always had that as a goal in the back of my mind, and thinking someday I would maybe have enough money to buy a farm. And it finally, of course, did happen. Didn't happen directly, it kind of happened indirectly, and I stumbled through a period of growing Christmas trees on Union Hill on some property I bought there, which was not very satisfying at all. And then I found out I was in the path of development, and we ended up swapping properties for the place I have now in Snoqualmie Valley.

There was something about the setting of that farm that I really liked. And I can tell you exactly what it is, it's on a road that connects nowhere and nowhere—that little spot at the bottom of the Tolt Hill. There's really no reason for people to turn left there, or where it comes out on the other side at the golf course, there's really no reason for people to turn there, except of course those two golf courses. But my farm is right in the middle. So people usually coming to the golf course to the north of me come in from Tolt, and the people going to the golf course south of me come in from 202, and we just don't hardly get any traffic. I looked at that, and it was quiet, with a big barn, and lots of land.

The flooding was something of an issue for me so I didn't buy it right away. I watched it for two years, through flooding seasons. And I looked very, very hard elsewhere: up in the Skagit Valley, further north than that too. I spent just weeks and weeks up there scouring, and going way beyond just talking to realtors, but going house to house. I'd see an area I liked, just go talk to people and see if there was anything available around. And I found some pieces that were tremendous buys and all that, but something kept calling me back closer to home.

I was now teaching and so I was looking for some place that would be close enough that I could teach school too. In the interim period while I was fishing, I also went back to school—had off-seasons, you know, in the academic year, so I went first to Notre Dame, and then back to Yale. And I really enjoyed teaching. It was kind of one of those indoor activities that's great to do in the winter, but I wanted something else too.

The only thing that really interested me was philosophy. It was the big questions that brought me to it. Certainly the personage of Socrates as presented by Plato is seductive above all things to an inquiring mind—the kind of honesty that.... I mean, usually you think of Socrates, if you don't know anything, as the stodgy person who knows everything; whereas in reality—at least the picture we get from Plato—and I always liked Nietzsche's assessment where he says, "When you're looking at Socrates, remember, it's Plato in front, Plato in back, and Plato in the middle." But we're not devoted to the personage of Socrates in the same sense that I suppose Christians are devoted to the personage of Jesus or something like that. Socrates was a great teacher. It's the thoughts that count. But the kind of humility that he really had. I mean, you think the day that he was gonna die, he had this *great* belief in the afterlife, and somebody came up, and they were having this little conversation, and said, "Hey, you're completely wrong about all this." And Socrates says, "Well, I've believed this all my life. But if there are new arguments that I haven't heard, let's talk about 'em, because I'm gonna be there soon!" I was just amazed by that, that a person could go through his whole life, and really believe something fervently, and not with the dogmatism that says, "This is it, I'm right, I know in the strong epistemological sense...." And that's what I found refreshing about the good philosophers, the really top-notch ones. There's a kind of humility. Because once you really do go beyond, you break through that barrier of self-confidence that says, "I *know* something." Then suddenly, it's frightening in a way. And as Kierkegaard said, it becomes lonelier. There aren't many people that will agree with you. And they'll look at you as being a little bit perverse, because you can't really definitively say, "I know."

So yeah, so it was basically philosophy. I took a course at North Seattle Community College, from a person who had no idea he would later become the best man in my wedding. Good friend, life-time friend, and he was the one that urged me to go take a Great Books course at the University of Notre Dame, which was just a wonderful experience for me. I was writing a letter of reference for a student last night, to Notre Dame, and I was kind of reliving some of those days. They were very, very exciting days intellectually, and I think that it's so sad that so many young people settle for being trained, when they could be educated. It's such a loss. But I'm thrilled that Seattle Central University, where I also used to teach, is now offering a two-year degree in sustainability, or they're in the process of doing that. And there's a board of directors that's setting up the program, which I'm on—the only farmer on it, by the way. I was kind of surprised to see that. And I'm kind of wondering what's gonna happen there. Are we going to be talking about training students? Or are we gonna talk about educating people, and also teaching them how to farm. Those are two very different kinds of endeavors. I mourn over the substitution of technical training for the kind of liberal arts tradition that once existed. I'm sure it will continue to go on, but there's so many people who are, as a friend of mine once told me (who happens to have a Ph.D. from Harvard, a medical person, taught in medical school) after we'd been friends and talked for quite a while, he said "Erick, I'm *incredibly* well trained, but I'm unfortunately uneducated, because at every juncture, I was in the lab, I was in the math class, I was on this narrow track." I'm a student of philosophy—how's that? A lover is not exactly the same as an obtainer.

Anyway, I was looking at land for a long, long time. And I looked at this piece, the one I have now, and it didn't feel right to me at first. There's a big lake in it, for one thing—right in the middle of it. It was very wet. It'd been abandoned many years before. The person that owned it—I hate to say this—was a real redneck, and wouldn't put it on the multiple listings, because he was afraid that a person of (whispers) *color* might come and express interest. Really! And that really turned me off. I don't know why, I thought maybe bad karma. But anyway, I kept looking at it. Its proximity to Bellevue Community College where I was teaching was a big plus. It was less than thirty minutes away. And yet it just seemed like....

You know what it's like when you get on that road West Snoqualmie River Road... You can look around and kind of ignore the houses on the hill and say, "Wow, I'm in rural America, in a rural agrarian-type situation here." So we bought it, we bought the farm. And the one thing that was real interesting, I was assured by the neighbors that I spoke to, of one thing, and that's that I would never find a way to make a living off the land—which kind of hurt, because way down deep, that was really one of my goals. I thought, "Here I've got"—what did we have then?—"105 acres"—maybe more. I think we bought a few more pieces too. Maybe 150 acres at that time. "Surely I could make a living off the land." And they assured me that I couldn't. And these were people who were in the stages of going broke. At the time I moved in there, that would have been the late eighties, dairies were dropping like flies. There used to be.... I don't know what the greatest number was, but there were many in Carnation; at one time, I heard there were twenty-six dairies between Duvall and Carnation. And ours was one of 'em. Leon and Pete Enger, the people who built the place here, they did well on fifty cows. They milked fifty cows on a flat line. So they told me I wasn't going to be able to make a living. And I got off to a pretty good start in proving them to be correct, because I went into the cattle business.

That also seemed romantic. But it finally occurred to me.... fortunately then the floods weren't nearly as bad as they are now.....we didn't have issues with, in the wintertime, with water getting into the barns or anything. That all came later. But it occurred to me that doing cow-calf operation on 150 acres, there's just no way I can compete with people in eastern Washington, who lease 10,000 acres, and just let the cows roam on 'em, and have no costs. I didn't know that then. Then eventually I found out, and then I got into raising calves, and raising calves is a difficult proposition too. They tend to die when they're taken away from their moms. And then I don't know exactly what it was.... Oh, yes, I do know what it was—it was Chua Pao Cha.

Chua Pao came in with the first group of immigrants—I say "immigrants"— they were the Hmong people who were our allies in the Vietnam War and after "we" pulled the plug, climbed on airplanes and just "beamed us up and out of there!", they were left to face the music, and it wasn't very good at all. In fact, at one time we sponsored not a Hmong person, but a Vietnamese person who had fought with South Vietnam, and that poor guy, he'd been in a concentration camp for like ten years and lost 50 percent of his body weight. He was still missing teeth. He was just shell-shocked. That's kind of what we left behind. The Hmong people also, they were mountain tribal people, but they were huge allies of ours, they did intelligence for us, they helped us get by in the jungles.

Anyway, Chua Pao was one of six brothers, and he came over here and settled in the first group that was sponsored by the Congregational Church in Carnation. And one day he came over to me—he's just a little short man—and he said, "I want to buy peeg." I couldn't understand what he was saying. What he was saying was—we had a pig—he wanted to buy our pig. I was raising a few pigs just to eat, and I said, "Sure, I'll sell you a pig." And we got to talkin' and then he said, "I want land." And I thought, "Well, go get yourself some land." But what he was asking was, could he rent land from me." At that time, there were no other Hmong farmers in the whole valley. This was the first acre of land that was rented out to a Hmong person. I said, "Okay." So we staked out an acre of land, and he rented it and I sat and watched him. I watched him farm and saw how he did. He did row crops very much like we do now. After watching him—he did some flowers and he did some vegetables, as they do now—I thought, "I could do that!" and I started.

The interesting thing was, I wasn't really organic at that point. I didn't really have a sense of being organic. I wish I could say, "Oh, yes, I started pure, and this was my goal, was to save the world," and all that. All I wanted to do was make a living off the land. And using chemicals didn't feel right to me. I'll never forget the day I went down to Wolf Kill in Monroe—it's still there, same building—and stood there and talked to the guy. I said, "I want to grow sweet corn." He said, "Well, if you want to grow sweet corn, I will tell you *exactly* what you need to do, and if you vary from this one bit, you will never grow an ear of sweet corn." And of course you start amending the soil. And then he put down—I can't remember which pesticides, Atrazine is one of them. You have your pre-emergent weed control, you have your post-emergent weed control, you have your pesticides.... And he had this whole spring regimen, and he said, "If you don't follow this, you will never grow anything in our Valley." That was pretty impressive, so I started doing that. But right away I knew that I didn't like it. And as fate would have it, I picked up the book called "*Seeds of Change*" by Kenny Ausubel, a wonderful book, very seductive, because it comes out and says, "We all gotta be organic to save the world!" He simply showed little vignettes of what's happening when we don't try to save the world, the downhill trend of agriculture: erosion, and of course agricultural poisons that end up in the water and the air and affect the fish and the environment and all this sort of thing. I was really totally converted at that point and started farming organically. There was nobody else farming in the Valley then. And when I kind of announced to a few of my neighbors I was going to be organic?....... talk about the laughing stock! They were also questioning whether I was going to be wearing tights out there.

Purple pants, yeah. They assumed that I was gonna come out of the closet; all sorts of little jokes. But I heard about this thing called CSA. There really was only one west of the Mississippi at that time. I didn't know who she was, though. I didn't even know she was there at that time. That's Claire Thomas, of course, at Woodinville at Root Connections. I didn't know anything about her, but they were gonna have this conference in San Francisco, and I thought, "Wow, I haven't been down to San Francisco since hippie days. I'll go back down there." And so we went down, went to this conference, heard about CSA, and it just hit me between the eyes. It just had everything.

And again, was there a little romance in it? Yeah, it was painted up to be community involvement in agriculture, but it's the real thing, it really is. I mean, I've done it now for fourteen years, and I would say the feeling I had about it then is exactly what it's come to be on my farm. And some of that may be because that's what I wanted and I made it happen, or it could be simply because when people come together around something as simple and basic as a primordial need like food, the hierarchies tend to disappear, and people really tend to become, I don't know, capable of sharing with each other, and being a part of community.

So it was a great thing. When I came back, I did find out about Claire. And remember, Claire, at that point, had been doing this for seven years. And there wasn't anybody else in the whole state doing it, and it just.... She was so amazing— and she still is to me. She is definitely—and I don't mind saying this publicly—she is my agricultural hero. And not just agricultural, but also—I don't know if I'd say ethical—in terms of a committed lifestyle, her farming has been reflective of the way she was involved in a marriage where her husband had Alzheimer's, and she hung in, and she cared, and she took care of him. And did the same thing with an ailing mother. It's just the way she does things. She's wonderful.

She was friendly to me, but not like, "I'm gonna tell you what to do." She became a model for me, and when I think back on my relationship with Claire, I realize that she was doing something really important there, and she didn't mind me coming to watch, but I think that she knew that she couldn't hold my hand. If I had what it takes to do it, I've got a model here. I knew she was gettin' by, she was makin' it, and I thought, "Well, if she is, I can too." And so we started with a CSA. I didn't know much, I hadn't grown very many things, and I never have taken a class in agronomy. I've never taken any kind of agricultural classes at all. But little by little I've picked up things, and so it's worked out well.

One of the big changes that occurred for me had to do with the issues around becoming certified organic, because when you become certified organic, you of course then become open to a set of rules and regulations about what you should be doing. I've never been particularly good at following rules and regulations. I've always had a pretty strong sense of one should do what's ethical or moral, and if it happens to be legal, well, that's fine, but if not, then you just do what you need to do.

But the thing about the certification, it actually, at two stages it initiated new levels of my relationship to agriculture. In the first instance, I'd been certified for a couple three years when the first serious effort came to have a national organic standard. Those of us who had been in it for even a little bit at that point, immediately saw the handwriting on the wall: this is something that's going to become subject to Congress. Congress, of course, is subject to the lobbyists and corporations. And we just saw that what would happen is, the corporations would get involved, and the organic standards would be changed significantly. And of course that's eventually what happened. But we got involved in the hearings that were held down here, and a big protest march as the hearings were going on, in which I almost ended up in jail because I happened to be the person that was in charge of organizing this protest, and we were marching around the Seattle Center—big snare drum, the whole thing, "Hell no, hell no...." I can't even remember what the cry was, but something like that. And I was in the back of the group when somebody in the front decided, "Well, let's just go right over to the building where the federal hearing examiners there were taking testimony." And so they were leading. I thought, "Where are we going? We're supposed to be...." All of a sudden we're marching right to the building, and they didn't stop at the door. Some people *tried* to stop them. They pushed right through, right into the hearing room, and we had about 200 people, everybody marched in there, still chanting. And of course they had to stop the hearings. And the cops were hot, and everybody was hot, and there was a lot of tension, because there was this really strong feeling amongst people who were doing farming then, that things were gonna change drastically. And of course I think that that's right. I dropped out of the certified organic program. Number one, for CSA I don't really need to be certified. My members know how I farm, and it's not like I'm wholesaling where that certification means something. I don't mean just to badmouth the certification program, because it really is important in many instances, and we have to have it, so that when you go into a PCC or *any* store, and you see the "certified organic," at least there's a much better chance that it's really organic. And so in that sense I'm in favor of it.

On the other hand, the standards have been diluted to the point where it just.... I'll tell ya, it's really sad to think of how little it takes to become certified organic. And this, of course, was the second stage of my dissatisfaction. The big change that came in my farming career also had to do with that certification process when I really realized, and I just couldn't deny, that for all the talk about sustainability, there really is no essential relationship whatsoever between being certified organic and sustainability. To be certified organic is kind of like the rabbi that I was talking to, who came out to my farm, and I was asking him, "What about kosher dill pickles? What makes 'em kosher?" And he was kind of a rotund man, and he kind of leaned back with a happy smile on his face. "It's easy! You pay the rabbi. I go out and bless 'em, and that's all it takes." And kind of in a way, that's kind of what certification is, too. You pay your money.... There's a few "thou shalt nots." And there's another interesting correlation here between the whole kind of religious phenomenon and certification for organic. I mean, there's "thou shalt not use herbicide, thou shalt not use pesticide, thou shalt not...." Those are the things you *don't* do. Just like in religion, you have all the "thou shalt nots."

But are the "thou shalt nots," is that the heart, the essence of what it means to be a religious person, the things you *don't* do?! Hopefully not! I once heard somebody say, "If you're doing what you *should* be doing, you won't even have time to do the 'thou shalt nots,' you won't even think about it." And unfortunately, the organic movement, through the certification approach, really doesn't have much about what we should be doing, how we should be healing the earth. I use those words "healing the earth"—it may sound melodramatic, but I'm actually quoting Rudolph Steiner. And he has a wonderful little refrain that shows up over and over again, where he says, "We do these things that the earth may be healed." We don't save the earth, but we can heal the earth. Why can we heal it? Because we're the ones that have wounded it. And it is possible, because the earth is very resilient, at least to a point, that we could enact some healing.

So as I drifted further and further away from certification, I thought, "Well, what else is out there?" I ran into the whole bio-dynamic group of people. Rudolph Steiner, who died in 1925, was kind of a seer. Really, I've come to see him now not so much as an originator of a farming method, but as kind of a collator of older traditions that still were alive in Germany and Austria at the time, that he particularly gleaned. And he wasn't shy about this. I mean, he was probably one of the most erudite men in all of Europe, wrote prolifically, gave some 10,000 public lectures, and yet would go talk to old women who really carried the **"agri - culture"**, folklore, the women who stirred the pots, got hauled off regularly by the Catholic Church and burned at the stake for doing things like making organic biodynamic preparations, like we do today.

So in Steiner I heard the words for the first time that "if you really want to be a"—and he didn't use exactly the word sustainable, but it's what we mean by sustainable—"but if you're going to continue on with the health of the farm, you have to maintain the fertility of the farm." That's a big one. But Number Two, you have to do it *from* the farm itself. If you bring it in from someplace else, you just can't do that, because you're stealing from some other place that needs that fertility.

In the first instance, just to say "you've got to replace the fertility of the soil," is kind of shocking. There are a lot of farmers who go out, and they farm for years and years and years on very rich soil, and they really don't have to replace the fertility, because there's so much fertility there. However, it's exactly like someone buying an auto parts store. I shouldn't say that, but if you've been in any auto parts store, you know what I mean. So you get a big inventory there, and suddenly you start selling off your inventory but not replacing it. And everything can be great for quite a while, maybe years, but eventually you run out of inventory and you don't have anything left. And the fertility of the soil is the farmer's inventory. And what *so* many farmers are doing is they're selling their inventory, they're selling off their capital, and acting like it's profit, but it's really not profit at all, because they're giving away the value of their land, and when they're done, there's not much left. We have a lot of land in America that's in that state, or to some degree in that state.

So I started thinking about, first of all, the fertility of *my* soil. It turns out we have river bottom soil that is just absolutely wonderful. And you don't have to be much of a farmer to grow stuff down there, you just have to put the seeds in and figure out how to keep the weeds out, and you can look like you're a good farmer.

I don't feel like I'm a very good farmer. I know some people with green thumbs, but I'm not one of 'em, but I work hard at it. But the soil is very, very rich, but no matter how rich, it can't go on forever. So what do I do for fertility? That's a big issue. But then the bigger question is, "Can I really learn to provide the fertility for the farm from my own farm?" And that's just an enormous challenge. It's the kind of question and problem and real life conundrum that keeps me going, that keeps me searching for an answer, because I feel like if I can't do it on this farm, if I can't model it on this farm, what chance do we have anywhere? I need to learn how to do that.

This is where you get into this kind of paradox. I mean, I guess I've been farming longer than anybody in our Valley, and everybody says, "You should be doing this, and you should be teaching people, you should be making change, you should be on all these boards of these organizations." And another part of me just says, "You know, what I really need to do is really learn how to be a good farmer, and really take sustainability not just as oh yes, I'm organic and sustainable, like I hear...." I hate to say this, but sometimes brand new farmers, people who've never farmed, they're certified organic already, and they say, "Oh yeah, we're organic and sustainable." Boy, that sustainable is a *really, really* big word, and it takes, I think, so long to develop it, and initiate it. It's not gonna happen in *my* lifetime on my farm, I know. But I want to head that direction. And I think I'm doing that, and trying to be an example. We have lots of really neat younger farmers in our valley. And I don't feel like I need to tell *them* what to do, but I feel like I need to show them in some way that it *can* be done. Because for most farmers, it's pretty daunting. I mean, you buy those plastic bags, it's pretty easy. Bring 'em out, cut 'em open, get 'em onto the soil, and there's your fertility. But that's not really sustainability. And of course it uses and squanders a lot of fossil fuels, both in its creation and its transportation. And it mitigates the kind of full creativity of the human being as a farmer. I often call that painting by number. You know those little painting by number things? That's really what farming has become for a lot of people. And getting back to the thing about training these kids—are we going to train them to paint by number, or are we going to turn them into agricultural artists? And that's what I want to be.

I want to have the kind of artistry so that I don't have to have a book that tells me everything, because there's gonna be situations that I just haven't seen before. But I want to develop that sense and that competence that we can deal with that, we can find an answer to it, and we can find it with a means that *can* be sustained. And that's really what excites me more about farming than anything else. And it's what kind of prevents me from wanting to get out and be beating the drum for getting on all these national boards and things like that. I know that there's a place for that, and somebody's gotta do it, but oh man, we have *so* many people trying to help farmers. I'm sure in King County there's *way* more people who are drawing full salaries by the way—way more than any farmer makes—to try to *help* farmers, than those of us who are actually farming, and actually making a full time living from farming. There aren't many. There really aren't, when it comes right down to it—a very, very small handful. But I think it can be done, and so that's what excites me. That's what I would say is my real goal.

Along those lines, there are some political things. I really have a vision for trying to make the Valley so that it *is* possible for young people to get involved. And I just don't want to see our Valley end up like another Enumclaw that just gets hacked up and carved up into little hobby farms all up and down the Valley, owned by people who are very wealthy, and who have no intention whatsoever of farming.

It's kind of interesting, I just read in *The Capital Press*, down in Oregon you can build a home on a farm, but only if you have an income of ... what was it? ...

something like $80,000 for a twenty-acre parcel. They have some kind of a—you have to show that you have had an income off that farm, by farming, before you can build a home. Which is something just designed to prevent people who just want to come out and sit on big pieces of land. And I understand why people want to do that. But boy, that land is sacred, and it's a desecration of it, I think, to either use it wrongly agriculturally, by using poisons and that sort of thing, or to not use it at all. It seems to me that both of those are desecrations. But you've gotta be hopeful, there's gotta be some source of hope, but honestly, I don't know how much hope I have, I really don't. And it doesn't follow from the fact that I don't know that I have that much hope that I'm gonna become a quietist and just sit back and hold my hands and say, "Oh wow, all is lost." And I would like to think that those small incremental changes would make some kind of difference. Just look at the twenty years that I've farmed here. When I started, organics was nothing, and now it's *huge*, and everybody wants to *be* it. I mean, even the national corporations—Monsanto has an organic division! That hurts, doesn't it?

This is why we need to educate people, not train people, because as E.F. Schumacher says, "The essence of education is really the evaluation, analysis, and transmission of values." And that doesn't mean any particular value, it just means that we evaluate our values. And coming up with what is it that we really want in life? And as Schumacher says, the unstated and unquestioned value in our society, is that more is better: more money, more things, more stuff. And so many of us don't stop to think about that. We somehow or other breach that, so that instead of saying, like the subtitle of Schumacher's book, "Economics as if people matter." And that's really so much of what it comes down to. Our society is set up so that the mass population doesn't matter, except insofar as they become the consumers for the goods that the wealthy then will sell to the people and become even wealthier. Schumacher talks about the two cultures that exist. And there *are* two cultures, and never before have they been more disparate, and becoming *more* disparate, widely spread, financially, all the time.

And so the question then is, can a fringe group of the people on the bottom somehow or other affect the whole? In the U.S. we would like to think that that would happen. It doesn't seem to be able to happen politically, because we know where the political power is. Where I hold hope, some little bit of hope, I suppose, is through litigation in our own—coming back to the local—in our own county, we are farming in the Snoqualmie Valley on lands that have been specifically set aside for agricultural production. And if we could get the courts to do what the politicians *won't* do—the politicians won't do it because they want to placate the people with money who *do* want to sit out there and not use the land—but if we could get the courts to come along and say, "Hey, this land has been designated agricultural." Legally, this is the code, it *says* it's agricultural land. Not just agricultural, but agricultural production, *commercial* agricultural production. If we could somehow or another get the courts to take a stand, that seems to me to be the biggest hope. Short of that, we have hope only of some kind of semi-apocalypse. For example, I was hoping when the price of oil started going up, and when gas hit, what, four bucks a gallon, I said, "Keep goin'! Keep goin'! I want to see ten!" And *then* we're gonna see some change. So there is that kind of hope. It's a really sad hope, though. It says that we need to be driven to our knees before we'll change. But better than nothing, right? But the question is, can we have a semi-apocalypse? We couldn't stage one. Could it be gratuitous enough, could the gods just say, "Smite 'em, but don't kill 'em?" Is it gonna be semi, or is it gonna be enough just to wipe us out?

It does seem like, for whatever reasons, the constituents of the earth tend to come together into life forms, just for whatever. So if we had a burnout or an ice-out, as we've had in the past, I think that it would start again, I really do. And it's kind of interesting, all of a sudden we're down to Buddhist cosmology, the huge cycle. And maybe that's where it's at. Obviously, as you get older you think more about things like that. And I'm much closer to the end than I used to be, and I feel it, I really do. And those questions become amazingly interesting to me. I don't feel like I'm going to have any kind of dogmatic answer one way or the other, but I love exploring the possibilities and thinking about it. But at the same time, I want to have my hands in the dirt. I like that.

You know, one of the questions we face is, "How do we feel about raising products that are largely for a kind of elite affluent consumers?" I've thought about that a fair amount. I get that kind of a question a lot, as well as—and this might not seem like a direct analog to everyone, but it seems like it to me—is when we have extra crops, people say, "Well, are you donating those crops to the food banks?" There's kind of the expectation that we ought to do that. My answer to this may not be quite as warm and fuzzy as it ought to be. It's not that I'm unconcerned about the poor. I really am. One of the things I don't like about living on Earth is the kind of system injustice that exists. Boy, you don't have to travel very far before you see it. *But*, we also have to realize that the reason that we are selling food that is very high-priced is because all the rest of it is subsidized. And it's awfully tough to come to a farmer and say, "Hey, you're competing with subsidized stuff. You really should sell yours at less money, even though you're not subsidized." You go, "Wait a minute! I'm just *barely* getting by now!"

The solution is not to try to get the farmer to get his or her prices down, but to get other food to reflect the real cost of production, which it *in no way* does. We are right now—we got a little taste of it, again, in a semi-cataclysmic event. I'm thinking of the Katrina event, where we kind of realized, everybody stopped and looked at the Mississippi River. It drains away 14 million acres of corn production soil into the Gulf, and we need to realize that we are polluting not just our streams, but our groundwater, the oceans, the atmosphere as it evaporates—everything! And there's a *tremendous* cost there that's going to have to be paid someday, we're going to *have to* clean it up. Just like these smelters, the one down at Tacoma, what did it cost? Six *billion* dollars or something was dumped into that black hole. People make little trinkets, whatever they made there, for years and years and years, and put a price tag on it that in *no way* reflected the cost of the environmental damage being done. And in agriculture, that's *exactly* the same thing. Nor does it reflect the price of the fertility that's being stolen from the soil, or the loss of topsoil, or the health issues that are accruing. And it goes on and on.

Everybody in the United States should have a picture of the Easter Islanders cutting down the last tree, kind of looking at each other and saying, "What now?" It really becomes kind of a sad thing, and it's true, I totally agree that we *are* selling to the people who can afford it, *because* they can afford to pay for nonsubsidized food. And once again, it's the gap between the haves and the have-nots: what can we do? And I don't know that I really have an answer to that. We have to change the whole of society.

We need to try to get urban agriculture going. That's another thing I'm personally really excited about. One of the major colleges here in town is wanting to start a farm—not just a garden, but a farm. And it's right down in an area of a lot of poverty. That's really exciting. And we've talked before about the whole kind of Cuban model in Havana, a city of 2.5 million that feeds itself through urban agriculture now, although they do have the tremendous advantage of having two growing seasons a year. They *never* see single-digit temperatures! But we could do it here too. I see things like this Seattle college starting an urban farm in proximity to people who need. They're doing it, and with a little organization—and I'm kind of excited, because I don't feel like I know a lot about farming, but I'm a pretty good organizer, and I've really learned how to set up a farm, and I know what they need to do to have a lot of success, and I believe they will. So that's really an exciting sort of model, I guess.

Steiner said, and Sir Albert Howard also made this same observation, and, "When people don't eat well, they don't think well, and they don't behave well." They said it before there was any evidence—and now there's getting to be more kind of scientific evidence—there's a correlation between eating all this junk food and misbehavior. People just are wound up. And you get people who are wound up, in situations of real social injustice, and you're gonna have the kind of thing that you see, and some of it's gonna be ethnic, because we have a real, real shameful history of ethnic relationships in our country. For all of our claims to the contrary, what we've done has not been very good.

So it's exciting to see things like that happen, and I'm hopeful. But I don't want anybody to get the idea that farmers are, number one, getting rich on this, and that it's wrong to charge.... Let me restate this. I think that the consumers need to recognize that replacing fertility of the soil is a valid cost that needs to be borne in the act of selling. People say, "Why don't you take all the extra food that you have, and take it to the food bank?" Well, that's interesting. You think about that for a minute, and you think it through, it sounds really noble, and I have done it, but there's a problem there too, because that food that's not used, were it to be composted and put back into the soil, which is what we do—or just worked back into the soil—it becomes a part of the fertility bank *of* the soil. So what's being asked of me is basically to say, "Because you happen to be a grower of food, you should underwrite the cost of the poor in a way that the rest of us aren't really asked to because we don't grow food." But it's money. It's money. I've got to replace that fertility one way or another. And if I take it off the farm, I've got to get it back into the farm. I know that may sound really hardnosed and all that, but as I thought it through, I just thought, "It's not like the farmer has some kind of special imperative to share that food." But there's a common imperative—we all have an imperative to help those who don't have enough. And farmers should certainly be involved, but not to the detriment of the soil.

I know a lot of farmers right now who do not put back. The law of the return is being violated, because they just don't have the money to do it. They just can't seem to make ends meet. And, you know, the soil *is* forgiving, it'll forgive for quite a while. But I also know farmers who haven't done that, who just these last two years have gotten caught, and they can't grow crops anymore. Their crops are *really* diminishing in their quality, and it's very obvious. And then suddenly they look back at six or eight or ten years of abuse and suddenly now, "How am I going to replace six or eight or ten years of a fertility program that *should* be going on *all the time*?" And that's something that we just don't teach enough in our Ag schools or wherever it is. We just don't articulate it.

You know, you can't separate the person from what the person thinks. And my person is getting tired. I've never before in my life experienced much tiredness. In Alaska I would sometimes fish for five days straight, without a break, without sleep. Not without food—we did eat. But with no sleep, and it wasn't that tough. And when I first started farming, I could farm, easily work twenty hours a day if I had the daylight, and feel great! I'm goin' downhill, can't do it anymore. And maybe that's a good thing. It encourages me to delegate more, and try to get other people involved. The other thing it does, though, is that having had my head down in the trenches for a long time, maybe it's time for me to come up, and say that some of the things that I've learned and gleaned about agriculture, and maybe also about education, need to come together now. You know, in the Hindu tradition, there are those who go off into the forest and spend time reflecting, and then come back.... this usually happens in their fifties and sixties, and they come back, and they become servants of society in a way. They don't charge for it, but they just help people because they've been through it.

I feel like in a lot of ways, intellectually I'm at the top of my game. Physically I'm not anymore. And maybe that's saying to me personally that it's time for me to get out of the trenches, so to speak, and do some of the things others are enjoining me to do at other times. And that's exciting, because I would like to be involved in this university project, the one down at Seattle Central. I'm really glad to be on the board. And I would even think personally maybe getting back into teaching and trying to teach. I think there's a huge philosophical component, an ethical component, of any kind of agricultural endeavor, that *needs* to be there so we don't end up growing farmers who never even stop to question whether more is better, or even whether more is going to make them happier. They don't even ask the question! It's just assumed.

Where do we go from here corporately? What I really see us needing to do, is, again, it's the notion of communal existence. It's one thing to have a successful farm, and that feels good. It would be another thing to have a successful agricultural community. And when I started, like I said, on my road, my little road, it's just a couple miles there, but I was the only one. And now there's like probably ten of us there, up and down the road, and that's the start of a community. And there's a lot of power in community, there's friendship, there's the kind of thing that makes life ... I want to say worth living ... but helps us get through the hard times, and we share the hard times, and the joys. And that sort of *re*-establishment of community is something that I really look forward to, and hope will happen before I draw my last breath.

Wendy Haakensen

10 December 2009

I'm Wendy Haakensen, and I was born on May 24, 1960, at Seattle General Hospital, which is no longer there. I grew up in the Wallingford area with my mother and father and one brother and three sisters. We were across the street from an elementary school, McDonald Elementary, which is where I went to elementary school at. I spent all of my summers at my grandparents' farm in Longview, which is a two and a half hour drive south, just forty-five minutes this side of Portland. That was always my favorite place to go, I loved it. I could not get enough of it. My mom would try to hold off telling me that they'd planned a trip to the farm, because she knew that I wouldn't be able to sleep if I knew that I was going to the farm. So she would wait until the day before, try to not let the cat out of the bag. Because if I knew that I was going to Longview, to Grandma and Grandpa's farm, that I would not sleep one wink, and I would be so excited to go. I just always loved it there.

As I got older, I would spend my summers there. We'd always go down every summer the first of July, and bring the hay in. So that was something that was a big thing for my family, because we did it every year, and that was our summer vacation, is going to Longview. I just absolutely loved it. And when I think back now about the days that we spent there, bringing the hay in, it's so different from now. I feel so blessed to have had that experience, of watching the hay being cut, with my mom riding with the little trailer on the back with the sickle bar and the seat. One day she was bucked off and broke her ankle in like six places. From then on, the sickle bar was attached to the tractor, we no longer did it by the little trailer hooked on the back. And then we would go through and make the shocks of hay by hand, all of us, just mounding up hay. We'd go through and rake it with the buck rake, and then come through and mound it up into shocks, and then come through after it was fully dry, and we'd put all of that loose hay onto a skid, this long wagon. It just had two big tree skids on it, and you pull it over to the barn, and then you winch it right up into the barn. It was all loose. And then we just had a blast playin' in the hay, playin' with the animals, and it was just wonderful.

They were subsistence farmers, so they always had a garden. It wasn't that they had a lot of excess produce to sell, but they always had stuff that they would trade out. We'd milk the cows, and they'd have excess milk to trade or sell to the neighbors. My grandma always had a little strawberry patch, so she'd always have people comin' in to pick strawberries. And then they had cows and milk cows mainly, and sheep, and ducks, and chickens, and sometimes they'd have geese. Never had pigs. So there was just a little of everything goin' on there. It was just a true subsistence farm—at least early on.

So from the time that I remember, my planning, my thought, was always that I would be a farmer. I just, for some reason, knew that, deep within, that I was gonna farm somehow, some way. And then I got to be a teenager, and that thought—I don't know where it went, but it got buried somehow, I guess, with the whole friends and having fun and being a teenager. And farming wasn't a thought that I had at that point. I guess as I graduated from high school and went on, my thoughts turned to having a family. So I got married fairly young. I was twenty and married for a couple of years when I had my first daughter, and that was in 1982. And then I had my second daughter in '84. Started teaching preschool. I don't have much of a background in schooling, other than I'd gotten an A.A. degree at Bellevue Community College, in early childhood education. So I went on to teaching preschool for fourteen years. But when my youngest daughter was graduating from high school—it was actually a year before my daughter was to graduate from high school, I had taken a trip to Costa Rica—a teacher educational trip—and it was a "save the turtles" kind of thing through the Woodland Park Zoo. And it was a wonderful trip, but it reminded me, it brought back that desire to farm. And it just came up so strongly for me.

And about the same time, right after I got back from that trip, I was at a bookstore, thumbin' through some books, and found this book called "*Seeds of Change*" by Kenny Ausubel. And I started reading that, and oh, that just completely turned that desire to farm back on again. So it was about a year and a half that I was really thinking strongly, and kind of bothering my friends about this whole idea of "I want to farm! I really want to farm!" And I'm trying to work this out to how I could go back to farming, or get back to that place that I wanted to be at, and that I thought I would be at, years and years before. So what happened from there was I was living in Woodinville at the time, and like I said, my daughter was getting ready to go off to college. I decided that in order for me to farm, I needed to get a little bit more education under my belt, as far as knowledge of farming goes. I'd always had like little gardens and kind of kept my hands in the soil, but not to the degree that I wanted this to occur.

The other book that I was reading at the time was Barbara Kingsolver's "*Prodigal Summer*". Something about those two books and that trip to Costa Rica just opened up this window for me that I just had to do this thing. So my intention was that I was gonna go back to my family farm, which my grandparents' farm had been in my family for over a hundred years. My great-grandparents homesteaded it. Then my grandparents lived there. My uncle has never left. He's still there today. What he's been doing since my grandparents passed away is that he has had a small herd of beef shorthorns—more of a hobby for him. So there's not been a whole lot going on, on the farm these past ten years or so. My brother still goes every year to hay in July. He still carries on that tradition with his two boys. That's where their connection stops there, to bring the hay in for this small herd of cows that my uncle has. So my uncle was giving me some land, about ten acres, and my intention was to go and build some sort of living facility there, and to start farming that area. But before I went to that step, I thought that I should find a local CSA, because that was really the model that I liked the most: an organic CSA/Farmers Market type situation. So I wanted to get myself immersed in that area, and see what other people were doing with that—you know, visually and hands on.

I had given my notice at the school that I was working at. I was working on Mercer Island at the Mercer Island Learning Lab, and teaching there. I'd been there for about five years. I had a wonderful friend there that I was teaching with. This is through Bellevue Community College. And so I'd given her my notice that I wasn't going to be back the following year. I thought during that whole summertime I'd be able to get immersed, and then decide where I was going to go from there. So I made it possible, in that the house I was living at, that I had a mortgage on in Woodinville, would not really be a place that I could feasibly stay, farming, when I made this next step. So at that time, my daughter, like I said, was getting ready to leave for college, so I brought in a couple of roommates and just scaled back on any expenses that I could, and went on this search for a farm to intern or work at. Even if it was just volunteering, I figured I would somehow get my feet wet. So I had a good friend, Jim Newton, who I was always in communication with, "Oh, I want to farm. I'm sure you're gettin' really tired of me sayin' this all the time. I want to farm. How am I going to do this? Should I go back to school? Should I get some agricultural degree?" He just kind of pushed me to just get out there and do it and see what you think—kind of took the loftiness or the work I was.... I was making it too hard for myself, instead of just doin' it. So I had e-mailed a few local farms, and in waiting for some replies to that, he had set me up with a very good friend of his who was a member at this farm out in Carnation. He said, "You should go out and meet Diana and see what she knows about this CSA farm in Carnation." So I met her out at Jubilee Farm. So she walked me around the farm and told me how it worked. I just *loved* that model. I mean, short of having animals, it was the perfect model for me. I just thought this was the greatest thing. So I didn't get to meet Erick at that time. I thought that was great, went back home and was watching my e-mails, and here comes an e-mail from Erick. And this was, I guess, probably in the fall that I went. I think I went in October and I guess I e-mailed him early spring. I think it was like the end of February, first of March, so there's a little bit of time in between there. So he e-mailed me back and said, "I don't have any spots open for employment, but if you want to come out, I would be more than happy to talk to you about how I got started. So I met with him, and he walked me around the farm, and told me in a nutshell how it worked and what he did. And one very important thing that I remember him telling me was that when he started he knew nothing, he didn't know a thing about farming. So that made me feel really confident that I'd be able to pull this off—not that I had a lot of experience—and I didn't. The little experience I had, was, like I said, just small, having gardens of my own, and helping my grandmother in her garden, and helping with the butchering of chickens, and kind of just a general food canning, processing, making jam, that kind of stuff. I didn't really feel like I had a lot of large-scale farming experience. I could drive a tractor, I could run a lawnmower, I could work a weed whacker, so I wasn't unfamiliar to the labor part of it. I was in pretty good physical shape and felt like I was a good hard worker. So I guess Erick really inspired me with confidence, knowing that I could make this happen, however it was to look, whatever form of farming, CSA, marketing, I was led to.

So from there, he left it pretty wide open, other than, you know, "I don't have any room for employment for you, but if you want to come out and volunteer, you're welcome to do that." So I made arrangements to start comin' out to volunteer, and it was, like I said, early spring, so I started coming out once or twice a week. We started out with another gal that was also volunteering, so her and I and Erick would prune the apple trees in the middle of March—freezing—but learning a lot. I really enjoyed that time. We just had great conversations, the three of us.

And then as the weeks progressed, he had one of his interns—I think this intern was from Finland or Sweden or someplace, and just got very, very homesick and needed to leave immediately. Just one night, he was gone. Erick took him to the airport, and he just had to go home. He couldn't be there any longer. I think he was pretty young. So anyhow, then Erick had a space available. And I think the other part of it, too, was that he really wasn't sure.... He had a lot of people come on the farm saying, "I want to farm, I want to farm." They'd work a couple days and then see that it was more than they could handle, and would disappear. So I think that was part of his concern, too, was he didn't want to offer a job to somebody that he didn't know would be able to stick with it or do the work.

Anyhow, he hired me and I started working there as soon as school was done in June, full time. Of course by that time one thing was leading to another, and we'd gone out for coffee a couple of times, and I remember the time my daughter said to me, "Well, does he take all of his employees out to coffee?" Thinking, "Mom, I think there's something going on here." I said, "Well, no, I guess not." So one thing led to another and we became involved as a couple and were dating. Then a year and a half later we got married, and we've been married for five years now.

I've just finished my seventh year at the farm. That's kind of how we got together, and how things have transpired for us throughout the years. I know it seems like such a short time when I say it's just five years, or seven years, I feel like I've been farming for a long time. But I don't know, just the excitement of fulfilling that desire kind of brings up emotion for me. I wouldn't want to do anything else.

It's been a little bit of a challenge collaborating with him because Erick had really done it on his own for so long. To get him to give up a little piece of it, even just the market—you know, just the market side of it.... And also, I mean, I think he's always felt very confident in my abilities, but he's also relied completely upon himself to make sure things are done the way that they need to be done. So that's kind of been a little challenging, in that he needs to give up a little bit of that responsibility, because I *need* a little bit of that responsibility. And so.... I don't know, I think at this point we've kind of delegated certain roles for each other. I have a real strong pull for the animals.

In fact, part of our herd was just recently acquired from my uncle. He really got to the place in his life where he could not take care of the animals anymore. It was just getting to be too much work for him. He's in his mid seventies, and he was just ready to be done. I think he felt very comfortable.... It was hard for him to give up his herd of thirteen cows, but he also, I think, felt very comfortable that they were going to me, to Jubilee. So having the animals on the farm is a big plus. And I see that as.... I feel myself taking a big part in the caretaking of the animals. And we both definitely share that responsibility. They are a lot of work. So now that the summer is done, and we're packing boxes, and we're done with our off season, our fall session, we still have The Cows. And so they take a lot of our time. It's a *big* commitment to having the cows, but anyhow, I love having the animals on the farm, and I feel like that has completed things for me as far as the type of place that I want to farm, the type of place that I really feel is complete, is to have some animals. And I know that's not possible for everybody, but I'm glad that we have the infrastructure that we could make that work for us.

I still have a lot to learn in the area of Bio-Dynamics. I've not done quite as much reading as I should, and I need to. So I need to kind of pull myself back into that again. I feel like we kind of go in and out of that, but the wintertime is for us to get caught up on our reading, and that time now is coming, so I see that happening. But yeah, as far as the bio-dynamic.... The cows, of course.... The bio-dynamic process led us to having the cows on the farm, but to me that was just a given. It was just a matter of when that was gonna happen. I just felt very strongly that that *would* happen.

I do a lot of the organizing of the market side of it. You know, we both sit down in the winter and pick out the types of seeds and what type of produce we want to grow, and what varieties. We have a lot of fun doing that. We usually go someplace warm and kind of snuggle up with our seed catalogs. So yeah, we both share that responsibility. And the same with.... I do a lot more of the paperwork type of organization with the members and applications and contact with our members, as far as e-mails and the whole financial side of it goes—and not so much with the work-share load—you know, the folks that come in to do work shares—but also then work alongside of those people, as far as weeding and transplanting and seeding.

For "work-share" people who are interested will contact us in early spring and we'll send them a little flyer that gives them kind of the low-down. Basically it's a twenty-week commitment. Then they come out once a week starting in mid June and going through the end of October. They come out once a week for four hours, and work mainly transplanting, harvesting, weeding. And for that work they get a week's supply of food. Towards the end of the season it's basically all harvesting, so it kind of depends on what day they come out, too, as to what jobs they do. But last year, just this last season, we ended up with about eighty-five work-share people, which is the most we've ever had. The year before, we had fifty, and we cut it off at that, because we weren't sure if we'd be able to organize everybody. And now that we've also got *two* full-time employees, that helps us with the organization of that as well. That's made this eighty-five number possible. So it'll be interesting to see what happens this next year, as far as to how many people.

Mainly we get people that are—I don't want to label people as a Microsoft kind of person—but maybe it's more of in the technology industry. But we're in the Microsoft community, outside of that community, so we get a lot of people that sit at a desk, stare at a computer all day long, and they need to reconnect with the earth, and that's what their goal is, is that they need to get their hands dirty, they need to get themselves back in connection with the earth somehow. So we get a lot of people that are in that situation. And then there's also people that are interested in farming themselves. We have some people that started probably about three or four years ago, working with us, with that desire to farm, and they ended up now farming in the Valley, and they're doin' it! So it's just so wonderful. I think they did a three-year work share for us, and then at the end of that third year, they were working with us part-time ... well, less than part-time ... but they just went on to farm, and it's so exciting to watch that happen, somebody so interested, or a couple so interested, that they actually are able to fulfill their dream. That's really exciting to be a part of, for us to have a hand in that, and to see that manifest. That's really exciting.

We do a lot of education on the farm and are doing more and more all the time. And that has a lot to do with the organization. As we get more organized, which I feel we are, it frees us up to have more educational experiences. So part of that is the Waldorf Schools coming in. Part of that is doing spring tours. And a big part of it is our October tours that we do. And I have to remind myself, those are very educational. It gets really busy in October, there's a lot going on, there's a lot of kids that come out during the week. There's a lot of people that come out on the weekend. That's a really busy time of year for us. But there is a lot of education going on, and a lot of that isn't real formal education, it's people comin' out to the farm, and maybe they're coming to get a pumpkin, and see, "You mean you actually *grow* things here that people can *eat?!*" That sort of, I don't know, enlightenment. But we are getting more formal in our education, and that's exciting to see opening our doors to having more young people come out, high school classes, college classes. We do quite a bit of that now too, where people will come out. And we basically would rather have them work while they're out there, plan on doing a couple hours worth of work in trade for the ... usually Erick will spend an hour with them, conversing about what we do, and about farming. And so we'll trade his time for some work time, which works out really well for us. It's a good trade. And I think they're still learning more, maybe more so, when they get out there and get their hands in the soil.

We also have "Farm School" on each one of our pick-up days—we have four pick-up days. So every day we offer a different time to have the kids come with their parent. Normally what they'll do is go out and harvest something. We also have the cows. We like to talk a lot about the cows, because they're exciting, and of course kids love to learn about cows, or just to go out and see cows, and then to.... It's such an easy work in the compost, you know. Kids love poop, you know! That's great, talking about cows to compost, it's perfect, it's a great setup. And then also to do a little spiel about insects, which I think is really important, because unfortunately our society doesn't like to get dirty, and a lot of our society doesn't like things that crawl. Bugs are typically right up there with mud—especially for adults, not for children. So it's good to kind of bring that to the attention of the adults so maybe they're gonna be a little more open to getting dirty, and discovering what that creepy-crawly thing.... You know, how many things does that thing have? And it's got a purpose. I think we tend to shut kids down a little bit too much in that area. So yes, that's part of the educational part. And kids will always eat what they harvest. They just can't help it. It's kind of like they can't ever walk around the mud puddle. Well, it's hard for them not to eat something they've harvested. And sometimes we'll joke about it and tell 'em if they take this, they have to eat it. More often than not, you hear the parents come back that next week saying, "Gosh, he ate every bit of that. He didn't like broccoli, but now all he talks about is broccoli, and was it grown on the farm; or 'Did this apple come from Jubilee?' or 'Who grew this apple?,' 'Where'd this cabbage come from?'" So it's exciting to hear those comments from parents.

I'd really like to learn a little bit more about the microbial life and to step up the whole insect collection with some microbial collections. I have a small insect collection of the insects that we find on the farm. I like to try to educate myself about their purposes. But more so, I'd love to get like a microscope of some sort that we can learn a little bit more about the microbial side of our compost, and of the soil. That's one of my big interests, so I'd like to do a little bit more investigation with that. But to actually bring that to the eyes of the people, the educational side of it, and somehow incorporate that, just to take it to another level.

And the other thing is that I want to reach out more towards the community. Here, a lot of people say—there's a lot about, "How can I use this produce?" That's always a big thing. And something I've been thinking about for a while, but I'm really gonna do it this year...to bring, somehow connect with the senior center and get.... You know, when you have seniors come out to the farm, and we don't have a lot of that, because it's not a really easy place to get around. There's things you can trip on, and it can be slippery. But when seniors come out to the farm, when they do just happen to stop in with their family, they sit on the porch and they think.... I hear this a lot: "I grew up on a place like this," or "My father grew up on a place like this." And there's this connection that they had at one time. And I feel like they now don't get the connection of food. And just because they don't eat as much as a family would, it's not feasible for them to be a part of the farm, to be a member and come out and get this big box of food every week. It's a lot to eat. So anyhow, I wanted to connect somehow with the senior center and maybe just bring them a box each week, just to start something, some kind of connection with them. I have a strong feeling and desire to do that this year, but that's kind of a small thing. That's one of the things I'd like to do.

Erick is Big Picture guy and that's why I think we work pretty well together. I'm seeing the little things crawling around on the ground! I mean, I have to remind myself to look up and see the rest of it, because I get really singly-focused on this little area, or just getting this harvest in. And he's really good about seeing the whole thing, and he brings that back to me, which is good. And I think we feed off of each other that way, which is a good thing for the farm. So yeah, we've got some pretty big things in the works, and one is having a safe place for the cows. And it's a pretty big thing for us in that we do need something that's up out of the floodplain, someplace that we can safely have the cows. When it does flood, we won't have to be shuffling them around. It's not safe—for them or for us—especially now that we're a little further away from the barn, with our house. And the compost. We want the compost too. That's a huge part of the farm. It's all a balancing act, and we've seen what happens when you kill all the insects and all the microbial life in your soil—which happens way too frequently. It's all a balance, and that compost is a huge part of the balance, in giving back, to keeping the soil, the ground, the farm, healthy and whole. So that needs to be in an area that's not going to be infiltrated with flood water.

The main purpose of the cows is for the manure, which is then to make into compost. And that compost then is put back out into the soil every year. Right now they're in the barn, where they spend four to five months, depending on the weather. And that's where we collect the manure to make the compost. But in the summertime, from March until into November, they're out in the field, and we move them every day from pasture to pasture, so that they're always eating fresh clean grass. Yeah, they pretty much get a fresh plate of food every day. So it's a lot of work, but I think they really do well with that process. And we don't have to bring food in. They've got fresh grass to eat every day in the summer and fall and early spring. And then in the winter months, they're in the barn, in the loafing shed, eating all of the hay that we've cut off of our fields. Starting last year, we started growing sugar beets, and this year we added turnips and rutabagas to their diet. And they're also eating squash, of course. They feed off the extra pumpkins that we have in the fall. And we bring them into the loafing shed then. We also bring in whatever leftover pumpkins that we have. They *love* the pumpkins. They love the squash and the turnips. So we're adding to our knowledge. I think as the farm grows and matures, I like to think we do too, and to learn more, learn from our animals, and of course from other people. I hope every year we do a little better job.

I don't know, maybe it's a yearly thing. Maybe if you ask me in the spring I'll have a different attitude than I do this fall. But I don't know. I worry about the future. I worry about there being enough of us—"us" meaning small farmers, and even smaller than us. I feel like we are probably on the cusp of the larger side of what I think of as farming, as, I don't know, healthy farming. I think we're probably on the larger end of that. And I think it all relates to what your space, your farm, can produce at a healthy level. And that, for everybody, is different. I worry that there's not enough small farmers. And it doesn't have to be a 400-member CSA. It can be a 30-member CSA. I just feel like we need a lot more of us out there. I'm concerned about the future. And I see in our own little world, I see farms coming back to life. Where there used to be farming, and then there wasn't for many years, I see that coming alive again. And that's encouraging. I feel we need a lot more of that. And so I worry about the changes, and there not being enough, soon enough. Agri-business is not where it's at. It's not gonna cut it for us. It's not a quick fix to saving society.

The green revolution hasn't been so green, it's been a browning effect, but I think, you know, you feed something enough nitrogen, it's gonna turn green, but it's not *really* green. So it's really.... I think at this point.... Is there a chance, I think, of saving the soil? Is there a chance that we can do that? Which is saving the earth, however you want to put it. Bringing the soil back to life from death, which is, I really think, what agri-business does, abuses Mother Nature, abuses the land to where you couldn't grow anything on that spot if you wanted to, it's been so neglected. So neglected, but yet so stepped on. Neglected but abused. But really the question is—I don't know, I feel it goes so much deeper, not just saving the soil, but saving our souls. I feel like the more we feed ourselves cardboard, the less human we are, the less soulful we are. And that's what I feel we've lost, is our spirit. When I say we're eating cardboard, it's that processed food. I really feel like.... And even myself, in my past, I lived that route, I'm certainly not a purist by any means. But there's something about eating food that's alive, that we need to do, and I think we were meant to do that. And I think we *have* to do that in order to survive. We can't continue eating stuff that's not healthy. And it's not healthy in so many ways. Not only is there a nutritional deficit, but there's also some.... This lacking of aliveness may be keeping us alive to some degree, but it's not feeding us spiritually, and I think there's more to the food that we eat that we know about: there's something there that feeds us spiritually. When you eat a fresh apple that you know has just been picked off of a tree, that you know where it came from, where you know maybe what it looks like where it came from, that feeds you so much more deeply than something that maybe was shipped in from who knows where, and has been sitting in a box for who knows how long. There's just something about that, that we need to have this connectedness with. And it's whether we actually get out there and put our own hands in the soil, or at least connected with a place that does that for us. Or know the people that do it, yeah. We need to have that connection someplace along the line.

Not everybody can do that. But that is a good feeling, yeah. And it's not like we don't eat out. We eat out. We get busy. But there's something about that—also bringing that connectedness with your neighbors and family and friends, you know—sharing those meals. There's something very deep about that, and enriching. Yeah, just to have that conversation, have many of our members relay those same kinds of messages as they sat around the table, knowing that Farmer Erick and Wendy grew this. "This is what we helped harvest at farm school today." Yeah, there's something deep about that. And I think for children that's going to be a lasting memory for them.

I remember sitting, eating turnips with my grown father, and picking out a lamb's quarter with my grandmother for dinner. One of those things we need. Yeah, farming has definitely changed my whole thought process about a lot of things. But mainly, I think the biggest thing is about the balance. You know, that things aren't good or bad. I mean, sure, we look at bind weed as not being a good thing, but it's necessary for some reason. Just because we don't know what that reason is, doesn't make it a bad thing.

And it's not like it's not hard work, because it is hard work. But there's something about that, at the end of the day, feels really good. It's remembering to take time—at least for me personally—remembering to take time to also reconnect and renew my spirit. You still have to take care of yourself too, even if you do work in the most beautiful of surroundings ever, and you have the best job ever, you still need to take care of yourself—which when you get so busy farming can be a challenge. But that's something that I have to remind myself of.

I feel like for me personally, my lifetime is not gonna see the real bad part of what we've done to this earth. I feel bad for the next few generations to come, because we're the ones that had this grand party and fling at the expense of them. And I feel like now.... And part of that, I think, is what led me back to that desire. I don't want to do any more harm. I feel like just living kind of what I used to think was a normal life, was not having a positive.... Not that I was.... I felt like I was having a positive effect, but there's also, I think, some negative effect. And I feel like now it's like a double positive in what I do and how I live—at least as far as my relationship to the earth goes. And of course there's something more I could do. But like I said, I'm not a purist by any means. I'm just trying to do my best.

Farm Journal

27 April 2009
Local Roots Farm

We walked up and down freshly seeded rows of veggies. Jason Salvo and Siri Erickson-Brown sort and spread the long tangles of drip-line (survivors from last year's flood) and talk with quiet enthusiasm about their accidental adventure into farming. They are recent partners with Dan Beyers who owns the land and the three of them have been planting and marketing vegetables here for the past three years.

Jason has a law degree and passed the Washington Bar; he could be practicing. Siri has a Master's in Business Administration and could be doing whatever it is business administrators do in Corporate America. Yet here they are on the flood plain of the Snoqualmie Valley actually making a living (be it ever so humble) growing vegetables and selling it at local Farmers Markets, to restaurants and CSA clients.

Why?

Why forego a Law Practice and those handsomely billed hours or abandon any number of management opportunities to eke out a living from farming? Both answered simply, "When the opportunity to work the farm and share resources and skills with Dan appeared, we said 'yes' without thinking." There is more to it, of course, and that's why I've come to talk with them and this whole group of "New Farmers" who have established the Snoqualmie Valley as a new Mecca for those who want to devote their lives to "sustainable" agriculture.

As one who came of age in the 1960s and bore witness to the debut of the "Whole Earth Catalogue" and all the attendant "back to the land" efforts of the day, I'm not sure what I expected to find at Local Roots Farm, but it bore no resemblance to the "anti-establishment", political fervor I experienced forty years ago. Instead, these young people are surprisingly without declarations or political agendas. They are clear-headed, practical and completely certain that the life they have chosen will support them and, beyond that, provide a raison d'etre that the corporate world could never offer. Nor was this a religious or "spiritual" reaction. Rather, it is simple acceptance of a deeper unconscious response which asserts the "rightness" of a particular course of action; the Journey recognized because the steps leading to it dissolve as quickly as the steps forward lead on.

Perhaps that is reading too much into it. Yet, theirs is an intellectual response as opposed to a purely emotional one. That is, the choice to relinquish one mode of economic behavior over another is made here from a point of personal rather than "universal" enlightenment. The "greater good" being served is their own; the choice to live a life with "adequate" means rather than one striving for opulence. Preservation of self and preservation of environment are equivalent: I am my response to the world. I am what I grow, what I eat and, therefore, what I provide for others is a communal connection rooted in the premise—the over-arching response resident in the details; the quaking of butterfly wings that precipitates systemic change.

Local Roots Farm

Siri Erickson-Brown

2 December 2009

My name is Siri Erickson-Brown. I was born on October 26, 1978, in Seattle, on Capital Hill where I now live. And I've been farming here in the Snoqualmie Valley for three years.

I grew up in the city, I went to Seattle Public Schools all through twelfth grade. I went to the University of Washington, twice. I got an undergraduate degree in history, and then I got a bad job, and then I thought perhaps if I went back to school I could get a better job. So I got a Master's in public administration from the University of Washington which means you are trained to run bureaucracies. Usually in government, and now increasingly in nonprofit. It's kind of like a business degree for the public sector. So you learn a lot of economics and statistics and also policy analysis and human resource management, which was the part I was like, "Oh, I don't really care about this stuff, whatever, managing people." And now that's my largest challenge in life. And then after I graduated, I got another bad job. And then my husband was studying for the bar exam so that he could become a lawyer, whatever that's all about. And the summer that he was set to be studying for the bar, I took an internship on a farm down the road from where we are now; Nature's Last Stand, John Hushley's. And I worked as an intern for all of two months, and in that two months I learned everything I needed to know; and the next year I started my own farm.

When I was pretty young, probably between the ages of two and eight, my parents, together with my mom's sister and my grandparents, my mom's parents, all bought kind of together a collection of acreage that had a farmhouse and some kind of pasture and a big garden, and also had some woods. We spent a lot of time out there on the weekends. I think my parents envisioned some kind of homesteading thing, as well as a nursery. My mom's a landscape architect, so she and my grandfather were doing a lot of plant propagation, and they ran a wholesale nursery business there for a couple of years, but I think *there* is where I really imprinted on being outside and playing in dirt. My mom has a picture of me where I had picked—she had this kind of wildflower garden, cosmos and bachelor buttons and stuff—and I picked all these flowers and I planted them, just the flower itself, like in the ground. So I had this patch of dirt with all these flowers. So there was that, and I don't actually, unfortunately, have any great food memories about going out and picking the fresh peas and eating them. I just don't remember. I remember planting stuff, I remember playing in the dirt. There's a picture of me buried in a compost pile like up to my neck.

But by the time I was, I think, probably twelve or thirteen, we had in this back yard of the house we lived in, in Green Lake in Seattle, I had taken it upon myself to plant a little garden. I was growing spinach and beans, and I was reading up on all this stuff, and trying to find a sunny spot in this yard that was totally shaded by apple trees. So I don't know, it's kind of weird, it's like that's what I was supposed to do.

Many of my grandparents grew up on farms or in farming communities. Both my grandmas are from North Dakota. My dad's mom grew up on a farm where they raised potatoes and some kind of grain for kind of commercial sale, but then her mom also had the cow that made the best butter, and they'd take it into the town and trade for stuff at the general store. And they raised turkeys. So both my sets of grandparents always had gardens. I think it's just there's this kind of genetic stuff.

So, I had my little failed garden as a young adolescent, but then Jason and I traveled in Europe together—I think right after college, basically, a year or so after college. We graduated, we worked, we saved some money, we went to Europe, and we spent six months, mostly in Italy, and part of the time there we were living on a farm in Tuscany that grew ... was it an olive tree farm? But when we were there, it was actually like this time of year, late November early December. All the harvest was in, so we ended up just working in the garden, chopping wood, and playing with kittens, and eating all this really kind of hearty winter stuff. We'd go out and find wild arugula. When we got home several months later, we were like, "We want to eat all these foods. We should grow 'em ourselves." Because they were really expensive and not very good in the grocery stores. So we started a *very* small garden in our back yard that grew and grew and grew. We would plant, I think we had twenty or thirty tomato plants. I mean, this is like an apartment back yard, not big. And I read a lot. I really like to read about farming and gardening. I definitely didn't go seeking out an internship. We actually had been chatting with John Hushley at the farmers market, because we used to buy a lot of stuff from him. And he said, "Oh! Why don't you come work for me?" This is February probably.

I don't really remember. I mean, it's like this mythology that we've created about, like the origins of our farm. And I don't really remember the details, but it came about that I was like, "Oh, I'll work on a farm for a summer. Jason will be studying for the bar, and he'll be really busy. It was the spring that we got married. We got married in May, and then a week later I started working on the farm. And for our wedding we had grown tomato plants as the centerpieces for all the tables and decorations. We put them in terracotta pots. So we, at that time, were growing under lights in our closet, in our 400-square-foot apartment, a hundred tomato plants. So I mean, I don't know, I was definitely on somewhat of a path, but I didn't have any intention of doing this, it just sort of came about.

When I was working for John, he was growing on about maybe half an acre on Dan's property. He was borrowing some acreage there, because he had earlier leased the farm right next door to ours, where there's a bunch of horses now. So he and Dan, when Dan was first out there, kind of puttering around and trying to be a farmer who didn't know what he was doing, John shared a lot of information with him about tractors and techniques, and Dan would just go over and help 'em out, and so they had kind of an ongoing farming relationship. So John, even though he'd moved a mile or so down the road, was still using some of Dan's ground. So me, the couple of interns and I would come down to Dan's farm and harvest beets and talk to Dan. Dan was always there, he didn't have anything to do. All he would do is hoe. He had his little hoe, he'd go around and weed. He would never bend down and pick anything. So we'd be there weeding, and he'd be there ostensibly hoeing, but mostly just chatting. So the summer passed, I was no longer working out there. I didn't really know what I was doing. Jason and I, after he took the bar, we left town, we went and drove around the country for six weeks. And when I got back to Seattle, it was like late October, and I got a call from one of my fellow interns, this guy named Larry, who used to live just down the road from you here. And he said, "Hey, I think you should talk to Dan. I think we should start a farm together." Dan had moved and bought the farm, bought all these tractors with the intention of being a vegetable farmer. But he got out there, took out all his life savings and bought this eighty-acre farm and was like, "Well, *now* what am I gonna do? I don't want to leave, I don't want to have to go sell things. Here I am." And he would plant stuff. He'd plant like 80 bed-feet of basil, and just admire it, just enjoy the basil, it's beautiful. He didn't sell anything. So he was also not actively seeking farming partners, but the universe just brought us together. So yeah, that was three years ago just about now.

  We didn't really even know where to begin. I use a lot of spreadsheets, I'm an Excel person. So I thought to myself, "Okay, how much money do we need to earn if we're gonna be farmers? Well, how much money can you make if you go to a farmers market?" Well, I've been to a farmers market before and usually it seems like people will buy maybe like thirty bunches of beets and thirty bunches of radishes, so if we did that every week for a season.... I mean, we went to three markets, and we sold all that stuff, well how much would we make? Okay. And then maybe we could do this, we could have a CSA. We could charge these unwitting people who are gonna just hand us their money. We could say, "Maybe you should give us $300 this spring, and then we'll grow vegetables." Okay, so I did that. And then based on all those things, what we had to actually grow in order to supply sixty CSA members and three farmers markets, I plugged that all into my magic spreadsheet, I looked in the seed catalogs, and they said, "If you plant 100 row feet of peas, you'll get 20 pounds of peas." So I was like, "Okay, let's see how many row feet of peas we need to plant." And I made a farm on my computer, and then we attempted to implement that farm. And we did okay. We did actually, our first year we were like, "Okay, we didn't know what we were doing at all," and it was like we had weeds six feet high over the whole five acres, but we picked a lot of food, and we sold some food, and we *did* manage to get sixty people to give us $300 each, and we gave them boxes of vegetables for twenty weeks in the summer, and they came back, most of them came back the next year. It's crazy, I don't know what we were thinking.

  And we felt awed at the time, like we're unnecessarily starting from scratch, when there is actually, especially here in the Snoqualmie, there is quite a bit of a community of knowledge. After our first year, we got more hooked up with the little group of farmers out here, and I think it's helped. But on the other hand, not knowing what you're doing, and just trying to say, "Here's the goal, we're going to try to grow this food, and these are the resources we have available to us, let's just figure out what seems like the best way." And through sort of trial and error you figure something out. Maybe that's *better*. Maybe not just reading a book and saying, "Here's what I'm supposed to do," or going to Ag school and following some totally bogus formula handed to you by the fertilizer company—might be better. Maybe, I don't know. So yeah, I mean, it is challenging, because you know what you want, you have seeds, you have soil, plants pretty much grow on their own. But I think the big challenge for market farming, like what we do, is matching what the people want to buy and pay money for, with what you can grow and when you can grow it, and how well you can do that. And because the external world is always changing, the weather is always changing, you can *think* you know what you're going to do, but then every single day you have to improvise. It's not really that hard to grow vegetables—they pretty much just want to grow. But then growing them at the right time in the right way, and actually being able to sell them, is I think what is challenging.

  The soil here is great—I think. I don't know anything else, though—except for our yard in Seattle. When we first built our vegetable garden there, we brought in some three-way topsoil mix, and we grew like all this spectacular stuff our first year, and then it was like (ahhhh), and then we'd get these little scrawny kale plants that wouldn't even—they'd be all bug infested and we're like, "Hm, I think we've depleted our soil. That didn't take very long." Yeah, here, it's a lot of stuff in the soil that plants like. You don't have to add that much.

We are not strictly organic in the sense that we're forbidden by the federal government from using that word unless we pay for it—so no. But we don't use any synthetic inputs of any kind. We don't use any things that kill life, besides our tools and our bare hands. So we don't use herbicides, or quote unquote "natural or synthetic." There's plenty of bad stuff that's allowable under the organic rules, but we don't use those things.

The whole certification business is a little shady and I'm afraid it's getting shadier. We made the decision our first year not to apply for organic certification, and it seems to be working out well for us. It's actually kind of cool, people come to the farmers market and ask us about whether, "Are you organic?" "Well, no, but we follow the same type of practices." Well then they ask, "Well, do you spray?" And we're like, "Well, no, but just because somebody's organic doesn't mean they're not spraying some stuff you probably wouldn't want to eat." And it's cool, because it leads to a dialog. And most of the time I think people appreciate it. Sometimes I think all they really are looking for is the seal of approval, they don't actually want to know anything, because they feel like food choices are already hard enough, and everyone's telling them all these rules, and they feel afflicted by it, but that's their problem.

You know what's interesting is, I think a lot of people don't know quite why they care, but they do want, they're seeking chemical-free food. Most of the time I ask them, "Do you have environmental concerns, or is it personal health? Is it you don't want to be dependent on petroleum products? Why do you ask?" And they don't really know. I think most of them, it would have to come down to like a personal health thing. They want to know that nothing bad has been sprayed on their food. But once you get past that.... Mostly people are more interested in talking about the vegetables themselves, and what they are and where they came from and how you can cook them. People love to talk about food.

We do a fair amount of educating. Yeah, there's a few items that I think we've probably given the exact same recipe for now, over the last three years of going to market, like a thousand times maybe.

They say, "Oh, turnips! Oh, what are these?" "Oh, they're a Japanese variety of turnip. They don't really taste like a storage turnip. They've got really fine-grained flesh, they have a texture kind of like a radish, and they've got a little bit of a bite, but they're really sweet, and you can just cut 'em in half and sauté them in a pan. Because they're really high in sugar, the cut surface will caramelize. So just take 'em home, trim off the greens. You can eat 'em if you want to, or not. Cut the little turnips in half, sauté them in a pan with some olive oil and garlic until the cut surface starts to turn brown and they're kind of soft. And then if you want, you can chop up the greens and add them to the pan and mix them all together, and then you get a nice color contrast, and you use up your greens. You'll love them, you'll come back and buy them every week." And they do!

The farmers market clientele is definitely a self-selected group. But my favorite people are the ones who will come and they'll be like, "Well, I've never been to the farmers market before and I don't really cook vegetables, so can you help me?" We probably get a couple of those a year, and they're great! Because they really want to learn, and they're like, "I've made a change in my life, I'm going to eat vegetables now. Tell me what to do." Yeah, they're the best people.

I think I've had a life-long struggle with the search for meaning. So everything that I considered seems inadequate until now. And it was really hard for me, applying for jobs, trying to be like, "What is this all about? What does this even mean? What's an administrative assistant? Why should I care about this piece of paper? And what *should* I care about? And *is* there anything that I care about? Is there something wrong with me that I don't have some kind of driving passion that I'm following in my life?" And so I got really lucky, because I don't think I would have necessarily pushed myself in this direction if it hadn't just happened. But I feel every day like I could not imagine anything else that would be better. I thought I was just going to have to be kind of ... what's the word? I thought I was gonna probably be unsatisfied with the options available to me my whole life.

    People have to eat. I mean, I think so. I don't know what else I would do. But there's so many ways that you can be a farmer, and I think people right now—and I'm sure they will continue to be for many years to come—have an insatiable need for good food and information. And so if I'm either growing mostly, and also talking to people; or if I'm growing a little bit, or in charge of other people who are growing, and talking to people more, I'd be pretty happy. Because it's all the same. Just because you can grow something doesn't mean that you've done your job. Because if you hand it to the person and they don't know what to do with it, then it's just as though you'd never grown it, because they don't eat it anyway. Yeah, I think education is essential. When people say, "Oh, the farmers market is so expensive (mutter, mutter) organic food." I really feel, like at least the way *we're* doing things, people get added value when they come to our stand at the farmers market, because it's like a cooking class on top of the food. You get the food too!

    We're keeping our eye out for property of our own. I think we're going to solve it through this really tedious process that we're all involved in to some degree— all the farmers out here—with trying to change, in small ways, some of the regulations about how land is used in the Snoqualmie Valley to make it more available. I think things are happening. Clearly things are happening, actual regulations are changing. I think it's just going to be a process, because every individual who starts a farm comes to it with a whole bunch of totally unique circumstances that allow them to do this or that or whatever, so it's really hard to say, "This is what aspiring farmers need: they need grants and they need technical assistance." Like, who knows what they really need? They're all different. But every farm needs a critter pad to keep their equipment safe in a flood. Every farm, I think should have a place where the person who owns the farm lives. That's a big problem. The ability to irrigate. Stuff like that. And I think progress is happening, because the people in King County who like to eat food are, I think, gaining an appreciation of the complexities of trying to manage the rural areas as resource lands, but also as productive farmland. And I think for a long time the mentality has been that those two uses were not very compatible. But I think people are, through a bunch of different organizations: the Stewardship Partners who do the SAM and SAVE certification, and some really excellent people on the staff of the Ag department at King County itself, work is happening, and people are learning. It's going to take a more nuanced approach, but I think that all the parts are there for it.

    You know, I try not to think about the bigger picture too much.... Well that's not true, I think about it a little bit. I mean, you could really get discouraged about a lot of things, and it might make it hard for you to do the things that you're doing every day—so I just do the things that we're doing every day. And when people ask me, I try to have opinions about whether this policy or that policy is good or bad, but I don't let it, like, control my life. Getting rid of subsidies for this terrible, terrible food is probably the first thing, I would say. It's ridiculous to try to fund these little grant programs for schools to buy carrots from farmers with a couple thousand dollars here, where with the other hand we're giving *millions* of dollars to people to grow, in the worst possible way, the worst possible food, that we don't even really need, and that we're going to turn into a bunch of additives so we can make junk food for the poor people. I mean, I would just like to see what would happen if we *just* got rid of agricultural subsidies, and *then* we'll see about all these other problems. That will never happen, but....

People have been talking about this, how expensive oil is going to get. I'm like waiting for it. I would like to see that happen. Where is it? Any day now, it's gonna happen! I mean, I believe that. Then, we'll see what happens after that. In the meantime, I think that the more of us doing this kind of work that there are, the smoother the transition will be, because it's going to happen eventually for some reason. Maybe in a hundred years, I don't know.

The difference between who we are and what our stand at the farmers market looks like, between our first year and our third year, is vast. So we're doing better, we see more people, they buy more food, but I think a lot of that is probably attributable to changes on our operation, not necessarily changes in the outside world. I mean, statistics on the farmers markets in Seattle is that most of them experienced decline in sales and shopper visits between 2008 and 2009. But I've also read.... There's just not a lot of data collected on any of it: whether people are joining CSAs because they perceive there's a greater value to it, or what. This is the thing that's kind of peculiar, but I think a lot of the research I've read says that food sales are down, people are buying less food. Maybe they're throwing less food away, I don't know. So how can farmers market sales *and* supermarket sales be down in the same year? They're buying less. So I don't know, I don't have an answer for that one.

The intern program is a pyramid scheme. You hire interns, and you tell them you're going to train them to build their own farm. And then when they get their own farm, they're gonna hire some interns, and they're gonna do all the work for them. We had twenty people already apply to work for us next year. A lot of this batch seems to come from the Midwest. We got a lot of, like, Wisconsin and Kansas. But they come from all over. They find us through the listing service on the Internet. It's actually, surprisingly, housed in this little tiny branch of the USDA's website. It's called "Alternative Technology Transfer for Rural Areas," ATTRA. And it has a bunch of sustainable farm resources, little fact sheets and things. And then it has this listing of internships nationally. You search by state.

What do they say they want? It's different for every one of 'em. And I don't think they all really know what they want when they come. They think it would be cool to work on a farm for a year. Little do they know, they're just a brick in my pyramid.

Dan is the master puppeteer of the farm, because he has all the power. Nothing can happen unless it's permitted or actually executed by Dan himself. So I write the plan, and I say, "Okay, if you would like to earn this much money this year, we need to do these things and if you want to make this *other* amount of money this year, then we have to do these things *and* these things. So do those things—or not." And then he does them—or not. And that could be anything from constructing a greenhouse, making sure we continue to have running water, plowing the field on time, planting the seeds, etc., etc. He operates all the tractors, pretty much, although he's beginning to let other people be involved in that a little bit. But yeah, he's the crux of the matter. I think he secretly really relishes his position of power, but he tries to pretend like he doesn't. Like, "Oh! I just can't get it all done on time! (mutter, mutter, mutter)" I don't really know. We have a great relationship. I actually think he and I have very similar personalities, which is very frightening for me. So I understand him and all his different ways of not getting things done. I sympathize. But that doesn't mean I don't think he should get the things done. So yeah, he's a little like negotiations about what's gonna happen in this off season, are we going to be able to build a couple of new greenhouses? Because I really need to know before I start taking new names for the CSA next year, if we're going to be able to grow, you know, 500 tomato plants or 1,000 tomato plants, because I need to know, if I make these plans. We sit around and talk a lot, a lot, about all that stuff. And then eventually sometimes we reach a conclusion, and then sometimes the conclusions that we reach turn into corporeal realities.

I am happy with the relationship. I mean, it works out for us, it's perfect, because Dan never wants to leave the farm. He stays there, he keeps all the chickens and the seedlings alive. And it means that we can be more freed up to go into the city and sell the food to the people, and not have to worry that if we don't get back to the farm in two hours and water the seedlings, they'll all die. So we actually have really quite compatible interests in the matter.

We have a trailer, we stay in our trailer probably like half the nights of the week. But there's really no habitable dwelling on the whole farm—even Dan's house, which he continues to live in. So anyway, many days of the week we drive into the city and bring vegetables to people in various ways: restaurants, CSA, we go to market. And then having our place in town means that when we're done, we just go home, instead of driving an hour back out to the farm. So it works actually pretty well. And it's pretty common, I think, for people out here.

It would be good for Jason and I to try to invest in some property of our own. I don't have any fear of our relationship going badly with Dan, but just from my kind of practical standpoint. I would like to have my own place. And the infrastructure on Dan's farm is minimal, and he's really limited in what he can build there. So it'd be great if another piece of property ever came up that had non-floodplain part of the farm. It lets you be more flexible. Lots of things would be good about that. I would like to stay in this Valley. That would be my first choice.

It's funny, we talk about flooding a lot, with people who come to visit the farm, but I always say that I'd much rather live on an undammed-up river where when a flood comes, you know it's gonna come—instead of some kind of infrastructure failure upstream, and then you're drowned. So yeah, the reason that we have this farmland as a resource here is because of the flooding. I mean, initially, primarily because that's what created the farmland in the first place, but also because it has excluded development, because of the FEMA regulations. But above all that, above the county and other local regulations, and the Growth Management Act and all that stuff, the FEMA flood insurance regulations rule all, in terms of getting a permit to build some things. So as long as FEMA says this is a hundred-year floodway, you can't be insured here, then no new development's going to happen—even if something crazy happens at the county.

Jason Salvo

2 December 2009

I'm Jason Salvo. I was born on March 1, 1979, which makes me thirty years old. I have been farming with my wife, at Local Roots Farm, for three years. I was born in Boston, Massachusetts, or actually, technically, in Newton, Massachusetts, was the town where the hospital was. I grew up in a small town north of Boston called Swampscott, population like 10,000, very small—except all of the eastern seaboard is like one big town. The town itself was 10,000-14,000 people, but the houses went right up to the border, and then a new town started, and so it might as well have been the same town as Boston, because there's continuous people all the way. We're about fourteen or sixteen miles north of Boston.

My mom is from Seattle, and when my parents got divorced, we moved here in 1991 or so. I think I was eleven or ten. My dad remained in New England. He moved to, literally, the next town over. And so I would spend my summers in Marblehead, Massachusetts, with my dad, and I went to school here in the Seattle area. Went to Garfield High School, where I met Siri. Actually, we met in middle school. We have been together since we were about sixteen years old.

I went to the University of Washington, I majored in history and political science, and then I went to Seattle University Law School. I'm technically a lawyer, although if I don't take my continuing legal education classes, which are really expensive, I probably won't be for much longer.

The first year of the farm, in fact when Siri was saying, "Okay, how much money do we need to live on?" we decided that even if the farm didn't make any money, I had a job. Actually, I think she decided in November that she was going to start a farm, and I didn't get a job until February or so. But it worked out quite well, because I worked for a woman who only wanted somebody to work part-time. So I was on the farm three or four days a week, and then I worked in an office the other three or four days a week. At the end of that year, the work in the office waned. She had hired me because there was a really big case that she had been working on, and just needed more people. So the work at the end of that year waned, and we decided that the next year, the second year that the farm was in existence, it could make enough money to support our household, our needs being few, and the farm providing for many of them. And so I did not continue to work as a lawyer, and I have not since. The farm has supported our household completely for two years now. Which I think is unusual. I think most of the people who farm—I don't know if this is the case in the Valley—but they have either a partner who has off-farm income, or they come to it with a whole bunch of money that they've earned over their career, which enables them to afford the lower income that farming brings.

Siri has *always* wanted to farm. I think her vision of life, from when she was much younger, was that she wanted a little homestead—certainly not the sort of farm that we have now, but some, you know, inspired by the Nearings, Scott and Helen Nearing, and that kind of lifestyle, a little cabin in the woods where you grow your own food and all that sort of stuff. We, in eighth and ninth grade, would talk on the phone for hours and hours, and she would often say that that's what she wanted to do. And I thought it was just a terrible idea! I didn't have a better plan in mind, but definitely not that. So as far as farming being on my radar, once we graduated from high school and went to college and were sort of in the current that I think most people get swept up in, in life, which is that you are supposed to get a job, and you're supposed to work in an office, and do normal things with other normal people. And

I don't think that we really talked about farming again until, well, I guess at some point we sat down.... I suppose when we were sort of trying to decide what careers we could have in life that would be acceptable—you know, what are the things that don't contribute to any sort of harm or badness in the world—and there aren't that many of them. Most things we had decided were in some way environmentally harmful or socially harmful, or at the very least were neutral. You know, you're not creating any kind of good in the world, you're just coasting, I guess. And I think at some point along in our, I guess early twenties, we decided that what we would do is work and earn enough money to buy a farm. I remember one day we wrote a timeline on a piece of paper that had twenty years out we would own a little farm. And I had really no interest in it, but I knew it was what Siri wanted, and I figured in twenty years lots of things would change, and so it wasn't much of a commitment to make.

Well, I *did* fall into her trap, because before we started graduate school, we went and we traveled in Europe, and as Siri said, I organized two stays on farms, one of which ended up not happening because we got to Rome and we really liked Rome a lot, and we rented an apartment and took language classes and decided we didn't want to leave the wonderful lifestyle we were living. But before that, we'd worked for about a month on an organic olive orchard with a crazy person who hated Americans. This was right before the Iraq War, so it would have been in 2003 or so. And we just couldn't do anything right, the person hated us. We chose this particular farm, because in his ad it said "no English spoken." And I, in retrospect, realized that what *that* was, was his way of trying to prevent Americans from being on his farm, because he actually spoke perfect English—maybe not perfect English, but he spoke well. And in fact, I wanted a no-English-spoken farm so that I could get really good at speaking Italian. And he, in fact, mostly spoke to us in English, even though I tried to speak to him in Italian.

Anyway, we left that farm on somewhat bad terms with this guy, because he didn't want to let us use his telephone. Siri wanted to call her parents on their birthday or something, and we weren't allowed to use the phone. Anyway, it was bad news. But, as Siri said, while we were there, we became.... I mean, I think not just being on this farm, but just living in Italy for four or five months you get acquainted with all sorts of different and amazing foods, which when you get back to America, they're expensive, or mostly they just don't taste as good. They don't have the same flavor or richness, because we were eating things that were picked much fresher. When we were on this farm, we were going out to the little vegetable garden and picking fennel and chicories and all these things. And if it's sitting in a grocery store for three weeks because nobody wants to buy those things, and then you buy it, it's bad. It's not the same experience.

We really like cooking. I think cooking and eating good food and having people over and sharing that food as a social bridge, a way to connect with people is something that we've never consciously, but as I'm talking now, it has been our way of interacting with our friends. And so when the opportunity came around to start this farm, it was a really easy and natural progression of what we'd been doing—just cooking and eating food. And we had had this really large, for the small apartment that we lived in, an elaborate vegetable garden which we were pretty proud of.

It *could* be pretty lucrative being a corporate lawyer. Although even when I was in law school, I didn't do any of the things that one would do to pursue that track. I had no interest in the hours that are required to do that, or.... There's no way that I could live with myself if what I was doing was helping the wealthy companies do things that essentially are screwing the public or screwing a person who's been harmed by the company, or anything like that. And, you can't fall into the corporate track, because it's highly competitive. You have to choose to do it, and you have to work your ass off to get hired by these companies that will pay you your first year $120,000 a year, and all you have to give them is your soul and eighty hours a week. Finding a "meaningful" career is not really something that I ever talked about with anyone, except for Siri. And I would like to imagine that if you went to a career counselor, that they might put those sorts of questions to students, but I never went to a career counselor, so I don't have the benefit of experience in seeing what happens when people who are feeling wayward, seek help.

All through law school my goal was to find a part-time job. And there aren't any part-time jobs. Nobody wants to hire you. You can't be a lawyer part-time, I don't think. Nothing interested me. None of the actual, on-the-ground lawyer jobs interested me. When I was in law school I was much more interested in abstract, intellectual, constitutional law theory, which I think that not that many people get to pursue that line of work. And I think you have to be really lucky and really smart, and have gone to an Ivy League college. And so not having gone to an Ivy League school, it seemed obvious that the thing I was really interested in wasn't going to happen, and I wasn't really interested in doing anything else. So I didn't ever try that hard to find a job. What my thought was, "If I get a part-time job, you make enough money to...." I didn't *need* to make $100,000 a year. "If I make $30,000 a year, and I only work thirty hours, twenty hours a week, I'll have lots of time to do enjoyable, rewarding, fun things in my spare time." As it turns out, I work as much as if I had chosen a corporate law career! But it doesn't feel the same, and I think that what we're doing is really meaningful and beneficial.

Siri is the ultimate decision-maker and the planner. As she said, she has created really excellent spreadsheets that detail what the year is going to look like, how much of whatever we're going to plant. Because the first year I was working part-time, and Siri created, just sitting in a coffee shop, over the winter, she created this plan. Since then every year she's been refining something that was created a number of years ago. So the first year my input was zero. And each year we've been collaborating more, but Siri is the author of the plan ultimately. And so when it became clear that I was not going to be a lawyer and I was going to work on the farm full-time, I felt—because the dynamic among Siri and Dan and I is such that Dan owns the property and he owns the equipment, and as Siri said, ultimately he is the final arbiter. He also is very, very ... peculiar, in that he's not always willing to do what seems to be in the best interest of the company, because he has various hang-ups and peccadilloes that he has to overcome before progress can happen. Siri, as I said, is the author of the plan; and Dan is the hurdle that the plan has to get over. And I felt like I needed to have my own role, something that was mine, because one of the things that I learned about myself is that I'm not very good at working for other people. I'm too arrogant or something. I don't like being told what to do—ego—I have too large of an ego. I don't think it's arrogance.

But I don't actually think that highly of myself, I just think I'm always right. So anyway, the area that I have carved out for myself is I'm the, I don't know, restaurants accounts manager, to give it an official-sounding title. I really like the unusual things that we grow, and I really like cooking. And Siri is not the farm's communicator. She's not as good at answering her phone as some people. That is to say, she doesn't like to answer her phone. She just doesn't like to respond to e-mail. And for whatever reason, I'm more prone to do those things. So when it came to communicating with people on a regular basis, sending out an e-mail saying, "Hey, this is the food that we have".... Plus the cooking side of the farming stuff is of more interest to me—or at least an interest that goes farther back in my life than growing food. And so that is my unique role on the farm.

I could not imagine doing this without Dan. He plays a really key role—not just because he owns the property, but he's.... We fit together, the three of us, in a really interesting way, whereas I think that I'm much more, I'm very goal oriented and I'm not process oriented. When I have decided that something needs to happen, I'm focused and I want to start immediately, and I will start putting all the things together that I think need to happen. Dan is extremely process oriented, where I think the pleasure that he gets out of a lot of projects isn't so much in completing them, but in thinking about them, and thinking about them, and thinking about them, and thinking about them, and thinking about them; and talking about them, and talking about them more, and reconsidering, and measuring, and really coming up with an excellent plan. And so I think that we wouldn't mesh very well, really, if it weren't for Siri, who's like a negotiator, I think. I think I want to take something and run with it, both fortunately and unfortunately, I think, because it's Dan's property and he has ultimate veto power on anything happening. I think our trajectory has been much slower and more deliberate. When I said "Dan's peccadilloes," I think it's because he's deliberate to a fault. A lot of things I think don't get done because there's too much considering and not enough doing. And it probably is a function of it being his property and him believing that if he's going to do something, he wants to do it once and he wants to do it right. And so not just the process, but actually I guess the outcome is more important to him, whereas I guess if—and I'm speculating here—because I *don't* own the property and I say, "Oh! we need these things in order for the business to function more smoothly, in order to make more money, in order to work less and have something built that will help us be able to, like, use our time more efficiently." I would be perfectly happy to throw up a slap-dash, jury-rigged whatever, in order to have this outcome which is ultimately something happening more easily, something happening, whatever, with less work. And I think for Dan, he doesn't care about that. If he's going to build something, it needs to be perfect and well thought out, and part of some overall plan that he might have, or vision. So that's what I mean when I say peccadillo.

Actually, I very much appreciate, having worked with him for the last few years, because I'm.... It certainly makes me try and be more deliberate and thoughtful and things like that in my life.

I think the parts of it that are the most satisfying are that, well, I work for myself, which is, like I said, I've never liked working for other people. This is definitely the most—you know, from *that* perspective—the most satisfying job that I've ever had. One of the things, when I said I wanted to work part time, I love the outdoors, I love the mountains, I love being outside. And so that is also a pretty important part of what we're doing, to me. And maybe more than anything else, but I didn't know it, going into it, is the communicating with people, bringing new ideas and new foods, and telling people how to cook, and just being an evangelist, I guess, for good food. It's probably my favorite part about all of it.

Through the whole other series of random occurrences which play some role in the creation of this farm, we're friends with a number of people who are in the restaurant industry. And one of them, a woman named Emily Crawford, two years ago said, "Hey, we should do some dinners on your farm." She was, at the time, hired to work at another friend of ours' restaurant, but it hadn't opened yet, and I think she was looking for something to do. So two summers ago she cooked, I think seven dinners, out on our farm. It was totally her idea. We went in as partners ostensibly, but she basically did all the work. We just did the dishes after she was done cooking. And they were just splendid. She's unbelievably talented, and just very detail oriented with creating really beautiful and amazing foods and creative with things that she uses and puts together, the flavors and that. And this year the restaurant that she was hired to work for, opened, and she didn't have the time to do them, and so I sent out an e-mail to all the restaurants that we work with and said that we were looking for chefs. I think we did about eight this year too, with only one person who did more than one dinner. So it was seven different chefs, seven different restaurants that we worked with, that came out and did these dinners. It's just another way for us to—you know, we look at it as a way to interact with people, and have people come to the farm.

You know what? One of the parts about it that I like the most is that we are a working farm, and it is not clean, and there is shit everywhere, and there's holes that people could fall in, and a dog that might bite you if you are a child. That happened! And I think people are looking for these real experiences, and a lot of places are trying to do a really good job of approximating reality with their décor, and it's supposed to look like a French farmhouse, and it's supposed to look rustic, but it's all contrived. And we do these dinners with a big long table out in the middle of the field. Or when the temperature gets cold, in our greenhouse, which has drip tape piled up in the corner, and plastic trays that we seed plants into, in the corner. It's a dirt floor, it's an uneven floor, there's no square right angles anywhere. It is real, in the extent that we don't pick up very much before people come. And we're a working farm, and there's just crap everywhere. But I think I really like the exposure. People come, we give a tour, we walk around, we show them the vegetables, have them meet the chickens, and blah, blah, blah. But it's in a really honest environment, which is pretty unique. And then we eat dinner with everybody, and Siri and Dan and I split up, so we're at different parts of the table, and we answer the guests' questions and talk a lot.

It is really rewarding. Siri was talking about farmers market customers who come, who don't know about cooking, and they know that they feel some sort of, I don't know, their super-ego tells them that they should be eating this food. And they're like, "But I don't know what to do with it! I don't like broccoli. I don't like this...." And luckily, I guess, we like cooking, and we read a lot of cookbooks and cooking magazines, and just have in our own life, I guess, been able to distill things that we cook into just a few sentences, that are simple enough and easy enough to remember, that you can say, "Okay, take this home, put it on a cookie sheet at 450° and roast it until it's crispy." And then people come back and they go from being somebody who didn't think they liked broccoli, or didn't think they liked brussel sprouts or whatever, to being a regular customer and the gratitude that they express when they come back, and they say, "Oh, we just love that recipe so much! It's the only way that we cook broccoli. Tell me another recipe, tell me something else that I've never heard of. Teach me how to cook that." And it's *so* amazingly rewarding, to have incrementally improved somebody else's life in that way.

There is a really cute couple that are customers that are at the Broadway Sunday farmers market. I think they're both art historians, and I suspect that maybe they teach at the U. Because we lived in Italy for a short amount of time, and speak Italian, are into that cuisine—we grow a lot of really weird Italian stuff that I suspect that there's probably only a handful of farms in the country that are growing some of these weird things that we grow....Such as puntarelle, which is in the chicory family. It looks a little bit like red-root dandelion, which is on the chicory.... But before it bolts, it makes this unbelievably weird.... Or I guess in its process of reproduction, it makes this gnarly, bizarre, central stalk that looks sort of like a lot of heads of asparagus all clumped together. And in Rome.... I think it's a vegetable that they only grow and use in the region of Italy in Latsio, which is where Rome is. And they push these puntarelle through like a wire mesh, so that they're thin strings of chicory stem that they put into acid, like lemon juice, water, and then they curl, and they dress it with anchovy dressing. It's really good. It's something that we ate probably once when we were in Rome. And a friend of ours who opened a restaurant in Seattle who really also loves Italian food and Italian things recommended that we grow it—he said, "You should grow this."

We'll go through seed catalogs, and sometimes we'll order things that maybe we *kind of* know what it is, but we only vaguely know what it is. And then it turns out to be something really great. So this couple has been coming, and they're buying treviso radicchio, and they're buying puntarelle, and they're buying romanesco broccoli, and all these very Italian things, and they said.... We were chatting with them, and they said every Sunday they go home from the market with their bag of stuff that they got from us, and they think that they must be the luckiest people on earth, because they have found us; or that we have this stuff that reminds them of Italy, which is where they also have some emotional connection to. It feels really good when you can make somebody's life happier in any kind of way.

At a lot of meetings and sort of policy things that we attend every once in a while, there's kind of two tropes that you hear, and one of them is: "Farmers need to make more money. Farmers need to earn a living wage. Farmers need to be paid what they deserve." And also: "Healthy, nontoxic food needs to be available and affordable to the poorest elements of society." And those are, unfortunately, in many ways, opposites. In some ways they're opposites. You know, how could we make more money? We could be bigger, and at some point there's economies of scale, where just by virtue of selling a lot and only making a penny per head of broccoli, but if you sell a hundred million heads of broccoli, you've made a million dollars. But the larger you get, I think the lower the quality of what you're producing—just simply because you can't pay as much attention to each individual thing, and you start doing things which make you more money, or which sort of increase your efficiency, but which lower any number of virtues broccoli might exhibit. And then the other way to make more money is to charge more. I think some farms are really much larger, and they are able to charge less for their food, but to my eye it doesn't look like it's as good. It's surely better than what they're getting from the Safeway. So it's something that I think about a lot, is what the appropriate price for our food is, and whether it's too expensive, whether it's not expensive enough. I think that last year I would have told you that food needed to be a lot more expensive. And this year, as we got better at doing what we're doing, we didn't get *much* bigger in scale, and I think our quality went up, and we sold a lot more food, and we made a fair amount more money than we did the last two years. And it's gotten me thinking about whether there *is* an appropriate, you know, hitting just the right size farm, so that you can grow really beautiful wonderful things, and also grow and sell enough of them that it *is* affordable and accessible to lower-income people.

The problem, though, is even if it were less expensive, I think there's a culture shift that has to happen, really, before the people who I think need it the most are gonna go out and buy vegetables. If a value meal at a McDonald's costs a dollar.... *And*, I think, beyond the value meal costing a dollar, if you have gone for so long in a family or in a culture that doesn't value cooking. If you don't know what to do with it once you get it, even if you think it's something that you should do, maybe you're not going to make that choice because you don't know what to do with the beet when you get home.

As with all problems, there's a lot of factors contributing to it. And I think there's no one answer, and there's probably no five answers. It's incremental, and probably more than incremental changes in a lot of different places that have to happen before the stars will align right, and everybody can afford healthy food and there's demand among the people who need it the most, for healthy food. We live in a world where convenience is a pretty compelling reason to make a choice. Something takes less time, you're probably willing to spend *more* money, because you'd rather be going to the movies or playing video games; or you're busy, you have a job, and you have children to look after, or whatever. And I think maybe one of the biggest hurdles isn't price, but simply that we live in a world that doesn't value that sort of cooking at home, eating dinner with your family, these sorts of things, family values.

We talk a lot about ways that we can bring people to the farm and help them have these experiences. And I think right now the sort of people that are coming out to the farm are a *fairly* self-selected group of people who are interested in our farm dinners, or who are members of our CSA. They've already drank the Kool-Aid, so to speak.

We are doing a program with a group called Global Visionaries, which in Seattle Public Schools, and I presume other school districts in the area, because some kids came last year from Mercer Island High School—you have to earn a certain number of volunteer hour credits, service learning credits, in order to graduate—and so a number of groups sprang up, of which Global Visionaries is one, that sort of provides a structured environment for kids to get these service learning hours. And this one, they ultimately go and work on a coffee plantation and do some work in Guatemala. But the service learning component in Seattle is over the last couple of years I think they've done trail maintenance and restoration through the, probably, Student Conservation Corps, and then there's some other sort of outdoorsy pull-ivy-off-trees things. And then last year they contacted us and they wanted the kids to go out and work on a farm. So just because we knew somebody who worked in that organization, we ended up being the farm. And we're beginning our second year with this group. It's interesting, kids who are sixteen, who are sort of forced to do some sort of volunteer thing, and they're like, (lackluster voice) "Oh, maybe a farm would be fun." I'd like to think that we'll provide some sort of meaningful, life-changing experience, but I don't really think.... I don't think that that happened last year, and I doubt.... At best, I think you provide people with some exposure to another way of being or thinking that doesn't resonate when you're sixteen, because I think when you're sixteen you only  are thinking about yourself. But maybe one day in the future, some other event or person or thing that you read or something will remind you of an experience you had when you were younger, and it'll hopefully resonate sometime in the future—and maybe now, I don't know.

We don't necessarily have any particular grand agenda, but I think that we think a lot about ways that we can be ... I guess bring more people into the community that we're a part of—whether it's through education, or just providing them with good food, and maybe just exposing people a little bit to some of the things that we do and think. And hopefully it will spread.

Dan Beyers

12 January 2010

My name is Dan Charles Beyers, and I was born March 5, 1948, at Swedish Hospital here in Seattle. My family lived in Seattle. We moved to the Eastside by the time I started kindergarten. Went to kindergarten in Issaquah. Then I spent the next three years bouncing around elementary schools on the Eastside. I guess it was a dynamic kind of changing population then. I spent several years in more than one school, in parts of gyms, I guess. And then in the fourth grade we moved to Issaquah and I went to school in Issaquah all the way through high school, and graduated there in 1966. Straight to the U., and graduated from the U. in 1970, without debt, which I don't think that was that unusual then.

About the end of my third year they took me in and said, "Listen, the idea is that you major in something." I had realized that I really only had a year left in me. So I looked at my situation, and about the only thing I could graduate on time, the only degree I could get and get out of there in four years was social cultural anthropology. So that's what I got my degree in. No employer has ever asked me about my education, so I guess it was a liberal arts education, I loved it.

Issaquah was a wonderful place to grow up, but it wasn't very worldly. It was a very nice little community with family-owned businesses. I received, I thought, a very good education. It served me well, it prepared me for the university. I was very happy about it. But when I went to the U., I was exposed to other nationalities, races, languages, ethnic clothing—it was just wonderful.

So after I graduated, the friends that I met at the U. and I, we wanted to farm. I'd always wanted to farm. When I was a child, at the dinner table, this was what I would always contend I was going to do, is have a farm. I don't know exactly why that is, except for the fact that my dad blessed me with a garden every year of my life. No matter where we lived, we had a garden. We ate from the garden. I grew up on home-grown vegetables, moose meat, salmon, sea bass—simple food, good food. So I have many fond memories of working in the family garden, and filling my pockets up with peas and things, and climbing up trees and sitting there and eating them when I was kid. In those days they just told you to leave the house in the morning. I was a little kid, our days were ours to fill up in the woods. It was wonderful. So I've always been more comfortable in the bushes than I have in the city. But I thoroughly enjoy the city.

When I was growing up in Issaquah, my dad was a small-time contractor. And to get away from the family business, they purchased fourteen acres just south of Carnation in the Snoqualmie Valley, and they bought a little trailer, and in those days without answering machines or cell phones, all they'd have to do is go over the hill from Issaquah, and they could be in the trailer for the weekend, away from the family business. In those days you always answered the phone. There was nobody to screen calls. I can't remember *ever* the phone not being answered if it rang. So the only way to really get away and have some free time was to get out of the house. So that piece of property, after I graduated from college, my friends and I, who had been reading Rodale since we were in high school—that family's publications—and were already at that point convinced that that was the way we wanted to grow food, and that there was a problem with commercial agriculture already. This was back in the 1970s when I graduated from the U.

We went out to this family property of mine. My family generously just donated its use. And it had previously just been cow pasture. And we bought a Troybilt rototiller and put in a couple acres of vegetables. Did it for several years, grew a lot of wonderful food, but made no money, because we were naïve and there was no market. As I remember it in those days, PCC was a start-up remodeled house in Ravenna, was one location. And there were very few places that appreciated our food as being any different, and they wanted to mark it way up, and we didn't do it on the scale that you could make a living at it. So eventually, we all had to move on to jobs that would sustain us economically, unfortunately. And also, my main partner there, that I had gone to junior high and high school with, also passed away at a very early age. It's actually what kind of precipitated the end of that farming experiment. He had a horrible melanoma on his head, and passed away. It's very ironic. He was the most vital life force I've ever known. He was really the force that got us all together and out there, and maintained the energy that it took to do it. So we all went our separate ways.

But while I was there, I met the neighbors and my current farm was purchased somewhere near the turn of the century and it's just 300 feet from being contiguous to the family property. It's a seventy-five-acre farm. And it was a previous dairy farm, and I knew the individuals that were my neighbors, the young couple that were renting the house then. So that's how I became aware of the property, and I knew the property. So after we quit farming on the family property, I was a one-man contractor, basically, using the skills I learned from my dad and his employees. Ended up with two children, and I was a single parent with two sons, and it was difficult. A friend of mine who I had done much work for, encouraged me to become an employee of his business, instead of doing spot work for him, to actually become an employee, and it would stabilize my income, allow me to get benefits, healthcare for the kids, etc. So I took him up on that and spent about twelve years as an employee there. He sold the company, and then it was sold again, and I ended up with him not managing me anymore. I loved him, he was a mentor, a wonderful man. I met him also at the U. And he was often at the family farm, he was a part of that experience. He didn't farm there, but he was one of the people that was always out and supportive.

After my kids had grown and were out of the house, I was stuck with this fully vested corporate job which had paid the bills, but it wasn't what I ever imagined doing in life. And I came home one day and one of my kids had left a flyer on my bed, a real estate flyer, for this farm that I'm currently living at. It took a couple days, and I realized that I wanted my future to be there, not at the house that I had paid off in Duvall, where I was living. So I took a risk and purchased the farm. And then I spent well over a year—some of it still working—preparing and trading assets to pay for them—cashing in and preparing my property and selling my property in Duvall, to get to the point where I was finally on the farm. So it was quite a period of time where I actually owned it but wasn't actually living there. And then I lived there for four or five years, visiting other farms and allowing some other farmers to occasionally farm part of my fields.

The owner of the farm had not lived there for many years. So the house was rented out to one group of people, and the fields were rented to a local dairy family. And that had been, I think, thirty years of them using those fields almost exclusively growing silage for their dairy herd, using traditional agricultural techniques. They were wonderful handshake farmers. So a couple years into the ownership, when I was prepared to start working the fields myself, I'd gotten rid of my other assets and was *there* and ready to focus on the property, I felt uncomfortable about it, but

I was going to ask them to not farm on it anymore. I didn't have to, because they announced to me that they were selling their herd of thirty years and quitting the business. This was a very established family in the Valley, brothers that were dairy farmers for decades and decades. And so they lived up to their handshake deal and cover cropped the fields after their last use of it, for me, and went on their way. And then for several years I kept cover cropping the fields. I could not certify them as organic immediately, and it was during that time I started trying to meet other farmers, because gardening is not farming, and I had to scale up.

So after a few years of that, when I was letting one of the neighboring farmers use part of my field, and kind of experimenting in terms of whether he and I could be partners, I spent a portion of the summer conversing with his interns that would be harvesting in the field—my field. And at the end of that year, and after their relationship with him had ended, and I had decided that he wasn't the person that I wanted to farm with, and I determined I needed a partner, the interns approached me and I'd gotten to know them, and we decided that our goals were similar. I was very impressed with them, so the three of us formed an LLC and so we have just completed our—this spring will be our fourth year together as an LLC. One of our founding partners has since—and his intention always was to move on. He was here because his wife was going to school here and furthering her degree. So they basically left on schedule. Last year I took.... My partner's husband became the other partner, so we're still three partners. And so I farm with a couple, basically now. Wonderful, intelligent, dedicated, I couldn't be happier about the people that I found to farm with.

Siri Erickson Brown, and her husband Jason Salvo. They went to school, they've known each other for many years before they were married. They both have graduate degrees. He's actually a lawyer, but now he's a farmer. What I owned was ground and equipment, and I had this desire to farm vegetables. They were better consumers than I was. They were knowledgeable consumers of local produce. They were veterans of going to farmers markets, which I was not. They are intelligent, and they/we worked out—Siri and I, basically—worked out the first year. We worked up a business plan, and she's continued to take the lead. She is really the one who writes the business plan. We get along very well, so we bring complementary things to it. They bring the off-farm presence, which I was unwilling or incapable of being. And I provide the farm and the equipment that they didn't have.

I maintain the equipment. Well, we've had three very successful years. I don't brag about my knowledge of farming or my knowledge of equipment, but I'm doing it. This is what I'm doing. And I'm capable of persisting. So we have exceeded every economic goal that we set for ourselves, and were forced to set those. But that isn't why we farm. We'd be a fool to farm to try to get rich, or even make a living. You farm because you have to farm. In fact, if you do not have a sustainable economic model, you can't continue to farm. So it's a necessity. When I naively moved to the farm, somehow I got to the farm and owned the farm and really did not have a business plan. And it's absolutely vital. I think it's a mistake many young farmers make. They grow it and then they try to sell it. We sold it in our minds first, in detail, week by week, all the way through the growing season. And then we reverse engineered the entire business plan so that we would have what we imagined selling, when we imagined selling it. And then we continued to expand our plan within the confines of my farm, and the opportunities it allows, and have continued to exceed our goals every year. In that sense, we feel quite successful. And I think they're probably as good at what they do as anybody I've ever met. But I would not brag about my farming skills. The main thing I bring to it is that this is what I wanted to do, and I'm actually doing it, and I realize that I can't do it alone, and I've managed to find people that I can successfully partner with to do it. And that's everything. I could not do it alone.

I farm because I want to, completely selfishly. I farm because that's what I want to do. I did not want to have a corporate job. I *had* to have a corporate job and pay the bills. And I made the best of that, and I loved the people that I managed in my corporate career, that I worked alongside and that I managed. But the job that we were doing, I had no interest in.

I don't really know what it is about farming that got me goin'. I would say that never being without a garden as I grew up, is a big part of it. My fondest memories are about having a family garden. From the time I was in diapers, I never was without a family garden. I think that is really probably what…. But also I never have bought into the culture's definition of success. I don't really care for possessions. "Things are in the saddle and ride mankind," as Emerson put it. I care more about doing no harm, and carrying my weight, being a productive member of my community, and I care about my own sense of integrity. And farming is something I think is productive work, it's an honorable thing to do, it's a needed thing to do. And so since I want to do it, and I'm now capable of doing it, why not do it? It brings me great pleasure to do it. And I happen, I think—it's just fortunate—unlike 1970 when all that was the case, but the community I lived in didn't care about locally-grown food, and there was no developed market, and so for that, and the reasons I explained earlier, we quit. My family retained the property, and it's now mine, so I own the original farm and the farm I purchased. They don't quite abut—they're 300 feet from being contiguous to each other. We currently farm both pieces. In actual productive cultivation right now, we have six acres. Next year we'll have a little over seven. We will most likely continue to expand until we have reached the point where we are using the farm properly. I have fields that I'm still not using properly.

We basically grow our food by the guidelines that you can certify as organic, but we do not certify. I see it as a marketing decision, and we do not need to certify to market. It's time and money that we don't have to spend to sell everything that we grow. The marketing opportunities that certifying opens up aren't necessary to us, we're not drawn to them. And we're completely honest with anybody that we sell to about all of our techniques, and we have no difficulty marketing our produce at this point. So we also feel that I think the Rodale family's intent to push for years and years and years, to try to distinguish organic produce from commercial produce, was quickly co-opted by the large economic interests, and now you need to be very careful. Just because it's organic doesn't mean it's what the Rodale family would have blessed. Luckily for us, the local community now also values local food production. I think they value that almost as much as having the word "organic" attached to it. And I think they're also learning that you don't actually, technically, have to qualify, certify your food as organic, to be wholesome food. And I doubt that we will certify.

Others in the Valley have been certified, and have talked to their customer base and decided that they didn't have to. I don't have any problem with the people that do. We grow without herbicides, pesticides, or any chemical fertilizers, basically. I think technically we would…. Except for the fact that we don't do the paperwork and pay the fees, we grow by all the approved techniques, and used all the approved substances only, etc.

On my farm I'm blessed with what I consider to be world class agricultural soil. And it is the floods that created that soil. But the floods make it *very* difficult. They add a whole 'nother context in which we have to farm, that many farms don't face. They are an undeniable reality that our infrastructure has to make peace with. And within the last three years, we've had *two* record floods, all-time record floods.

We survived them. Our success has happened. We've only been farming for three years, and two of those winters we had record floods. So, so far, so good.

But it is a challenge for start-up farmers for that reason. And I think it would be very difficult to purchase a farm now and pay for it. I own a farm. I'm a business partner, but I'm also the landowner. So our business compensates me for the lease of the ground and some of the equipment that we use. And that money doesn't attempt to pay—there's many, many acres of my farm that our business does not use, that I purchased separately from that. And so it's hard to find small acreage for start-up farms. A beautiful world-class piece of soil, you could sit there and look at it, but to farm it you need a certain amount of road, you need access to irrigation water, to water that you can use in your wash station. You need to be able to protect your equipment. You need equipment. You need equipment to transport your produce to the market. I think the difficulty—it's a start-up difficulty—and you won't become rich doing it. And so you have to find a way to have more than passion. You have to find a way. And I think there's much fallow ground on this Valley floor. I think much more of it would be used if it wasn't so expensive to start up. Our experiment is we are attempting to farm with as little capitalization as possible. We are attempting to farm with as simple a tool kit as we can. We do that partly out of necessity, but I also think it's a very timely, interesting experiment, because I think for the reasons I just stated, that the young start-up farmers really need ... *that's* the technique they need to witness, not a mature farm that's twenty years old. How did they get from the beginning to that?

I think the future of farming in America is not corporate farming, it's third world farming. There's a certain inefficiency to the way we farm. *All* of our harvesting is by hand. We use as small of equipment as we can. It's amazing how many people you can employ when you do intensive market gardening, which is what I think you refer to our farming style as. We grow a *very* large variety of vegetables, and we grow them very intensively. It takes a lot of man hours to do it.

This year, well, we've had a couple interns for the first couple of years, and also spouses of my partners. But this last year we had five interns. It was a wonderful summer. I was completely, by the end of the summer I just felt *so* fortunate to have those five individuals share my farm and the whole experience. I don't know, I think we were lucky. They were intelligent dedicated people. Some of them want to farm, some of them were experimenting, they were trying it out. In America right now, two of our interns came straight from their graduation ceremonies to the farm. And they were not looking forward to going to the job fairs that their friends were going to. But more importantly, they were looking for an alternative way to have a life. Their future isn't the future I faced. I've lived my entire life in King County, and I've owned *a* piece of real estate since I was nineteen. And I just kept rolling over the increased value of what I held. That's partly why I, as a single parent, received no economic help raising two kids, ended up owning a farm. So I was very frugal, but also the macro-economic environment was in my favor. I do not think that's the future these youngsters are facing. And I think they're well prepared. My interns all understand that, and will thrive in this environment. They, in a sense, don't value corporeal possessions. That's not what makes them happy. They all have their own sense of themselves and integrity. Several of them I know will farm. One of them is already interning in his home state, Vermont, on another farm. Eli. Just got a letter from him today. He got the job there. So I'm very happy for him. I was very, very impressed by him. We receive countless applications.

Somehow we had a wonderful time. It's hard work, but.... Farming, to me, is a way of life that right now I have no plans to ever move off the farm. I'll farm as long as I can, and then if I can't, I'm hoping to have wonderful partners like I currently have, that will farm and continue to farm, and I can be there—just be less instrumental to the success of the farm, and enjoy all the benefits of the wonderful people that the farm draws down the driveway, and the wonderful food that we get to consume, and enjoy their wonderful perspectives. I just stay at the end of the driveway, and the best part of the world seems to come to me. It's wonderful. Because one of the *worst* parts of my corporate career was the commute. I feel very fortunate to have survived.

I think I'm encouraged by the number of young people that are exploring this possibility. And I am absolutely impressed by their intelligence. Not only their intelligence, but many of them are highly educated. You would think that it would open other doors. They're not interested in those doors. So my hope in the future has to do with young people like these interns, and my partners that are half my age.

I think agriculture has as good a chance here as anywhere. A *very* small percentage of the vegetables consumed in King County are grown in King County. The farming community that I'm a part of is not competing with itself. It feels like that when you're at a farmers market and you look at your beets and you look across at the other guy's beets, but the truth of the matter is that we're competing with imported corporate food. And luckily, the willingness to buy local food is staying ahead of the ability to produce it. So we get a good price for direct marketing our food. It's appreciated, and we really aren't competing with each other. I don't feel that way at all. And there is a lot of cooperation and a sense of community amongst the farmers in the Snoqualmie Valley here, which is wonderful.

Before I moved to the farm, I think I lived almost twenty years in one house, and I barely knew the community. I, like most of the other residents in the community, drove out in the morning, and drove back late in the day to a family that I hadn't seen and had needs. I had no sense of community at all. And now I know everybody up and down my road, and have a reciprocity of some sort with almost everybody. And it's *very* satisfying, and it's the way it should be. I hope to just continue to nurture that relationship. Then, beyond my road, I would hope that King County would embrace the Valley as a valued agriculture source of food. And up to this point, that's happening. I realize that we sell food for top dollar, basically, and that the current economic situation, macro-economic situation could force people to make very hard decisions about the quality of the food they buy. We'll see. But *we*, my partners and I, haven't seen any evidence that that's impacted our business model yet. We'd still be growing wonderful food. We would just have to alter our business plan and find some other reciprocity, some other way to be compensated for producing the food. We do not quit producing the food. But there is this unfortunate reality, you have to make enough money to pay the undeniable expenses of life, or you can't continue farming. So we'll see how this goes.

I worry a little bit about other uses that would vie for the ground, that could raise property prices. I don't involve myself personally too much in the local politics, but I'm aware of it, and my partners are more involved than I, and so I get to participate in the conversation, and I guess witness the process. It's fascinating and a little discouraging at times, but we do have an Ag production district. It is converting from dairy, which is almost dead in the Valley. My farm was a dairy farm originally, before it was used by the farming family I mentioned, to grow silage, there was a small dairy right *on* the farm. There's a lot of fallow ground in the valley floor right now.

We have no metric, but my partner Siri keeps *wonderful* records of virtually everything, and she would come up with a fairly educated guess, but we just spoke about that today at lunch, we *don't* know the tonnage. It'd be nice to know.

It's interesting, because my partners and I farm because we're passionate about farming, it's what we want to do. I think most of the people that buy our produce buy it because they want to buy local produce. There are many people with means well beyond our customer base that choose *not* to spend their money on local produce. We drive by a whole lot of them to get to the markets that *we've* found, that are willing to support local produce, and for us it's Seattle.

I'm living the dream. I feel very, *very* fortunate. I'm happy to wake up every day. I have had *many* wonderful friends that are gone. And I not only wake up, I'm capable of going out and putting in a good day's work on a farm. And I don't have to drive anywhere. When I get out the door, my commute is opening the door and stepping to the other side of it. And that is absolutely wonderful. I'm not trying to inspire people. I'm not trying to save the world. I happen to think that what I'm doing is a big part of the solution. I just have no idea what America thinks it's going to do to go back to work. We're near the bottom. And so it seems to me that a lot of people could take the place of huge equipment. I'd love to see the Midwest fill back up with small towns and local farming communities. I don't know how that's ever going to happen.

Farm Journal

7 August 2009

Changing Seasons Farm—as it happens, a group of three high school students from Bellevue, WA show up to volunteer. Laura Casey met one of them at the Issaquah Farmers Market and he asked if he could help out on the farm. Later that week, he called, set a date and brought two friends.

They are "up-scale" kids from Clyde Hill—a very posh upper crust, nearly gated community with its own police department. Nonetheless, they are curious and willing, trying to deny the upper class stereotypes and, unabashedly ignorant about how vegetables grow and are brought to market.

A quintessential moment—Laura squatted down at the end of a potato row and pulled a plant from the dense, loamy soil. Three large Yukon Gold tubers hung from the stem and the boys stared in amazement.

"What are they?"

"Potatoes."

She handed him one and proceeded to explain how this was in effect a seed and each of the little "eyes" would, if the fruit was returned to the soil, produce another plant.

"You mean, if I put this in the ground, I'll get more potatoes?"

"Yes."

And then the epiphany………"And I can keep doing that and get more and more potatoes?!"

"You could get hundreds," his friend chimed in……….

"That's right." Laura smiled a teacher's smile.

He turned the potato thoughtfully in his palm.

"I never saw one of these before."

………………………………………………………………………

8 August 2009—Farmers Market, Issaquah, WA

Laura and Dave Casey have their booth set up. The Market is huge and bustling. Cars are backed up on the main road—lined-up to get in. It takes me ten minutes to get in and park.

They are happy to see me and we talk briefly about the potato Pentecost; Dave is deeply pleased by the whole encounter—confirmation of one of his goals for the farm. Business is a little slow but they have their loyal customers who take pride, as I do, in knowing the one who grew the food they will eat tonight.

Dave and Laura are in their element………they work, I take photographs.

Changing Seasons Farm

Laura Casey

22 November 2009

I'm Laura Casey. I was born December 24, 1957. So that makes me fifty-two shortly. Born in Seattle, one of the few natives left. My dad was also born in Seattle, and my dad's father was a vice-principal over in West Seattle, so I've got roots here. My mother was born in Ohio, I think, and ended up here in Seattle and met my dad, and they got married. So we lived in Seattle for a few years, and then we moved to southern California for a few years, and then moved to eastern Washington for six months, and then back up here for high school. So I've been here ever since.

I went to high school at Edmonds, being a local high school. It's now Edmonds-Woodway. I went to college in Walla Walla, got a Bachelor of Arts in biology and environmental studies. A few years later I went to grad school at Wazoo, Washington State University. I have a Master of Science in environmental science. And I'm a certified professional wetlands scientist—when I'm not farming! But I'd rather be farming.

We always lived in suburbs, but my father liked to garden, and so he always put in vegetable gardens most of the places we lived, and I would help him out. When I was twelve, I got my own first little patch of vegetable garden. Actually, I think it was flowers, it was nasturtiums. That was my own first little garden. Once I got out of college—actually, sometimes *in* college—everywhere I've lived, I've put in a garden and grown vegetables, just because I like to. It's what I do. We've been out in the Snoqualmie Valley now for a little over twenty years. We live currently in a little house on an acre that I built twenty-plus years ago. I had it built. I drew the plans up and had it built. We put in a very large garden there. Dave has also always been a gardener, but you'll hear that from him. So we put in a vegetable garden there, and a small orchard. Then we expanded, and we found a farm, and it's been slowly growing more things every year.

The biology fits really well with our farming. The fact that there are wetlands on the farm property, I can use my education there. We are surrounded by the river on three sides, and so one of the things we're doing is working on enhancing the river buffer, which also ties into my non-farm education and experience, because we're putting in native trees and plants. I'm a naturalist, I guess would be the word. And also I've been an environmentalist since high school, maybe junior high.

Actually, at that time, it was the late sixties, early seventies, and there was a lot of people paying attention to the environment and observing. I think we had a lake burned in the Midwest. That was when all those sorts of things were happening. People were actually starting to pay attention, cleaning the air, trying not to continue trashing the planet. It fit well with me, it's what I believe in. Growing food is part of that. I'm not religious. If anything, I would say Tibetan Lamaism is the stuff that is the most interesting to me, but I'm more metaphysically inclined, but I'm not religious—unlike my husband, and my stepdaughter.

As I said, we had a very large garden. I mean, large enough that we were giving *lots* of food away every year. And a small orchard which produces lots of apples. I always thought we should just look and see if there's a larger piece of land out there. So I was always driving around. As part of my non-farm job, I get to drive around and look at properties that are going to be developed but aren't yet. And so I get to do a lot of driving around the county. On New Year's Day, the piece of land that we ended up buying went up for sale. I came home and told Dave, "Hey, you know that road I'm always driving up and down? Well, there's a farm for sale on it." I told him, "Don't worry about it, it's a junker," and that's the one we bought! And we bought it because it is relatively flat, it's surrounded by the river on three sides. It's got total solar exposure, so it's really good sun for growing things. The soil's marvelous, it holds water, it holds moisture almost all summer, so I don't have to irrigate a whole lot. So we decided we would try it, and we bought it. And then a few years later the opportunity came up to buy a couple more pieces of land attached to that piece, so we did that. There's one piece left we want to buy to buy this whole peninsula of land that's surrounded by the river. And then we've been expanding. The piece of property that we bought was—the farmhouse has been there since the late 1920s. The barn had been built in the 1930s. It was sinking into the mud when we bought it. The farmhouse is old and moldy, but they're existing buildings in the floodway, and because of *my* background, working with the county building department, I knew the rules, and you can't build anything out there unless there's something already there, or if it's an existing farm, then you can actually replace it. So it had great value to us, even though it wasn't in very good condition, because it grows *great* vegetables, and the buildings can be replaced or remodeled, which we're slowly working on.

We replaced the barn. Dave and some high school kids and some buddies tore it down piecemeal, saved a lot of the wood, and we've put in a new barn, which we're still building. We put in a new drain field that is just complete as of two weeks ago, maybe a month ago. We're going to put an apartment upstairs in the barn so we can actually move onto our farm and live there. And we're in line for a grant to raise the farmhouse up. Last January it had three and a half feet of water and mud inside the farmhouse. We have met people who lived there in the eighties. We asked them, "What did you do when it flooded?" They said, "Oh, we just went upstairs." They raised a family there. I'm amazed! The previous people who had owned it, had owned it since the sixties and had been renting it out. It had had pastures on it, but it didn't look like anybody really had grown much of anything—some little garden plots, but not on any big farming use.

I can't be around a lot of chemicals, I can't eat a lot of chemicals. So all the food we've ever grown has been organic by default, because we can't use the chemicals. My poor husband would *love* to use Roundup, but I won't let him use it. So growing things organically is just part of what we do, it's part of my life. We can't grow them with the nasty chemicals. I can't be around them. Why we decided to be a farm, I really don't know. We've always grown things, we just expanded, we grow *more* things than we used to grow. We seem to be pretty good at growing vegetables. And we're learning a lot from our neighbors on how to do things larger scale. The shift from gardener to a farmer has been kind of interesting.

When we first got the farm, we felt like we needed to weed everything, because when you have a garden, you have to weed everything. With a farm, that's not so much what you do. Don't worry about it so much. You knock down the big infestations, but you don't have to take out every single weed, for example.

Community is important, and the neighborhood that our farm is in has a wonderful community of other farmers, just up and down that road, that are extremely helpful to one another, and educate us, which is great. We've been doing this since—this is our eighth year. So we've been doing it for a while. We still think we're rookie farmers, I feel like a rookie farmer, but we still keep learning things every year. We also think that it's important to grow food locally. In the *long* term—one of your *very* last questions—but in the long term was what do I think is going to happen to agriculture in the U.S.? As the prices of fuel, such as oil, keeps increasing, as they will, because we're going to run out eventually, as these prices increase it's going to become more and more important for the U.S. to grow its own food again—and I don't mean corn, soybeans, and wheat. I mean the stuff we can actually eat. And it's going to be important to grow it locally so people can get food that they can afford. We aren't necessarily going to be able to ship everything from California to the rest of the U.S. in another fifty years. Of course I won't *be* here in another fifty years, but we're working, it's a process. We're working towards.... I think where we're going as a country is we will need to return to many more small local farms than the large agri-business farms that concentrate on making money, and only growing commodity crops. When I was a kid, you wouldn't go to the grocery store and see every single kind of fruit and vegetable all year round, like we can now. And we can now because they're coming from other parts of the planet. Well, when the fuel costs become excessive, that is not likely to be able to continue, or people won't be able to afford food. So that's another reason we think it's important to—*I* think it's important—to grow food, and to grow food locally.

A farmer starting out in this area has to overcome the main thing, which is land's really expensive. Farmland is way less expensive than developable land on the hillsides. Nevertheless, it still costs a lot of money. If it doesn't have structures on it and it's in the floodway, you can't *put* structures on it. Because King County in particular has very strict rules on what you can and cannot do in a floodplain, in order to earn themselves a very high rating on their insurance rating through FEMA. And they're very proud of that, and so they don't want to allow people to do a lot more things in the floodway. Recent changes that have become a *little bit* more flexible are that people are now allowed to put in farm-pads, piles of fill in the floodway, in order to put their animals or their equipment, or their seed and fertilizers, up higher than flood elevation—especially if they don't have any other land outside the floodway. If a person wants to build a farm on a vacant piece of land, and it's in the floodway, they can't do it, they can't put in a new house, they can't put in a new drain field, and they can't dig a well. That's state level—the well restrictions. They don't want new wells in the floodway. So it's really tight. The reason that we've been able to do what we do is we bought a piece of property that already had a house, a barn, and a well. So that meant that we had existing infrastructure. It had a drain field, it's just nobody knew anything about it. To put *in* the new drain field, we had to let them deny us, because it's in the floodway, so the health department regulations don't allow for a new drain field in the floodway. We appealed it, because that was their process. They don't have a variance, they have an appeal. So you have to appeal it. We appealed it, we monitored the groundwater levels in several septic pits over a year, over a winter. We went out every week and kept track of it all, put it all on a spreadsheet. We won our appeal, and we were able to put in our drain field. But it took about three or four years to get there, from when we started. So it's a long process.

We're not going to turn into subdivisions, the Snoqualmie Valley is not going to become subdivisions, it's not going to become Wal-Marts, it's not going to become Green River Valley. We don't have levees, we don't have a dam on the river, it continues to flood. They can't bring in that kind of development. But if the citizens of King County want to support local ag, and getting their food locally, then they need to look at being a bit more flexible about what kinds of activities, development activities, farmers are allowed to do out on this land. Otherwise it will turn back into just wild land. It's great habitat, and it's good for the fish, but it's not growing food.

As the climate changes in this area, what the scientists are expecting to occur is that the snow level in the mountains will rise, so that the average snow level every winter will be higher. That means that, for example, Snoqualmie Pass level or below, there will be a lot more times where there will be the occasional snowstorm, and then heavy rain. That *can* cause more flooding where we are. So we have *that* to deal with. Because of where our river valley is, we're not going to be affected by sea level rise. We're still seventy, eighty feet above Puget Sound. It's not gonna get us, we're fine. How it affects the presence of wetlands or the amount of water in the river, is another issue. And that depends. We're supposed to have drier summers—drier, droughtier summers—and a lot more flashy type rainstorms with potential for flooding in the winter. That can be a problem for agriculture if you're trying to—if you have to irrigate in the summer, that's one thing. And if you have to deal with flooding washing out crops you're trying to overwinter. I know there's at least one farmer—I've *heard* there's at least one farmer in the Snoqualmie Valley who's quit growing garlic because their farm gets scoured so often by floods that the garlic washes out. There's no point in planting it. It's going to be interesting.

I know, for example, this past summer, which was very warm and dry, farmers on both sides of me pump out of the river for irrigation in the summer—with or without water rights. And you could tell, because usually they don't do that until late August, and this year they were doing that in mid July—they were starting to pump to irrigate their fields. That makes a difference, depending on how many people are pulling water out of the river, how much water there *is* in the river for salmon habitat, which is important as just a piece of the puzzle, but a piece that gives us a clue, a key, to the rest of the ecosystem. If the water level drops and the water's too hot, the salmon can't live there. If the salmon aren't there, all of the rest of the ecosystem that's tied to salmon, their eggs, their food, their nutrients going back into the environment, will also feel the detrimental effects of not having enough water in the river, and therefore not having enough salmon. I don't have an answer for it.

All I know about the property that Michaele's farm is now on, which is part of Puget Consumer Co-op's Farmland Trust, that was an incredibly wet piece of property to begin with. And if it's that wet, and it stays that wet late into the growing season, I could see where her concern is. That, and it floods early. To my way of looking at it, it's definitely not an ideal place *for* farmland, because it's too wet. And I don't think the PCC people knew that when they were buying it. There's lots of other farmland up and down this Valley that doesn't experience that kind of flooding that early. And I believe there is information in the county farmland preservation program about which kinds of property are wetter. The ones that are really the wettest, you really can't farm on, and they really might just be left as natural. But I think there's some 14,000 acres of farmland that isn't being used. So I think there's plenty out here, you just have to find the land that will actually be dry enough when you need it.

If I had an answer, what would it be? Well, the county or some other organization could do an analysis of the farmland up and down the Valley and figure out what's the best farmland in terms of the amount of water that's going to impact it. They could consider the potential effects of climate change. I know there's a lot of controversy about climate change—at least in the newspapers. The county has to look at it, because the county is responsible for building and maintaining roads, and they have roads in places like around Vashon that will go underwater in another fifty or a hundred years, if the forecasted changes occur. And they may not. Or they may be different. Graphs are really nice, but they don't necessarily portray reality. But they're not really looking at it in terms of land use.

In Washington State, land use is addressed at the local level, the State does not have any say over land use, specifically. It's all done pretty piecemeal. Each jurisdiction has their own set of land use rules. The State may have some guidance, but it doesn't have regulation—not much, anyway. Growth Management Act, I suppose, would be the one that's made the biggest difference, as saying cities have to draw a line, "that's urban, this is rural." Also, the Snoqualmie Valley isn't the only agricultural area in King County. There's a *large* area that's designated Ag land down by Enumclaw, most of which is not *in* floodplain, and so they have a completely different.... But their soil's different, too. Their soil is derived from mud flows off of Mount Rainier, whereas ours out here in the Snoqualmie Valley is river deposition over hundreds, thousands of years. I love our soil, we don't have rocks! There are no rocks in that dirt, unless it was brought in by humans.

I think that the farmers and the citizens in this county are doing a really good job right now of making sure that the county council, for example, is aware and protecting agricultural issues. As you know, just due to where we are in the economy, very bad economy we've been having for the last year or two, all the local jurisdictions and the State are having budget issues as to what they can fund. So they're all looking at what they can cut. The farmers and concerned citizens did go to the county council and managed to save several agricultural programs by bringing it forward and expressing their concerns that it was very important. In a local jurisdiction like King County, it is amazing what a few people can do to actually make changes, because the council members only hear from a few people, and that's the basis they have to make their decisions on.

Dave and I don't have any plans for the future. We haven't got any serious plans, other than finishing the barn and trying to move there, eventually perhaps being able to raise the farmhouse up. We expect to stay there. There's no guarantees in life. We expect we'll keep farming until we get worn out and can't do it anymore. We could always lease out the land to young farmers that want to buy it.

I don't think we can make a living *just* as farmers. I've seen my fellow farmers. It appears that they either live at very low poverty level, or they have another job. Most of the farmers that I know of work another job, or part-time another job, because Americans don't pay the full cost of food, and therefore you can't take what you're growing and take it to the market and sell it for what would actually provide a farmer a reasonable income. Although I do know there's other farmers who are doing great. I don't know how to do it yet. I haven't gotten there yet—possibly because Dave and I are part-time farmers, we have no employees.

What I would like to do, my plans, my hopes for the future, what I would like to do is reach a point where I can cut back or quit my other job, farm more hours, possibly go to another market. We're going to try, we're thinking we're going to try doing a CSA next year, getting some farm members, because we have a lot of interest, people have been nagging us for a while to get on it. But there's only so many hours in the day, and I can only tend a certain amount of area, in terms of growing food and harvesting the food and weeding, irrigating. I don't see how I can expand a whole lot further without having employees, and we don't want to have employees.

And another interesting factor is the farmers that I know that go to the Seattle markets can sell their organic produce for virtually twice the price per pound as what farmers like us can get at the east side markets. If I go to the Issaquah Farmers Market or the Redmond Farmers Market, we're competing with farmers from eastern Washington who are not organic and sell for much cheaper prices. We can't sell.... Our produce would not sell if we asked the prices that are asked in the Seattle farmers markets. So that's another option, we could always go to a Seattle market instead. I really don't have an answer, because the Issaquah and Redmond markets have *lots* of customers, and they're drawing from a lot of different places, so I really don't know why it's easier to get more money for the same potato.

I've read Bill McKibben and Michael Pollan—halfway through one of Michael Pollan's books—but there's a shift in being more community oriented, as well as the economic reasons for needing to get food locally instead of getting it elsewhere on the planet. I think that may be coming. But in the long run, I don't see our economy returning to what it was four or five years ago. There aren't enough resources on the planet to support the population of this planet if they all want to live as the traditional current American citizen does. It can't be done.

We have a couple of people who have been informal work sharers, who come out and help me harvest or help me weed. I've had a lot of people who *say* they're interested, but other things get in the way. But I think it's a very positive experience. It's very positive that we have people who *really* are interested. They are interested for reasons that they're concerned about local food, they're concerned about organic food, they want to know where their food comes from, they want to make sure it's grown without chemicals. The people that have come to our farm have completely varying levels of knowledge about actually farming or gardening, and yet the ones that stay are the ones who are willing to learn, and learn along with us learning. And I know you saw this summer we had the three high school guys who showed up one day, who'd given me a phone call and decided they wanted to come out, because they'd talked to me at the market. And we're open, we're willing to have people come out, see our farm, learn what we're doing. They came out and they spent a day, and they worked their buns off, and they did wonderful things. The one who was the leader wants to come back and do it again. School's in session, he can't do it right now, but I wouldn't be surprised if he comes back next summer.

I was very excited to see young people who were interested in learning, and who were knowledgeable, or wanting to become knowledgeable about the importance of growing food locally and organically. I felt that it redeemed my impression of the younger generation. Not all into video games. They came out and worked, they volunteered. They asked to come out and work. They spent a couple of hours weeding our cabbage patch, which is a lot of work—it's a lot of hard physical labor. As I said, there've been a lot of people who expressed interest, but don't show. They wanted to know some things about.... Well, the leader, the older guy, he wanted to know some things about how we grow things, and why we were growing things that way, and whether we were forming any sort of a community, because I think they've been reading some of the books that are out there now on changes in the local communities and in farming—which I think is wonderful. One of your questions related to this was about educational opportunities on the farm. We're always educating. We go to the market and people are asking these questions. They don't just want to know what the food is, they want to know how you grow it, they want to know how come you've only got garlic scapes in the spring, how come we can't grow okra. Because of the climate. We don't live in the South. So we're always educating people, just because we're there, and they're asking us questions and we're giving them answers. People come to the farm. We're *always* delighted to have people come to the farm. We'll show them around, we'll show them what we're doing, and of course slip in some of the philosophy about why we're doing what we're doing. Which I think is marvelous. It's a great opportunity for us, and it's a great opportunity for them. And some of our customers have become very good friends. They now come back to our farm regularly. They drop by to see what's growing. They come by to spend a half a day doing some weeding. And that *is* building a community, which is a wonderful thing.

The people who go to a farmers market are already somewhat educated into being interested in local food, whether or not it's organic. I don't usually run into people at the farmers market who say, "Oh! I don't believe in organic!" because if they didn't, they wouldn't bother looking for local foods. I run into that in the grocery store. I don't run into it at the farmers market, because you've already got.... We're getting such a particular slice of the population who's interested in buying food from us, that they already have the knowledge, or are interested in the knowledge.

I think our farm is particularly fortunate this year that we didn't lose a lot of customers with the economy. The biggest difference I noticed is that the Issaquah Market has a great deal of ethnic diversity, but this year there were many fewer Eastern Russian, Eastern Europeans, and Indians and Pakistanis. In previous years, that's been a substantial portion of the market customers. So I don't know where they went, or whether it's the economy that's changed that or not, but we also have a lot of steady customers who've been buying from us for the five years we've gone to the Issaquah Market.

But I fear that it will be countered by the economic realities that if people don't have jobs, they can't really afford what they perceive to be more expensive local organic food. Whether it is or isn't, there's a perception there. I hope that as the economy eventually bottoms out, that things will improve. I don't know. What I've seen in my few years watching things happen on this planet, is things go in cycles. We are, I believe, right in the middle of a cycle where local organic food's really popular. I don't know that that's going to carry through. I don't know if it's going to become an actual shift in the way that everybody lives, or if it's going to shift to something where people are willing to pay more, but they're happy to pay for apples from China, instead of from eastern Washington, for example. I believe 70 percent of the population of the world still feeds themselves off of their own farms or garden patches. The more quote, unquote, "civilized" ones don't, but I think what has to happen in the United States, and possibly other places, is a shift away from the giant agri-business scale, back to not necessarily everybody has their own garden and eats everything out of their own front yard—but somewhere in between.

I have read of certain farmer entrepreneurs who are doing some really interesting things in cities and in inner cities, where they will take vacant lots in the big cities, and they will turn them into community pea patches, and that gets people interested in growing their own food, learning a whole lot more about their food and what it comes from—tasting a real tomato off the vine, so they know what it really tastes like. In Seattle, for example, there's a group that leases portions of people's yards and they operate as a farm, but they go down and harvest from like ten or twenty people's yards. The people who own the land get a portion of the produce. The farm gets the rest and takes it and sells it. That's another interesting way to deal with that. Part of the issue probably has to do with different cultures, and people coming into the U.S. from many different places. For example, my stepdaughter is now living in Leschi, which has got a large Somali community, and they're not used to this climate. So to teach them how to be able to grow their own food, they would have to learn a lot about the climate and then about the land. They have to live in a place where there is the available land. I think there'd be some great advantage to having a government, like city, to support expanding pea patches in areas where there are large communities of the poorer people, so they can learn about growing their own food, and also to save money. It's much cheaper to buy seed than it is to buy the produce that comes from that seed. What our farm does particularly is we have abundant produce in the summer, and we donate to food banks, which are usually quite delighted to get fresh produce, and to take it and distribute it.

A lot of the poor people are living in multi-family type housing where they don't have access to the land, or they don't have a landlord who's willing to let them tear up something to put in some vegetables. There are some new communities being built in the city and in King County that I believe are actually incorporating some pea patches into them. That's what I think, you have to be able to grow your own food. That way it's so much cheaper. And you don't have to go to the market and buy it and pay the premium price for people who are bringing it in from the countryside. You have your own, right there.

We learned how to expand from gardening, to grow a larger area. We have expanded from—we now have at least three fields, two greenhouses that we're growing things in. We have a whole 'nother field we're going to do something with next year. I went to the North Bend Market for two years, and then was convinced by one of my sister's neighbors who said, "You *really* have to go to the Issaquah Market." So we tried it, and now we go there. And now we're reaching the point, "Okay, what's our next step? Do we do a CSA? Do we do another market? What can we do with the amount of food that we grow, and the amount of time we have available?"

101

David Casey

12 December 2009

My name is David Casey. I was born Friday the 13th, 1955, in the month of May, at the Columbus University Hospital, at University of Columbus; that's in Ohio. My parents were kind of the black sheep in that most of my mom's side were dairy farmers in Virginia. Actually my dad's side was really not in the farming community. My dad was working on his Ph.D., and soon after I was born moved to Austin, where he taught at I don't know which university. And then we moved to the Bay Area. But, pretty much, my mom was a Miller, my dad was a Casey. And we're the only ones out of those two clans that moved to the West Coast. And from that point on, we were pretty much all just urbanized.

I remember a couple of times when I was *really* young, we would go to what was called the cousins' picnic, which was on one of the dairy farms, and we'd take a long drive in our 1956 Buick Special, all the way across country, and then go to this cousins' picnic, and then drive back, and kind of resume with our lives, and that's pretty much the only association that I ever had with farming or anything like that.

My parents didn't have much. My dad had a back injury and couldn't work, and so my mom worked. One of the things I'm really proud of about her is that when we were in Berkeley, California, she noticed there were a lot of unwed mothers who were dropping out of high school, and she started a program called the Parent-Child Education Center. She got partnerships, and actually it was one of the last social oriented bills that Ronald Reagan signed as a governor, to provide funding for this facility. And both my mom and dad have since passed away, but that facility is still going on.

I went to grammar school three years in San Bruno, and three years in Berkeley. It was actually Redwood Elementary, which was a *gorgeous*, gorgeous elementary school in Berkeley. All redwood. And then, junior high in Oakland, California, down in the Fruitvale area, which is now a completely different neighborhood. I had high school at Skyline High School. For college, my parents didn't have any money, so I was pretty much on my own. I spent a year at junior college, and then I had an opportunity to go to Alaska and work on fishing boats. Long story short, I graduated from high school in '73, graduated from college—my diploma is '85, but I was the Class of '84, because I was one humanities credit shy.

I spent pretty much the entire seventies working up in Alaska, canneries, off-shore platforms, and then Prudhoe Bay on the pipeline. I'd go up there, I'd work a winter, a summer. I'd work a summer, winter, summer, and then quit. And the company I worked for was really generous in letting me leave for nine months to go to school for a year. And so I didn't know really what I wanted to do, so I was in economics, pre-med, all that type of stuff. And finally I was working on the job, I was managing a welding shop and they had these engineers from Texas, and I realized I could do a whole lot better job than these guys can, I just need to go get my education. And so I went to U.W. and changed a little bit. I wanted to do mechanical engineering, but I didn't have the grades to get mechanical engineering, but I had the grades to get into the physics program or civil engineering.

I met my first wife, Nancy, during one of the times I was going to college in the Bay Area. We decided we wanted to get married, and I was thinking, well,

I'd like to move to Alaska. And she's goin', well, I'd like to stay in California. And we compromised on the Seattle area. And so she had just graduated from UC-Berkeley. I finally got into the U.W. and went through that program. My area of expertise really is hydraulics and hydrology, which are water resources. And so that's something that has *always* been my passion. I was just so blessed with the professors and the mentoring. The bottom line was, we weren't so focused on grades as we were focused on relationships with our professors and the process. This was recognized by the professors, and they really enjoyed that.

Nancy and I were very involved in the church. We were in University Presbyterian at that time, and because I had been an intern at First Pres. Fresno, I think in '76, just with a junior high group, I had developed relationships with those people. And they had developed relationships through Fuller Seminary with some young men who had come over and gone through the Ph.D. program, who were associated with the African Inland Mission, which was AIM, which was basically a United States driven organization. And as people basically matured, came to the United States, became educated, and had their cultural understanding, they realized that they didn't want to be a part of the AIM anymore, and so they developed the African Inland Church. And so the project that I was involved in was called the Kenya Water Project, and we had funding, we had complete support.

I went over there for about three weeks to do some reconnaissance in the Machos area, and basically looking at water systems, catchment systems. How come this dam that somebody paid for all the equipment for them to build, never held water, the catchment area wasn't big enough? Simple things, like how come this pump keeps breaking? Well somebody installed a pump with a capacity "A," and they were operating it with a capacity "B" and it keeps breaking. They're trying to pump too much water too fast too far up the hill. And so I came back with a whole list of things. We were getting ready to go—Nancy's parents were medical doctors, and they said, "Well, Dave, take a full physical." And so I took a full physical and it came out that I had a blood condition, so I couldn't leave the country. It's under control, it's not a big deal.

That's kind of the background of my passion for water resources, and part of that's sustainability. So I've always had a little bit of that foundation. Things didn't work out with Nancy and I, and I was working at King County, and Laura kind of swooped in for the kill. Didn't even have any time—and it's on tape!—didn't even have time to mess around or anything. It was just like, boom! She had a place out here, she had just built a house. I remember just helping her move out, and there was an attraction there, and we kind of worked on that. So we got married.

We've always been frugal, I've always been frugal, and I think a lot of that has to do with the fact that my parents didn't have anything. But I always had money when I was in high school, because I went door to door in the neighborhood—I had a paper route—I went door to door in the neighborhood and said, "Can I take care of your yard?" I always had that resourcefulness. One of the philosophies that I've always had, and it helped me in getting my jobs in Alaska, is that opportunity comes to those who seek it. A lot of people sit on their rear, waitin' for somethin' to come to 'em. You have to get out there and seek it.

Another thing that started in Oakland when I was growing up, I always had chores. I knew every Saturday morning I'd get up really early, five o'clock, do my paper route. Then I'd come home, and I'd say, "Mom, what do you want me to do," and she would say, "Okay, vacuum the house." I'd vacuum the house. And I'd get it done efficiently, and then I'd say, "Mom, what do you want me to do?" And she'd say, "Go outside and weed for an hour," and I'd go outside and weed for an hour, really enjoyed doing that. A lot of times it had to do with folding the laundry or doing the dishes or that type of thing, but inevitably, about noon, I'd say, "Mom, what do you want me to do?" and she'd say, "You're free." So I always knew that there was that responsibility. And sometimes it involved sweeping the driveway, washing the car, cleaning up the dog poop for the dog, that type of stuff. I always knew I had an obligation to do some chores.

So I had some basic skills and abilities, and Laura had some basic skills and abilities, and of course that's a dynamic tension when you bring those together in gardening. And so we basically took an acre that had nothing and completely landscaped it. We have one cedar tree that's probably two feet in diameter now, and I remember planting that tree. We've had to move our greenhouse a couple of times, because other trees are starting to shade it out.

Laura had her place. It's off of Northeast 24th, which is old Lake Lange Lost Road. We had an acre there. So we were in the Valley at that point. We had always kind of thought of getting something a little bit larger with a little bit better dirt, so Laura probably told the story that one day she comes home—and we would drive on West Snoqualmie River Road Northeast, because it's just a bucolic road. Everybody loves that road: the Miata clubs and the Harley clubs and the bicyclists, everybody loves that road. It's just a nice road, it's a relaxing road. You drive down it, your blood pressure goes down ten points. And she came home one day and said, "Well, Dave, there's a place for sale over there, it's all kind of junky. I don't know if you want it or not. You probably don't even want to look at it." So I went and looked at it. And it was a mess, just an absolute mess. But that basically started that.

We did not have a plan that we are going to do this. I would have been happy as heck to have built a garage where we currently live, with a little office upstairs so that I could tie flies and just be content. But once we got into it, we had no idea what we were getting into, in terms of the amount of work, in terms of the cost—but, in terms of the benefits.... Because there wasn't Michael Pollan back then.

When we bought the farm, I think it was in 2000. This groundswell was just barely beginning. And I don't know if we really knew what was going on or not. We knew in our hearts, we knew in our bones, that what we were doing was a good thing, and it might have been kind of the concept of the whole earth, you know, trying to be self-sustainable and just eating better, because after you've had a vegetable garden, suddenly something happens where it gets hard to go back. I don't eat tomatoes in the wintertime. So the thing that we had *no* idea that we were getting as a bonus, was the community of that road. And I remember one of the things I really enjoyed about being in Alaska was the sense of community. There's a *huge* sense of community, where if someone has a need, they're not afraid to express it. A lot of times people will start out, and they have great intentions that, "Boy, I'm gonna start workin' on my cabin in June. And then by September, August, I'm gonna have the roof in." But come September, there's not even trusses on the top, and the community, kind of the word gets out that this guy needs some help. And the community comes together and knocks it out in two or three weekends. It's the old barn-raising concept that doesn't exist. We have people who live in cul de sacs. They can brush their teeth and reach out their window and almost touch the house next door—but they don't even know their neighbors. On this road, Van Strom's probably a quarter mile away from me, and then Erick is another quarter mile, and then between them there's Matt and Deanna, and we know each other intimately.

It could be that the flooding issue brings people together, that kind of adversity. But we had no idea. If that community did not exist, I don't think there'd be half the farms on that road that there are. People help each other out—share--drop what they're doing to help somebody. I'm sure you probably heard about Van Strom and his contribution to the community—it's *huge*. I mean, he's been blessed hugely in his life, and he's very generous with giving of himself and giving of his expertise. What's interesting, everybody brings to the table their skills and abilities. And that, I think, is a wonderful thing, in terms of advocacy of farm issues that could impact what we're doing, in terms of, in my case, on the farm-pads, I helped two or three of the neighbors complete their applications on a short deadline thing, because that's something that I can do. And reciprocity, like I helped Erick on something else, raising one of his houses, and he comes down and plants three acres in a cover crop, and so it all works out really well that way.

Laura and I are essentially building a farm. A lot of people would think we're crazy in that we both have very good-paying jobs. We don't have to be doin' what we're doing, but we believe in the whole concept of sustainability and local and kind of the whole Michael Pollan thing, but we are spending a lot of our time building a farm, and hopefully we'll be moving into the farm within a year. That's our goal. And that'll be a *huge* thing, because we can rent out our small house and then we'll start looking seriously at finances so that maybe Laura can quit her job and start farming full time.

Why would someone who has a good job, doesn't need to do it, get up at six o'clock on Saturday morning—work until dark on Friday night, get up at six o'clock on Saturday morning, some days earlier, and load up the truck and go spend all day at the farmers market? For us, it's not really about the money. Part of it is I believe in what we're doing. I could stand on a soap box on the corner of a street and talk about sustainability and all of the things that are good for farming and that type of stuff, all day long and no one will listen to me. But when they walk into my stall at the market, I have an audience. And a lot of times I get questions about, "Why aren't you certified organic?" "Because we're certified naturally grown." We adhere to the exact same standards as certified organic—and I explain it to 'em. And most people get it. There was one time—and this is also part of the dynamics of a market stall—there was one time I explained it to this guy—there was a guy and a gal, probably in their fifties—they were walking away, and I heard the wife ask the husband, "Well, did you understand that?" And his response was, "Yeah, he just wants to do it the easy way." And Laura heard that, and Laura saw me, and she just.... "Dave, let it go." Same thing with shoplifting. We just let it go. When kids come in and smash the.... Everybody wants to squeeze the tomatoes. I don't know why. You know, they pick 'em up, they put 'em right to their dirty noses. I'm cringing! Like, "Argh!" Everybody wants to squeeze the tomatoes, and I tell 'em, "I want you to know, those were picked last night." But it's so exciting when I'll tell someone how to cook something, and then they come back next week and say, "That was just yummy! I want to buy some more of that!"

You know, the stuff that you see in QFC and Safeway and Fred Meyer and some of these other places, that you see all year round, they're all homogenous, they're all uniform. You just don't get to see any ugly potatoes or things like that, but they're still yummy. It was really funny, it took me a long time to learn how to actually harvest potatoes. It's really kind of funny, because I was harvesting the potatoes, just tossin' 'em up in the wheelbarrow, and then I hosed 'em down, they were all just nice and purdy [sic]. In two days they had brown spots everywhere, had to throw 'em all away. And so I've actually learned to be *really* careful with my potatoes, and really possessive of my potatoes. And so we basically, when we harvest potatoes, we don't even wash 'em anymore. We leave dirt on 'em. And it's interesting how some people will walk up and they'll pick up a potato, and they'll say, "I *know* this is a good potato, because it still has dirt on it." And then other people will walk up, and they'll take the potato, they'll start banging it on the side of a basket to get the dirt off. And usually with them, I would try to tell them, "Well, we keep the dirt on it because it helps protect the potato. And if you think I'm leaving the dirt on because I'm charging you more, get some potatoes, and I'll throw a couple more on to make up for the dirt."

That's, I think, one reason why I like doin' it. I actually like interacting with people. It really does take a team at a market stall. I think it'd be very difficult for one person. With *our* type of produce, one person can make—at least at our market—$500, maybe $600, because it takes time to interact with the customers, to explain why we have four or five different varieties of garlic. And I like growing four or five different varieties of garlic, but I've been tempted just to grow one. You know, I have six, seven different types of peppers. Okay, which is the spiciest? Well, then some people say, "Which is the hottest?" And then every once in a while you'll have the—it happened—some guy says, "Which one has the highest Scoville unit?"

We came to farming as an adventure. We came to it as here's an opportunity to do something that we've never done before in terms of taking a farm and turning it into something. I feel that since I have gotten into it, it's—you could use the word "cause," you could use the word "passion"—a lot of that is founded in education and knowledge. We subscribe to a lot of different periodicals. And so we read about issues related to farming, and the more we read communicates that farming, not only in the standard methods of farming, not only in the United States but the entire world, is not sustainable, and actually has not been sustainable for many, many years—even before we got our farm—water issues being one of the biggest ones, because water is going to be the limit to growth. Of course, that was before climate change. But we don't really know how the two are coming together and that type of thing. So I did not come to it with a cause. And I've had a conscious decision that I am going to build myself a farm, and here's the reason why I'm gonna build myself a farm.

In the midst of that, Laura was the one who actually went out and first started doin' the farmers market. I mean, she was at North Bend. I said, "Darlin', that's your deal. You're goin' to the farmers market, I'm goin' fishin'." And it's kind of evolved. I've been brought into it because I realized if you have two people in a stall, you can do *hugely* better, because you need one person to be weighing and doing a little bit of "boy howdy" over here and taking the money, because that's kind of one reason why we're there. But then I'm up front doin' the *big* "boy howdy." You know, talkin' about recipes, and explaining the difference between these types of garlics, and that type of thing. Anyway, Laura would go to the farmers market in North Bend. She'd come back.... I mean, she was so dad-gummed persistent. She'd come back and say, "I spent $25 for the stall, I spent $30 worth of plants"—you know, like tomato plants or something like that. "I only made $10. I'm not doin' this anymore!" "Fine, darlin'." Then she'd do it again. And then she'd do it again.

It almost reminds me—and I don't know if this is.... I listen to Garrison Keillor whenever I can, and every year they have kind of one whole thing on jokes. And there was a joke that—and I don't usually remember jokes—and it goes so fast! I mean, it's goin' so fast! And one just got stuck with me, and I think at first because it was funny. But afterwards, I realized it has so much depth to it.

The joke is: A blond is walkin' down a sidewalk in Beverly Hills. She sees a banana in front of her on the sidewalk and she goes, "Here we go again!" It's kind of a funny joke. It puts down blonds, but then I started thinking about that. I'm goin', "How many times in our lives do we continue to choose to step on the banana?" It's almost becoming part of my bones in terms of that, and it's good philosophy for farming. You hear it constantly, "Whall ah been doin' it dis way for twenty years and ah'm not gonna change now!" The guy keeps steppin' on the banana. We step on the banana in personal ways or something like that. But I really have used that, because a lot of times I'll go out to the farm and I'll just be looking at something that I need to do, and I just say to myself, "Dave, don't step on the banana! Don't plant it the same way you plant...." And just kind of mix some things up. And sometimes you mix things up and it doesn't work. Well, we planted our eggplant *outside* this year, which should have been a good year, but I think because it was too hot, we didn't get any pollination, and so we had a crop loss. And every year, at least at our farm, there is one or two crop losses. And that's why the diversity keeps the farm going. If we relied on green beans for the whole farm this year, it wouldn't have happened—or eggplant. It has been shown, and a lot of people don't really like to hear that, but on a per-acre basis, the smaller farms that have more diversity using methodologies that are actually healthier for the soil, produce more dollars per acre than the large corporate farms. But I like the banana. I wanted to get that banana thing in there.

    I know that there have been times when a lot of indicators point towards imminent disaster, and it has been averted, through conservation, changing in farming practices, the green revolution. While theoretically it was a good thing, I think now it's been determined that it was a failure. The big banana is being stepped on while we speak, and those who are attached to the foot are more interested in money, in my opinion, or the status quo. I'm very concerned. And that's one reason why my farm is looking better every week. But of course when everything goes to heck in a hand basket, it doesn't matter. You know, there's no amount of guns to keep your farm safe—that type of thing. You know, it's that type of thing. The whole climate change thing just really throws a loop into it. You know, the Gates Foundation getting into GMOs, that just scares the livin' tweedle out of me. There's enough knowledge—I mean, our whole food aid policy has destroyed food productions in so many countries in Africa: the fact that, yeah, we'll give food aid at a subsidized reduced cost. We'll give the government money, but they can only buy from *us*, and by the way, it takes us four months to get it there. We should be giving the *farmers* the money, and the communities the money, to have their own local contained silos.

    If we had four hours, we could probably get through some of the topics, but I'm not very optimistic. I am concerned. The peak oil, the groundwater depletion, the concept.... There was an area in India that they put in all these wells, and they had the green revolution, and it completely destroyed the entire economy, and not only that, they're running out of water, but what they're pumping out has very low concentrations of arsenic and selenium. Those are the two biggest chemicals that can become an issue. But when you bring it up.... and it's in a form that's not that bad, but when you bring it up, due to the pressure changes and the methods of irrigation, you start to accumulate it in your soil. And that's what's going on. And it will *never* go away. There's I don't know how many square miles in Texas—and it's *still* going on in some cases. The Ogallala Aquifer—that's an issue, that is a crisis that I think in terms of United States economy is more critical than potential climate change, because it's something that could have been averted, with changes in farming practices, CFOS (Confined Animal Feeding Operations, i.e. Feed-lots). We didn't have e-coli in the seventies! You could eat beef tartar, have a rare hamburger. It was no big deal. Then there's other diseases ....Crone's disease, I think, that never even existed before the CFOs. That's *so* unsustainable. I actually quit eating beef a long time ago.

    I don't have any answers. Like with China.....that's just a wild card nobody knows anything about, in terms of pollution and the importation.... What is basically happening is we don't have enough inspectors. So because we don't have enough inspectors, the beef lobby and other lobbies go to the FDA and say, "Okay, it used to be that you could cook beef to this temperature, so just to keep everybody safe, let's just raise it five degrees." Well, you're cookin' out nutrients, you're cookin' out flavor, and you still have tainted beef. I was really hopeful with Obama comin' in. Michael Pollan wrote a *wonderful* article, it was an open letter to the next president. It was called "Food, Food, Food." When Michelle put in the victory garden on the south lawn, I'm goin', "That's a good thing!" But I see it goin' by the wayside. I don't see any significant initiatives addressing our food security in this country. Just the Ogallala Aquifer itself. We will not have any more high fructose corn syrup when the Ogallala Aquifer dries up. Actually, that's a good thing! Dang! We will not have any more CFO beef feedlots in Nebraska! Dang! Maybe that's a good thing!

Most change starts at the margins. And I believe that with a lot of the tainted food, things that have happened with China, and even we had spinach, and then it's been mushrooms, and wait a minute, then it's peanuts. And of course the ground beef keeps coming and coming and coming. People are becoming more aware. Will that change consumer habits? I don't know. I see a society right now that scares the livin' tweedle outta me in terms of what people give their children, in terms of what people buy that they don't need. And I was *really* hopeful that this economic crisis would have shook some people into being more frugal. But mainstream, everybody talks about, "Well, gee, people are spending more this month than they spent last month." But I just want to scream! I just want to absolutely scream. That's not what it's about. Shoot your TV!

I am, however, very optimistic about farming in the Snoqualmie Valley. I'm concerned about the Hmong, because the children are not getting into it. But it is so difficult, farmland is so hard to come by, and a lot of the farmland that the Hmong have, it's leased. Some of them do practice organic methods, some don't. You don't eat flowers, so it's not a big deal. But I know that some landowners are requiring it, because they want to make sure that if they convert a portion to something else, that they can do that in a seamless way.

Farming is hard! I mean, farming is just hard enough as it is, without a lot of the roadblocks and without a lot of the regulations. Everybody says, "Oh yeah, we love our farmers, we want to support our farmers." But many times I just don't see it. Case in point—you don't have to put this in the book—is this whole PSE re-licensing up at the Snoqualmie Falls. That slipped through the radar. King County knew about it, but no one talked to us, the stakeholders, downstream. We're gonna get more water. But on one hand they'll say, "Oh yeah, we're gonna do whatever we can to protect the farmers, we're gonna do whatever we can to support the farmers." When push comes to shove on a big issue, they disappear. And I'm fighting that.

And here's the other thing that I never thought that I would get into. Living out here in the Valley *requires* participation, and it's not just farming. I do not have a choice, when people call me, but to get involved in a cause. And sometimes it's *extremely* time consuming. Like the farmers market commercial kitchen. I donated all my time as a civil engineer to prepare the site plan, working with the architects. Well, it didn't happen. It's gonna happen *sometime. As you become part of the community, people learn what your skills and abilities are.* And it's really hard saying no when it's a just cause. And I think that Laura and I have always been—we have always felt that having been blessed to have the educations that we have, there is a responsibility to give back. She has helped different people with their critical areas designations. And I help people out where I can. And it comes back. It's that "what goes around, comes around" type of thing. And I'm not whining or anything, *but it takes a lot of time!* It's a *lot* of effort. And I never knew that that would occur, moving out here. But having known that, I just tell Laura, "You know, I can only handle one crusade a year." I don't have a problem getting involved, but I can only handle one a year. And some years it's two or three simultaneously, and then I feel bad when I don't give it my all. But it's a whole lot better than people doing nothing. So I think there's a lot of potential.

Everybody approaches it with their different knowledge and experience and background. And I would just say that we are building a farm. We're hoping to farm more, maybe full time. But Laura and I, it's really interesting, everybody who's had anything to do with that farm has told us that there's something special there. When the guys were doing the framing, they didn't want the job to end. When the sider was there, he said he almost cried, leaving. And I could tell it in the skill and the quality of their work. They got their heart into it. And then there was a friend of ours that used to be on the historical society. He's now retired. And he said, "Dave, you are building the barn for the next generation." And then all of a sudden it hit me, this is not my farm. It's not. Then that kind of scares the livin' tweedle outta me, because I have a lot more responsibility. So Laura and I, our philosophy is, we are building a farm, and we want to keep our small house, so that we can retire to the small house. And if Kara does not have any interest in farming, that farm will go to a foundation, or we'll create a foundation. It's not going to be sold for some horsey people. It is not going to be sold for that, at all. That's something that one never thinks about when they start getting into this. They're actually getting involved in something much larger. I mean, you've seen the way we built that barn. Obviously it needed a meeting area upstairs. Obviously it needed a sales area. I mean, so many people said, "How come you just didn't make that your beautiful house?!" I said, "I can't. The farm needs these things." Because even if we weren't going to pass it on, even if we were going to sell it, the farm still needs certain things. Then why do you drive by so many farms, and there's a double-wide mobile and a beautiful barn? They put all their money into the infrastructure. The farm needs that stuff to be successful. And it's interesting. I had no idea, honestly, what we were getting into.

The Ogallala Aquifer covers approximately 10,000 square miles from Texas to the Dakotas, and is a major source of water for the High Plains. Unfortunately its water is being used faster than it is being replenished, and the result is predicted by many to be serious eco-centric pressure on the area in the not so distant future. Many people assume that large groundwater formations may temporarily run low, but will fill again when rainfall is plentiful—as do lakes, rivers and reservoirs. However, unless the areas impacted are unaffected by the factors that contribute to high evaporation—such as minimal rainfall, abundant sunshine, low humidity and periodic strong winds—this assumption is not even remotely correct. Therefore, it is imperative that we find solutions through research to water problems and maintain the aquifer as a continuing resource. By the time we know whether today's conventional High Plains farmers can live with less groundwater, it may be too late to save enough to keep them on the land. Pumping the Ogallala is still a one-time experiment, unrepeatable and irreversible.

An example of the aquifer's water depletion in the Oklahoma Panhandle area is in Texas County. Texas County consumes almost all of its water from the Ogallala Aquifer flowing some 200 feet beneath the Panhandle. In 1990, approximately 363 million gallons per day of groundwater were pumped from the High Plains Aquifer. Throughout the High Plains, the water table dropped 9.9 feet from 1980 through 1995……..there were approx. 54,400 acres in irrigated corn in 1991; there were 90,000 in 1998.

Texas County has more than 380,000 head of feedlot cattle, a ready market for the corn. While corn is a particularly thirsty crop unable to grow without irrigation in Texas County, it yields up to 200 bushels per acre with 22 inches of irrigated water. With an estimated 90,000 acres of corn in 1998 and each acre using approx. two-acre feet per year, Texas County uses approx. 58,653,180,000 gallons of irrigated water a year on corn alone. Corn is fed to both cattle and hogs…..While livestock water usage is 3% directly, livestock feed accounts for 92% of water withdrawal from the High Plains Aquifer.

The Kerr Institute for Sustainable Agriculture, 1st Publication, July, 2000 **(Author's note: The Oklahoma-Texas Panhandles produce the bulk of beef and pork products for American use and export).**

Farm Journal

10 August 2009

    I have been in a persistent epistemological quandary over rich boys and potato plants. Clichés abound; you can't know what you don't know sits at the front—behind it, another—you don't know what you've missed 'til it returns. In one instant, the boy found the entire life cycle sitting in the palm of his hand and was visibly moved (or so it seemed); life feeding on life, the entropic system of birth, growth, death and regeneration before him, tangibly resident in a potato. But I wonder—was he as moved as I? Or do I wax poetic wishing it were so? Was the experience merely one more oddity buried inside a kaleidoscope of sensations and discoveries fueled by hormones, adorned by his new "cool"—his plaid winter ear-flap cap (to be worn year round—best in summer)? Or was it, as I and Laura Casey hoped and wanted to believe, a transformative moment? Maybe......who knows? Who knows which "meme", which ideational virus, will take root and grow within an adolescent mind and shape a life?

    I still believe that the root of change is "direct experience"—as a friend of mine once noted, "If it ain't in the muscle, it's just rumor!" As I wrote somewhere, love is behavior, not pronouncement—the touch, not the word—love is beyond injunction—love is lawless and abjures the commandment "thou shalt love."

    If you teach a man to grow his own food and you learn his name and taste the fruits of that grower's labor you will not be tempted to do him violence. This I believe but find its proof hard to demonstrate. I am deeply uncertain about the epiphany of the boy who learned of the potato at Changing Seasons Farm. After all, when his day as a volunteer worker at the farm was over, he got in his shiny new car and returned to Clyde Hill and the neighborhood; clean, quiet, protected, manicured with lawns, graced by swimming pools; each house isolated, each person essentially alone, separated from more or less unknown neighbors, far from Whole Foods Market or IGA, caught in the dream of television and the Internet—each more solitary than the last, each far from the farm he visited—all of them devoid of flesh, sweat, earth—the scent of life.

    We are told we don't need those things—we need the erase of acquisition and the speed of consumption—that other place, within the "potato myth," if you will, is a nostalgic diversion at best; a teaching moment for the youth as a substitute for therapy. The myth is poetic, but in our technological world of the "bottom line," poetry is not practical. I have always rejected that injunction. I prefer the voice of the poet, William Carlos Williams:

> "Look at
>   what passes for the new.
> You will not find it there but in
>   despised poems.
>   It is difficult
> to get the news from poems
>   yet men die miserably every day
>   for lack
> of what is found there."
>
>   Wm. Carlos Williams, "Asphodel, That Greeny Flower", 1955

So much depends upon a young man with a new potato in his hand.

Farm Journal

06 June 2009

Cool weather this morning after a hot week and a light rain—with these comes a curious thought.

I observed the moist grass, darker sky and felt the mist in the air; Pacific Northwest sunshine—rain forest air. All of these awakened and brought to mind the question, "What do you think of when it rains?" My answer at that moment, "I'm wondering if George Magnochi will get his hay in before the rain ruins the cutting now on the ground." We had spoken just yesterday and he was watchful and a little worried about the weather. The hay is his buffer against rising feed prices which further reduce his very small and sometimes non-existent margin when he sells the milk his cows produce.

What is novel for me is the chain of associations: (>>>>rain>>>>>George>>>>>hay>>>> cows>>>>>milk>>>>concern for him>>>> his farm and all the attendant connections). All this has happened as consequence of my work the past few weeks, i.e. getting to know each of these famers and their world and, somehow, becoming invested in them. Perhaps this is the "hook" for the book after

all. From now on, when it rains, I will think of George and the hay and the cows and not about rain impinging on my schedule or my vacation. I will think of Erick and Wendy, Jason, Siri and Dan, Dave and Laura and their farms and those I've yet to meet. Maybe this is also a possible source experience for paradigm shift for "suburban man" who looks at rain as an impediment to his morning commute.

What would happen if everyone could change those chains of causation that occurred when they observed the first drops of a June rain; if they thought about seeds being nourished or washed away or hay lying wet and useless in the field? How would their lives proceed?

Two Sisters Dairy

Lena Magnochi

29 January 2010

I'm Lena Magnochi, born January 20, 1985, in Carnation, Washington. I had a small town, simple life, not too exciting, not too crazy, just nice, simple, fun to grow up in. When we grew up, we had a few cows, a few 4-H animals at the home place in Carnation. And then they kept growing and multiplying and stuff, and we always had chores and responsibilities growing up. The older we got, the more chores we had. We always got our school work done and then had to go to the barn and take care of our animals. And we've always had cows and chickens and a few horses. I have one older sister. She's like three and a half years older than me, and that's all there is, just the two of us.

When we were little, we started off feeding calves. That was like our first chore. Or putting grain down for the cows. Then as we got older, it was helping with hay and milking the cows and cleaning the pens and just all the chores—never-ending chores. I did pretty good in school. I was always probably like a "B" average student. I liked math, it didn't always like me. English was more of a struggle, but I got through it and graduated high school from Cedar Crest, and then continued on to college and Walla Walla Community College, and did their animal science and Ag business program there, and actually enjoyed college more, because it was more something I was actually interested in, and classes that I was looking forward to going to, instead of, hello, I have to go to class. But no, I was a good student and graduated in the top half of the class.

I've always grown up on the farm. It's not just a hobby, it's your life, and your lifestyle. So it's what I enjoy, and I couldn't see myself staying in a little office all day, and doing computer work and paper work all day. I'd go crazy! So I just took my hobby and took it further and did my education in that. And then came home, and now I work full time on the farm. My sister works for the county and she does farm planning and plans nutrient management plans with the farmers and stuff like that. So she doesn't work *on* the farm anymore, but she still works with farmers.

For my senior project in high school I did a job shadow of a vet technician, and I thought about that for a while, but I couldn't handle putting the animals to sleep all the time. Like the one rule on the farm, I don't touch dead things. That's Dad's job. And he always jokes, like what's gonna happen if something happens to him, and he's not there to take care of the dead animals anymore. And I said, "That's a requirement for the boyfriend list. They have to be able to touch dead animals." So yeah, I don't touch the dead ones.

We've been milking on our farm in Carnation where we are now, I think, for eight years. We started there on the farm we're at now when I was in high school. So it's probably been like three or four years now that I've been out of college that I've been at home on the farm. It's hard work, but it's rewarding work. It's fun to watch the little baby calves grow up and go to the different fairs and stuff and see them grow and mature and then turn into the cows. That's fun. It's rewarding. It's hard work, but it's fun. It's not for everybody.

It's challenging sometimes, 'cause the prices go up and down. It's not a set price. Here and there it fluctuates. So that's a challenge because I can't.... It's hard to budget to match your prices. But it's also fun because it's not just an industry you're in, it's more of a family you're in. The different farmers, like everybody competes against each other to have the best cow and the most milk and all that, but at the same time, if something happens at one farm, everybody rallies to help each other. So I like that, because it's not.... Like if you're at Microsoft or something, Apple computers are running over to help Windows. So I don't know, I like that part of it: it's not just an industry, it's a family.

The organic dairy is for a niche market, but I think with the economy now, the average person can't afford the extra money to buy the organic, so I think you might see it plateau or go away just a little bit, but it's gonna stay there, because everybody's more health conscious and everything. I don't see our farm going organic anytime soon, because when you're organic you can't use any medicine or anything like that. And we don't use a lot of medicine, but when a cow does get sick, or a heifer gets sick, it is nice to be able to have medicine to give them. It's just like if you get a cold or an infection, you want to have medicine to take to get better. It's not that you take it all the time, but it helps. Organic dairies can use like natural medicines, like herbs and stuff like that. But they can't use penicillin—that's not considered organic, I guess. There's different rules and regulations to everything. And just because we use medicine for like when a cow's sick, it doesn't actually go in the food system, because we're required to hold that milk or that meat for so long before it's taken for human consumption. So actually you're not getting any of the antibiotics that we treat our animals with. If they're sick I'd want to be able to treat 'em, not just watch 'em get sicker and sicker. And if they do treat 'em with something, then they have to be taken out of the organic herd for like, a year—I don't know the exact thing—or be sold to somebody else.

We milk about sixty cows, and then we have dry cows and heifers on top of that, and baby calves. So there's probably like around a hundred or so, with the milk cows, heifers, dry cows and stuff. I milk 'em twice a day, every day, that's my job.

Out here we're one of the smaller dairies, and so sometimes it's a little challenging for you just to be able to get.... Like, well, since there's not as many dairies around anymore, it's more of a challenge to get supplies to you, because you're further out from more people and stuff. But, I mean, right now it's the same, everybody loses money; or everybody's making money. When the price is bad, if you have less cows, you're losing less money each day, rather than more cows you lose more money every day. But still, it's a challenge, and you have to try and cut the budget and do the stuff as inexpensive as possible. It's just not like making the big fancy living, but still.... I mean, it's happy, and everybody has a good time and stuff. I don't know, you have everything you need, so you don't need much more.

I don't know, there's always more cows, more cows, and there's always more milk, more milk, so then the market gets flooded, and there's too much milk, so then the prices go down. And I don't know, Canada has a quota system, and so each producer knows how much milk they can produce, and if you produce over that, you get paid a little bit, but not very much for it. So I think if we had something like that in the United States, it would make it so everybody knows what their price is gonna be, and it's more stable and less fluctuation in the price and stuff, and it would make it easier. But nobody wants it. Well, like people want it, but then they say when the price goes up, "Oh, we don't want it, because then there'd be a cap on our price or whatever." I don't know, some people want it, some people don't want it. But the government has to step in and put that in place, because it's more of like a government thing, I think.

Our feed and stuff now is pretty much organic, because it's all off our farm and we don't use commercial or anything like that. Like the other stuff, I mean, we don't get grain or anything that's like full of chemicals. I mean, they spray their crops and stuff, but it's not like horrible. So I don't see our feed changing. I mean, our goals are always to get more milk, and get a fancier, typier[sic] show cow, because we take our cows to the fair and stuff and compete that way. And like my goal has always been to get a typie[sic] enough cow to someday take her back to Madison, Wisconsin, and that's where the World Dairy Expo is held, so that's always been my goal, to be able to go back there and compete with the high class and win back there.

The typier and showier cows you get, then you can market 'em, 'cause ours are registered. And so you can market your animals and sell them in different sales and stuff like that, and their calves and embryos and all sorts of stuff. So it's just another side of the dairy. If you have a champion cow, then different bull studs will want to take and put contracts on her to get bulls to put in their stud to sell to different people. So there's always different stuff. Or you can sell embryos to people to implant in their cows, and then they have a daughter of this cow. A lot of different stuff. If you sell a bull calf, you get so much. But probably the females are worth more, because there's more of 'em. If you had the bull yourself, and you were sellin' semen, then.... But hardly anybody does that. They go to the stud.

We went to a lot of fairs. We did 4-H, FFA, and now we do open class. But we used to go, we'd start early in the spring and go to the Southwest Youth Fair down in Chehalis. And then we'd go to the Enumclaw Dairy Show. And we'd go to the Savanna show, and Monroe, the Evergreen State Fair. And then we'd go to Puyallup; we'd finish there. And we'd do the Western National Jersey shows there. And then like another week later we'd go back and we'd do the 4-H and FFA. But now we go to the Evergreen Fair and we go to Puyallup for the Western National. And then I've been going to the Yakima. That's the Central Washington Fair. So we only go to like three now. We've cut back a little. It's kind of like a beauty pageant, I guess. You want 'em to have like the tall and sharp over the shoulders, and show dairy character.

It's boring to people who don't know what's going on. Like their udder, you want it to be high, and wide in the rear, and lots of veins, and definite crease down the middle, and their teats placed squarely and properly, not shootin' out to the sides. You want 'em to walk on a good set of feet and legs. You don't want 'em to look like German Shepherds, and you don't want 'em to look like a fence post, but just a good angle to it. And then like the dairy character is how sharp and clean they are over the shoulders. You don't want them to be really fat. You want them to be kind of slender, because that shows how much they milk. Like if they're really fat, then it doesn't look like they milk, because they put that energy into their milk instead. So I don't know, you learn it once you're around it forever. Like "sharp and clean" means their shoulders come up to a peak, kind of like a little mountain. You don't want it to be like a round hill. You want it to be sharp. You don't want them to have a lot of extra skin and wrinkles and stuff under their chin. You want it to be smooth and clean and look pretty.

It's really practical stuff, because the udder has got to be well attached. And the veins, the more veins means the more blood goes through there, and the more blood means more milk being made. And if they're sharp and clean over the shoulders and don't have a lot of fat on 'em, that means usually they're putting that energy into making the milk. If they're not making the milk, then they're putting the energy into fat on their body, instead of in the milk. I mean, it all ties together.

I think it's important to save the land, because if there *isn't* any land, no one's gonna farm, because there's nothin' left *to* farm. I think it's important to support your farmer, because if there's nobody wanting to be a farmer, or everybody keeps pushing out the farmer, then there's not gonna be anybody left to make you your food, and you're gonna turn around and go, "Well, there's no milk today." And it's gonna be like, "Well, you pushed out Farmer Joe down the road, so no, there's not any milk." But I think there's a place for everybody, small farms and big farms. I just think there needs to be some regulations on how much you can flood the market with your product. I don't know, it's a challenge. I just do my thing and I'm good. I listen to everybody else and then I'll make my decision.

I think people get hung up on the organic stuff. Really, I don't think organic's that much more better for you than non-organic, because I think our quality of non-organic stuff is right up there with the organic. And people go, "Oh, it's organic, it must be better for you." I don't think it's really that much difference. I think if something happened and we couldn't import food, people would wake up and realize, "Well, where's my farmer to make my food?" And there's less than 2 percent of the population in America are farmers. So I don't know, I think people just need to kind of realize there's only 2 percent feeding America. If something happens, where are you really gonna get your food from? I think that's kind of a wake-up call for people.

I don't know really that much about crops and stuff like that, because we stay mostly towards the dairy. And we don't use any of that stuff, so I really don't know that much about it. I mean, if those big farms aren't there right now, then who *is* gonna produce that, because the little guys have been pushed out. And nowadays the younger generation really usually doesn't *want* to take over. And because it has been made so hard for people to keep continuing farming and stuff like that. So I don't know. I think it'd be nice to try to turn it around some, and help try to encourage the younger generation to come back to the farm. I think most days most kids *don't* want to come back.

My nickname at school was always The Dairy Princess, because I was always the cow person. My friends always come to the fair and visit and stuff like that. I think I was the only person in high school that did come from a dairy farm at the time. I mean, there were other kids, like in the past, they'd been on farms, but not anymore. I don't know, everybody, we all grew up together, so it was just kind of like the given thing, like, "Oh, you do cows." These people do dirt bikes or whatever. I don't know, they always thought it was cool to come see the cows on the farm, but they didn't really understand all the hard work that went into everything. The teacher would always—like you'd take notes in to get off time from school to go to fairs, or different trips that the cows took you on, stuff like that. They were always like, "You're really going to the fair for your cows?!" They always thought it was kind of weird. I remember Dad called one day, and the one cow had just calved, and she was down, and she had milk fever—it's a lack of calcium in their blood—and they can die from it if you don't treat it. And so Dad was home by himself, he needed my help, and he called, and I was in Spanish class. They called up to the classroom, and they're like, "Something about you need to get home, your cow has a fever, your dad needs your help." And I started laughing because I knew she had milk fever. They thought she just had a temperature. So it was kind of funny. They were understanding about stuff when I had to go places or do stuff. But at the same time, they really didn't understand *what* I was doing. They were pretty lenient with it, so that was kind of cool. It was nice, because it was a small farming town, people kind of gave you leeway.

I'd like to keep on as a dairy farmer. I mean, if not, I always see animals in my life, or cows in the back yard or something. I'd like to continue farming. It's my passion. I like my cows. They're my babies. They all have names, they're all pets.

The organic is a niche market, different things for different people. And I think it works for some people, and it doesn't for others. I'm glad that they're exploring the opportunity. I think it's good for different people, and it works for some and it doesn't work for others. There are some people up in Bellingham that we know that do the raw milk—or they were, last time I knew. They were doing that and stuff. And we have some friends that make cheese and sell that all over, and stuff like that. So I mean it works for them, but I don't think it would work for us. It's another challenge. And we do everything ourselves, so it's just challenging enough between Dad and I, just to get milkings done and calves fed and pens cleaned, and keep everybody happy. Maybe someday way down the road, but I don't see it anytime in our near future happening. But it's always a possibility.

Hopefully we'll stay at this farm if the water doesn't push us out. That's the only bad thing about where we are, is we get flooded. We've got a little critter pad started, so hopefully it'll keep something dry if it floods again.

George Magnochi

make it up in volume. And if they don't do somethin', and they don't control this price some way, so that it's a stable market that you can plan.... If you want to build a new barn or whatever, you want to borrow money to improve, you know what that market's gonna be down the road. This way you haven't got a clue. And this is no exaggeration. The price of milk can be so much this month, and tomorrow morning you walk in and your paycheck is a *third* less. And that's what's happened. I mean milk has been almost $20 a hundred, and this last *year* it's been $10 a hundred. So your payments stay the same. It don't make no difference, that cow keeps right on eatin', the price of hay is high, they don't really care.

I think they're figurin' in the $15 a hundred range is break even, kind of on an average. Some days are more, some are less. If you can grow a lot of your own feed, that cuts your cost down. If you've gotta buy most of your feed, then your break-even is a lot higher. And if you've got a lot of labor and stuff, that figures into it. I've always said if the price of milk was good, we could *all* make a livin'. You want to milk 5,000 cows, that's your business. If I want to milk 50, that's my business. We can all make a livin'. It just depends how high on the hog you want to live. It's a mess. It ... is ... a ... mess. We're seein' it right now: milk is startin' to climb, and the guy that was bitchin' and moanin' about the government's gotta do somethin', we've gotta do this, we've gotta do that—he's already talkin' about puttin' on more cows. And we'll be right back in the same hole. Whoever's figured this out with oil, if they've got too much oil, they cut back. Not the dairymen! If the price of milk goes down, he milks more cows so he's got more cash flow supposedly. Price of milk goes up, he milks more so he can make more money.

And these guys, a lot of these big, big ones—we're talkin' *big* ones—they figured, "We're into the bank so far they'll never let us go." Well, that day came and went. And what a lot of the California guys, or anyplace, they *did* that, and they could be losin' money, but their place, the land, was worth a zillion dollars, so the banker didn't care. He figured if you went belly up, he was gonna come out, because he got your place. And now, when the land prices dropped, the housing industry went to hell in a hand basket, they're in a world of hurt. That ain't holdin' water anymore. And there's a lot of big dairies that are gonna fold. And the bank has said that old theory don't hold water no more.

It's a problem. I've said this a lot of times: You were competin' with some of these big guys. They were broke—really, essentially, broke. But they were gettin' money. And then a lot of these big, big outfits, they'll tell you, "Hey, we don't care. We didn't have nothin' when we started. If it goes under, big deal." And they paid themselves a wage, the farm's losin' its ass, but they paid theirselves a wage, so they come out. And they're not all that way. And I keep sayin' I'm not against big dairies. It depends. California always has had bigger dairies because that's just the way their business has been. And there's a lot of big dairies that are family farms that work hard and do a good job. But there's some of these big outfits, there's one guy in Idaho milkin' 50,000-60,000 cows. Well, my question is, how many cows do you have to milk? Average dairy in Washington is about 400 cows. That's a good-sized dairy.

There's really no subsidy for dairy farms. The milk can only go when it hits the port price, and that's about nine somethin'. It usually don't go below that. And there's a government program that kicks in and they'll pay a little bit you'll get, but it don't amount to a tinker's damn. But we don't get a government check or anything else. I mean the price of milk can go—well, it got up to $20—and it can drop down there into that $9 and $10. And then the government *will* buy like butter and cheese. If that milk has got to go to surplus, it'll go into cheese and the government will buy the cheese. It gets down to a certain level, and they'll stockpile that cheese.

And that's where we're at now, we got a lot of cheese that is stacked to the ceiling, and a lot of butter, stuff like that. That's what happened this last time because these other countries had money to spend, and they were buying protein, and that was powdered milk and things like that. And of course everybody was like, "Oh boy, we're sellin' this!" So they produced to beat hell. Well then the bottom fell out of *that*, and they're all standing here goin', "Now what do we do with *this?!*"

The Canadian system has worked. The only problem with the Canadian system is if you want to start in the dairy business it's almost prohibitive. To buy quota, right now it's approximately $20,000 per cow, if you want to buy your way into the dairy industry in Canada. And basically the only way you're gonna start up there now is you marry into it or you're born into it or whatever. But it has worked, it has stabilized the price of milk. They know what's goin' on, and if you want to see a good example of it, you just drive up to Linden and you look at the farms up there. There's a farmer on this side, they're holdin' everything together with balin' wire and duct tape. And you drive across the border, and everything's new, because they.... Yeah, it costs a lot of money, but they know how much milk's gonna be ten years down the road. We ain't got a clue. And there's a lot of different plans in the works now, but nobody can make up their mind. And the whole thing is, "Well, yeah, we want a program to stabilize, but we want to expand before that gets in. So we want to make sure." And the mentality of the guy down here is, "You're gonna go broke before I do, so I'll buy your place and I'll get bigger and you'll be gone." And it's a joke, it's just a joke. And you can cry and whine all you want, but if you want to stabilize the price of milk, there's really only one way, it's some type of a quota system, whether you like it or you don't. And if you don't want to do that, then shut up! and go up and down. We're gonna diversify. We're gonna buy stock in Kleenex because when the price of milk goes down and everybody's cryin', they'll be needin' a lot more Kleenex, so we'll make money off of stock in Kleenex.

But...I've always liked it, I like the cows, you see those calves comin' up, you're tryin' to breed a certain type of a cow. And it never used to be this volatile. Of course it's more of a worldwide market now. It used to be a local market. And now you've got New Zealand and Australia playin' into it. And China's big. All this thing. And these big creameries are trying to market powdered milk here and there and everything else. When you had these local creameries, they knew about how much milk they needed, and the farmer produced about that much. In the springtime you had a flush of milk. In the wintertime you were less milk. And then it got bigger and bigger and bigger, and creameries got bigger. It's just a rat race.

I think there was one creamery in Kent—well, the processing plant—and then of course in Seattle. When I grew up, there was Carnation, Vita-Milk, Foremost, Arden, Darigold, and I think there might have been a few more. But there was five, six creameries, and you could choose whoever you wanted to ship to. Now there's one. So either you ship to Darigold, Darigold, or Darigold. And I don't know what would happen if *they* were to go under. You'd just be SOL. And there were a few juggers in the Valley, which they processed their own milk, but they're gone. That's another ball game.

Like Billy Vinn, up here in North Bend. It's when you have your own dairy, you have your own processing plant, and you milk your cows, process your milk. We called it juggin'. They had all the different—they had skim milk, whole milk, chocolate milk. And then you either sold it at the place, or you put it in stores, or both. Bill's Dairy, around here now, there's nobody left. Bothell at one time over there, there was probably five guys. There was Thenos, Muller, Galitary Dairy up on the hill, and Bill's Dairy, all right in that same.... And they sold, they did really well. And here in the Valley was Bill Vinn. He was in North Bend. They jugged their own milk. But that's not an easy game, because if you don't sell it all, they used to, some of the creameries would pick up the surplus milk, and pay you little to nothin' for it. You tried to produce about what you sold. And then you had to have somebody runnin' that creamery and keep all that machinery goin'. So you really had two things to do. And now there's been a few people doin' some raw milk sales, but that is just—the liability of that is unreal. I mean, you just lay yourself wide open. We have some friends in Sequim, they did a really good job, they built their creamery, had done an excellent job, put out a *super* product, and they had a problem with.... It wasn't e-coli, was it? It was salmonella. And I mean it just kills ya'. They don't know where it's comin' from. It wasn't in the milk, the cow didn't have it, so I don't know how they come out. But it's really touchy.

We are *very* regulated. When the milk truck picks us up, they take a sample of the milk, and pull butterfat for leukocytes, which is the white cells in the milk—you want it low, and you want your bacteria low—and they check for bacteria and antibiotics. And when they get done pickin' up whoever they pick up in that tanker, that tanker goes to whichever plant. Before that milk truck is unloaded, they take a sample out of that tank and check it for antibiotics. If the tank is okay, then they unload the milk. If for some reason or other that tank showed antibiotics, then they go back and they check each one of those samples of the shipper, and if you have antibiotics in your milk, you just bought yourself a tankerload of milk and you're off the market. There's *no* tolerance for antibiotics in the milk—*none*. And this is what a lot of the organic people, that are buyin' organic, don't understand. And the organic person that's sellin' milk, they push that, that they don't have any antibiotics, which is true. But *no* milk, nationwide, has antibiotics—*none!* There's no tolerance for it. And then of course the growth hormone BST, the organic people don't have that. And now most of the big creameries, you can't use that either. So milk-wise, what's in it is pretty much the same. And then the state inspectors, they come around twice a year and check your place and stuff. So as far as the product, it's very regulated and safe as far as human consumption.

Most of the organic dairies *are* on the smaller side—most of 'em. There's a few big ones, but they've had some problems with them. But most of them are smaller dairies. But it's a lot of hassle, unless you've been set up for it and stuff, because it's hard to find your feed, you pay more for it. You get more for your product, which is true, but it's not all roses either.

I'd say we probably grow half of our forage. We buy all our grain. We don't grow any grain. But we grow hay and silage for the cows. And then we pasture, which is a big help in the summertime. They're out six months of the year. Good for your cow. Easier to have the cow go out and harvest the feed and bring the milk back, than you go out and cut the feed and bring it to the cow. So we do that. And of course it takes machinery to do it, but it works pretty good to let that cow go out to pasture. And then we buy some alfalfa from eastern Washington.

In our grain, I couldn't really tell ya' but I don't think there's an abundance of pesticides in it. Our grain is comin' from the grain farmer. We run a pretty basic grain mix. We've got cottonseed, corn, mill run, distillers grain, beet pulp. It's just a basic feed. And our hay, the same thing. I'm sure they spray the hay over there. But on the other hand, if you *didn't* have some of these pesticides and stuff, you would not have near the production, you would not have near the food on the market that you've got—the bugs would be gettin' most of it. I mean, yeah, you don't like to have a lot of pesticides in your food, I agree there. But if it's done right.... And that's the thing that people don't realize: you can be on the Mexican border, and on this side you can't use this pesticide, and they can grow that tomato on the other side and spray it with that same pesticide that you can't use here, and they ship it right up here. And people think in the grocery store it's all the same. Well, it's not! They can tell you whatever they want to tell you. The food system in the United States is pretty well regulated, really. It's probably the safest food system in the world. Ask the Chinese. They've got that bad stuff in the dairy.

We don't put commercial fertilizer on our fields, and we don't use pesticides. So I kind of classify us as "natural." We're not organic, and we're not the other end—we're kind of in the middle. And we don't use hormones on the cows. If they're sick, they get treated. Otherwise, we don't use the BST and all that kind of stuff.

I think you have to educate people, number one. You have to tell them this. The bad thing is, I can sit here and tell you or anybody how we do it, and then there's twenty-five people talkin' against you, sayin' anything they want to say: the animal rights people, the this, or that, or whatever. And they put out propaganda that's not true, or twisted to their deal, and the average person ... does ... not ... know. And you can't blame them. "Well, I read it on the blog." Well, yeah. I mean, you got people that are against animal production or this or that. I don't care, if you want to be a vegetarian, that's your business, that's fine. If you want to eat meat, that's fine. But I keep sayin' a lot of the people that are talkin' against these things, they didn't get up one mornin' and go on a crusade—somebody's payin' 'em. So there's money involved someplace. The only thing that agriculture can do is do the best job they can at educatin' and showin' people how it's done. And the farmer has got to do a good job, and practice what you preach. You gotta take care of your animals, and you got to do a good job. And if you think people aren't watchin' ya', you're nuts. People know what's goin' on. You gotta put out a good product, and that's about all you can do. We live right on the road, and I don't know how many zillion cars go by a day, they see what's goin' on, and they see your cattle. So if you think you're gonna put somethin' over on somebody, you got another thought comin'!

I don't think you'll see the dairies come back here. You *could*, but I don't think you will, because the regulations to get started and all this and that, and there's nobody gonna come in here and do it. These valleys that had a lot of dairies that have left—they're done. I never thought you'd see the Carnation Farms be out of cows, but they are. About the only one that started here would be Eric Nelson, and he quit, but he's back in again. And you might have one or two little ones come in, that are gonna maybe make cheese or somethin' like that. But basically what you've got is what you've got.

This is a good valley, this is a good farming valley for cows. Western Washington is about as good a place to milk cows as any. You've got urban people to worry about, but if you did it right, you save your farm ground, and you farm there, and you've got your houses over there, and that's the way it is. But the climate, you can grow just about anything you want to grow. The weather's good for the cattle, and it's a good valley.

I would hope this valley stays agricultural. With the people worryin' about their food and things, if they don't, there ain't gonna be anyplace to grow it. The truck farmers have helped a lot of this ground to grow somethin' on. If people don't wake up and smell the roses, why once that ground's gone, it's gone, and you won't get your food here. In a way, the economy the way it is has helped. It's took the pressure off of land development for a while. And some of the programs where you could sell development rights to the ground, that does help, and stuff. So it's a constant battle.

I think it can, if you can get this ground set aside and stuff. If you've got enough people wantin' food. If anything ever happens as far as screwin' up your transportation or your food chain or whatever, that's when a piece of ground or whatever is *really* gonna become important. You ask the people that have come to this country from Russia—and we're not talkin' sixty years ago, we're talkin' now—people have come from over there or wherever the…. Well, it isn't the Iron Curtain anymore, but in that area. And I'm tellin' you, you don't realize how important agriculture is to them. When they were in the old country, food was the biggest thing, you had to figure out how to get it. They really appreciate agriculture, whether it be livestock or crops or whatever. They understand how important it is. And the average person here never gives it a thought really, because food is so abundant and easy to get, they don't give it a thought. They're worryin' about what ball game do we go to, or what show do we go to, or what new i-Pod or what new thing, and hey, no problem.

It's a problem. If anything ever happens, and the food supply is broken, as we would say on the farm, the shit's gonna hit the fan!

You gotta love farming. You gotta love it. And if you get married, you'd better make damned sure your wife or your husband loves it, because you're there. Crop farming is a little different, you get a break in the wintertime, but then you fix stuff. Cows, it's every day, every day. They'll tell you what, when, why, and how come.

Farm Journal

23 May 2009

     Stopped by Local Roots this morning early—took Jason a little by surprise—didn't expect to see me early I guess. He, Siri, Dan and three of their interns are just getting started—a little late for them.

     The light is beautiful—clear sky—cool air—dew still on the grass.......Dan is preparing a field for seeding with a beautiful vintage tractor he's restored. I set to work making exposures—they're harvesting today—chard, radish, lettuce—they've been to market twice since my last visit. We don't talk. I shoot, they work. There is much to photograph—got nice stuff—need to return for late afternoon light.

     Talked briefly with one of the interns, Everett. Told him what I was about and that I want to interview interns and workers as well as farmers for the book. He was excited by the proposal. He's a bit of a 1960s throw-back in that he has a similar naiveté and an oddly innocent face, full of seeking and unspecified need. He and the others are here just for the summer—a nice touch for the dimension of the book.

....

     I still don't know what the outcome or focus or even design might be for this work. There is "something" new here, but it's hard to pin-point and beyond that quagmire, the deeper dilemma; who is the audience? Who am I talking to especially now in the midst of global financial collapse which may well profoundly alter our economic structure forever? What is the story to tell here? Does this agricultural "movement" represent the "seeds" of a return to (if there ever was a place to return to) sustainable, steady state economics or is it merely a hopeful and inspiring response to strange times—our generally unfulfilling existence—i.e. our corporate world driven by endless growth, increasing profits, and accelerating consumption of useless goods and services? All of it pushing toward a poverty of art, craft and intellect. Is this the nightmare of de Tocqueville where the tyranny of the majority at last disposes of the "Elites" (as the term was recently coined by Geo. W. Bush)?

     If the surge is genuine and could find a wider following, is it too late? Have we gone too far down our unique road of excess, climate change, overpopulation and all the rest such that the answers offered here will fail even if implemented?

     Who would read this book beyond those already sympathetic? Is it useful at all to "preach to the choir?"

....

     Met Susan Schmoll at Game Haven Farm the other day. She does some restaurant sales, U-Pick pumpkins, plant starts and sells some grass fed beef. She's been here since 1951—went to school with George Magnochi—both are transitional farmers (part of the traditional farm community as well as the "New Farmers") who know a lot about the history of farming in the Valley; both necessary for the project.

     I've decided to follow each of the owners through an entire day on each farm, just photographing and getting a more comprehensive sense of their routine and work load.

Game Haven Farm

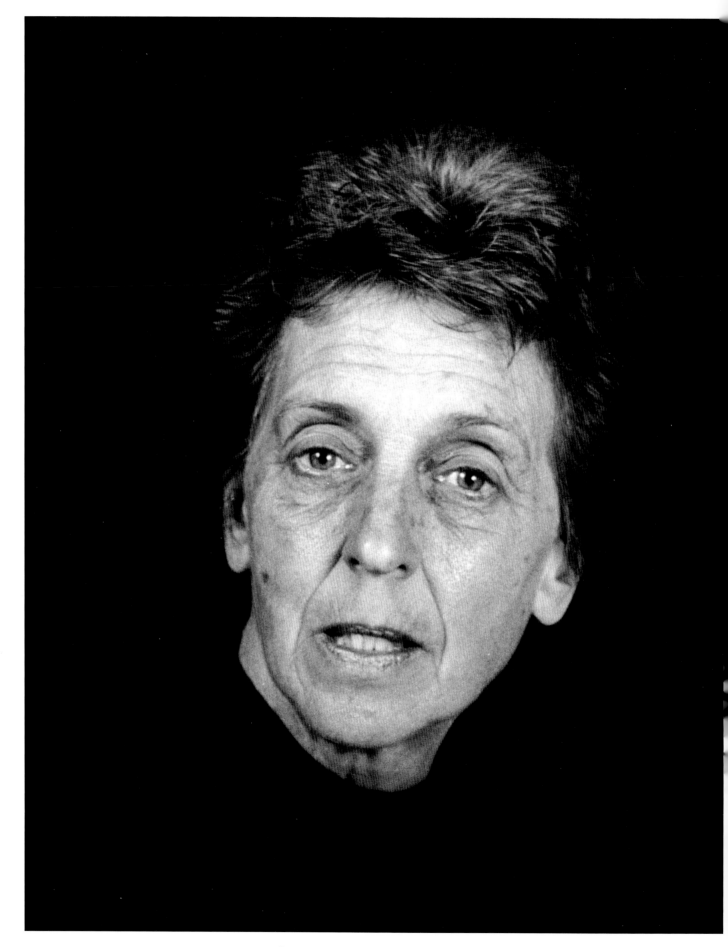

Susan Schmoll

25 March 2010

I'm Susan Schmoll, I was born in Ellensburg, Washington, 8-19-46 and now live in Carnation, Washington. We moved here when I was in kindergarten, so I can't remember too much of it. We were on a dairy farm in Ellensburg. And my folks moved here because my dad thought it would be a better place to dairy at that time. And now all the dairy is back *that* way! We moved to a dairy farm, and that's where I live now...on the same farm.

Back then most of the herds were probably around fifty cows, so that's what we had. I was the youngest of four, with three older brothers. My dad always worked out, and then worked on the farm after work and weekends, etc., etc. So we did as much of our own feed as we could do, making silage and making some hay. Everybody got up and did their chores before they went to school, milked the cows. My job was to feed the calves before and after school. So it was a very busy time. But when I went to school, a lot of the kids in my class were on dairy farms.

My mom and dad went out of the dairy business when all the kids were gone, because it was too much work for them to continue. I went to college and then got married and lived in California for a couple of years. My husband and I and our two children moved back up to the farm, and have been there ever since.

I went to school in Carnation all the way through kindergarten to high school then I went to college for four years and graduated with a degree in nursing, and used that for a few years until we moved back on the farm and had young children and I stayed home.

When I was growing up there were a lot of dairies and some row crops. I can remember up on 60th.....I'm trying to remember, I think they grew beans there, because my brothers used to go and help. I'm not sure if they picked or if they hauled things or what. I think Reitmans grew beans there. Harvolds did row crops. They did broccoli, I know that. I don't know what else. Truthfully, when you're young and on the farm, in the 1950s you don't drive around the Valley. You know, you don't go see everything. I understand there were row crops at some time in Duvall, but I don't remember it. In the thirties and forties there were canneries still in Carnation....into the fifties also. But I think maybe by later than the fifties, late fifties, early sixties, Reitmans had their cannery running, but then it was more of a custom cannery, because we used to harvest our garden and go down there and take care of all of our stuff and put it in the cans, and then they'd send it through. And when everything was canned, then we'd go pick it up.

We had a *big* garden. And of course my closest brother and I, our job was to weed and do all that stuff. And then the other thing that was in town was lockers for rent, and a lot of people used the lockers because not everybody had freezers at home. So we always had a locker. Out in the front part of the locker they had a cooling room. And so when we would slaughter our meat, it would go into the cooler to hang, and then we'd go down some evening, and it was set up with a big block table and a grinder, and we'd cut up our meat and wrap it and make the hamburger. And then the locker's right there and you would put it in the locker. And my dad wasn't a butcher, but he cut it up. "Florence, what cut do you want out of this one?" he'd say to my mom.

They were wonderful parents, but they were very hard-working parents, and expected their kids to be hardworking. But we always tried to get away once in a while and get a picnic in, and go fishing. Mom and I used to go fishing down the river quite a bit. That was one of the things we liked to do, is go down to the river and go fishing. So long evenings in the summer were really good for that. We were a close family. My dad was mainly Irish and my mom was mainly Swedish. Our name was Meehan, M-E-E-H-A-N. Irish name.

Years ago, none of the farms were very.... Well, we probably had one of the smaller farms, acreage-wise. But you know, now there are small vegetable farms and big vegetable farms in the Valley. So there's quite a range there. But since the dairies moved out, it's good to see something growing. And it's good to see the land being used and taken care of, one way or the other. I've noticed in the last years there's sure a lot of hay being made in the Valley. When I was a kid, making hay was a *very* difficult thing, because if you got a summer rain, you couldn't get it dry. I can remember making hay was very hard to do, so my dad did a lot of silage.

The floods back then were not nearly as bad as they are now—not nearly. There was one flood; in '59 I believe was a high flood. And I'm not sure how high it was, because when we did get floods, my mom would have me go from school to stay with a friend in town so that I wouldn't miss school. So I wasn't home for all the floods. I was once in a while, but not very often. And when we first moved here with *our* kids, and the floods would come, I would go, "Oh, wow, this is a good reason to stay home. Nobody can go." And I'd bring out the bag of walnuts, and it was time to crack walnuts! So I think it was probably, especially the flood of 1990 that changed *that*. After that, I never thought of floods as being, "Oh, well this is a reason to stay home." Or, "A good reason and we can relax." Because after that, there's no relaxing with a flood. There's been too many bad floods from there on. I think '86 maybe was pretty high, but not that bad. The barn that we milked the cows in never had water in it. So they always had an easy time with the cows. Now that we have beef cows and they're not in the barn—and that barn would have been underwater—it's always a hassle every time it floods. You have to keep your mind on what's going on, and then make sure you have your cows on the best place, before it floods.

We did get a critter pad in, and got a fence around it, so that is the good thing now, is now we can walk them in. But the flood last year, which was 2009, that actually topped our critter pad. So our cows were standing in water for a while, and we did lose some calves. I mean not calves that were born. We had cows that were pregnant that lost their calves. Right now we have about twenty beef. We raise them for beef. They wouldn't tolerate you milking them. We raise them for sale.

Just as a little bit of history, when we moved there, my mom and dad had started a nursery, so we took over the nursery. Because my mom had had a stroke when we were going to take over the nursery anyway, so they could retire. But she really wasn't able to come and work and keep it up anymore, but she did come and help me an *awful* lot, the stuff that she could do. So we did that for many years, and then a friend and I thought something would have to be easier than lifting all the heavy, heavy stuff. So a friend and I started a business and we grew salad greens and other produce and marketed them to restaurants and to grocery stores and to individuals. So that has gone on. I'm kind of at the tail end of *that* business, trying to scale down to what I can handle. So mainly what we do on our farm now is I still have a big garden, and I grow a multitude of vegetable plants—tomatoes and peppers and things like that—that I sell in the spring to the public. Then we put in a pumpkin patch, so we grow pumpkins. And then during the summer, keeping that weeded and doing those things, and taking care of the cows, and doing hay, and getting that stuff done. Yeah, we keep ourselves busy.

A lot of the farms now do a lot of CSAs. I don't know how many of the farms in the Valley *do* CSAs, but I know there's a lot. And I thought about it one time myself, but I didn't ever get it organized or do the research to pursue it. And so for many years I've thought it was a good idea, and I think they're people that really enjoy it, and I think they work very hard to put together a good batch of produce that the customers will come back year after year. It's a lot of work to do that. I think it's a good idea. I really do. We're in a good place here, because we're so close to a lot of population, that it *is* an opportunity. I mean, there's farmers in the Chehalis area that are bringing their produce up to the Seattle area. So the metropolitan area really aids the ability to do that. And I think there's more people doing a little bit of their own gardening.

There's this whole movement against the large corporate factory farm, importing vegetables and all of that from miles and miles away. Then there's the controversy over organic food as opposed to food that's fertilized and treated with pesticides and all the works. I agree that it would be *much* better to use the local food. I think some of the public has a problem perhaps with the cost of that. And the thing is to try to educate the public. And I think they're trying to do that, that buying locally is good, *if* they get stuff that is good. And then you can say it hasn't lost its nutrients in the truck. I don't go into a lot of stores and look at their organic produce, but I know a few years ago, three, four, or five years ago, there were some stores, when you looked at the organic produce, it looked really, really sad. And why would somebody buy that over the other? But I do notice some of the stores in the Valley, when you look at some of the organic produce that they have, I think they're doing a *much* better job of presentation and keeping it looking good. I think the other thing with long hauls is people are so used to going into the store and buying whatever they want, to cook whatever they want, and if you really have a commitment to local, there are things that aren't available, unless it's hauled. So there again, it's trying to educate the public to eat local. But it is a hard thing to try.... And I know some of the farms are trying to do year-round cropping. But I know this year in the beginning of December everything I had *covered* in the garden froze. And you think about a *big* farm, I don't know, they'd have to really spend some money on equipment to be able to mulch, because they can't go out and hand mulch like I do, and throw out a couple bales of hay over everything.

I think people are becoming more aware of eating more fresh vegetables and fruit. Like I don't think as growing up, or as somebody who has cooked, I have hardly bought.... I don't think I've ever bought beef out of the store. I truly believe that the grass-fed beef is *way*, way, way far superior. I think organic is better. All of the food that I grow is grown organically, but fresh is good too, you know. When you cut that broccoli out of the garden, you've never tasted broccoli like that from the store.

I think it will take time. And I questioned that at one of the tilth meetings: Is there enough land here to grow organic food to feed Seattle and Bellevue? So I don't know that answer. See, I questioned. And then you have winter. And then you have a lot of your farms in the flood plain, and if it floods, you don't have any food, because then they can't sell their food if the flood waters have been on it. I mean, that's a big question. My brother-in-law lives down south of Bakersfield, so one of the biggest carrot growers down there bought out Cal Organics. Now that's a big farm. The first one is a big commercial Ag, more conventional. And then they bought out Cal Organics, and they're growing organic. So to me that shows that even those big guys know that there's that slot that they need to get into. So I look at that as a positive that they're looking at. And so they're working at practices on a big scale to do that.

In the stores that sell "local" it would be nice to know what "local" is, how far around it goes, because, you know, a lot of people are saying, "buy your food within 50 miles or 100 miles." So could that be local? But I really do—that is one thing I would really like, is to go to the store and have something there that has a sign that says where that product came from. And local might be okay—and not just with organics, but the other produce. I would like to see signs there that said, "These plums come from Chile, or they come from eastern Washington, or what it is." Some stores are doing it, yeah, but it's not a requirement. I think some of them are listening to the people.

There was a lot happening before the global warming issue. I have gone to meetings for years and years and years and years on the flood issue. When they put in Snoqualmie Ridge development, I went to those meetings and said, "You're going to cause us a problem with flooding." "Oh no, we're not, we're going to retain all the water in storm sewers and ponds, and there won't be anything extra added to the Valley." And then when we went up to the meeting after the final plan came out, it was all being tight-lined into the river. So all the assurances we had, all the meetings we went to, meant nothing at all because they changed it to what they wanted to do. So I've seen a lot happen around the Valley in my years, and one of the big issues is a lot of the development. You've got to look at, when you drive over, how much is in the skiing, that as soon as it rains it comes down. You know, there's no trees left to hold the water. There's a lot of development locally on all the hills, where it used to come down slowly. A lot of things have changed. And maybe the rain events have changed. I haven't gone back and looked at the flows and what the rain event was like and that type of thing. But generally in the winter, if it gets to be fifty-some degrees, morning and night, you just know it's gonna flood and rain.

So they say global warming will just add to it, which is scary. And I think what would threaten the growers in the Valley to not be successful is mainly going to be flooding. They can put in critter pads, but that's not going to protect their crops. And that's gonna be the toughest thing. We can raise our houses, we can put in critter pads, but the flooding, it just does so much damage, and people lose a lot of money when they can't sell their crop—especially if they put in.... I mean, you've got two, three months or more into that crop before you're selling.

I don't know why zoning couldn't prevent development. You know at one time there was supposed to be a dam. That was proposed and that was put down. I don't understand why zoning cannot prevent that from happening. I don't know if there's farmland *out* of the floodplain. There are some people, I think, that are up on the hill with some, but those aren't very large, and they don't have good soil. And, in the Valley, the reason the people are farming there in this Valley is because it has good soil. That's probably one of the reasons my dad moved over here, was for the soil and being able to grow. And that's why there *were* a lot of dairies here, is because the grass was so wonderful.

I think Monsanto is scary because of the strings that they have on all of their seed. That's really kind of scary. The other thing is, it's becoming such a monopoly. So as far as world food goes, you go one way and you go the other, because you read "We're not going to have enough food." And then you read that there's surplus of food, but then there's still countries that don't have much food. Then I was reading the other day that a lot of agricultural land might be taken out of agriculture to sell for carbon credits. So I think if anybody's gonna look on down the line they need to look at keeping ahold of the good land for food production.

My husband's retiring this year, and so I'll have more help on the farm. So we really don't know what we're going to do. As you get older, you have to start readjusting how much you do. But we will be working on.... Hopefully we'll have a little time to spare if we *both* work on stuff.

I do a little bit of selling my produce to restaurants. I've worked with this restaurant a long time, and I know if I have something, what the chef likes, and I can call and see if he needs it, and that type of thing. When we were really doing it, we used to put out a list every week of what was available, and then they'd order. We had a delivery day, and then they knew it would come to them at that time. I don't know if you've ever worked in the restaurant business at all, but most of the people when they deliver, everything gets checked. But after we worked with some of the restaurants long enough, they never checked our produce to look and see if it was in good shape or not, because we didn't send them anything that wasn't good. So when we were doing that, that was really what we strove for, was to have really nice-looking stuff that went to the restaurant, and they didn't have to…. And we felt like they had very little prep to take care of it.

As for our children, I don't know if they want to farm. One lives in North Carolina, and the other one is living on the farm right now, but long term, I'm not sure. So that's why I said we have time to figure that out and see how that works. I don't know what else it would be but farmland, because it all floods. During last year's flood, there wasn't a dry place there. All the high ground that was always the safe ground, everything was covered. That would be the one thing. That is a very discouraging thing when you go out and the only thing you do for months is clean up. I wouldn't try to predict what will become of the Valley, because you never know what's going to happen. There is a lot of the growers, you know, they're very dedicated. I don't know where a breaking point would be, but the ones I've met, they definitely love their garden and their growing. It would take a group to address the issue some way or another. If it becomes something that becomes a problem to everybody, I think then it would have to be addressed, if the flooding does. This has been a wonderful winter. I know everybody is just thrilled—not only because we had such nice weather once we got past December, maybe, and everybody can get out and get stuff done and get started early, just because we didn't have a flood to deal with. It just gives you so much more time to get your work done. That's one of the main things. We're just lucky we don't have the spring floods like they do back east. I think the latest…. Well, I shouldn't say that. The latest flood I've seen really is March, but you know one time we had a small June flood—strictly a rain event. But that just came into the lower fields.

We have our U-Pick pumpkin patch on the farm. It's picked at the farm. We grow other things that go along with it—winter squash. And we make some little hay bales to go with it. And we do corn stalks. We have gourds. I'm thinking…. Some specialty little gourds that we sell. I'm trying to think what else I was going to say. Oh, and the Indian corn. I grow Indian corn, so we have Indian corn. That's available. And then all the vegetable starts that I sell. I sell them off of the highway on Highway 203, right up at the corner. So it's amazing how many people see me there, and they go, "These are your plants?!" So that's worked into a big business from when I started it and just did a few. So every year it's a few more and a few more. And then with beef, we usually sell to individuals. And they are slaughtered on the farm, and then they go to where those people want them to go, to be cut and wrapped. We'll have one shy year this time, since we lost a lot of calves last year. I mean, it put us behind.

My dad would not mind the fact that there's the growing going on, and that perhaps the use of the land has changed to a different type of farming, but while he was alive, he would be at *all* the meetings. You know, the recent project that the Corps of Engineers did up at the falls—that I think was first up in the seventies that that was up. We had a meeting downtown, he spearheaded that. He went out and talked to people to get 'em to the meeting. We went into the Corps' office and talked to them. I mean, he was very active in letting people know. He would have loved to have seen something to help the flooding situation. And anything that came up that he thought was going to cause more flooding, he was very vocal on that, because he saw some increase in the flooding and how it did affect the farm, and when he was milking cows and stuff.

I think our boys had a good life here. They had to learn how to work also.

According to the US Department of Agriculture, April 2003, three states dominated cattle feedlot production: Texas had 2.7 million cattle on feedlots; Kansas, 2.3 million; and Nebraska, 2.2 million. Combined, these three states accounted for two-thirds of all beef cattle feedlot production. These three states rely on the Ogallala Aquifer to supply water for their animals as well as the corn used to feed them.

The total number of beef cows in the United States in April 2003 was 33 million. One third of the nation's beef cattle (10.7 million) is produced on large feedlots. The remainder are either grazed or raised on smaller feedlots with a capacity under 1,000 head. The early 2000s continued the trend toward larger feedlot operations. However, the industry exists under a cloud of environmental suspicion regarding the damage caused by waste runoff, as well as the effect of growth hormones injected into cattle to promote quick weight gain. Encyclopedia of Business, 2nd edition (**Author's note: Feedlots are the major source of all meat and poultry products stocked in supermarkets, restaurants and fast food chains in America.**)

The increased use of confined animal feeding operations for cattle, poultry and hogs has raised concern regarding the possibility of groundwater pollution. Full-grown hogs, grown under confined conditions, produce 15 pounds of waste per day, per hog. Since hog manure is disposed of as highly liquid slurry in confinement operations, the cost to transport it is prohibitive. Therefore, it has to be used in the local area. Although there are many systems to handle hog waste, lagoons are the cheapest and least efficient. The current regulations allow lagoons to be constructed to hold the waste and to seep at roughly one-quarter inch per day. The Oklahoma Department of Environmental Quality translates that into a total of more than 500 gallons per acre per day.

Thus more area is put into irrigated corn which is a high user of nitrogen, a key component in manure. Irrigated corn, in the course of consuming enormous amounts of water, produces nutrient runoff particularly high in phosphorus because of the use of animal manure as a source of nitrogen. There is no procedure in Oklahoma to monitor how much and where nutrients are spread on the various crops and grasses grown in the Panhandle. And one does not need to speculate about where this runoff finally travels, i.e., into the Ogallala Aquifer. The Kerr Center for Sustainable Agriculture, Poteau, Oklahoma, July 2000 (**Author's note: The Aquifer also is the primary source of drinking water for the region.**)

Farm Journal

19 August 2009

Spent the day with Michaele at Growing Things Farm. Although she's been more than supportive of the project, she's also touchy about me dogging her steps for a day. Finally agreed only if she could reserve the right to tell me to "go away" if it just got to be too much; with four workers, three of them new to farm work and the pressures of tending chickens and pigs, harvesting and getting it to market, a nosy photographer could stress the system indeed. I assured her I understood "busy" and had been rejected before and only asked that she not throw dirt or manure on my cameras. I arrived at 5 am (as instructed). She'd been there since 4 and they were all about to head out to the field.

It was a morning at the cusp of autumn; the air betraying the chill to come—fog rising off the river, sun blotted into a shimmering smear, fields wrapped in mist and stillness. We moved silently for the most part, she harvests the last of the radishes and directs Shauna, Emma and Colin as they push through their individual early morning fog and let consciousness find its way to them.

Michaele is always "on", always several steps ahead, trying to salvage and/or stay on top of crops that want to bolt. And then the sun began to burn its way through, a sudden white disk trapped in fog, Michaele walks in the distance, minute at horizon's edge—everyone shimmers in the half-light.

The afternoon was warm. They harvest the last of the potatoes, repair sprinkler heads and drip-lines. Shauna and Emma (cousins), clearly worship the ground Michaele walks; she is their Maven yet she seems unaware of their admiration; they have much to learn. She will work until dark; there is always more to do.

Growing Things Farm

Michaele Blakely

26 January 2010

My name is Michaele Blakely, I was born March 31, 1954, and I live in Carnation, Washington. I'm from all over the place: Portland, Oregon—I was born there. I lived in Portland, California, Bellevue, Duvall, Seattle, up and down California a lot. My family's all over the place too. They're in California, most of them, and, I don't know, pretty average family. My mom married my stepfather, who had a cattle ranch, and so we were introduced to ranching early on. I was the one who grew the vegetables and raised the chickens. Surprise, guess what I'm doing now? My grandparents had a market farm. They had a roadside stand that they sold their berries and vegetables. And so in the summer I would visit them. In the winter, other times of the year, I'd be with my family on the ranch. So that's how I got there.

I went to school, went to college, had children, went back to school after a while and started a Montessori school, got my Montessori training and taught school here in Duvall for ten, twelve years. That's about it. Then I started farming.

I've always had a vegetable garden, always had animals, and it just seemed a natural progression with my garden to grow something to support my garden, because I didn't want to buy all these perennial plants for my flower garden. So I thought I would sell perennial starts at the farmers markets to kind of take care of my "hobby" so to speak. And I also had at the school a vegetable garden for the children, that they would grow, and then we would sell things. It was sort of a business enterprise for them. And it was just a natural progression. When I decided I didn't want to teach anymore, I moved into selling flowers. And that was just about the time, I think I had sold flowers for maybe two years, when the Hmong community came into the Valley and into the farmers markets, and they pretty much wiped out all of the flower growers in the business, because they grew these big showy dahlias and they sold them very cheaply. So my next step was to grow vegetables, because they weren't, and so I started a CSA, and started the vegetable garden and began selling vegetables.

CSA is a movement that I had heard about. It hadn't really started yet in this area. There was one CSA in all of Washington, or at least in this area, that I knew about. It seemed like the thing to do. I don't remember what year. It was a *long* time ago. I know that Erick and I started doing the CSA within a year of each other, so it was well over twenty years ago. That was also during the period of time before anyone really thought that you could make a living farming like this. And so it became *my* goal, because I had just a small plot of land, to see how much I could produce off of an acre. And then I went to *two* acres. And when I discovered that I could really make a lot of money on a little bit of land, I decided that I needed to start sharing this information, and that's when we started getting the interns and started sharing. So that's how it went.

I have moved too many times over the years! I'm never moving again. I don't care if the place floods all the time, I'm not moving anymore. I started on Stossell Creek. I had about a half an acre there. And then I moved to Carnation. And then I moved to Duvall, and then I moved back to Carnation. Then we lost the lease on the property in Duvall. And at the time, PCC, the land trust, was looking for farmers, and they found myself and Andrew Stout and Fong Cha and purchased this particular piece of property and divided it up among the three of us. So that's how I got there. That was 2006. It wasn't long ago at all. I wound up with thirty-one acres. There's probably about, between ten or fifteen acres in cultivation; and then most of it is the animals; chickens and turkeys and pork and cows. Erick and I are kind of the pioneers here in the Valley.

I've always farmed organically, even with my family. My family farmed organically I would say 99 percent of the time, just because it was practical, and it was inexpensive. We always had animals, we always had cows. When I was a child, for the garden, one of the things that we would do in the afternoon, after school, we'd go pick up all the cow pies and take 'em and chop 'em up and then put 'em into the compost and make our compost. I was doing this at eight years old. So it was just a natural—I didn't think of any other way to do it. My grandparents also farmed organically for the same reasons. They didn't call it that. In some respects sometimes they were a little embarrassed because they didn't go out and buy fertilizer, like some people would buy Miracle-Gro or some fancy fertilizer, and they didn't.

How organic has grown? It's kind of disappointing, in respects that it has now lost its flavor, so to speak, because large corporations have taken over the name and taken over the meaning of what it is. It's sort of a mixed bag. It's a good thing that organic is now a big business, because that means that the planet is going to be a cleaner place for us. On the other hand, the integrity of the product is diminishing. My goodness, we have organic French fries now! Great that it's organic, but it's still not good for you. And yet somehow because big business is there, it's managed to create an image of food that isn't necessarily good for you, but it is. And then the regulations for organic standards are so bizarre sometimes they're not common sense, because of the large food chain. The big farms now have to be monitored and regulated. The standards are.... How to say this? Take a large food processing plant: it is so big it has to have just these incredible regulations to ensure the safety of the food. It's happening with organics as well. Our E-coli scare was from a large processing plant, so that now what they're doing is—one of the things in California they've decided to do to make it "safe" for us to eat organic spinach is to take out all of the hedge rows that they planted to create wildlife environment. So now all organic spinach fields in California are just bare, there's just nothing but ground that is kept clean, and that's going to keep us safe. And that's always what happens with all sorts of other regulations.

I just filled out my organic certification form. It's in the car; I'm going to go send it in. I was quite impressed this year that it's not so horrific, the paperwork is not so horrific. But there've been years when it's just been awful. But I am stuck now, because I made an agreement with PCC, I have to stay organic. I probably would still stay organic as long as the regulations didn't get ridiculous. For instance, if they ask me to start clearing all my land of wildlife habitation, I'd throw a fit! No way! Because organic has become such a buzz word for so many people, that if you don't have that qualification up there, at certain markets it's really hard to compete, because by law, you can't call yourself organic unless you pay that money. And that's disgusting, but that's the way it works now. And so I could be in big trouble if a customer came up to me and asked me if I was organic and I said yes, and I hadn't paid my money and gotten that certification and gotten that inspection too, to ensure that what I was saying was correct. I could be in trouble, I could be fined. So that's hard. And so a lot of small farms, they don't want to pay the money, and my goodness, my fees are well over a thousand dollars. That's a tax. I'm paying them money so I can have that sign, and they're going to come out and regulate me and they do, they do. I don't know if it's worth it. A lot of small farms don't want to go through that headache. They're small enough that it's not necessary; they can still sell all their product without that certification. I also sell wholesale, and I can't sell wholesale as organic either. If I don't sell as organic, then I don't get a good price.

I think this Valley is so special. When I was first here, there was nothing but cows. And then the cows went away, and then there was nothing. As far as I knew, until I met Erick, there was nobody but me out here doing this, and I was the weird chicken lady that sold organic vegetables. She was the weird organic chicken person, and people would talk about me. I would hear that people would talk about me, this crazy lady. First of all, I was a woman farming, at a time when there weren't any women farming. And I was also among a lot of old dairymen that were trying to figure out what to do next and that sort of thing. So I was kind of a bizarre case for most of the Valley. Very interesting that as the years progressed, I started getting a different feel for how these people felt about what I was doing. First, they got used to me being here. And second, we were slowly changing our viewpoint and our frames of reference about the food that we had, and how we ate, how we treated the land. I mean, this was twenty years ago that this was all going on, so we've gone a long way. And then it was almost like there was something that clicked. It's like we turned the page. This was the ground work, and then we turned the page, and then boom! We had these farms show up, and these people come, and they just kept coming. Every year there was somebody else that kept showing up. And I thought it was glorious! I mean, it was just wonderful. It was like wow! Here's this community.

I'm not the crazy lady anymore. And not only that, it was just wonderful to see this community building, and these people, like-minded people, committed to doing these things. Now, there are good points and bad points, like everything. But the vast amount of good that has been done is just great, I think.

As for the arguments against organic production—that you can't grow enough food that way to feed the world's hungry.....Bullshit! I mean, I proved, when I was farming on one, and then just two acres, how much money you could make. I fed a *lot* of people. It was a lot of work to do it on two acres, and it took an incredible amount of brain work, just constantly evaluating what you were doing, and focusing on being on top of everything, but you can feed a lot of people on very little land. And they're now proving that not only is organic food more nutrient dense, but you get the same yields, and sometimes better, than you do with conventional farming. And certainly even the large conventional farms I think do a great disservice as far as crop yields. I think you get better yield from well-maintained, small-acreage farms, than you do the large ones. And certainly the benefit to the soil. I mean, you go out and you look at a large farm, and you look at their fields, organic. They're treated just the same as the conventional ones. They're tilled to death, the drainage is so poor. It's night and day. The other thing I wanted to say is that because the large non organic farms treat their fields this way, the health of the soil is in jeopardy. That then slows down the crop production as well, or the yields.

I think we'll have quite a crisis for a while until it gets fixed, and figure out how to.... Because our food system is such that it would be hard to feed our society the way we have it geared up now. It would be very difficult. Those of us who are lucky to live close to it, like the Snoqualmie Valley now will be okay somewhat. But there's a lot of places that don't have areas to grow food anymore.

I have interns here every year. I think that's the best way to educate. I educate my customers as well, but the interns, we have between—there's been one to seven interns on the farm each year for almost twenty years now. That's a *lot* of interns. There's been a couple of years where I haven't done it, but for the most part, there's always been. And so there's quite a few farmers out there now. Or if not farmers, they have a really good grasp on what it takes to grow food and feed people. Basically they have to apply for a position on the farm—a placement—I wouldn't call it a position, but a placement on the farm. We go through the application process, and if it's a fit, then they come to the farm, and they stay between two months to six, seven, eight months on the farm. They live there and do hands-on learning. You saw an example of the hands-on learning. Some of these kids have *never* had an opportunity to even see.... I kind of like it when the kids *don't* have a lot of experience, because they come in with an open mind, and just a sense of awe and marvel at what life is like on a farm, and what it means to actually grow your food.

Each intern gets a tent. It's only the interns that are here for a short period of time that use the tents. The rest of them are in other living situations. They get paid a stipend, and I let them know that this is a learning situation, it is not a job; that it takes an awful lot out of me as a farmer to spend my time teaching them. And so they get a stipend for some spending money, and also there's a little psychological advantage to someone giving a little bit of money for what they've done, because they work hard, they really do work hard. They get fed, they have a place to stay, and they get a wonderful education. So that's how they get paid.

You know, they've all kind of progressed in the level of knowledge that they have about their food. Some of them have been pretty radical, pretty ranting against The Man and The Machine. And others have been very philosophical. This last group were just so sweet. They were just very sweet, generous people. Three of them were Mennonites and I had never actually met, that I knew of, someone of that religion. And it was very interesting. It was a great learning experience for me, to learn that philosophy, which was nice.

I grew up in the latter part of the sixties where you weren't supposed to make money. Money was all plastic stuff. And so if you were doing good, you weren't making money. So I decided that I needed to switch that. I needed to switch that so that you did good and still made money. So that was my take on it. "Well, let's see if I can do a wonderful thing by growing food for people, and be able to support myself doing it. I don't necessarily want to become rich, but I want to be able to pay the bills." So yeah, it was definitely—I wouldn't do it if it wasn't for my philosophical reasons. I'd be finding something else to do, to maintain that. And I think the two professions that I've had in life have been nurturing children and nurturing people—or feeding people and educating children. And so I think those two are probably in the top five of what you do for the world, if you do it right. It's definitely a very deep need inside of me, to be able to do that.

Interns don't talk about it with me, not a whole lot. I think those are conversations that they have between themselves more than with me. I get hints of it every once in a while in the comments and that, but they don't do a whole lot of philosophical talk. It's kind of we're already there and doing it, so we're in the moment. Reflection comes later, I think—or synthesizing it comes later. I think farmers are just naturally that way—except maybe Erick. He spends a lot of time talking about philosophy, but he has a right to it since he has a degree in it. He has a license to talk! But you know, when it's your life, that's just it, you don't spend a lot of time with it, I think. I don't know for sure.

I have a friend that I met in the very beginning of the Iraq War protests. We were some of the very few out there in Duvall and Carnation, and doing it. And we were in Seattle as well. I did it through the winter, and then I told them, "I have to go." They couldn't understand how I could leave this very important thing of coming out here and doing this. And I tried to explain to them.... Or that "this was the answer and we had to stop the war, we had to create peace." And I said, "I'm living this by what I do. And it may not work...." This was a while ago. You know, it's been almost ten years. And I had to explain to them that even though it wasn't quite—the lines were kind of jogged around, but they did connect the dots eventually to the way I farmed had a whole lot to do with this war, and that if I didn't get back out there and do that farming in the right way…. So it's hard for people to understand that, and it is so nice to know that by living your life with your beliefs, you *do* make a statement, and it *does* make a difference. And so I feel *very* lucky to be able to do that.

There are some times when I think, "Well, maybe the best thing in the world *is* that we just get this incredible crisis and the world comes crashing down, and it'll all be over, and we can start all over, and we can build it up." And I think, "Well, yeah, I'm kind of lucky, because I think I'd survive that. I'm not sure about everybody else, but I think I would manage it okay, if the world didn't crash on top of *my* place." I don't know, I have incredible hope for people and in their creativeness and their way of solving solutions. But also at the same time, the same amount of hope I have, the same amount of despair I have for the other side that creates these problems for us. So I think it's a toss up.

Climate change; that's a big one. I think we will always, until we come to another crisis like the age of the dinosaurs, where they all disappeared, and eventually the humans will disappear too, because we can't adapt any longer. I think we'll still adapt, we're pretty creative. And farmers, especially farms that farm the way we are, are extremely innovative. It takes a season sometimes to change it, to see it. But we in the Valley I think are getting really good at figuring it out. We've got the pads now, we've got…. I think we'll be okay until climate just does something to us so horrible that we can't make it work—and that's a possibility. What I think is the hardest thing for us are the regulations from the county. Makes it really tough. For instance, it took a lot to get the farm pads up, and there are still many farmers who still can't have farm pads because of the regulations. There's just all sorts of things, all sorts of little tiny regulations that get in the way of farming. We're always subject to the whims of politics. So sometimes it's good for us, and sometimes it's not so good for us. I'll just leave it at that.

I don't know, I'm going to leave it to other people who sit in offices and think about it. (Laughs) There's just so much you can do. I don't know. I don't know how that works. It's a long road, I think. It's a very gradual progression, so I don't know. No, I can't say there was a single moment of when it changed.

My customers are my friends now. It's a circle, it's a community, and it's a partnership that we have. They are incredibly grateful to me for growing the food that I grow. And I am incredibly grateful for them to buy my food. So it's a great relationship. You know, there's something absolutely magical of being able to feed somebody for over twenty years. You know? And have them come every week and buy your food. There's this one man, one of my very first customers, when I was really just selling eggs, started buying. He's a writer. He's quite wealthy. And he now can't see, he has cataracts. He doesn't write anymore, he doesn't do much, he's very frail, he's in his nineties. And yet every year—he now has a helper that comes and takes him to the market—and every Saturday I'm on pins and needles to see if he's going to be here. There are many of my customers who no longer come, because they're dead. It's sort of a magical kind of way…. I liken it to a doctor who has watched the children that he's helped come out, grow up and do that. So it's the same sort of thing. It's just wonderful.

Like during Thanksgiving, I think it's now on our third or fourth year, the Eat Local for Thanksgiving campaign, which King County and Cascade Harvest Coalition worked together to start this program. It's been really fun to see the customers coming to the farmers markets and the stands to buy their food for local. And basically the idea is to get everything local. And it's the same sort of thing. It's just grand, it's amazing. They don't have to go out to the grocery store to buy their food, it can just be right on their table, twenty-five miles away from their home. And it's a hard one—when they first started it, I thought, "That's kind of a weird thing to do." I started to think about it, my food *is* all from my farm. I'd say 95 percent of it is from the farm. I forget how often people don't eat that way. The other day I broke down and I bought some hot house tomatoes because I was craving a BLT. Had to do it. I figure I've got credit.

There was a time when two years ago I hurt myself, and I kept working, I didn't stop, and it got to where I was so disabled that I couldn't lift a fork to my mouth. It was really, really bad. And it wasn't that it was so painful, it's that actually it.... I mean, it *was* painful anyway when I was working, but I literally couldn't move it and make it work. And the doctor said that it was quite possible that I'd never get back the motion that I had. And so I reevaluated and I said, "Okay, I'll stop." That was one reason I took the year off and I went to PCC and I worked, because they have *incredible* insurance. You can't touch it anywhere else. Then went for physical therapy, and I'm still doing that, and have regained, primarily, almost everything doing the work that I have to do for my body, to maintain it. And during that time, I was so.... I don't know how to explain it. I thought I was dying. I was so out of my element and unhappy by the fact that I wasn't feeding people and doing this thing. Yeah, I think if I couldn't do this, I don't think I'd want to do anything else.

It is widely prophesied that sustainable agriculture would result in a heavy financial loss. This is however a misconception. Sustainable agriculture need not be less profitable than conventional agriculture. The farms using alternative methods had lower yields initially, but this was offset by lower costs for fertilizers and pesticides. Sustainably or organically farmed soils offer the advantage of greater water-holding capacity than conventionally farmed soils.

Sustainable agriculture needs to be seen more clearly not as a throwback to hundred-year old agricultural practices. Instead, it requires the farmer to be more knowledgeable about his farm's ecosystem and recognize its place in his life and society's. In most cases, sustainable agriculture simply implies diversification rather than specialization. The objective is long term self-sufficiency to sustain the farm environment and to reduce economic as well as environmental costs.

Low input sustainable agriculture is hampered by federal economic programs that do not recognize it----for example, the rotational system used by alternative-method farmers, who end up sacrificing income support payments available to conventional farmers. For decades conventional farmers have received federal economic incentives that distort their profit picture. What they need instead are economic incentives to change their current unsustainable practices. The Kerr Center for Sustainable Agriculture, Poteau, Oklahoma, July, 2000

....

A Faustian bargain with the water is now coming due; it created a prosperous irrigation economy based on levels declining ten times faster than any recharge. But we have no historical experience from which to predict the future of high production industrial agriculture or the small-time farmer on the High Plains without the continuous massive infusions of groundwater. Nor have pragmatic alternatives been devised, much less tested. Pumping the Ogallala remains a one-time experiment. Opie, J. "OGALLALA: Water for a Dry Land." University of Nebraska Press, 1993, p.294

Farm Journal

08 September 2009

Nice morning with Luke at Oxbow Farm; the edge is off—he'd been a little guarded most of the times I've visited the farm (maybe just preoccupied). Whatever, he takes a bit of time to make up his mind and is protective of himself, and the farm; in good ways.

He is clearly the manager/administrator and works hard at keeping the details organized. And yet, he is compelled to go out into the fields and tend the rows of beets, carrots, cucumbers—whatever has come or is coming on, still despairing over those plants who suffered during our long dose of hot, dry July heat. He still moves his mind like a farmer—things get born—everything dies—some sooner than others.

It is a slow, graceful Pavane these farmers dance—dignified, precise steps whose origins reach back to those first seeds fallen and germinated under the eye of a human transfixed by the wonder of it all—the still miraculous, even after seven thousand years, spectacle of death and regeneration—the quiet, persistent wink of immortality that drove him madly from seed to sacrament to poetry. And, as much a cliché as we have made of it, the regeneration of the seed was the spark to fuel our most desperate hope; that somehow, the death we see all around, stepping and stopping, touching and holding, finding its way to each of us, somehow we too can be reborn—as grain, as all vegetation is reborn; and with that, our many artful frauds are hatched—those myriad paradises which try and fail and try again only to give birth at last to the real crux of poetry—the tragedy that is our relentlessly denied mortality play.

Oxbow Farm

Luke Woodward

13 January 2010

My name is Luke Woodward, born February 5, 1966, in Walnut Creek, California. I was raised in Maranga, a suburb of San Francisco, Oakland Bay Area. A former agricultural area, I would say, but I grew up having nothing to do with agriculture.

It was a very beautiful place, and my dad was in World War II, and came home and went to school on the G.I. Bill and did the whole fifties World War II vet. Got a job with a corporation and raised 2.3 kids—no! Raised three kids, including myself. We were in a nice.... They moved all over the place, but it had a real pretty beautiful area that was surrounded by watersheds. There were reservoirs, so it was all protected, East Bay Municipal Utility District. Our house, out the front yard was just complete suburbia—which is nice, lots of kids, very safe, nice environment to grow up in. My back yard was just miles and miles and miles of wild lands, which was great: hills and cows and horses and oak trees and creeks and reservoirs. So I think I spent my youth getting lost back in the hills part of the time. Then the other part of the time I put bicycle cards in my spokes and rode down to the store and bought SweeTarts and Pop Rocks.

I went to U.C.-Davis Agricultural School—did not study agriculture! Studied international economics, with a minor in communications and rhetoric. Sarah would agree on the rhetoric part. I focused on third world economics and I learned a lot in school, but I think from the day that I received my diploma, I don't think I've done a single thing that has anything to do with my education. I moved up to the Northwest. I love the Bay Area, but I was just getting a little itchy, ready for something new. And my sister and her family had moved up here. I was just starting to get a little bogged down by just the population of the Bay Area. And then the big earthquake happened in '89, and it just was crazy after that. Three of the five major freeways of the whole Bay Area were basically shut down during that time, and so it was right after that, that I moved up here. I wanted to get involved in the environmental movement, and didn't have any history or education or job experience, and so just waited tables for a long time. When I realized I just couldn't find a job in the field, I just started calling people who I thought were doing interesting things, and asking if I could come and just talk to them. And people were really open to that, which was really nice. And so I went around and talked to all these different people who were working in the environmental field, and eventually I ended up with a job at the Pacific Science Center. That was great experience for me and led to other things. I met Sarah. She was a singing and dancing waitress, and I was a bartender.

I eventually started working full time at the Science Center. I started out on the floor, and that was kind of part time, and it only paid like $6 an hour. So I got a gig teaching the after-school science class. I waited tables, I bar tended. I think at one point during that time I had five different jobs, and one of them was bartending on the *Spirit of Puget Sound*, where I met my lovely wife. Lucky me.

And during that time I'd applied to the Peace Corps, and I ended up, Sarah and I were dating, and I ended up going to the Peace Corps anyways. That was a real transformative....you know, it just is so with us to this day. It was nineteen years ago, now, that I went, and sixteen years ago that I came home.

I lived in a small village in Senegal, West Africa. But still, we lived, as they said, "*ahm bush*" or "*chiavi*," in the bush. And I lived in a little village that was a subsistence farming village. I mean, not only did they grow what they would eat for the most part, and raise what they would eat, but their housing was made out of what they ate too. They grew millet and peanuts, and their fencing and their housing was made out of millet stalks, and the roof was made out of bound-together millet chaff. And then they had some cement buildings in the village here and there. And it was a real very simple life, and the people were just so fantastic, so wonderful. And their life was so hard, but they just had this spirit of just kindness and humor and light-heartedness and generosity that I think they needed to have to survive, and it just really gave me a pretty huge perspective on my experience back in the United States. And Sarah ended up coming over to visit, and then came over the second year and got a job in the capital and got to experience that as well. It was just a tremendous experience for me.

Senegal was where I decided to get into organic farming, like so many of the sustainable farmers these days, a lot of us don't come from farming backgrounds. But in Senegal there was just a lot of chemicals, and a lot of the development agencies were promoting fertilizers and pesticides to make life easier, but I had just learned, for instance, that DDT had been banned in the United States, but the manufacturer of DDT had *not* been banned in the United States, it was still being produced in the United States and just shipped overseas to places like Senegal where you would find piles of DDT, crystallized DDT in the market, and these sweet women sitting in front of them, and would pick piles up with their hands and put it into bags, and then we'd go down to our village garden, and I was working with them in the garden.

There was a big garden project. It was a very dry, arid area, very hard to grow anything. And that's a whole other story. You'd see everybody down by the well, and women with babies on their backs, pulling water to drink, while the guys were just, with no mask, no nothing, just spraying clouds of DDT upwind. Clouds of DDT were pouring down toward the well. To them, it made their difficult life a lot easier. It made the crops grow better, and the pests were a big problem, and it really helped, and it was way easier than going out at night with flashlights and squishing the bugs. So that kind of inspired me to get involved my second year, in trying to promote organic gardening practices within the village. It's hard to really, I don't know, coming from the privileged background that I had, to try to articulate to them, "You guys gotta be organic, man!"

It was interesting, because it just so happened that Rodale Institute had at the time I think eight international offices around the world, and one of them just happened to be in Senegal, not even in the capital, in the next big town, which is about an hour away from the big town that we were in. So I got involved with them. And then another French organization that was promoting organic agriculture in Senegal was also in Chaz, which is where the Peace Corps training center was. And I just started contacting them and working with them. There were Senegalese that worked in these organizations, so it was by working with them, and them coming out, it kind of helped bridge that gap a little more, and we started working on composting projects and just getting them understanding this stuff. I just explained to them that this stuff that they were using had been banned in the United States because it was toxic and was killing people and causing cancer and all these problems, but it's still legal here. You know, for being real world people, they understood how the world economy kind of worked that way, and that wasn't like a foreign notion to them.

Some people listened and some people didn't. At any rate it was an eye-opening experience. And not only that, but slowly I realized that the area that I was in, the chief of the village, who is, to this day, although he's passed on, is one of my favorite human beings. When he was a boy, the region was forested and there was a river that flowed behind our village, that fed into another big river in the main town. Around the turn of the 20th century, the French colonized Senegal, and the main crop that was grown there was peanuts, and so they realized a great peanut-growing zone. I didn't even realize—peanuts to us are for eating and peanut butter, which was big, but they also set up factories. They make soap and bleach and vinegar and all kinds of different products out of peanuts. Well, as I learned, the mono crop, cash crop world for the north, whereas before the advent of that economy, the culture pretty much grew what they needed to eat themselves or trade locally. And in my opinion, that probably fit into the environment a little better than the cash crop economy did. And once that was introduced, it was the more you could grow, the more money you made, so the trees started to get cut down, and peanuts started to be grown, and there was a big income spike for a little while, and people were really prosperous, and so the population grew, which caused more pressure on the trees for firewood and heating wood, because it would get cold in the winter. So now people say it's desertification, or you often hear in the press in this area that the African people are deforesting, they're chopping their forests down. Well, you know, the real story why they were doing it was to grow peanuts to send north, to Europe and the United States, and Skippy and all kinds of different things.

And so I became aware of that and started to see that. And at least in the north it was peanuts. In the south it was cotton, and that was *real* chemical intensive, and one guy down there, when I was down in the south, said once to me, "You can't eat cotton." So I think I started to realize, "Ah, that's what goes on all over the world, is that people are displaced." I think that's what the Zapatistas are all about. So that just inspired me to want to come back and get an internship on an organic farm and be a farmer someday. Little by little, it ended up working out.

It's incredibly easy to get very depressed about the state of the world. But you know, what can you do but try to keep putting good energy into it, and try to do good in your own little way, and support the things that you believe in with your money and your heart and your hands, and promote them.

So I came back, and I think like Sarah said, we always had the goal of being farmers and how to get to that we weren't really sure. So we got internships on farms. We wanted to get back to the land and have a community, and all that. And so we worked on farms in California, and then moved up to start this bakery, thinking that could be a business that would spin itself into us being able to have some land to supply the bakery, and that didn't quite work out the way that we'd planned. Although it's quite interesting, that full circle, the sister and brother-in-law that we started the bakery with now have the Grange Café in Duvall, which is supplying all local organic—or not necessarily all organic—but all local sustainable product for the most part. And so that's an interesting turn of events.

> The Zapatista Army of National Liberation is a revolutionary group based in Chiapas, the southernmost state of Mexico. Chiapas is one of the richest states in Mexico but suffers from massive inequality and poverty. Since 1994, they have been in a declared war "against the Mexican state", although this war has been primarily nonviolent. Their social base is mostly rural indigenous people but they have some supporters in urban areas as well as an international web of support. Their ideology combines libertarian socialism, libertarian municipalism and indigenous Mayan thought. They align themselves with the wider anti-globalization, anti-neoliberal social movement and seek indigenous control over their local resources, especially land.

So when the bakery didn't really work out, Sarah had a job as a gardener, and then got the job at Seattle Tilth. I knew we couldn't suddenly buy land and start farming, so I thought, well, what I should do is become a carpenter and start learning those skills, and I know those skills will come in handy for me if we ever do get to our dream of being able to have or run a farm. I think I spent two weeks at a desk in my whole life. I just knew that I didn't want to do that, from an early age. I saw the stress. My father died at an early age when I was fifteen, and I just saw that he was a very good, sweet man that came from the hills in Placerville, and I don't think he was ever really very happy in his 9 to 5 corporate downtown job, and his commute. And I think that that in part, as well as not good health, caused an early death for him. And so I always took that with me.

I was down in California trying to work on farms and I got injured and couldn't work for a little while and had to do something, and so I worked in an insurance office doing a temp job for two weeks. I was supposed to stay, but one day I just got up and walked out and left and I never went back. That's the only time I've sat at a desk. And I just knew that making money wasn't necessarily a passion for me, but living, working with my hands, and trying to help do work that would promote good. And so I got the job as the carpenter and worked at that for a while, and was planning on sticking with that, just because I believed in the trades. I still do, I think it's a great occupation for any young person, is to be in the trades. It gives you a sense of fulfillment. And this opportunity came up where we didn't necessarily start our own farm, but the opportunity came to us where this family, the Albergs, had this piece of property, and they just wanted to do something, they wanted to steward the land, and there was an actual job announcement that said a Seattle family is seeking a property manager to try to research planting natives and restoring this land, 100 acres on the Snoqualmie River, and grow crops and put in the infrastructure that's necessary. And I just thought, "God, did I write this job announcement myself?!" This is like my dream job! And it was. And at the time I was also considering going into environmental restoration. Farming and restoration were the two things I was interested in. And it wasn't "come start an organic farm on our property," but that's kind of what they got with us.

I'd just come from working on a farm in California that was a 1,600-acre wilderness preserve called Hidden Villa, that has a working, about fifteen-acre organic farm with animals and crops, but then also has trails and wilderness, and real established educational programs, where school groups, two classes come in a day and do garden activities, do activities with the animals, and then go up into the woods and do environmental activities. I spent a year there and just had a fantastic experience and thought it was a great program. Just trying to fuse the sustainable agriculture with the environment has always been a passion of mine, and I think they go hand in hand. Early on I just thought that food is something that we can all really agree on—conservative, liberal, whatever—anybody appreciates a nice box or basket of home grown, local grown produce. A lot of the neighbors around here that we've had, that aren't necessarily New Age, liberal, organic farmer types, they're really nice, and you show up with a basket of potatoes and carrots that you just harvested that day—and lettuces or whatever—they're going to be very, very appreciative. Food, to me, is kind of the panacea for all our ills, our depressions, and brings community. The farmers market here in Carnation is a great example in this little teeny microcosm of the community coming together and having a good time. It's what we need more of, in this country especially. And we need to eat better, clearly.

The first year we started, it was just me, with a lot of Sarah's help, because she had more experience with growing food, and she pretty much steered the ship, and I just kind of did the work. And then I started to learn about it as well. I was more the infrastructure guy. I could put the plumbing in and build the little sheds and do all the stuff we needed to do, and put up the fencing, and drive the tractor. And the first year we actually put in.... You know, we didn't know—we tilled, we should have plowed. Created a huge weed problem for ourselves, but that was all right, we turned up some land and planted most of it to cover crop and started a little garden that was probably an eighth of an acre, and put in some crops. We didn't have a greenhouse, we didn't have water, we didn't have electricity, but we just pumped out of the lake. Actually, that was a really wet summer so we didn't really have to water too much. And we would harvest the food and take it all into Seattle. And at the time we were also remodeling our house. That had started before this opportunity came, so we were staying in a friend's house who was away for the summer. We would bring all the food back, and we had this big Styrofoam box that we would fill up with water, and then in their front yard we'd wash all the produce and distribute it. We had twelve CSA customers, and distributed it at my sister and brother-in-law's bakery. That was the year of the squash, the zucchini. And there's two people from that first year that have been in the CSA every year since, that are still in it.

Mike and Molly and Barrack and Nancy, thank you, original members of the Oxbow Farm CSA. At the time it was Alberg Farm, and then we changed the name to name it after the Oxbow Lake, which is kind of the central feature of the property. And it's grown really incrementally and naturally since then. In some ways we need to grow into ourselves now. Our operations need to grow into our size. The first year we had twelve CSAs, a small garden. The next year we kind of got it down a little more. We had thirty CSA members, and that first year it was just maybe about ten weeks. That second year we did a twenty-week CSA with thirty members and went to a farmers market—pulled that off pretty well. Sarah was more involved then. I think it was the third season that they hired Sarah full-time. We grew the CSA again, and went to another, started the Ballard Farmers Market in that second year. We just were able to grow, little by little. Got our first intern. And it's just grown pretty naturally. It wasn't even a science. Each year we thought, "Okay, we can expand what we did last year. Let's just do half again what we did last year." So we ordered half again as many seeds, and planted half again as much acreage, and didn't really have a lot of science to it, just did it, and thought, "Okay, we did this with this many people, then we need one more person."

It was kind of customer driven. Now, with the economy, and now there's a lot more people doing it. For the glory years, it just seemed like anything we grew, we would sell. We couldn't grow enough. We just could set the prices really high, and sell like crazy. And now things are a little different, so you have to innovate, like any business does. About three years ago we had a little girl, Pearl, and so Sarah stepped out of the full-time operation, and then Adam came in. Suddenly there were two guys, instead of a guy and a gal, and the guys were like, "Let's grow more! Bigger! Let's get more tractors!" That's kind of what happened. And he had more experience with bigger acreage and mechanical cultivation and more machinery, whereas I was more kind of the carpenter, infrastructure. He had more of an engine mechanic background, as well as great farming experience. And so we've kind of taken over the mantle. And we did really expand the acreage and what we were doing—and this year we're not. We really expanded what we were doing last year, and realized we didn't really have the infrastructure to keep up with it. We did, but it was pretty crazy. And this year I think we're just gonna hold steady, and our philosophy is to just keep doing exactly what we're doing until we get it down, and then we'll grow once we get it down and we figure out how exactly *to* grow. That's where we are at this point.

You know, most farms have such a slim margin, and you hear that—if you go to business school, they'll tell you that your labor should be at about 30-35 percent. Well, pretty common for a farm of our ilk is 50-60 percent. I think last year ours was maybe 65 percent, and that was because we had a lot of equipment go down, and a lot of problems, and we had to do a lot more hand labor than really we should have. That's not to say that those employees should be displaced, but we would have rather those employees were just harvesting and washing produce for sale, rather than out there weeding and hand fertilizing and stuff like that—organically, of course.

The thing about this farming community that is so admirable, is that none of us are in it to get rich. It's just something that we believe in, and most of the farmers really believe in the movement, and they're giving back. The farming is incredibly hard work, but then you've got people like Sarah and myself, and the farmers who actually are involved now with Sno-Valley Tilth and are coming to meetings and volunteering to put on fundraisers to try and further the education—not to benefit just themselves and their own farms, which it does in the long run—but just because we believe so strongly in the movement and what it means for society. Somebody was just saying they were at the QFC on Redmond Ridge, and now it's not just the organic section, but they have the local organic section now. I haven't seen it, but I just heard about it. That's really heartening. Sometimes you can step back and be like, "Aw, it's still a drop in the ocean." But at first it *was* just, "Oh, I want to eat organic for my health," and now it's people are starting to really see the big picture and how the industrial food industry is toxic. That's not to discredit the family farmers who are raising corn in the Midwest and have been struggling for years to just get by. I don't know what that's like. My hat is off to them and I have a lot of respect for conventional farmers as well as organic farmers. And I think a lot of those people, if they suddenly could switch completely to organic, probably would, because farmers understand what's going on in this country too. You get strapped when you don't know what else to do—no disrespect to the conventional farmers of the world. It's more our system that needs to change, and it's the people who need to do it, because the companies are making so much money they're not going to stop. They don't care about the food and the farming. They're so removed from it.

    I think people are coming around to realizing that, you know, paying for food is really important. I mean, I think as an industrialized nation, we're last on the list of percentage of income that we pay for our actual food. That's too bad. You see that in the rise of the diabetes and cancer and obesity and all the health problems we're having in this nation. But sadly, when people are making money off our bad health, we can't rely, I think, on the government and the corporate structure to make things work. It's individuals who are going to have to make those choices. And so little by little it's happening and turning around.

    Three years ago we were struggling to find people to come be interns on the farm. The last two years, the inquiries have just been phenomenal. Some internships have more of an educational slant. We don't really do that, it's just kind of like your education is by doing. Just by working on the farm you're gonna.... You know, we're not gonna take an hour or half a day and just sit down and go over books and different things. It's just your education is getting in there and doing it. And so our internship, as it stands right now, which hasn't really been in operation, because we've had the same guy back for two years, and he's pretty experienced. He's more of an employee, just lives on the farm. We have one trailer, and it's a stipend, and you come in and you work five days a week, and you're working pretty much in all aspects of the farm. When it first starts, you're in the fields, weeding, planting, maybe working in the greenhouse, pretty much in all capacities where we need you. Then you go to market. You're driving. A lot of young people who come to it, they want to learn everything about it, they want to start their own farm, and they want to know about the finances, and how do you order it, and how do you plant it, and how do you do all that? You just can't learn all that in a year. And then the first thing you have to understand is just how the day-to-day.... You know, understand the work and understand how to use a shovel, and all that. It's amazing how a lot of people don't really know how to use a shovel. They think they do, but then they don't actually.

    They are paid, and they're paid a stipend, and then they're given free room and board. It varies from $600 to $1,000 a month. But then you factor in free room and board, and then food from the farm, it works out pretty well.

Being a non-profit farm is an interesting new development, and it's great. To be honest, it's the family. And I think that they have always really thought that what we were doing was great, but they're busy, they've got their own lives, they're not farmers, they live in Seattle. Tom's the head of this venture capital company. He's very, very busy, and Judy's involved in all kinds of things—that's his wife. They're busy, and so I don't think that they ever really.... They thought it was neat what we were doing, and something to talk about, but they didn't really get it. I shouldn't say that. They were just busy with other things. But in the last few years, they've really become really interested and knowledgeable about what's going on—not only on our farm, but just with the sustainable food movement in general. They read *"The Omnivore's Dilemma"*. We read it, and I learned tons of stuff by reading *"The Omnivore's Dilemma"* that I didn't know before, and highly recommend it to anybody. Their kind of line of interest and involvement in the property has evolved in the last few years, just into a great area. Now they see it as just this fantastic thing that we're doing, and they want to further the message, so they've turned us to a nonprofit status, just to become more of a research education facility. And it's a phenomenal spot for doing that, and I'm really, really excited about it: not only bringing kids in and trying to give them an experience with environmental education and sustainable farming, but also doing on-farm research to promote organic sustainable methods to make it more accessible to more people, and to try and promote the economy, and just promote the movement in general, which is what it takes for it to grow.

And so again, back to labor, I hope that for young kids it's a viable option. I think if this economy could really grow on a local level, that there's more access to work in the sustainable food industry that could actually allow you to raise a family and have that as a career, that's a goal of ours. And if we had an infrastructure in place where people could come out and work on a farm and feel good about themselves, I think it would just do great things.

I think it's a big inspiration that Sarah and I both had many, many years ago as we saw a woman named Katherine Sneed speak at the Bioneers, one of the first Bioneers conferences in San Francisco. She was this woman who, I believe—I don't have the whole story, but from what I remember—grew up in Hunter's Point—not Hunt's Point, but Hunter's Point in San Francisco, which is a pretty rough area, but just a beautiful community. No access, a lot of violence, a lot of crime, a lot of drugs, no good food, no trees, convenience stores and fast food is it. But a lot of those neighborhoods spawn just amazing community as well, and great positive people working for change. I take it she was probably involved in that, because if I remember correctly, she was diagnosed with cancer, she wasn't given much time to live. She went totally on a macrobiotic organic diet and was cured. I don't know if I have that story right, but that's how I remember it. It inspired her just to see what was going on in her community, and she started an organic farm at the San Francisco County Jail—and it's still there, and it's still operating. We went to it, and it had these criminals who came from these horrible backgrounds, who knew nothing but cement and violence and roughness, suddenly they're raising a little seedling and planting it and seeing it grow into a broccoli, and harvesting it and eating it, and it was really transformative. You know, they'd had nothing to nurture, nothing that counted on them, or no one they could count on, and suddenly their responsibility, their hands are in the dirt, and "this little plant is my responsibility." So it had an incredibly successful result—so successful that they started a post-release garden in Petrero Hill that's still going, and they would hire inmates to work and grow food and sell it. And then they also did a landscape and arborist training program, that the City of San Francisco is using for contracting companies that would hire people.

And so it's just this incredible story. One of the directors now.... When we were down visiting, which was years ago, one of the main gardeners was this *huge* black fellow who had grown up a pretty violent guy, and his life had turned around. He was just this amazing horticulturalist now, just this big, huge, sweet guy. That story in and of itself, I just think that was a huge inspiration for what the land and good food and getting back to it, and giving more people the access could do for our depressed, violent, overweight, unhealthy, isolated society. That's not everybody, but you know....there is a lot of us. And we're all that way, even me at times. I don't know if that's a little too preachy, but that's what I feel.

We have paid workers and so it seems like most farms have to rely, because there's such a thin margin, have to rely on intern labor, but you know, we're really trying. Adam and I are both paid. We're really trying to create a farm economy that supports paid labor. Still, we pay $10-$12 an hour, which is a lot, but is not a lot. I remember being on a panel with Tom Douglas last year—he's a big restaurateur here. He supports local farms a lot, but he was kind of listing all the reasons why it might be difficult. "I have a company. I'm paying healthcare," this and that. It's like, "Well, that's great, but none of the farmers you want to support have healthcare, and if you really want to support farming, you've got to just buck up and be willing to pay a little more and be a little more flexible." It's not just that they're, "Oh, we've got this local organic farm thing. It looks good for my menu." There's a lot of chefs out there that are like that, and they're a pain in the ass to deal with. But then there's a lot of chefs that are really dedicated and get it: Peter Burke at Ray's Boathouse, John Sundstrom of Lark, Maria Hines from Tilth, you know. Seth Caswell.

Most farmers have to pay for their own healthcare. We're fortunate to be offered it, but we're paying for.... Up until Sarah started doing this, we're paying for Pearl's healthcare, and none of our labor has healthcare. We can't keep them employed year round. So it is really a goal. Someone like Full Circle, they *are* keeping people employed year round, and that's great. They're really creating a pretty big business. Someday, if we had more of an infrastructure and just more behind it, we could grow year round, I think, but it's just too difficult right now.

I kind of like where we are now. I think we have room to grow. That's part of me. You asked Sarah if we'll always be farming, and I feel like now there's times when I'm like, "God, wouldn't it be great just to have a job that you go home and forget?" But now that we farm and kind of know how to do it fairly well, I feel like I really enjoy it. It's easy to say in January. In the middle of July it can be pretty—especially August, September—it's pretty exasperating, but still rewarding. But I feel like we kind of owe it. I just have these skills now, and I feel like I just have to keep producing food for people. And out along the lines, how big do you want to get? It seems we have more land than we could grow on. And I want to do it healthily for everybody involved: myself, my family, all the work, the land, the environment around us. So there's part of me that's, "Oh, let's just keep doing what we're doing." But I think little by little, I think we'll grow if we can, because, you know, why not?

It's all about choice and economy, and you look just in this Valley alone, how much gorgeous farmland there is. I mean, we can put people on the moon. You think about how sophisticated and complicated, and we just gave $800 billion to a multi-billion-dollar industry, and if we wanted to just change our tune and just say, "Hey, why don't we put $100 million into creating university extension programs where people are actually starting farms and providing food for the local populace?" I mean, just this Valley alone, which is a stone's throw from a major population center. I don't know what percentage of it is being farmed for food, but all you gotta do is drive up and down the Valley and you see empty fields everywhere. And it's beautiful farmland, so a lot more food could be grown locally here.

If we suddenly wanted to make it happen overnight, the government would need to be involved, and people would say, "That's communism! That's socialism! You can't do that!" But that's kind of crazy. You know, our tax dollars are going, *my* tax dollars are going to all kinds of things I don't really want them to go to, so I would love to know that my tax dollars were going to creating institutions that were setting up local food systems and growing local food systems. But with the free market the way it is, it is a lot easier for a gigantic corporation to grow a thousand acres of one thing and spray it with a bunch of chemicals. And now chemical companies are making a lot of money, and they're all in.... And there's people who work for it, but there's not nearly as many.... There's not nearly as many people as who would be working in a local food system. It's just we're so far into this economy that we have now, that the thought of changing it is pretty complex and daunting. We can do anything if we just set our minds to it. It's just a matter of getting the public behind it. I think nothing's going to happen overnight, but slowly but surely I think it can. I mean, it'll have to. Sometimes I think, I don't know, we're screwed. But I'm still gonna keep working, trying to do good.

And then as far as the rest of the world is concerned, you know, most of the people around the world know how to grow their own food. But this so-called green revolution is displacing people from growing their own food. They say we need corn to feed the world, but really what's happening is in India, in Senegal where I was, the whole north was growing amazing amounts of rice, displacing people from growing their own food, and growing rice. None of the rice stayed in Senegal, it was all exported. And they imported cracked cheap rice from Pakistan and Thailand. And they're getting displaced from good farmland, to put cattle, to raise hamburgers for McDonald's in the north. So by promoting genetically engineered rice in India they're displacing diverse village farming societies that are growing and supplying their own food for their own economy, to grow a mono crop for the world cash economy.

I'm no agricultural economist, but I know that people know how to grow food, and if they're allowed to, especially in the third world, rural areas, that they can do it. But a lot of those people are getting displaced. Like in Senegal, it was the peanuts. They used to be able to grow food there, but now it's a desert. That was created by humans, and the green revolution kind of cash mentality. So I don't have much stake in that sustainable organic agriculture can't feed the world. I think it can. It takes thought, though, and it takes a new way of thinking. And it takes more compassion, and I think just letting people be. And it takes getting us away from this huge global economic mess that we're in, and trying to focus more on our local communities.

Sarah and Adam and I are just gonna keep farming.....just gonna keep doing. I think we've landed in a pretty amazing place. You know, we've got a great community here now. I mean, all these farmers, and it's just a pretty good life.

Sixty percent of water used nationally goes toward agriculture. California's Central Valley produces the substantial bulk of the nation's fruits, nuts, and vegetables yet receives virtually no rainfall during summer months, relying overwhelmingly on irrigation. But the snowpack on the Sierra which provides much of that irrigation water is declining, thanks again to global warming, and the aquifer that supplies much of the rest is being drawn down at many times its recharge rate. If these trends continue, the Central Valley may be incapable of producing food in any substantial quantities within two or three decades. Other parts of the country are similarly overspending their water budgets, and very little is being done to deal with this impending catastrophe. Richard Heinberg, "Fifty Million Farmers", Twenty-Sixth Annual E.F. Schumacher Lectures, October, 2006 (**Author's note: As of this writing, no comprehensive studies have been completed regarding the water table for any of the agricultural areas in Washington State.**)

Adam McCurdy

14 January 2010

My name's Adam McCurdy and I was born in Portland, Oregon, October 1, 1976. I was born in southeast Portland and grew up just not necessarily inner city but not suburban either, in the nice town of Portland, Oregon, right off the Willamette River there. Grew up doin' what kids do. Baseball was a passion. That was kind of my early, I guess, lesson in self-motivation, and passion, and setting goals for one's self, and compassion—all those things we live by. Graduated from Franklin High School there in, I guess it was 1994 I think, maybe '92. Didn't go right off to college. At that point I was kind of not sure what my passion was, but I was still playin' baseball, had been thinkin' that maybe I might not be goin' to the show anymore, but I didn't really know what was happenin', but didn't want to fall into the just goin' and gettin' into debt and goin' to school since I didn't know what it was I wanted to go to school for. So I worked for a couple of years out of school, just blue collar, workin' at a waterworks and irrigation place, which is applicable to farming now—just an understanding of moving water from "A" to "B" and pipe fittings and pressure regulators and things along those lines. Learned how to drive a forklift there. From there, as far as recreation went, I was just really into partying quite a bit with my friends, going to shows, music. Portland is a wonderful city for the ocean, the mountains, the desert. Similar to Seattle here, you go in any direction and you've pretty much got one of nature's wonders right there. Spent a lot of time up at the foothills of Mount Hood. Never got into technical mountain climbing, but a lot of camping and a lot of sittin' by rivers, and poetry and reading and playing harmonica. I haven't advanced in my harmonica playing since I was about nineteen. But if I'm sittin' by a loud babbling brook, I can really rock!

But from there, I wanted to figure out, without workin' at a ski lift or workin' at a restaurant how I could move out of the city and move closer to the out of doors. So I found AmeriCorps. Amazing programs. I ended up moving to Trout Lake, Washington, right at the base of Mount Adams. Just phenomenal experience there. I was working with the Forest Service in a lot of different programs; working with local schools out there. Again, it was kind of my first hit of moving into the rural realm. I started to get into some environmental education, all the while completely learning about the environment myself and educating myself. And got into trail work there, got into environmental education, got into natural resource preservation, spotted owl surveys. Started doing some work with carpentry as far as a kind of rough cut, you know, log ladders and log bridges and using resources in the area of the trail you were building. I got into some chainsaw work, small machinery maintenance. You know, all of those are skills that I use every day now—or maybe not every day, but every other day—something comes up where it's handy to at least fire up the chainsaw, fix that tiller, or this or that. I really loved that.

It was a year-long program. So that kind of began the journey of seasonal living and seasonal work, which in a professional realm has proven to be a bit challenging, because you think about simplicity in life, and you think about how you're going to be bringing in your income in this day and age where you're being spoon fed to go into debt and support the world around you. How do you stay hand-to-mouth and not be a backwoods recluse? And as a raging Libra, balance has been something that I've been seeking my entire life—not to put my values on other people, but I believe in some degree we all do, conscious or subconscious, and active or passive. So that was kind of the onset of that from there. I also really, as I mentioned earlier, I love traveling. Any chance I got, "Hey, I'm not gonna go to college, I'm gonna go work and make some money. I'm eight to five, honey, and I'm bustin' my hump." And I really enjoyed that, I love workin' hard. But I couldn't wait until the weekend came to go check out the Columbia Gorge, to go check out a new spot on the ocean, to go check out the mountains. And so after my year up at Trout Lake I was a backwoods wilderness ranger. I stayed there for the winter, just pickin' up odd jobs, a lot of chainsaw work and this and that. Then that next summer I was a backwoods wilderness ranger, in the beautiful wilderness areas around Mount Adams, and in that whole national forest, and that was a wonderful experience that I wanted to continue on with. So I did another year in AmeriCorps and went out to Maine. It was a great experience, because I was really the only one who was in the residential AmeriCorps program. So most everyone there was *from* Maine, and everyone kind of still lived with their folks, or they were still living in their college housing because they were kind of overlapping all of that.

I didn't have enough money to be renting a place. I was hitchhiking around—I would work, and wherever we worked was where I would live. And we'd work, it was a great thing in that we would do programs in a certain region for about a month, month and a half, sometimes ten days on and then we'd have a week off. So it worked out just great for me as far as traveling around and seeing different areas. I got to see more areas of Maine in a year than I did my whole lifetime living in Oregon. I did a semester of college there, which I would say at this point I probably have sophomore status now, as far as college goes, and I've just pieced that together over the years. I had done a semester in park recreation. That could have led down some roads to park management, but it was very much in natural resource management and environmental education and continuing on with those things. So that was wonderful. And actually, in the kind of nomadic living that I was doing in the hitchhiking and the tenting and all that, I spent a lot of time camping on the edge of fields, and a lot of potato fields up around mid to northern Maine. And I was spending all my time out in the woods, starting to be curious about, "Oh, I just sprained my ankle! How do I heal without Tylenol?" As I'm sleeping and I wake up and I hear this tractor fire up. I look out across the field and I say, "What *is* this field? I'm sure that the potato bread that I just bought at Safeway has nothing to do with the potatoes that are being grown here." And so just slowly there was starting to be a link between the value that I was finding in the natural world, and the disconnect that I was probably needing, the disconnect of the supplies I was needing to survive in that world. So my Lipton soup packets to go off into the woods for two weeks. I don't go without Advil and Tylenol, in case I blow out my knee or sprain my ankle, so I can get back to an area where I can get some medical help. And so it spurred a strong interest in herbal healing: what are the plants growing around me, so ethnobotany; it fired me right into that. I didn't even need to go to school for a year and pay thousands of dollars to do so. So I've always been a firm believer in learning from experience. That's proven to be a little challenging when I've decided, "Okay, well maybe I'd like to buy a house. Oh, what's my job? Oh, I'm a farmer. How much do I make in a year farming? Ooo."

A lot of people ask me, now that I am farming and I'm in my twelfth year of farming, "How did you get into farming? Did you grow up on a farm?" "No." I grew up with a small…. My dad was very much, and wasn't intentionally into organic gardening…. Well, he was, but it wasn't a coined term. And so I grew up with my dad gardening. And after I got into farming, I realized that I planted my first—you know, carrots have always been my favorite, which is kind of a coincidence, because at Oxbow where Luke and I have grown 15-20 acres of produce, carrots are really kind of one of the crops we're known for. Our logo is a carrot. And that's been through the evolution of the beginning of Oxbow with Luke and Sarah, workin' that. And then now us growing together. And so I found out that I was growing carrots, I planted my first bed of carrots when I was about four. So I had no memory of even, "Hey, I really love gardening. I'd like to get, quote unquote, 'back to the garden.'" But once I started farming, it was amazing, and the conversations that my dad and I could have. It was a real honor to be able to start teaching him about soil science and seed germ plasm and growing cycles and seed saving—all of it. And so that kind of got inspired when I was in Maine, on the edge of these fields. Spent a lot of time out in the woods and thinking, "What is the connection?" And I had my first thought there of "What's our food system, where do we get our food?" When I went to the supermarket, I was totally unaware of farmers markets, I didn't know the coined terms of permaculture and organic and all of that, which is so funny to think about, because that was fifteen, sixteen years ago. And now I'm eatin', sleepin', breathin', teachin', learnin', all of that! It's also been a real growing movement, so it's been a great time to get into that.

I was actually working in a recycling plant at that point. My AmeriCorps program was volunteering there occasionally, but I really connected with the fellow who ran it, who ended up being an organic farmer in Maine. And I had forklift driving experience from my waterworks and irrigation experience, so I started working with Ed—Ed Hamill was his name—I don't know if he's still farming—but I started working with him. In the process in the recycling plant, moving around the pallets of recycled goods and loading up trucks of all of this, my skill really helped him out, he pretty much was volunteering, but. It was a do-good thing from his end as well. So with him I started learning about organic farming. There were a few county fairs, and we would go to some farms around and glean some of their excess produce to sell at the fairs, that would go to donate to that township. It was very interesting. And I would go to these different fields. It was just very early touches of that.

And from there, I ended up moving back to the Northwest. My aunt and uncle lived here in the Snoqualmie Valley, which is how I ended up back here. All I knew of Seattle though was from holidays, family weekends. My aunt and uncle lived out here in Carnation: Germaine St. Germaine. When she married my uncle, it was Germaine Findley, and my uncle Michael Findley. My uncle and I were like best buds.

It was clear to me that I needed to get back out of the city, so I went to Hawaii for about six months. My mom grew up in Hawaii, so I have some roots in Hawaii, roughly—*haole* roots. There, I was checking out farming, and with my trail work and my little interest in farming, I found some real trippers gettin' back to the land, and helped them terrace hillsides and plant this and that. We'd go around gleaning avocados and macadamia nuts. It was very romantic at that point. Didn't need to make any money, other than just a little bit here and there, which I could do by bustin' my hump for someone for a week. That old simplistic life.

From there I was thinking about my AmeriCorps funds, because in volunteering for AmeriCorps I had not accumulated student loans, so all of a sudden I had this money that I had to spend on school. It was great, because I love learning, but I didn't want to go into debt to do so. So I had $10,000. It was a lot of money. It had a lot of restrictions on it, how I could spend it, and $10,000 in the education system is a spit in the bucket—a spit to the side of the bucket. So I started thinkin' about that. I was looking at schools in Hawaii because I thought, "Oh, how cool, if I could start to set up some connections here, and live so close to the ocean." But energetically, I didn't necessarily feel it. And looking at the school programs and where my funds could go, I didn't see too many links. So I started thinking, "Man, I've always just visited my uncle on the weekends. What if I could go live with my uncle for a while?" And I know there's a whole lot of agriculture going on in the Snoqualmie Valley. I know there's still some dairy farms goin' on, and boy I'd like to learn how to work with cows. It's not really my forte, but I could spend some time milkin' some cows and schleppin' through some shit. But more so, I'd like to just go live with my uncle and I know that I could make somethin' work. I'd like to pick up some carpentry skills, I'd like to keep learning machinery skills, and I'd like to be close to farming. Sure enough, we had some dialogue, and it sounded like it was gonna work just great. And also at that point I knew that there were more schools back here on the Big Turtle Island than there were on the little islands of Hawaii, and I could use those funds. Ironically enough, I used my funds through a school in San Francisco, but I used them primarily to go study and travel in Thailand, which is now a huge part of me.

So I moved back to the Snoqualmie Valley for, boy, I guess it ended up bein' a couple of years, two and a half years, because when I moved back, I was living with my aunt and uncle, which was just wonderful quality time together. Great time of my life to do it, wasn't stressed about "what am I doing with my life?" I'm living here in this little trailer in the back yard, and they weren't stressed about it, and so it was just a beautiful, beautiful thing. And I was apprenticing. It was a job, but very low pay. I only had experience maintaining my old Volkswagen, as far as wrenching goes, and the little bit of wrenching that I was talking about through small engines. But I was basically working minimum wage, apprenticing with a mechanic south of Carnation, which was tremendous, tremendous value. The shop is no longer here—Gary's Magic Pro-Lube. He's a great guy.

It was a wonderful time, working with him. I think I only ended up working with him about six months. And again, like so many things I've done in my life, if I stuck it out for a year, what I would have gained. I would be willing to drop a clutch on most vehicles now if I would have stayed there for a year. Right now, it's selected vehicles, and only if it's the right time. But I know enough to say, "Hey, you should farm that job out to a shop." But it was just tremendous, and I use those skills every day on the farm.

So in doing that, and in living here, I ended up making some connections with my buddy John, who's still farming here in the valley, and I started farming with John, John Huschle. Nature's Last Stand is the name of his farm now. We were Cabbage Ranch, which was a continuation of an old farm here in the Valley. I had no business running a farm. I had just helped on a couple of farms. But we ended up getting together and we were good buddies and I wanted to start farming again. I had worked on a couple of his trucks in the shop, so we kind of made the link there, and I stopped workin' in the shop. I was up to my ears in grease, figuratively and literally, and I knew it wasn't for me, I was just pickin' up skills. So then I started farming.

John had farmed on a bunch of different farms at that point, and had started some different operations. So he actually went in a little bit heavy, a little bit over his head for what he could handle, and so I jumped right in and I had experience as a crew leader with the trail work and things along those lines in education, and so I jumped right in, to kind of crew lead. The folks that were comin' out to help, I was showin' them how to do things, and they would ask me questions. "What's the life cycle of these onions?" I'd say, "Well, as far as I understand...." I'd spell it out. But then that would inspire me to realize that well, I was very limited in what I could explain to them, so I wanted to learn more. What *is* the life cycle of these onions? What does it mean to be a "set" instead of a "start," a "seedling"? So we worked together, just chewin' on it wholeheartedly for a couple of years. And then in my third year together with John, I started to think, "Maybe this is a good match, we can go into business together," but I had all these curiosities. What are other farming systems? and this and that. So at that point I was somewhat of an intern there, but I took on way more responsibility than an intern would, because it was a small enough operation, and it was roots enough.

You know, it's amazing the support and the interest in the resurgence of agriculture right now, and the almost celebrity status of folks that are farming. It's neat. From our end as farmers, it's a real honor. But if you're not careful, you're *so* overcommitted. And even if none of that was going on, and you were just working with your customers, your employees, your interns if you've got an internship program, and growing your products, your fields, your soil, the roots of your livelihood, you're completely maxed out. Even if you're solo, or you've got a support team, no matter what your scene is, you're pretty darned maxed-out. Like anyone can see, growin' a garden at the height of the summer, your garden is a lot of work, even if you thought that you were conservative in sowing your seeds in the spring.

So it's very interesting, now that I'm operating Oxbow Farm with Luke, and we're going into our fourth season together, and when I came on three years ago, technically now, in the winter of going into the fourth season, four seasons ago, we were cultivating, oh, between five and seven acres. And now we're, depending on when you look at the fields, as far as what's in production during the time of year, we're between fifteen and twenty acres. So in those few years, we took the operational skills that I've gathered from going around and working on different farms and operations, to the evolution and what Luke and Sarah were building there at Oxbow Farm, and the fact that Luke has been there since the beginning, twelve seasons ago, for Oxbow Farm—I mean, there's a lot that has gone on, on that land. The current landowner and what's going on there, that started twelve years ago with just a little garden plot. They had, I think, three or four CSA members. And at that point, Sarah wasn't even working with Luke. Sarah was still the plant lady, working with Seattle Tilth. But working with Luke, yes, they were partners. If you're farming and you've got a partner in life, you're working together on that farm. So it's been a tremendous evolution.

My third year with John, as I said, I was curious about other farms, and Luke had come down and we had met each other through the farming community. And so Luke used to come down to the fields where John and I were working. We were sharing seed notes. "How do you grow this? What's the spacing? What do you space broccoli at? When do you start it in the greenhouse? Do you direct seed your peas, or do you start 'em in the greenhouse? What happens if the pigeons come and pull up every one of your transplants?" And so we all really started farming together twelve seasons ago, eleven years ago. So that was amazing. And so in my third year of farming in the Valley, I split my time with John. At that point he was Nature's Last Stand, so we were Nature's Last Stand. And at that point, Sarah was working with Luke, so it was Luke and Sarah, and John, that I was workin' with, and I was still livin' with my aunt and uncle. So here I was, loose visions, loose dreams, but I was livin' back in the Snoqualmie Valley. That's what connected me back here, and I was farming at Oxbow Farm and with John at Nature's Last Stand.

In that year, some things had happened. I was working farmer's wages, which are real low. It's super difficult. Now I am, and I have been for some time in different capacities: I'm an employee, but I'm also an employer, so I have to hire folks and work out those wages. It's very difficult, because people work very, very hard, and we wish that we could pay them more. So if it's someone who doesn't care about growing food and farming in that movement, then the farm really isn't the place for them, because you really can't compensate them monetarily for their work. It's very difficult to do so, I should say. Some people have figured it out, but very difficult.

I was making really low wages, I needed to make some more income. Thankfully I had other skills to do land clearing type stuff. And so I found some other work that would bring in some more income. That season I had to stop farming with both Oxbow and Nature's Last Stand. I was in a partnership with now my beloved wife, Shira, and we moved back down to Portland because she was in midwifery school. I wasn't committed to anything, but I was on my farming path. I was committed to Shira, but still in the early stages of that.

When we moved back down there, I was still workin' on "What am I gonna do with these AmeriCorps funds?" They're gonna be expiring soon. I worked really hard for the country, for the government, for these communities, I have this $10,000 which is for education, what can I do? I really want to travel. And so I started looking at what I could do. And it was a tremendous feat to pull off, using those funds to go study abroad. But I found a program through San Francisco State University, an extension program that had this wild-land study program in Thailand, and I thought, "Wonderful!"

I didn't know anything about Thailand. I just got all amped up that I could use these funds, and I'd be working with the indigenous people, working with ethnobotany, I'd be working with the agrarian systems. Once I got there, I realized there was a tremendous tourist path. I really didn't want to be on that route, so I really got into the language. I was able to tap in with the growers over there, and got fired up on that. And at the end of the little program we were doing, which was a very great experience because I was really the only individual.... No! There was one other fellow, an older fellow, who had been working, making a living, and then was on that program. Most folks were in the final years of their college years—went to high school, went to college, and then they were on the study abroad program. Everybody was there for different reasons, but a lot of them said, "Hey, we're gettin' credits for our final semester of college, travelin' to another country. Hoo-ha! I worked the system!" And so it was great to see that perspective for me. And for them, to have me in the group was good for them as well, because I wasn't in the college scope. I was farming then, I was doing other things with the land, and just trying to figure out what I was doin', but really tapped into the growing there.

At the end of the program, we had to do an independent study, and it was a no-brainer, especially since I was tied in with education, how could I make that link, what education programs are going on to convert conventional farming practices to organic farming practices here in Thailand? Because Thailand is one of those countries that unfortunately is getting our pesticides with the information packet shipped to them, saying, "Hey, grow this product without pests!" I mean, traditionally, they *all* grew organic, we all did. But in the green revolution, and in the industrialization of agriculture that we have here, in this wonderful developed nation where we got so mechanized so quick, and we came up with all these tricks and all these tools, and we can feed the world, and we can grow all of this without any stinky poop, and without any pests. And then we could get into the whole chemical byproducts of wartime and lah-de-dah. But anyhow, not to go off on all those tangents, Thailand is one of those countries that receives chemical aid. And already we were starting to see bad epidemics of things that are happening from going into this mono-cropping idea, and this chemical Ag. Let's go back to our crop rotations and growing soybeans after we've grown our corn—doing things to replenish the soil through crops rotations and minimizing the monoculture.

So I thought through the educational perspective I could tap right into some farms and do my studies. And sure enough, I was able to. I found a couple of NGOs, non-governmental organizations, which I think is kind of the term for nonprofit internationally. So really, that was wonderful, because I was off for just a couple of weeks to do this program, but that tapped me into a bunch of different regions of agriculture in Thailand, and different farmers, and I wanted to help them. I wasn't on a two-year Peace Corps program. There were some U.S. Peace Corps volunteers as well, coming in with those ideas, and coming in to implement systems. But I wasn't coming from that perspective. I was willing to bend over in the fields with them—not to say that those other volunteers with those organizations *aren't*, but they're coming to help put in water systems, coming in to put in a new crop rotation system. I was curious as to what they were doing, and curious as to what we were doing here in the Snoqualmie Valley with organic agriculture that I had tapped into for a couple of years.

I really started working on the Thai language, which was kind of a ticket into some of the rural areas, because then it showed that I wasn't just on this tourist's path, I wasn't just coming to take a picture of who they were and how they were living, and then ride off into the sunset on my motorcycle. Sunset motorcycle rides were wonderful, but I enjoyed more spending a couple of weeks with those folks and helping them—and helping with the language barrier, teaching them a little English, because they're all curious. I learned a little bit more Thai. Unfortunately it was all regional, so I learned that in this region the word for orange is the word for tomato down in that other region. And so after a while, more confusion than good was coming out of this, but it was a lot of fun, and very valuable education for me. And I still kind of hold onto my heart somewhere that maybe at some point I can end up over there. It would be much less nomadic now. It'd be an experience with my daughter and with my wife, to see how these international Ag systems, how we can bring that together.

So after six months I was missing my sweetie and I came back, and it was back to Portland, and I worked with a friend down there on a farm. He had a seven-acre farm that he had been growin' on for...oh, I can't remember how many years. And I didn't know him at that point, but he and my wife had made a link together because they were fellow herbalists. So I started a dialogue with him in Thailand, because I didn't want to just come back to Portland blank, because there were lots of opportunities for me in Thailand to stay there and carry on. And again, if I would have stayed for a couple of years, my experience would have been entirely different than my six months—just like my time in the auto shop. But if you're curious about the world, there you go.

So I was back in Portland, workin' on the outskirts of Portland in the west hills on this kind of...it was a rural-residential area. Traditionally, a lot of farms out there had supplied a lot of the food supply for Portland, through farmers markets. And there used to be a lot of dairy out there. But fields got paved, fields got built on, there were houses.

You know, it's difficult if you haven't made a living before, to start off now and make your living farming, paying land taxes, being close enough to an urban metropolis to sell your product, if you're going to direct market. To be a small-scale farmer, kind of a balance of "I want to make my living doing it, but I'm kind of on this homestead scale. I want to grow diverse crops, I want to be growing organically, I want to be doing this right social justice thing, and treating the earth right, and treating the community right." You kind of have to direct market, if you're on a small enough scale. You know, there are folks that are doin' it on larger scales. It's the new agri-business, which is a beautiful, beautiful thing. We've got an example of it happening right here in this Valley with Andrew Stout at Full Circle Farm. And then you just break it right on down, to how folks are pulling it off. You've got a lot of farms here in the Valley that are from hundreds of acres to one to two acres, four acres, that are doing it for production. And maybe you're supplementing in the winter, and you're baking. Wow, what a glorious glamorous life: you're the village baker and you're supplying food at your local farmers market. So there's a million and one ways to go about it. But it is very, very challenging. And that was one of the reasons I left this farm in Portland. I did one and a half seasons there, so it was the third season, but it was the half season when I got back from Thailand. I kind of came in mid-season, and then I had that whole next season where I operated the farm in kind of a loose partnership with the fellow who was operating it, to that next year.

He was getting burned out. He wanted to come up with a different idea, different system. Some of the challenges working on that land, not being able to live there, having to pay city rent, having to commute to your farm, all of these things, having the local politics there where you're rural-residential, and we'd get our delivery of compost, and sure enough, the one neighbor next door would be on the line an hour later, "When are you gonna spread that? It's gonna stink like high heaven when you spread it. It stinks like high heaven now. If we get a rainstorm you'd better not let that wash off." There were a lot of challenges that he was pretty much fed up with, I was willing to take on. So I actually took on that operation as my own in the business realm and in the operational realm. So that was, again, a tremendous experience.

So I operated that farm not entirely on my own—I had an amazing crew. On seven acres you've got a lot of balls in the air to juggle. But it was a great experience. Within that time, I was still in touch with everybody up here, and really, pretty much every year Luke and I would talk on the phone, or Luke and Sarah and I would talk on the phone and share notes. "How was your season?" You know. "Did you try any new varieties this year?" Ironically enough, when I ended up not continuing on, on that farm, to take it on for that second year, which was a tremendous heart break, I didn't want to see that farm go, had a lot of nice business relations, wanted to keep supplying those customers, had a *tremendous* amount of support; from the local restaurants, from the weekly customers at the farmers markets, the CSA members. They were just phenomenal as far as not wanting to see you go, you know. Just praising your hard work for the food you're growing. "Oh, my children never liked carrots. Now they *love* carrots." Or, "They never liked lettuce. Now they love lettuce." And in Portland it was really neat, because I got to—a lot of my family members were CSA members. Of course I wanted to help them out, and "Oh, I'll *give* you a share," but it was my business, and they wanted to support my business and they understood, and so they bought a share: my aunt and uncle, my mom and dad, good friends. And I started being able to feed my niece and nephew, now feeding my daughter, feeding ourselves. It really keeps you going, and all the challenges, and all the different things, and trying to figure out how you can keep this rolling. "Oh, it's too stressful, it's so much work, and the income is so seasonal. How can you possibly make a year's income in six months?"

In Portland I could extend my season a tremendous amount. But in the microclimate where I was, the winds would come howlin' through. The thought of puttin' up more hoop houses was a tremendous financial investment where I would really need to come up with a good insurance plan, because I would lose those to big winds. Here we've got the flooding in the Valley. We've got those early fall, late spring, or mid-winter heavy snows. Might not see 'em, we *might* see 'em. You know, you just have to plan for all those natural miracles or natural disasters, however you want to look at 'em. It's super-difficult to figure it out. *Fun* to figure out, but difficult. And so this being said, I had a really hard time not carrying on with the farm in Portland, because I wanted to see it continue to be cultivated, and tried to pass that on. There were still loose ties between the fellow who started the farm and me, and then we were just leasing the land from the landowner, so a lot of parties were involved, and everyone was struggling, wanting to do the right thing. From there I wanted to keep farming, and the movement was happening. As I had mentioned earlier, I have no regrets, but there's times that I thought if I would have gone to school and I would have got into computer programming, and been computer programming for five years, done the right thing, got into investing in the big boom, and I'd just have a little bankroll to sit on, to, "Hey, look at that beautiful piece of land. That's fertile soil. Let's pick that up and in five or ten years I think we could have a system in place enough to where we could be generating income, we could be paying our land taxes, we could build a little house on that raw piece of land."

  A lot of us who are into these sorts of things and local food systems and earth stewardship and all of these things, want to do the right thing in our hard work every day. And everybody works hard in every day: life is beautiful and life is hard. But there's been some thoughts of how could I have done this differently? Pretty much wasted thoughts unless you think, "As I go into tomorrow, how can I do this differently so that if that didn't work out, what didn't work? How can I make this happen for tomorrow?" And so I started to look at the movement that *is* happening, and a lot of the farm link programs, the PCC land trust that's in place, everything that's going on on the East Coast, the West Coast. I was primarily looking West Coast, but from California right on up into Canada, the different programs that were helping first-time farmers get their foot in the door. How can you make this happen? Because at this point, I wanted my own operation, or I wanted to be a major entity within an operation. My back was getting too tired just to be a field laborer. I shouldn't say *just* to be field laborer: field labor is the labor that keeps the wheel of the farm turning, are the spokes inside the wheel. Just from the ground up, figuratively and literally speaking, everything that goes into the farm operation is absolutely necessary, and there's not one of those roles that isn't of tremendous, tremendous value, and a tremendous amount of hard work.

  But I was really looking at how can I make a living doing this? How can I be preserving my body, thinking about the future, thinking about the finances that I'm making while I'm farming, and continuing to be working my passions? And there's a lot of, through the movement of the agriculture these days, there's a lot of programs that are linking. There's old farmers that want to retire because farming is hard, and a lot of the old family farms, the children aren't wanting to take on that farm. They've lived out their parents' dreams of going to college and getting an education and they've gotten some skills that they can work maybe equally as hard, or maybe much less and make a lot more income, just moving with the times.

  So there's these farms that are amazing. There's amazing systems in place, and there's amazing years and years of blood, sweat, and tears, and love that have gone into these fields. I started thinking, "Maybe I should start looking in this realm." I'm young blood and I'm not tied into any place yet. I'm not tied into a bunch of debt. Take a look at what opportunities there are with farmers that want to retire. Originally, when I got into farming, it was one of those things that, as I had said earlier, was a link to the desire that I started to recognize in Maine, and in rural Washington, that I wanted to live a little bit more rurally. And so farming was one of those things that I recognized through those steps that I got very passionate about.

  I ended up going to Twisp, which was very, very rural, eastern Washington. And you want to talk about a short growing season?! You think we're limited with growing seasons here, with the potential early flood, or that early frost, or that late frost, or those heavy winter rains, or those big winds I was speaking about in the west hills of Portland? The Willamette Valley has a much longer growing season than the Snoqualmie Valley here. All of your microclimate, you can work hard and you can extend your seasons, is the term that goes around with season extension ideas.

So out to Twisp. And my wife, Shira Jacobs, who got into midwifery, is a trained midwife and herbalist, her original roots of wanting to do that were wanting to do good through believing in natural home childbirth, and also knowing that she wanted to live rurally, or thinking that she wanted to live rurally, just like I was thinking I wanted to live rurally, and so got into farming. Neither one of those really drove the other one, but they were professions that we had gone into looking for the opportunity to be in a rural setting, appreciating nature and appreciating smaller communities. And so it was a good match. Hey, an opportunity to go very rural.

So we ended up coming back here and living in Twisp and seeing just a tremendous amount of folks that were living out the homestead dream, and growing their food. They had their livestock, the hand built homes that are out there. It's just a beautiful, beautiful, amazing, amazing area, with an amazing community. And so we were tossing around, do we stay out here, do we stay here, do we move there, where do we go from here? And it was one of those things where we still really felt ties to this area. In all of our bouncing around, we've kept links within all of those areas, through friendships and through business relations.

One of those connections, friendships and connections that we've kept is our friendship with Luke and Sarah. They've continually been working on the Oxbow operation. They were pregnant with their little girl, Pearl, and we were at some crossroads, and I was starting to go into kind of my next realm of wanting to continue farming. I know what it takes to operate a farm. I know a lot of the monetary expenditures that are there to buy a piece of land and the cost of doing business. I know kind of from my experience in working, operating the farm in Portland, and then being a major part of these different operations, what it takes to run that business, to get infrastructure in place—you know, those initial capital investments have to come back. And so I knew that we weren't looking to go into a tremendous amount of debt and look for our own place. So we were kind of not back to the drawing board, but looking "where can we go?" Where can we go where we can keep farming and where is there a midwife needed, and an herbalist needed, and just keeping an evolution of our livelihoods together? And so with Sarah being pregnant, and all of us being in touch throughout all these years, it was a real natural transition.

Going back to the beginning, where I had started really farming, got interested, and then started my farming career here in the Snoqualmie Valley, and having made that connection originally with John and Luke and Sarah, and then working with Luke and Sarah at Oxbow, and then with John, making that link all the while. And so I had already worked on this land and been a part of this operation in an entirely different time, and already had an entirely different skill set, but it was a real natural fit, because they would have been hard pressed to find someone to replace Sarah, and those are huge shoes to fill. And I wasn't coming in with the mindset of replacing Sarah at all, but keeping the operation going and the momentum that it's going, and being able to work with a friend, and coming back into a community and an area that we really felt attachment and connection to. So we ended up coming back, and now we're going into our fourth season here.

When I came back and Luke and I teamed up, with everybody else who's a part of this grander Oxbow operation, as it's evolving into a tremendous effort here on this piece of land. We were cultivating five to seven acres, now we're cultivating between fifteen and twenty. Looking at that scale, at least at this point, it seems like a scale that's large enough to supply the demand of still wanting to be, and dabbling in the wholesale market a bit, but wanting to be in the direct market supply, farmers market, CSA, and restaurants, food banks. On the land there's a tremendous amount of restoration. It's a hundred-acre parcel that's been in the family of the fellow who's owned it for years and years. He and his family really want to do everything to preserve the land, they really believe in the movement of sustainable agriculture, they really believe in the movement of education. So there's a lot of different parties involved, and a lot of different individuals working really hard to bring all of these visions together.

The itchy feet have been movin' every single year. Initially itchy feet with commitment in relationship with a loved one. And then having a family together. You know, the marriage, the family, the commitment to farming and how that can happen. And right now it feels like there's no desire to get out of farming. I believe in it.

I'm very proud to be farming. The itchy feet are not there. The challenge and balance of making a living farming, are still very much there—and while growing a family. You know, looking to buy a home, looking at breaking down those monetary commitments, looking at the resources that you've got, looking into the future, and what the cost of living is. King County and the Seattle area is a very expensive place to live. It's very beautiful, and there's a lot of wonderful things going, but it's a very expensive place to live. But right now there's no itchy feet to flee to another place. There is a lot of commitment, and there is a lot of passion and connection here. The farm community here is very strong. And that's a beautiful, beautiful thing, because we just all can really learn from each other.

I have a tremendous amount of appreciation for the journey—in the farming and just in living, and all the wonderful people that I've come across, and the youth that I've learned from and been able to teach, and the elders that I've learned from, and thankfully been able to teach. We all are on this journey so symbiotically, that it's wonderful to be able to keep that perspective. I see the bumper sticker that says "No bad days," and I'm like, "Eh, that sounds pretty dreamy." I'm a very happy individual, and very grateful to have found something that I'm very passionate about, and been able to be living out these passions and dreams in one form or another. As you can hear from the story, in many different forms and others. But I feel very grateful for that, and really 99 percent of the time have that perspective, and just a very positive, positive, bright light outlook in being able to continue on with this. We're in a very wonderful situation in that there's such an amazing team and amount of resources within that team here in Team Oxbow. We've just got a tremendous amount of support, and it seems like the sky is the limit. What we are pulling off, and what we will be able to pull off within that team, and then in the grander community of the agriculture going on in this Valley, and Sno-Valley Tilth, and all the supporters of that. I could have spent an hour and a half just rattling off names of individuals that have poured in a tremendous amount of passion, whether they're bending over in the fields, or whether they're on the phone making sales, or whether they're gettin' greasy in the shop, or whether they're linking farmers with land, or whether they're putting land into preservation so that it can some day be in the hands of a farmer and not to a developer—it's phenomenal. So I'm very happy to be a part of it, and I really have a lot of hope and optimism for where it can go. The challenges within the flood plain are very unique, but the beautiful soil that brings it about is amazing as well.

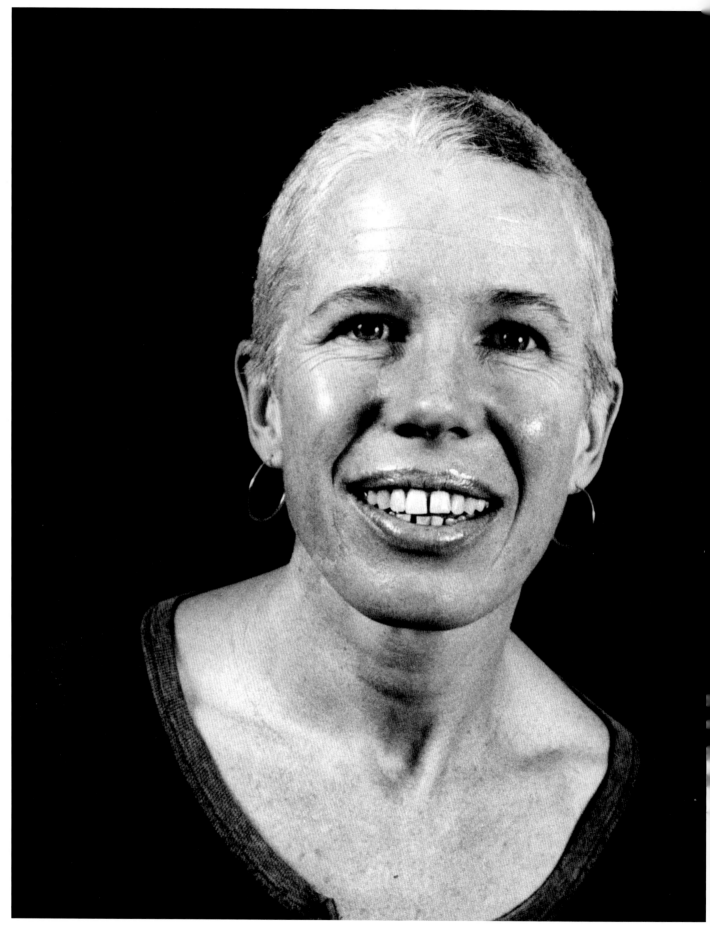

Sarah Cassidy

13 January 2010

My name is Sarah Cassidy. I was born October 6, 1967, in New York City, and here I am now. I was born in New York and lived my first two years in Greenwich Village, and then parents fled to the 'burbs after having their third child. So we lived in Rye, New York, and then moved to Old Greenwich, Connecticut, afterwards. I was basically raised in suburbia, in a beautiful area, an hour's commute away from New York City where my dad worked as a lawyer. So had not a lot of farmland around there. Very lovely rearing in a nice, if a little sheltered, suburban enclave. Then I went to college at Kenyon College in Gambier, Ohio, and studied English. In my junior year there, I went to Nepal, my second time abroad beyond the United States in my life, and it was just eye-opening for me. What a wonderful experience. And it has kind of shaped my perspective on life, I would say, and made me want to travel further and to different places. So I came back from Nepal and had one more year at school, and graduated in 1989 with my English degree and came out to Seattle forthwith to do who knows what. I was definitely not on a career path, nor had any idea what I wanted to do, and wound up—which is very humorous—as a singing and dancing waitress on a cruise ship (laughs) which is where Luke and I actually met, and he was a bartender there. So we met on this bizarre.... It was like a dinner boat. It would leave Puget Sound and take a three-hour tour around Puget Sound and come back at the end of the night.

I was singing and dancing, really cheesy, cheesy songs. But I loved it, because it kept me out of the professional world, which is what I think I was trying to avoid to begin with. And soon thereafter, Luke and I started dating, and he applied to the Peace Corps and got in, to go to Senegal, West Africa. So I was very supportive of that, I thought that was really exciting. We were together at that point for six months, but I said, "Go! Go! And hopefully I'll come over and visit," which I did, and I wound up staying there and teaching English in the capital of Dakar in Senegal, West Africa, for a year, but I would have lots of time off where I would come out and visit Luke in his village.

I feel that that was my first inkling about going into small agriculture, because the village that Luke was living in was an agrarian village. You know, you walk out of your hut, which you had made from your millet stalks that you harvested from that season, and walk out into your farmland there. And the women would run kind of a market garden where they would grow vegetables to bring to market to sell for extra money. And so it was my first taste of growing anything. My mom had a little garden, but I could care less about it growing up. So I was witnessing what was going on in this little village, and wanted to get my hands in growing. So I came back from Senegal after a year and I got an internship on a farm in Marin County in California.

I interned on a beautiful little farm on a ridge top called Mount Barnaby Farm, in the Lagunitas Valley, and just fell in love with farming. It was a very small farm, it wasn't by any means making its own money, but it was trying. But that's where I learned how to farm, basically, and farm in a very manual labor mode. There was no tractor, and so we were doing a lot of just like the digging and—oh, there was a walk-behind, but most of it was from us, we interns, who were young and excited about farming. So that's how we learned about it, and my first farmers market experience is there. It was Point Reyes Farmers Market that we would go to. Very exciting time. Bob Kinard was a farmer at that point, who was growing for Chez Penesse, and he was having these classes about farming, offered by the local community college.

So the interns on Mount Barnaby were able to go there once a week and hear this master, basically, talk about farming and how he farms, and starting to really talk about locality and what can be grown. West Marin at that point was really trying to come into its own as its own microcosm of farmland there, where you can basically get food, fiber, dairy, grain, anything that you wanted grown you could grow there. And so people were getting really excited about that. That was in the mid-nineties. The beginning was in the sixties, with the organic movement, but I feel like Luke and I kind of jumped aboard the organic farming movement at the like most ideal time. Just ten years ago it started really becoming very important in people's lives, and a household word, "organics." So we were luckily starting an organic farm at that point, but other people had kind of pioneered our way up to that point, which I salute them!

I was so floored in Senegal by the fact that everywhere was a farm. Everywhere you looked in the countryside, there were farms. And even in the city, there were little plots that people were farming. I never really made the equation in my head in the United States where our food was coming from. And so that was a drastic wake-up call for me. And then thinking back on the farmland that the U.S. has, it was so lacking animation, it was so lacking a presence. There was no one in the fields. You know, I drove through the entire state of Kansas with a friend on a road trip, and saw *nobody* in the fields; just corn, on either side of us, for the entire time in Kansas, but nobody was there! In Senegal, people were out there. There were *no* tractors, so everybody was working in the fields, and that's what you did. So it just really made me excited about food growing, and the prospect of, wow, taking it into your own hands. You know, not having an agribusiness bring you your food, but have people bring you your food. So I wanted to just get a taste of that.

Luckily when we were in Senegal, there was another Peace Corps volunteer there that was talking about intern programs on organic farms in the United States. I never considered that. When I heard it, I *knew* that's what I needed to do. And so I came back to the United States, and Luke was in Ghana. He went off to Ghana and we kind of separated ways then. But I came back alone and immediately started researching internships around San Francisco, because that's where my sister was living, and I was staying with her.

I had interned for a year on Mount Barnaby, and then the next year I was invited back to kind of assistant manage the small farm. And so I was doing that. Luke was down on the peninsula, working at another farm. We were both having different farm experiences, and we'd compare notes every now and then. So his sister and brother-in-law have always been in the bakery industry, in terms of bakery equipment. But they opened their own bakery up in Seattle, and they wanted us to manage it. So at that point I was finishing my season as manager of the farm, and we wanted to come up and see another exciting experience through, which we did. And it was a huge failure, at least for us, in managing a bakery. It was just not what we were about. We wanted to actually still be farming, and there we were inside.

The bakery was really hard work, and we were *far* from good managers. It was kind of a fiasco. But the bakery, luckily, is still going strong. And the interesting thing was it started over ten years ago—like twelve years ago, thirteen, fourteen—and the first year that we started it, we were very strident about using only organics. And at that point, it really wasn't in the purview of the mainstream. You know, it was not an important aspect of what people were looking for. So we really wanted it, so we were buying it from a CSA in Seattle, and we were trying to buy all these organic ingredients, but nobody cared. His sister and brother-in-law were like, "You're spending too much money on organic!" That was our mission, really. So we got out of that. And the funny thing is that now, thirteen or fourteen years later, they're all organic. They have switched out their conventional flour with organic flour. They're making organic bagels and bread and pastries and everything, so it's come full circle. But we were not awesome bakery managers. So we both left that and went on to doing our own things, still with our hands, because we really found beauty in working with our hands. I never wanted to look back on an office job from then on.

  I graduated college and I'd done this and that in the temp world and had to go downtown in Seattle occasionally with tights on and skirts and everything. I just felt like I was gonna die by the end of the day. So this really appealed to me, just hands-on everything. So I went back to gardening. I was working as a gardener at the University of Washington for a couple of years, and Luke got into carpentry at the time, and so we were both living our lives, doing that, and remodeling our teeny tiny house in Seattle. And that was suiting us fine. And then I applied to Seattle Tilth, that had an opening for their garden coordinator position, and I got that. And that was really exciting, because I felt like I'd come back to organic farming in the urban sense, in teaching people how to farm on an urban plot. So I got really, really into working there, and managing/overseeing the demonstration garden at the Wallingford Seattle Tilth Garden, and I loved it. We started another garden down south at that point. So I was very happy being back in the fold, the organic gardening growing fold.

  Right about the time that I got that job, I had just signed on to Seattle Tilth, and our neighbor, Carol Amberts, who has changed our lives forever, was working at Edmonds Community College at the time. It's a big community college for landscaping and horticulture. And so she had gotten a job announcement for a land manager/caretaker position in the Snoqualmie Valley. And she brought it over, and it read that this family owned a 120-acre property in the Snoqualmie Valley, which at that point I barely knew where it was. You know, living in Seattle, it was only twenty-five miles away, but I still didn't know it. And they were looking for somebody to farm it or do something on the property, as well as to maintain the property itself and all the outbuildings and the plumbing and what not. And she brought it over. She thought that I would be interested. And Luke grabbed the announcement out of my hands and he said, "I want to apply to that!" At that point I was happy at Seattle Tilth. So Luke applied for this job and got the job that is now farming at Oxbow Farm, which is very exciting.

  It's a wonderful family who owns the property, the Albergs. It's been in their family forever. Tom Alberg, one of the many siblings of the Albergs that have different hands in the Valley landscape around here. Tom just wanted to steward this piece of land that he grew up on, and he would bale hay, and just had fond memories of that area, and had two young children at the time that he wanted to bring out and introduce to the farming lifestyle. So it was a good gig for Luke to get involved in.

  At that point, Oxbow was nothing more than a little fenced-in garden with some new fruit trees and some blueberries and raspberries, and that was it. So he started breaking into the ground, and I was helping as much as I could, whenever I had a break from Seattle Tilth. By the next year, I was pretty much splitting my time between Seattle Tilth and Oxbow, and that was our first year of farming where we had twelve CSA customers, for like maybe a half-acre of land, and we gave them all a lot of summer squash. And they're all our friends, so they couldn't complain about it. Lots of zucchini bread for everyone! So it was a wonderful time.

We still have two of our very good friends who have their own families now. They're still members of our CSA from that momentous year. So it was pretty exciting, growing it from that. And we learned so much! You work two years on a farm, a year on a farm, and you think you know it all. And you do your own farm, and you know *nothing*! So we're basically starting from scratch. I think when we started ten years ago, the Albergs said that the property's been in their family for like seventy years, because it was Tom Alberg's father who bought the property.

That was ten years ago—well, eleven years ago. That was in '99, when we first broke ground. And we had that small field, and we were processing under the big-leaf maple right next to the small field, and that was our processing area for the next seven years, six years. We didn't have any outbuildings, per se, on the farm, so we were rugged at one point, but now we've got this palatial beautiful barn that's so helpful, and has a walk-in cooler and everything. So huge, huge differences. We're living the dream, we are living the dream.

About a year ago, the family who owns the property decided that it would become a nonprofit; which is perfect for a farm. It's a good thing, you know, in that it's making *some* money. We're realizing some money now, but it's still—you know, farming is never going to make you rich. So this is allowing the farm to cycle its profits back into the farm. So they are very interested in getting involved in farm education, as are we. We've always kind of seen the farm as—or we've desired the farm to be an education farm, and have had several groups out every year who want a tour, and get very excited about seeing the fields and everything. But now we are actually going to start programming, in hopes of getting regular public school groups on the farm during the fall and the springtime, and then having camp classes during the summer. So I have been asked to be the.... I don't know what my title is—Director of Education, something to that effect. Actually, I just like to see it as the person who makes a lot of fun things that kids want to do on a farm. So we're shooting for the fall of 2010 to begin some kind of programming for our kids on the farm.

What I would love to see, we're wanting to, of course, work with the farm aspect. And it's first and foremost a working farm, so we have to honor that. But I would love for kids to come out and harvest their own food. That makes them the most excited. And see where all their veggies and fruits and berries come from. And have not just an education place on the farm, but kind of a magical place of growth, and just being able to see a seed all the way through, from pumpkin seed to little vine, to the pumpkin itself, and to the compost pile. So just the things that kids love most: yummy food that they can pick from the farm; purple food, how exciting! Purple beans and broccoli. "Hey, I never knew it was purple!" You know, things that they love to just be able to eat fresh, pulling carrots out of the ground.... So to kind of just jump start a life of curiosity about growing their own food and if they grow it, they eat it. It tastes so much better. Absolutely. Yeah, that vested interest, "You're involved here, you're not just a passive eater, you're the farmer." So I'm very excited about where it could go. We also want to work with the developmentally disabled community and the food banks, in hopes of just producing lots of food that will go straight to the food banks.

I have to say that food in this country is the cheapest that it can be—in most of the world over it seems. I read a statistic that we spend around 9 percent of our income on food. And that is one of the lowest of any country in the world. Most other countries average 15 to 20 percent that they spend on their food. So I think we have been deluded into thinking that food is cheap, and so that's why I think people can't envision paying as much as organic asks for, because they think it's too much and it's going to break the bank. But I do think also, to circumvent the entire expense that organic food does call for.... I mean, we're barely making ends meet on our farm, and yet we're charging the premium for what organics are going for these days. So I can't even imagine what conventional growers, how *they're* making ends meet. Subsidies, I suppose.

But to circumvent the whole issue with paying what you think you cannot afford at the market, the base idea is to go back to the garden itself and grow it for yourself. And that, I think, is the number one goal in my hopes for our education program—you know, that kids catch the farming bug and the gardening bug, and they get excited about growing and eating their own food. And I think that if we enabled people in our culture, even in the cities, with pea patches to grow their own food, I think that we could really address the issue of prohibitively priced food.

In the era of WTO and NAFTA and this whole kind of literal farming-out of the farm jobs they say, "Oh, let some other agrarian culture do that, instead of us. We're going to specialize in computers." You can't eat a computer at the end of the day! And I just think this is lofty for our time right now, and we feel like we don't have to spend the man hours in the fields anymore, but I think that there's going to come a time. We're all witnessing peak oil and gas prices and just our heyday has kind of come to an end, or we're seeing the end in sight. So I think to rein our farming practices in, and to reignite the excitement, the *need*, for growing, and for growing our own food, is imperative in our country. So I think it's perfect timing for this agrarian renaissance to be happening. I think about open space, and the wilderness needs to be maintained too. You know, I think that they go hand in hand. I don't want to see the forests decimated to make way for more farming. The development is so encroaching that it's kind of concerning. How are they going to get back to all that soil underneath all of that development there?! But there'll be a way.

I always laugh at that bumper sticker in the Skagit Valley saying, "Preserve farmland: pavement is forever." And I think, "No it's not. Pavement is just preserving the soil for later years. And it's liming it all it can."

Whether it's in the field or in the classroom or in the field classroom, I *always* want to be doing this, because it's my cause, it's what I really believe in—that and music. No more singing on cruise ships, but it's like those two inspire me. It can be construed as a passing fancy, as so many things are, just in the food world of what's big and what's fashionable now. Organics is fashionable, but I can't see it going away, because it's where we *have* to go, where we're facing. So yeah, I'll just get deeper into it as it gets more and more a part of our culture.

I love the farmers markets—well, one, because Luke sets up the farm stand for me, and I don't have to! But it's my community, and it's all these friends that you've made in the community, and it's just a great gab time, you know, and great fun to hear what people are doing with your produce, and what they like, what they don't like; ideas that we have for them about what they can do with the produce. Now that we have a child, the whole petri dish of excitement and life and activity that farmers markets foster is so fun, and such an excitement. It's like a little weekly circus or festival.

People in our Valley seem to already grow their own a lot, and so they come to us for bumper crops of pickling cukes or stuff that they want to put up a lot. But a lot of people don't really know the reason why, the organic food that they're wanting to buy at the market *is* more expensive, and that's where we talk to them about that—that we're not just a wholesaler, you know, one of those corner produce-marts that's just buying the stuff in from Charlie's and selling it there. It's like we're growin' it!

I think that it's hugely important that people hear from their farmers, and hear how they came about, and that anybody can do this. Luke and I are from suburbia, and here we are. I always say, you know, farmers these days, or at least organic farmers, are not generational farmers, they're not third-, fourth-, fifth-generation. They're usually from suburbia or the city, and our first and foremost desire is to be green. And that's brought into the food movement through organics. So it's a lovely meshing of worlds.

The first principle of the exploitive mind is to divide and conquer. And surely there has never been a people more ominously and painfully divided than we are—both against each other and within ourselves. Once the revolution of exploitation is underway, statesmanship and craftsmanship are gradually replaced by salesmanship (the craft of persuading people to buy what they do not need, and do not want, for more than it is worth). Its stock in trade in politics is to sell despotism and avarice as freedom and democracy. In business it sells sham and frustration as luxury and satisfaction. The "constantly expanding market" first opened in the New World is still expanding—no longer so much by expansions of territory or population, but by the calculated outdating, outmoding, and degradation of goods and by the hysterical self-dissatisfaction of consumers that is indigenous to an exploitive economy.

This gluttonous enterprise of ugliness, waste, and fraud thrives in the disasterous breach it has helped to make between our bodies and our souls. As a people, we have lost sight of the profound communion—even the union—of the inner with the outer life...........There is nothing more absurd, to give an example that is only apparantly trivial, than the millions who wish to live in luxury and idleness and yet be slender and good looking. We have millions, too, whose livelihoods, amusements, and comforts are all destructive, who nevertheless wish to live in a healthy environment; they want to run their recreational engines in clean, fresh air. There is now, in fact, no "benefit" that is not associated with disaster. This is because power can be disposed morally or harmlessly only by unified characters and communities.

.......................The growth of the exploiters' revolution on this continent has been accompanied by the growth of the idea that work is beneath human dignity, particularly any form of hand work. We have made it our overriding ambition to escape work, and as a consequence have debased work until it is only fit to escape from. We have debased the products of work and have been, in turn debased by them.

Wendell Berry, "The Unsettling of America", 1971

Farm Journal

14 August 2009

 Stopped by Blue Dog Farm today, hoping to see Scott and Amy, take photographs. They weren't around, but Jen, their stalwart field manager, was there tending the U-Pick stand. A few young mothers and their children moved through the rows of bushes, gathering, filling their white buckets with purple sweetness. As I sampled a berry here and there and gathered candid, Zen-like photographs of moms and children blissed by the air and berries, I was suddenly standing before a child, maybe seven or eight years old, clutching her half full bucket which she seemed to offer me a peek inside, her face idyllic, somehow transcendent. Instinctively, the camera went up and I made an exposure. The camera went down and I faced the panicked lips and teeth, close to my nose, of the mother, clutching her child, demanding to know why I was taking pictures of her daughter. I calmly explained, handed her my card and she backed down a bit—still fearful, justifying her hysteria with fears of Internet child porn and the "one can't be too careful" defense and then held fast without apology. I moved away, shaken, searched and found again the enlightenment that hovered around the blueberry bushes.

 I remain shaken and troubled by the experience—perhaps making too much of it, yet wondering—puzzled as to how it must be to live inside that level of anxiety which is surely the presiding condition of her life. When I moved away from her, I encountered her friend, on her knees in front of a bush loaded with plump berries. She confessed she had brought her friend to the farm as another attempt to convert her to local, organic food. Her nervous friend jumped in and declared she was a slow convert—clearly worried about the "safety" of picking and eating berries not "sanitized" by the supermarket. Nevertheless, she was interested in my work and quickly revealed herself as a "true-believer" in organics, local growers and distributors and the "evil" tyranny of agribusiness and the mono-culture corporations who sustain it and would like to control the entire food production and delivery system. The entire interchange sent me searching this Journal when I got home to find an entry about a conversation I'd had with Erick Haakensen last June.

03 June 2009

 By chance, ran into Erick at Starbucks in Carnation—we both needed the caffeine and a break.

 The conversation turned quickly philosophical with him quoting Lao-tse and Wendell Berry in the same breath. The issue—the level of ignorance resident within our cultural paradigm; the perceptual filter built around the belief that ever-expanding corporate domination of food production (and everything else) is the only safe way to sustain a global economy. So well formed is the belief that, as Wendell Berry points out, small, local agrarian economies are regarded as aberrations or, at best, nostalgic reminiscences of an idyllic, "natural' life which never existed.

 A challenge to that paradigm is needed because local organic growers face a public demographically educated by advertising, corporate advertising and its commercialization of "the American Dream"; i.e., you too can grow your wealth exponentially and become a multi-millionaire. It is from that premise that questions about the value of community and the requirements for developing and sustaining local community rise to the front.

 Clearly, industrialization of society has "capitalized" individuality to the extent that each citizen is progressively more and more isolated and connected to other humans chiefly through various abstract "communities", notably, cyberspace network groups, Facebook, twitter, text messaging and Internet chat rooms (and yet, despite this apparent "connectivity", the woman in the blueberry patch is terrified in the field; plump ripe blueberries presenting not organic nostalgia but frightful uncertainty).

 The questions are few but telling and they all circle the problems of change and the relative epistemologies involving human behavior—i.e., the simplistic relationships of "nature vs. nurture" as they pertain to human nature and its dark companion, "free will". How much do we actually, individually "choose" at decision points? How do we know what is safe? Do we look inward to internal verification or outward to the behavior of others? I think the answers are systemic rather than individualized and the system to look to is the human one containing those deep, hard-wired unconscious elements that ultimately drive our social behavior. It is these basic tendencies (instincts?), finally, which the corporate ad-men utilize to create that abstract community which celebrates the illusion of individual choice by convincing the consumer that his identity depends upon his ability to acquire goods and services which s/he cannot have without the corporation—i.e., for "safe" food, only corporate agribusiness can be trusted.

....

"This exclusive emphasis on production will accelerate the mechanization and chemicalization of farming, increase the price of land, increase overhead and operating costs, and thereby diminish the farm population. Thus the tendency, if not the intention............is to complete the deliverence of American agriculture into the hands of corporations.
   The cost of this corporate totalitarianism in energy, land and social disruption will be enormous. It will lead to the exhaustion of farmland and farm culture. Husbandry will become an extractive industry; because maintenance will entirely give way to production, the fertility of the soil will become a limited, unrenewable resource like coal or oil."
   Wendell Berry, "The Unsettling of America", 1971

....

"This is a free country because compulsory education. This is a free country because nobody has to eat. This is a free country because not any other country ever was is or ever will be free. So now you know and knowledge is power."
   e e cummings, "i—six nonlectures", 1952—1953

Blue Dog Farm

Scott Turner

20 November 2009

My name's Scott Turner, born January 19, 1965, so that makes me forty-five years old. I was born in Chicago, but I didn't grow up there. My parents moved out when I was still a baby, so I don't have any recollections of Chicago, although I went back there to work for a while. My folks moved to Portland. My dad saw some advertisement. It was a Weyerhaeuser advertisement, a picture full of trees, with mountains in the background, and my dad was sick of Chicago at the time. He was a lawyer there in Chicago, and he said, "I want to live *there!*" So he looked up where *there* might be, and it was western Washington, western Oregon, for that picture. So he quit and we all moved out to Portland so he could get out of the city. I was one year old, so I don't really remember Chicago, just what my dad said about it, and then moved out to Portland, and eventually moved out to the suburbs after that.

I really didn't have any farming background at all. My dad was an attorney, and he ended up working at the Department of Justice as a prosecuting attorney. That was pretty much all he did. He didn't really have any gardening or farming experience—construction when he was in college. But my mom really liked gardening, so she.... We had a two-acre plot, and we were always growing a big vegetable garden and lots of flowers. And my grandfather, who eventually moved up to live with us, would always come up and garden too. So at least the gardening part of it, not necessarily larger-scale agriculture, was always kind of something that was happening around.

Initially we lived in Portland, and then my folks moved out to Tigard, which is basically a suburb that would be roughly equivalent to anything around here on the east side. But it was kind of on the verge of farm land, so there was still, at the time when I was a kid, you'd pick strawberries, because the Willamette Valley was the place where you grew lots of berries, a great berry-growing area. It was all Japanese farmers. So at that time we were still close enough to the farm land, so the trucks would come by and pick you up in the morning to go pick berries in summer, and drop you off. I had lots of friends who were sheep ranchers or apple orchardists, because at that time the Willamette Valley was pretty diverse. They grew wheat then. It's not that long ago. Apples, potatoes, berries—everything. I mean, you could grow anything there. That's why people moved out there from the Oregon Trail, because the Willamette Valley really was God's land, can grow anything you want there.

I mostly did it because I had to. But there was some stuff that I remember.... What was that book that my mom liked? It was "*Five Acres and Independence*". So she and our neighbor across the street worked at that kind of between the two of them. We had some cows that we would raise, and we'd go down to the dairy and get some Holstein bulls in, and raise those up for meat. What else did we have? We did the chickens and the turkey slaughtering, you know. We had chickens, and I took care of the chickens. I remember being part of the chicken plucking, which when you didn't know what you were doing, was quite an event. It's much better now that we know what we're doing a little more. I did stuff like a lawn-mowing business. And then when I was in high school, my mom got a job at a nursery, just a big, huge, forty-acre nursery where they just grew plants wholesale. And that was right out in the farm land of Willamette Valley. So I ended up getting a job there in the summertimes, working at a nursery, pruning trees, and weeding, and fertilizing. And then there was picking berries when I was younger but as soon as I could get out of picking berries, I had the lawn-mowing business!

My parents actually moved farther out into the valley, because typical suburbia was swallowing up farm land. Kind of ironically, they wanted to buy some land in kind of the Newberg-McMinnville area, which is farther down the Willamette Valley where all the pinot noir grapes are. I can remember being a high schooler and thinking, "Don't move out there! Because if you move out there, then I have to change high schools, and it's a big trauma for my little fourteen-year-old, fifteen-year-old self!" And I wish I hadn't been a typical teenager and only thinking about that, because if they'd bought farm land out there, it would have been a whole different deal. I might be growing grapes out there on their property. But instead they lived a little closer in.

But then I went to college up here at the University of Puget Sound, and met Amy. I remember one summer I wanted to stay up here, and so I got a job working for this guy named Pete Schulz. He is a blueberry farmer in Puyallup—older German guy—and boy, he ran the tightest ship of a blueberry place you've ever seen! There was nothing out of place there on this blueberry farm. And pretty much my job was to manage the farm, the picking operation. He had a family or a bunch of different people—mostly they were Asian immigrants that would pick, and I would just keep track of them, making sure they were picking thoroughly and managing their poundage and paying them and that kind of thing. There were quite a few U-Pick blueberry farms, and one in particular that I remember my dad liked. It was Lowlitch Blueberry Farm, and my dad liked it because there was a family of a famous baseball player named Mickey Lowlitch, and so my dad always wanted to go out there to talk to the guy. But anyway, those are my blueberry experiences.

I went to college, and my dad and my mom were both college graduates, and my dad was a lawyer. My grandfather, my mom's dad, was a doctor. So it's kind of just assumed that you're going to go on and do *something*. Even though my dad always said, "You should do what you love. You don't have to be in the corporate world. I don't think you'll be that happy there." But I kind of still felt that's something I should do. In the eighties, when I was in college, computers were the thing. That was where all the jobs were, and I'm working near Microsoft, which is just kind of startin' to spring up. So anyway, I ended up being a computer science major although it really wasn't what I love to do. I did it, you know, and I got through it, but I never spent any extra time there. I should have realized then it really wasn't what I like to do. But anyway, I did that because you've got to pay off your student loans, and that would be a good career. So I graduated with a computer science degree, and then I went down to Oregon State for a little while longer, just 'cause, I don't know, I guess I didn't really want to work quite yet.

I got my MBA, my Master's in business. I should have also used that as an indication, because I'm down there in Corvallis, Oregon, which is right in the heart of the Willamette Valley. Amy would come visit me, and she loved it there, and I loved it there, and we always talked about having a farm. But then I went to work for this computer consulting company just because, you know, that's what all my education was geared towards, so I'd better do that. It just wasn't a fulfilling career.

Amy and I went out to Montana for a while, in Helena, Montana, because the company I worked for, it was a national company, and so they were doing a job for the State of Montana, and we got to go live in Montana and travel around. That was the good part of that job. It wasn't the work, it was going backpacking and being outdoors and enjoying Montana. But then after that was over, then I ended up in Chicago, and Amy was back in Oregon.

But anyway, so after spending a lot of time in Chicago and traveling, flying back and forth, because Amy was in Portland, working as a teacher, we realized I've got to do something else, I don't know what it is. So I ended up quitting and looking at other things. We wanted to have property, and we kind of wanted to have farming, but it never really figured in as something that could be a full-time occupation. I guess we're wanting a little more security or something, and it just didn't seem like a feasible type of thing to do at that time, because we didn't really have that much money either, and buying land, even in the late eighties, early nineties, was still expensive.

So anyway, I was just trying to figure out what I was going to do for a career. I knew I didn't really want to be in an office. Anyway, I was kind of floundering around, and Amy says, "Well, you should look at this job. When I took an Alternative Careers for Women course, we looked at firefighting, and I really liked firefighting. I think you'd like it." So I looked into it and that's how I got involved with that. And it's kind of funny, because we talked about it as having a schedule suitable for being able to pursue other things, like farming.

It's kind of funny, because Amy and I had talked about it from early on, even when we were in college. We were kind of weird. Amy had a house and we would plant a vegetable garden and did stuff there. Most college students aren't growing vegetable gardens on their little tiny city lot. We'd talked about doing all sorts of different schemes farming, so it was never an epiphany, it was more kind of a steady, lingering thought that it's something we wanted to do, and it's something we wanted to pursue. And after I had done that work that summer on the blueberry farm, that became kind of an idea that seemed really feasible, something that we could do. Mr. Schulz, he had made a good living doing it, and so it seemed like it would be fairly lucrative, so that was the idea. So rather than one big like epiphany, it was just kind of a lingering idea that always was kind of in the back of our heads. And so most everything that we did, we kind of always had an idea. We kind of wanted to live in Portland, because I always thought that was where all the farm land was. You know, the Willamette Valley is pretty extensive, and it goes wide and far. I didn't think I'd really end up in Seattle, because I never really thought there was that much farm land there.

I ended up getting a job offer in Redmond. We actually talked about it, "Well, if we live in Redmond, there's not really farming opportunities there." I didn't really know Seattle. Even though I went to school in Tacoma, I didn't really know Seattle that well. And Amy was saying, "Well, you know, I know the Snoqualmie Valley, there's farm land out there." I remember actually driving around, looking to see if there would be available farm land, whether it'd be acceptable or not to actually take this firefighting job, because some of it was determined on whether there was a chance that we could do any kind of farming or not. We kind of thought, "Well...." It was just right before even farming in the Snoqualmie Valley exploded. It seemed like there was property out there. We weren't sure how that would work, but anyway.... The whole farming idea was always part of—especially the second career—it kind of got lost in the first career, but it came back more in the second career.

You know, it's kind of weird or just sort of an idea that started cropping up in my mind, and then Amy seemed like she was really interested in it also. So there wasn't really anything where the other spouse is saying, "Yeah, I don't know, that doesn't really interest me," because she was saying, "That sounds really cool!" So it kind of kept building. So this idea in *my* head ended up becoming an idea for us, between us. Amy grew up in a farming community too, kind of really similar, where it was losing out from fruit orchards to houses. So that kind of idea, I think, might have had some kind of effect in our interest in farming: farm land is going away, and it's something that's really precious and can't be replaced. Where I was on the edge of suburbia, I had a friend who had a 500-head sheep ranch, and another friend who grew potatoes, and there were still some apple orchards, and I worked at a nursery. There was quite a wealthy berry farmer, so I had all these kind of things that I saw. And when I was a kid, I worked on this other farm where he raised cattle and his own hay, and I worked, kind of helping out with the hay. So I had a lot of exposure to agriculture in kind of its more romantic state—not the big-time agriculture, but small farms. And we had examples of people, at that time when I was in high school, who were making a living at a small farm, doing things in a variety of ways. So I think that's kind of what made it attractive, and Amy likes gardening, and I like gardening. My parents, my mom in particular, did a lot of gardening. And my grandfather was a big gardener. So the idea of growing things was really comfortable. I mean, things grew, you know. It never really occurred to me, like some of our interns come through, and they don't know the process of putting the seed in the ground, and it comes up and turns into the plant; whereas I was always thinking, "Every seed, just about, sprouts." You just gotta grow it. So all of that stuff was just kind of part of who I was. I get people at work even, they're saying, "I want to grow a garden—what do I do?" And I'm like, "Well, start out small, get a ten-by-ten area and till it up, go get some seed packets and read the back of the seed packet, and put 'em in the ground, and start doin' some stuff." And they're like, "Oh, okay." They sound so amazed by it all, whereas Amy never thought twice about it. You just go out and you plant a vegetable garden. So I think it is more of an unusual thing for people.

When I decided to become a firefighter, it seemed like a good job to work with farming because most communities have firefighters, so you could be in a lot of neat places and be a firefighter *and* a farmer, as opposed to something where you had to be in a city to do the job. So when it looked like I might get a job with Redmond, we came up and Amy and I drove around, and we tried to figure out, "Well, are there any farms around here? Can we be farmers if I work in Redmond, Washington?" I remember not really being completely enamored with the Snoqualmie Valley right off the bat. I remember driving down 203, and it was in the summertime, and it was kind of hot, and it just didn't seem like there was really much goin' on out there. I mean, there's a few dairy farms, but I think that was kind of maybe comparing it to the standard of the Willamette Valley, which is a pretty tough standard, because there's a lot of great farm land with outstanding soils and it doesn't flood at all in Willamette Valley. So we kind of concluded that, well, there probably was some farm land in the Snoqualmie Valley somewhere, we weren't sure where it was, the job was good, so we moved up with the hopes that we would find a farm. Maybe we would have to go a little farther and wider.

Four years later we did find this dairy farm that should have been way out of our price range because it was a lot of acres, way more acres than we thought we would be able to buy. It had a little farmhouse on it, and Amy and I like old homes. It seemed like the perfect thing. One of the things we liked about the Snoqualmie Valley was at least the soils were good, and we knew that we were close to a lot of people, so that was going to be good for farming. This place was on, I guess you'd call it the right side of the river, so when it floods, you can still get out of there. And it was a *long* ways from the river, so we weren't gonna get floods. In fact, the farmer told us he didn't really have any floods.

I remember looking at buying the place in February, and there was this real estate agent that the farmer had employed, and he definitely wasn't a rural farming real estate agent. He was kind of a little, short, fatter guy that was obviously used to selling suburban homes. And so he wanted to know what I wanted to see. "Do you want to see the house? It's kind of old." I'm like, "Oh, the house is fine. But I want to go out to the field, it's February, I want to dig some holes and see what the groundwater is." And he's looking at me like, "What are you *talking* about?" But the funny thing is, the farmer, I think when he found this out, really ended up liking us, because he thought, "*Those* are some people that are really into the farm, because the first thing they want to do is find out about the soils and the groundwater." So this turned out to be the absolutely perfect place for us, because it had plenty of area that was out of the flood plain. One of my requirements, I needed to have a house that was out of the flood plain and we had to have a place where the berries could be, that wouldn't be completely obliterated by floods whipping through. And it had that; it had way more than we even wanted. I mean, it had woods on one side, and a big old barn that was just fantastic on the inside. And it wasn't too highly priced, because the development rights had been purchased by King County in the seventies, so that it couldn't be developed for anything else; at least the pasture land, the thirty-five acres on one side of the road, was gonna stay in farm land. All that actually made the price accessible to us, which was really neat, because that was the whole intent of this bond measure that passed in the seventies, was keep the farm land in the hands of people who want to farm, and not in the hands of housing developers. So it was pretty great for us. Otherwise, it would have been only accessible to rich people.

    At first we just wanted to have like a little farm, but I don't think we really knew what that meant exactly. We thought it would be a pretty reasonable kind of part-time thing. And then as the plants grew up, it became obvious that there was kind of a sweet spot there, that you had to have.... Because if it's too small, it's just not really big enough to be of value, at least in our current.... You know, we wanted to be a U-Pick operation, and we had two acres of berries, and just wasn't going to be quite big enough. But already you could see where it would get *too* big and you'd have to have a lot of employees, and we'd be bigger than we want. So we've kind of gone through a couple of different ideas with our farm. So the first one was have a real small farm with the quaint little U-Pick thing. Then we thought, "Well, that's not gonna quite work. We have to get a little bit bigger." And we planted some more berries, and we're like, "That's too many berries under our current management practice, so we need to have some people work for us." And so we got some people to work for us, and we thought, "Well, okay, now we got these people to work for us, but we need to make a little more money to help pay for these people, so let's look at growing some other stuff. Let's look at growing vegetables and doing a CSA." And then that was just too much while Amy was working and I was working. It was like, "Okay, that's too much. We gotta pare back to our core ideas that we want, and that's berries and U-Pick berries." So now we've reduced back down to blueberries and raspberries as our U-Pick for our main economic, and then we have our animals. So now our goal with the farm is to not run ourselves ragged, to make sure we're maintaining a great quality for our family life—especially while our kids are here, we can't spend 100 percent of our time on the farm, because they're gonna be gone soon. So now that's our main goal. And our second goal is to make enough money to really make it worth our while to be spending all this time and effort and thought on it. And then our third goal is to be able to grow as much of our food as *we* can, because that's become really important to us, this idea that—particularly any meat, because if we're going to be omnivores, we really don't want to be eating industrial raised food. And that became really important to us. I mean, I never really thought too much about it, about how a cow was raised, or how a chicken was raised, but it became.... One of Amy's and our biggest thing is like, "If we're gonna eat meat, we want to make sure that that animal was raised humanely with love and care." So that became sort of our third focus.

We became so blessed, because we got this great farm, in this great location in terms of market, because we have all these people all around us: Bellevue and Woodinville and Redmond and Snohomish. And then there's the community in Seattle that is really hard-core, organic, local foods. So I mean if we had been in Kansas City or something, I'm not sure.... I think it could be done, but not as easily. But the community in Carnation and Duvall and then all those suburbs, people are really coming on board with local food, and there's a lot of people out there that really think that's important. And so we kind of got in there right as that philosophy was increasing, and Seattle is, I think, kind of a hotbed of that idea. And people really embrace that, they're willing to pay a little bit more for a grass-fed cow, because they don't want to eat a cow that was raised the way they read about it in "*Omnivore's Dilemma*". They just don't want to do that. So I think we're fitting in with the community really well with that: high-quality organic fruit—because people still want quality, they don't want garbage—and people like to come out to the farm, they like to talk to us. I think we really work well with our customers, they feel good about it. And so I think to answer your question, we're starting to blend in with the community really well, and what the community wants out of their farms.

Actually, the mythology about farming is really what I want to have happen. I just like to think about our neighbors just down the road, the Rooshes. Lois Roosh and her husband, they had a dairy with twenty-five cows, I believe is what they had at first. And the guy that we bought from, I think he said he had 50 to begin with. But anyway, I mean, that was the way it was, and there were a *lot* of 'em all the way down the Valley. And then those dairies have pretty much died out. I mean, I think we could see five dairies from our home site when we bought in '97 and now there's actually no milking dairies. There's one where they raise dry heifers. We've just been part of this increase in the number of small organic farms in the Snoqualmie Valley, because there's people dying for this kind of food in Seattle, and this is the closest place. I mean, the Kent Valley is gone, and Snoqualmie Valley, I think it really could be Seattle's bread basket—or salad bowl, I guess would be more likely. So I think it's possible. I think there's a real conflict there between rich people who want to have their horses and want to have an open space, and it's still affordable there—that's kind of coming in conflict with people who really want to farm and could raise one heck of a lot of food on ten acres of Snoqualmie Valley bottomland. So I'm hopeful that the number of small farms is going to increase. I think of people like Siri and Jason; they're young, they moved in recently, and they're really making a go of it. There's quite a few other farmers.

I can be sort of skewed, I think, because you spend enough time in the organic farming circle, and maybe you don't really realize how it is in the real world, and so it's good to read Michael Pollan's book, because you realize, well, 99 percent of the people are still eating the way it was in his book, and that is probably going to persist for some time. I don't know how farms in the Midwest are going to break up into smaller parcels, but that's kind of really what it's gonna take, because the Snoqualmie Valley is just a drop in the bucket. It's really got to be taking hold in Iowa, Nebraska, and more.

I don't really worry about ADM and Cargill too much. I worry a little bit about some of the genetically modified stuff, because that can be a no-turning-back thing. But as long as we can keep some of those farms, especially in that farm belt area, I think, in the Midwest, in private holdings, then I think there's always a hope that there'll be a slow and steady shift away from just growing corn and selling it and putting it on a train and going down and making corn syrup. I really think there still is a future. I don't think it's gonna happen anytime soon, but.... I don't really appreciate those companies, but I don't think they're gonna be able to squash small farms. I mean, the Snoqualmie Valley isn't on their radar. I think if some significant chunks of territory got taken up to organic and small farms in the Midwest maybe they would start to think about it. But they don't really care.

I think Erick was a good example, because he was one of the earlier people around in the Valley, and maybe he kind of feels like I do, like I think. I constantly run into people that are supporting our idea of how food is grown. There's just a groundswell of people that.... You know, ten years ago if I had sat around at the fire station table, they wouldn't know what I was talkin' about. They thought organics was some kind of craziness. But now they think, "Well, I want grass-fed beef!" or, "I really want organic blueberries for my baby." And I really think that there's way more people in Seattle and all these areas that would want organic food, that actually have good access to it. I mean, they can go to Whole Foods, but I don't really think that's the model that people are looking for.

I think one of the answers to that is to create more urban farming. They can't grow *all* their food, but if people had their hands in the dirt and they saw the fantastic nature of growing your own head of lettuce, maybe they just had like three window boxes full of lettuce and peas, and they ate that. And the wonder of growing your own food, and that power of having healthy food that wasn't part of the whole Safeway thing—I think that all of a sudden then that kind of food would actually become a priority in their lives, and really they would want more organic food. Now the problem is, is that it's certainly more expensive than a bag of chips and candy bars.

So that's the difficult part, and I don't really know how to address that exactly, except that if people could grow a little bit of their own food, they might see how valuable that is, and value the outstanding grown food from organic farms. I think the problem is, if really, as a country, we think that that's the way to go, then we need to *stop* supporting corporate agriculture—you know, the ADMs and the Cargills—and start supporting organic and small farms. It doesn't have to necessarily be organic, it can just be a sustainable way of doing it. I think if you could shift the money from helping out those gigantic corporate farms that are destroying the farm lands, releasing enormous amounts of carbon, and using huge amounts of petroleum, to smaller farms, then all of a sudden, first of all, McDonald's could not produce a cost-effective hamburger; and second of all, if you could do *something* to kind of help the smaller farmer, then possibly their prices could be a little bit lower. If the cost of *land* wasn't so huge, right off the bat you could lower the cost of food, because it's so onerous right now to buy, even in the Snoqualmie Valley, ten acres. It's too huge for a young person, even though there's lots of young people that are dying to.... So I think it's just a matter of shifting resources from one type of farming to another, and that might actually flip-flop the economics. But I don't really think that.... I mean, we can't really sell our blueberries—our blueberries are kind of expensive—but we can't really sell our blueberries for any less than we do right now. And we are trying to reduce inputs and reduce labor, but it just *is* expensive to grow that way. But I also think it's worth it. So in the short term you definitely get this conflict, between people who can't afford to buy high-quality organic produce.

Amy's got the idea of work-share. It's kind of along the lines of adopting a row of blueberries. And that, at the very least, could get you better access to the blueberries, and maybe even a lower price. And so I think that's definitely a really good way, because frankly, when you go to organic, or sustainable, or biodynamic, you are probably increasing the amount of labor per whatever unit of produce. So if we can get the labor, then it stands to reason that you could reduce the cost to those people who are providing it.

One of our goals is to do a little more, especially in the fall, with some tours and stuff. We had a preschool come, and we talked as much as we could, about farming at that level. We've definitely talked about doing some more education, and seeing if more school groups might be interested in coming out. I had this thing in my head, and it turned out to be a lot of labor, but I still think it's a cool idea. It's not my idea, but it's having a pizza farm, which is basically you grow everything that is included in making a pizza. This one farmer did it, and he ended up charging money, but it's really highly educational. He did it, and we tried to do it in a small fashion. A circular plot, and then you have it in slices, so one slice would be wheat for the dough, and maybe several slices might be the cow for the dairy product, and you'd have to have a pig maybe for pepperoni, and tomatoes and herbs. But you know what's educational about that is the percentage of the land that is taken up for each one is very interesting. Kids kind of grasp that idea, so we've got *some* plans of doing more education like that. I think certainly animals as part of the whole system is important, and kids like to see animals. Blueberry plants only are exciting while there's blueberries on them—otherwise they're not too exciting. They don't move around or moo or neigh or anything.

We'll always farm in some fashion, hopefully as long as we are physically able to do it. I think Amy and I are really kind of moving to this philosophy, in terms of our vision of sustainable, and a lot of other people's, is that we have to reduce the amount of inputs coming onto the farm, because I kind of like to look at it in kind of like an apocalyptic sort of way, where if the world just went to pot, and it just wasn't viable to move fertilizer from eastern Washington to our farm, what would we do? Would our blueberry plants survive? Could we grow anything else? And we still use petroleum, diesel—especially in the winter, but we use bio-diesel. But this is all part of an enormous system that's out there. And so we are looking, in time, of trying to reduce the inputs onto the farm, by maybe using horses, and then being able to grow all of our chicken food, and create all of our protein for the animals, and to be able to grow nitrogen via legumes and clovers and things like that for the blueberries, and maybe live with slightly less growth out of our blueberries, but not have any inputs. And certainly that would sort of insulate us from the outside world, from having to have petroleum, and could lower the cost to make it more accessible to people also, but also make it so that our farm could be an island unto itself and be a sustainable unit, so you know that you're able to continue on.

It's really interesting, because the more Amy and I kind of talk about this, I really think the animals on the farm is really a critical element of it, which gets back to really that old-style mythological farm that you're talking about. "Oh, Grandpa has four cows, two horses, three sheep, and a goat." But all those animals played a particular role, and he didn't have 10,000 chickens, because he couldn't possibly feed 10,000 chickens. It doesn't work right, the proportions aren't right with the farm, but forty chickens are, and you have customers for forty chickens, and then your neighbor has their customers, and really.... So going back to that other question, I think if we can move that way, it *is* a model that could work.

O sweet spontaneous
earth how often have
the
doting

      fingers of
prurient philosophers pinched
and
poked
thee
,has the naughty thumb
of science prodded
thy

      beauty   .how
often have religions taken
thee upon their scraggy knees
squeezing and

buffeting thee that thou mightest
conceive
gods
      (but
true

to the incomparable
couch of death thy
rhythmic
lover

        thou answerest

them only with

          spring)

e e cummings

Amy Turner

20 November 2009

I'm Amy Turner. I was born in Cleveland, Ohio, on December 18, 1965. I am going to turn forty-four years old in a little while. So yeah, that's who I am.

My parents were from western New York State and western Pennsylvania, and they met in Cleveland, and got tired of urban life and wanted to move to a small town. And it always kind of strikes me how much of a parallel there is between my parents and Scott's parents, who essentially did the same thing: we want to get out of the Midwest and we want to go west. I always think of them as being kind of latter-day pioneers, even though both of us came from families where our parents had professional jobs, and they weren't farmers by any means. They didn't move to become farmers. So my parents moved to have a small-town way of life, and they moved to Emmett, Idaho. My dad was a CPA, and he trolled around through the professional journals for a partnership opportunity, and that's how we ended up in Emmett, Idaho, and it was wonderful.

One time a few years ago, I was having a conversation with my mother, and telling her one of those, "Mom, you know the greatest gift you ever gave me?" And she's like all baited breath, "Oh, my daughter's going to tell me the *greatest* gift I ever gave her!" And I told her it was making me a Westerner. The visits that I've had to the Midwest, the terrain, the topography, just the attitude of people just seems so different than out in the West. That disappointed my mom pretty much, but it's so true, I'm so glad to be here. I was so glad to grow up in Emmett, Idaho. It was a very small place. It's a fruit-growing valley and a sawmill town, so it was a lot of blue collar, and I think my parents felt like fish out of water sometimes—lack of cultural opportunities, there wasn't a good music program in the school, there wasn't a lot of advanced academic opportunities, but I had a lot of opportunities, for being from a small town. It was really fantastic.

I stayed there all through high school, so I graduated in 1983 also, and went to the University of Puget Sound, and that's where Scott and I met. A few years later, my family moved up to the Puget Sound area, to Bellevue. My mother was a nurse, and so she was working in the healthcare field, there was more opportunity up here. And it gave a chance—my older brother had gone to Seattle University, so it was a chance for the family to be closer together too. But no, no agriculture in my family.

My mother's parents had grown up on farms. And my paternal.... No, wait, how would I say this? My mother's father grew up on quite a prosperous, diversified farm—dairy.... In western New York State, just absolutely gorgeous: that kind of terrain where it's appropriate for grazing, and yet you've got those places where it's great for crops. I think their farm was pretty prosperous, and then my grandmother had grown up on a little sketchier kind of a situation, where her father part-time farmed, it wasn't really great land, it was kind of in the middle of nowhere. He did a lot of outside jobs. So my grandmother did not like being on a farm, and swore she would never live on a farm. When they married, my grandfather became an automobile dealer. So my mom went to Cornell, which she's very proud of, which is a highly respected agricultural institution, although she studied nursing. I always think that's kind of.... She knew some of the milieu of farming and yet it would never have occurred to her her daughter would grow up to be a firefighter and a farmer. Kind of freaked her out, I think. But Scott's parents did the same thing: moved out west, and then ended up being in this agricultural area.

When I was growing up, I never looked at farming as a viable way to make a living. It never occurred to me. I always loved stories of pioneers and all that "going west" stuff. It was so romantic, and yet I really admired that self sufficiency, that idea that you could take care of yourself, you actually could do these things. My mom liked to garden, so we grew a vegetable garden and flower garden. I had a horse for a while, which there's a lot to know about having animals, which we learned really fast. And you could see all the expense and infrastructure related to keeping animals, in particular, but also to farming in general. Making hay? Who knew that you needed all these different kinds of equipment to make hay! So the whole pioneer thing was very attractive to me. My parents weren't particularly interested in food, in the way Scott's parents were *very* interested in food. Well, his mother just impressed me so much. Where they lived across the driveway was fields of a strawberry farmer, a Japanese strawberry farmer who'd been farming a very long time. And so Mr. Hasawiki's field, she would just go over and pick strawberries out of Mr. Hasawiki's field and take 'em home, and make dessert out of 'em. I just found that so fascinating.

And the other thing I found very fascinating when I moved to Tacoma, was the wild blackberries *everywhere*. And Scott and everybody I met just said, "Ugh, yeah, blackberries, they're a weed." And I said, "Well, like, do they get berries on 'em?" "Oh, yeah, *lots*, and they're just everywhere." "And you can just go pick them and eat them?!" "Yeah, but...." Just so dismissive of this what looked to me like this *incredible* resource, *there* for the *taking!* And you could just.... Wow! It was mind-blowing to me. Wild blackberries! I still love 'em, and we *both* love 'em—as opposed to somebody who grew up with 'em as a weed. We did the same thing when—we weren't dating very long—also in terms of food, Scott's mom was a great baker. She baked pies, and she made jam, and they kept some chickens at home. And this was all very exotic to me—even pie. Sometimes every night, it seems like, they had a pie. It just seemed like really difficult. When Scott went to college and he wasn't there for his mom's pie every night, he started makin' pie, because that's what you do, you gotta have it. And pretty much now, we gotta have it! When we were dating, our first year, it was late spring, early summer...or I can't remember when it was, but we were in Tacoma, so we went walking at Point Defiance Park and came across wild huckleberries, the little tiny red ones. Scott's like, "Oh! We can make a pie!" It takes a *lot* of little red huckleberries to get enough for a pie. And that's very slow picking. But of course when you're young, and you're in love, I would have picked 'em for eight *more* hours. But we did, we picked enough for a pie, and we went back, and we made pie. I was done; I knew I was marryin' that guy!

And the other thing that happened was I took a backpacking class. And it seems weird to take a backpacking class, but I didn't grow up with an outdoorsy background at all, despite the fact that we lived on a few acres. But we were still very housebound people, I suppose. And we didn't camp. We would travel around and go see the outdoorsy sights, but we stayed in motels. And so this was also mind-blowing to me, that just regular people could just like walk out in the woods and mountains, and just *stay* there?! And eat?! And hang out?! And be at this place?! This just blew my mind. I just *loved* that idea. And so I think that really fed into this self-sufficiency thing that, "Oh!" It kind of was starting to build together. And Scott grew up backpacking and camping. So all that, again, was just really interesting to me.

But one thing that I learned in this class, and maybe it was even the second class where it was like *advanced* backpacking: the guy's focus was "imagine you're leading trips of people." And he told a story of—I can't remember the details of it now, but it really struck me. And I just have always remembered it, and I remember it now with food and farming: which is that one way to really turn people off of wanting to go out in the woods or backpacking or hiking is that nobody wants their inexperience or their unfamiliarity to be something that they would feel belittled about, or made fun of, and that it's uncomfortable when you're doing something new. So if you have to go and relieve yourself in the woods, and you've never done that, and here are some people who are on this, and they all seem like they all know, they're in the know about how to do this, or how to stay warm, or how to set up a tent so it doesn't get wet. And you don't know these things, you can just be overcome by the feeling that "I don't know how to do it," and then quit and not take enough time and experience and ask enough questions, and feel comfortable enough with your uncomfortableness to get beyond that. Like what Scott was saying about the garden: I think some of that happens to people about growing food, that it seems exotic; "I don't know how to do it; I might make some mistakes; I might not do it right; these people seem to know so much about it; I don't really want to ask them a question, I might look stupid." People, when they come out to U-Pick, I feel the same way. There's some people, they don't know *anything*. You know, they came in their flip-flops, or they came in their heels, or they came for they don't know what, they don't realize that it's just U-Pick, I don't have any fruit for you, but you could go out and get some that you would enjoy, and it won't take very long. You see it in their face that they'd like to, but they feel uncertain and like they wouldn't know how. Other people will come back and say, "There's a wasps' nest in this bush." Yeah, okay, Scott will go out and try to get it out, but there's going to *be* some wasps, there's going to be some weeds. You know, I don't want to shoot 'em down and say, (curtly) "Look, we work really hard at this! This is just what farms are like, so why don't you just relax or leave?!!" Sometimes I would feel like that, especially early when people would react to the price. I just wanted to throttle them and say, "You don't realize how many hours of my husband's life he's been out here alone, growing these for you, so why don't you just pipe down about the price?!"

But anyway, so when we were in college or a little after, when one of us moved into a house that had a yard, we made a garden right away. It's just what you did. We didn't know very much about it, we planted everything at once, so the lettuce is long gone before the corn even came up. We direct seeded everything. Then we bought our first house, we just started gardening like crazy. We did ornamentals, but we made a place to grow food. We started making jam, and we made salsa out of our tomatoes. Just one thing led to another. I just loved where his parents lived, I loved that end of the Oregon Trail. You know, "God's land," and anything will grow here. And it was so fascinating what variety of farms there are in the Willamette Valley. It's just an amazing place. I don't know, so somehow we kind of assumed that's kind of where we wanted to live, and what we wanted to do ultimately. We didn't know how'd we get there really.

I think it was conscious—definitely. At some point, and I wish I could pin it down, we would read things and.... Yeah, we just started kind of paying more attention to our world. I think we might have gone to a pruning workshop. Oh! I know what it was! We got a catalog from Raintree, because we bought some fruit trees for our house in Portland from the Raintree catalog, and may have even gone to like a growers' day or something there, or just saw in the catalog "Salad Gardening for Profit," by Susan Mosure. And we just ate that up. "Wow! This is amazing!" The scale of it looked human, and that here was somebody actually offering that you could make money farming. So sometime after that, that sort of became our goal. And it kind of coalesced into blueberries, because Scott had worked on a blueberry farm, and we both couldn't.... We didn't feel romantic about broccoli or salad greens really. I mean, berries make us very happy!

From the start, yeah! Even if you're trying to see 'em, people are happy. For people who aren't into produce as a way of eating, berries are *very* approachable. I mean, I think if you're selling vegetables, you probably already start out with a way more educated eater than we meet when you're selling berries. Because they're like candy. I could eat a million of 'em. It's good for me, but eh, may not have all the things that broccoli has, but it's pretty darned good. I don't know. So that's kind of where we got started. When teaching became...what's the word?...untenable for me, and computer consulting became untenable for him, we started talking about what can we do to be farmers?

There was a lot of things I liked about teaching, but I was a brand-new teacher, and certainly the first years of teaching are very difficult. I had a temporary job for my first job, and no guidance, pretty much. There's no curriculum, you just sort of make it up. So with teaching two different classes every day, making it up from Day One, it was a lot of work. And certainly English classes where I believed kids should write, but then everything they wrote...you know, I didn't have a system, and so there I was with this pile of papers. It was just an avalanche of work. And then the next job I got, I taught at a Catholic school, and I had *five* different preps every day. It was just an insane amount of work, and it was really stressful—dealing with the community, and dealing with just kids being kids. And I was young and didn't have a lot of mentoring. And certainly, like I said, there was no lesson, until I invented it. So it was hard.

And then Scott got hired by Redmond, because we had kind of decided, okay, we gotta do something different. And then that whole firefighting idea came along, and we kind of said, well, Scott would interview around at places in western Washington or western Oregon that we would be willing to live, and that would have some potential for us being able to get a farm sometime. And then after we moved up here, then I could also start a search for a firefighting job that I could commute to from wherever we settled with his job. I mean, he was more in a position to sort of just walk in there.

Mom went with it, she was okay. I think there's a lot of things she didn't say, but I think what she did say was, "It's just not ever what I would have expected." But she realized how difficult the teaching was for me. I mean, I just loved the idea with firefighting that you'd go and you'd do your job, and you'd meet problems, and then you left, and it wasn't your problem anymore! I didn't have to go back every day, and there's little Billy what's-his-name. Oh gosh! You know? Nine months, and we never really got to what Billy needed, but it was a constant drain. So it was so freeing to just say, "Oh! Well! I'm gonna go home!" Wow, that was a good feeling. My life got a lot better.

I was a firefighter for thirteen years, and finally it was too much, too much. And with the farm, we kind of had gone through different phases of trying to see if a farm could replace my income. I mean, because both of us having firefighting jobs was pretty critical to affording to buy that farm. I mean, for as ramshackle as it was, we needed both incomes. The farm needed a lot of things, too. The amount that we invested in machinery and supplies and plants and labor, and to do the same labor over and over. So many things we didn't know, and it was just way more expensive to establish than we ever could have dreamed. We thought, "First we'll plant our blueberries, and then we'll remodel the house." But here we are, thirteen years later, we never remodeled the house.

But we have great blueberries, and more coming. We tried various things with a CSA, and diversifying some of our crops to try to bring in more money, hiring more people for a couple years, and that didn't really seem like the right solution in the end. We finally just said.... Well, we do often kind of re-examine our goals and how things are going, and so we kind of had a big reorientation this year with settling on, "Look, we are growing a lot of our own food now, and that has become quite important to us. And we need to spend time with our boys while we have them." So what Scott said about kind of coming back to our core thing with the berries, and our own food, and raising our boys. And that's kind of where we are right now.

We home school, so that is also another reason to be home. So finally, we realized that at this point, this berry farm is not going to replace my income, and we just said, "Fine." So we'll do with half the money. We're just going to. Over the years we've simplified our lives a lot as it was. So, so far, so good. And I guess we'll simplify more, or I'll get some sort of part-time job.

I was hoping to be able to come home, once the children *needed* more from home schooling, and needed a more directed program, because between Scott and I, we could kind of handle counting and letters and beginning writing and beginning reading. Between the two of us, trading the kids back and forth between us. Originally we started home schooling—well, I convinced Scott, or he bought into it because of the firefighting schedule. I mean, we had 24-hour shifts. If we had a school schedule on top of it, then when would we all be together? So now it's still working for us, and we'll just go while it does. It's gotten much more relaxed since I've been home.

I think the romantic vision is doing good. You know, originally we got the cows because our farm was bigger than we needed to grow the amount of blueberries that we had in mind. And all of this land just.... We rented out to Hmong farmers for a while, and they would kind of come serially, because they weren't doing any soil building, and eventually the pests and lack of fertility would catch up with them, and then they'd go and find a new farm. So we did that for a while. And then they would move on, and we had all of this land. And we were buying beef from somebody else, so it seemed like, "Well, let's get some cows." Even before that, we started growing our own chickens. One thing led to another, and I guess slowly it sort of made a lot of sense. And then we started looking at the animals more for how can they work to help close those loops on our farm. Initially it was just them feeding us. And now, more how do we integrate them into the work that needs to be done on the farm. There's *some* income from it, but it's mostly to feed us, and to eat bugs, or provide fertility, or weed, keep the weeds down, keep the blackberries down. So I think it's going good, and I'm glad to be home because I can make jam, we want to make wine. More and more.... I mean, I've always been somebody who wanted to do it herself. You know, it fascinates me. Why would I buy...name something... curtains...if I could sew myself. Now I'm trying to learn how to tan, just because it's a resource, a wonderful gift of the earth and of our place. It's working good for me. Everywhere we go, we talk about farming, we talk about the land, we talk about what would it be like to be here, how would it be different, what do they grow here, isn't that interesting? It's just the focus of our whole life. I just love it.

As for politics, first of all, I think that a lot more eaters need to consider where their food comes from. And I totally agree with Scott, you can't get somebody much more Middle America than a firefighter, your average Joe Firefighter. He's pretty much interested in buying snowmobiles, and interested in going to Hawaii once a year, and interested in eating what he's eating, and didn't think that it got flown here from Chile or New Zealand or whatever. "I want the cheapest food. I'm going to go to Costco to buy all my food." So in a world where not very many people think about where their food comes from, for one, cost seems like it just becomes the driving factor. And nobody stops to think about, from the farmer's perspective, you can't survive on prices that get paid to subsidize commodity farms. You just can't. Second of all, it's not really *good* for you. This is just the average people, let alone people who aren't blessed with a middle class income. So I do feel that very much, that the food that we raise is pretty much out of the price range to people of lower economic status. It does, it bothers me. At the very last, we glean our fields with a U-Pick gleaning, and so all that is free, except that we share it, so no cash, with us with some, and leaving a third for the food bank, and then the customer takes home a third. U-Pick also, I mean, traditionally was a way to get food more cheaply. We definitely *can* sell at a lower price. It's not a great price, it's not a dollar a pound, and it's going up along with everything else, but that *is* an opportunity for somebody to come and get food more cheaply. And I think there's a lot of potential in that, even with tree fruits and with certain vegetables: get that harvesting and gleaning labor out of it, and you've got a lot more affordable food.

I like the work share idea. I think there's a lot of management of volunteers that's extremely time consuming. So on a small scale, I think it can work, if you find the right people and then you have an opportunity to train them and develop a relationship with them, so there's not intensive management of people who don't know what our farm is about. That's a concern on the work share end for me.

And then I think that ultimately if people can catch this bug to grow their own food, there is a lot of land in suburbia that's not anything to do with growing food. And that as people possibly can develop this idea that land is just—all it is, is a place to grow food, that why would we waste land? Okay, yeah, you need a baseball field and you need a soccer field, but you don't *need* a suburban lawn and planting strip. I think people can raise a lot of food, even in their own yard. And that doesn't really reach people who are living in high-rise apartments or in complete concrete jungles, but there's a lot of land in Seattle, and there's a lot of land in suburbia that's, for lack of.... There's a lot people who want to know about growing food, and that's what I hope happens, is that everybody's kind of a part-time farmer to grow for themselves and their neighbors. There'll always be a need for commodity farming of grains, probably—unless there's a *big* change in how we eat. Of course that's kind of my ideal. That's the kind of farm *I* want, so of course I think it'd be great for everybody. But, you know, I know some people who have started growing chickens in their yards, and that's a pretty popular model right now, the suburban chicken. I don't know, I just think there's a lot of possibility in it. And you're not so beholden to McDonald's to give you your food, or Safeway to give you your food. You have a lot more personal agency if you can contribute in a meaningful way to feeding your family.

I don't think I'm particularly politically savvy. I mean, I think that it's absolutely critical to preserve farmland, just because we're gonna need it. Over development of anything totally gripes me. I don't understand why anybody would build a new house instead of live in a house that's already here. I mean, just in our area, why would you do that? Why would you want to go out and.... If you have that idea that "I think I can go out to five acres and become food self-sufficient," I say more power to you. But if you want to go out to have five acres so you don't have to be close to people, so you don't have to live in community with people, I think that's a terrible reason, and I wouldn't choose you to be my neighbor! But I don't get to choose, and then I also think just gently, gently.... You know, you kind of hope that by example and by communication, you can sort of try to show a different way of thinking about where you live and what you want to do with the few resources that we have.

In the home school community, parents/moms sit around and talk a lot. You'd think that that community would be pretty open. I mean, I always think about it as being very conservative Christian self-sufficiency, almost survivalist types sometimes, and pretty liberal hippie kind of type people, but it surprises me sometimes how disconnected they seem to their food. Or even friends who are interested in good food—for instance I have one good friend, I had a conversation with her recently, and she used to buy eggs from us. We were talking about beef, and she said, "Well, my husband lost his job, and now this new job pays $700 less a month, so I can't buy your eggs anymore. So I'm learning all these different money-saving, budget stuff." "Like what?" So all us moms are listening, and she said, "Well, I go to Costco, and I buy all the packages of pork loins. And I buy big bags of organic apples, and *they're organic!*" "That's great." I don't shop at Costco. I don't think that everybody shopping at Costco for cheap food is really the solution. I mean, I think if I didn't have very much money, the *first* thing I'd buy is food, and then everything else would be the later priority. Anyways, I wanted her to think about *where did* those organic apples come from? Did they come from China? Because if you bought organic apples from China, well, it's not good for the earth, and besides, organic from China is just not the same as organic in the States, where there's *oversight*, so they're just selling you a snow job. And she's like, "Well, I don't care." It really shocked me that she didn't care.

So the things that people think are impossible for them.... I'm sure there are things that I would think are impossible for me. Like the chickens, another thing that comes up a lot, like with interns or other people who are interested in growing their own food, and they're meat eaters, they ask, "Well, how do you slaughter the chickens?" And so I describe how we do it. "Oh, I could never do that!" You know, for me, it was kind of important. It was a measure for how important eating meat was to me. And if I wasn't willing to participate in the death of this animal, that I thought we raised pretty humanely, it had a pretty good life for a chicken—if I wasn't willing to participate in that, then I'm not really sure that I deserve to eat chicken. I don't know, I certainly felt like that at one point, I only wanted to raise chickens for eggs. And it's hard, at first, I totally agree. And I didn't like participating in slaughtering them. But now, I kind of.... I don't know, it feels kind of sacred. It's like, "You know, you're giving a big sacrifice for me and my family. This chicken is important, and it shouldn't go to waste." The thing that bothers me most would be to waste any of the meat that we raise. This is really important stuff. And the same with the cows. I *do*, I love the cows. I don't want to shoot a cow. We pay someone to come and do the kill, because I just think knowledge is pretty important, and I don't think I could do that humanely at this point in my life. But I don't know. So that's my first question when somebody says, "How can you do that?" "Do you eat meat?" It's kind of part of that cycle. We eat a very limited amount, because that's what we can raise.

We've become much more, you know, returning to whole foods as much as we can, whenever we can. And so it just creeps up on us that over time we're buying a lot less stuff that's canned, or buying a lot less stuff that's processed. We're pretty much.... We're not on the hundred-mile diet, but that is very appealing to me, just that that's the right way to eat. We've got to figure out what we can eat that doesn't come from far away. It's a big job, and I think you can only really try for it incrementally; otherwise it crushes you with the enormity of it. I think that's how I feel about people that I want to have try more with me, with us, about eating closer to home, and raising some of their own food, and looking for local sources. I don't want it to feel so overwhelming. You know, like with Mary. I didn't want to burst her balloon and say, "I hope they weren't Chinese apples." But, you know, there's so many facets to it, and if we all can kind of pay attention a little bit to some of them, then maybe together we can come up with a better picture, because I don't think on my own I'm going to figure it out. And I'm probably not the right mouthpiece to share it with a bunch of people, because that's just probably not who I am.

I think we pretty much decided that we'll always farm. I just don't think we could get away from it. We talked about, "Well, how are we going to manage our lives?" And so there were only a few choices left. We had two jobs, we had our kids, we home school our kids, and we have this farm. And that was all we had. And one of 'em was gonna have to go, because we were down to what in our minds was the bare minimum. So moving from the farm was one of the ideas, but we didn't go there. It's our third child, is what I always say. And besides, when we travel, all we do is look at farms! So you know it's inevitable we'd end up there again. So let's not move off of this one now.

One way or another, re-ruralization will be the dominant social trend of the twenty-first century. Thirty or forty years from now—again one way or another—we will see a more historically normal ratio of rural to urban population, with the majority once again living in small farming communities. More food will be produced in cities than is the case today, but cities will be smaller. Millions more people than today will live in the countryside growing food although they won't be doing it the way farmers do it today and perhaps not the way farmers did it in 1900.

Indeed, we perhaps need to redefine the term farmer. We have come to think of a farmer as someone with five hundred acres, a big tractor, and other expensive machinery. But this does not describe farmers of a hundred years ago, and it's not an accurate picture of most current farmers in less industrialized countries; nor does it coincide with what will be needed in the coming decades. We should start thinking of a farmer as someone with three to fifty acres who uses mostly hand labor and twice a year borrows a small tractor that she or he fuels with ethanol or biodiesel produced on site.

How many more farmers are we talking about? Currently the United States has three or four million of them, depending on how we define the term. Let's again consider Cuba's experience (**Author's note: When the Soviet Union collapsed in 1989, Cuba lost the major portion of its financial subsidies, including the massive imports of Soviet petroleum to fuel its economy**). In its transition away from fossil-fueled agriculture that nation found that it required 15 to 25 percent of its population to become involved in food production. In the United States in 1900 nearly 40 percent of the population farmed whereas the current proportion is close to 1 percent. Do the math for yourself: extrapolated to our country's future requirements, this implies the need for a minimum of forty million and up to fifty million additional farmers as oil and gas availability declines. How soon will the need arise? Assuming that the peak of global oil production occurs within the next five years and that natural gas is already in decline in the United States, we are looking at a transition that must occur over the next twenty to thirty years, and it must begin approximately now.

Richard Heinberg, "Fifty Million Farmers", Twenty-Sixth Annual E.F. Schumacher Lectures, 2006

Farm Journal

14 August 2009

 Learned from Michaele that some of her interns were preparing to leave and if I wanted interviews with them, I'd best hurry. Went out to Growing Things Farm and found Luke in the cook shack (he's been cook for the crew this summer) and grabbed him for a portrait. We did the interview while he whipped up a favorite recipe (stir-fried greens, garbanzos, onions, garlic & spices). Lucky for me—good timing—he left tonight. The veggie stew was great!

 Luke Yodel is from Indiana, twenty-one years old, and listening to his story was like reading Thoreau's "Walden". He wants a life directed by himself only, one "off the grid", a simple one with honest work in the soil. His Mennonite heritage speaks to this and, indeed, all of his ancestors, save his parents, were farmers. He, like many others his age (as he testifies) cannot accept the life paths offered by the "Empire", as he calls it (the "Establishment" for my generation). His politics are local, personal and as such a general response to the wider societal issues. He has spent the summer in his tent—no media, no laptop and soon discovered he had no need of them and found, to his surprise, solitude and the company of Michaele's pigs preferable to his friends in Seattle. I was in awe and could do little but admire him and hope he represents a sea-change—the one all agrarian champions hope for; less is more, small is beautiful—this much and no more.

24 September 2009

 Interviewed five interns this week—have one full-time worker, Ryan from Jubilee Farm, coming tomorrow.

 They are amazing—all 23-26 years old, fresh, real, caked with soil—idealistic only to the extent they treasure self-reliance—growing your own food, tending, nurturing, harvesting, caught in the rhythm of the season, the earth, weather and sun.

 Politically, they are concerned but are more about reclaiming their individual autonomy. They know now, in concrete terms, that their lives are not controlled by the "Corporate Empire"—that they can live literally "off the grid". Each in his/her own way has come to a "Walden Moment"—Thoreau's voice echoes here as well.

 They are bothered by the cost of organic food and the irony that even with the local food movement, the poor still have little or no access to good food; they can't afford it. Those who can, as Rand Rasheed said last night, have become habituated to junk and/or don't know what to do with fresh food when they get it—any food that doesn't come pre-packaged—in cans and boxes. Corporate consciousness has effectively removed alternatives—even those once available to people during the Great Depression, many of whom at least had a garden.

 These young workers are very much aware and spend their evenings in their tents by the Snoqualmie River talking about the politics of food. They know that "revolution" probably isn't possible—that massive change won't happen over night or over years (if ever) and so there is a practical realism attached to the personal quest—living at the margins—changing the world by example, by rejecting as much as possible those ubiquitous tendrils of corporate dependency which have infected virtually every aspect of individual economics. And yet, they are undaunted, young enough to try, not yet disillusioned or willing to retreat into cynicism.

 This book has real promise now—here are people who demonstrate something alive—something which can provide a strong counterexample to the status quo. Perhaps the "movement" they represent is more pervasive and stronger than even they understand. It is indeed "viral"—a "counter-infection", if you will—one rich in diversity of behavior and mind—like the steady march of Paradigm Shift that transformed a geocentric, Ptolemaic consciousness into a Copernican one with its embedded death-knell for the idea of man as the center of his own private universe.

I have lived some thirty years on this planet, and I have yet to hear the first syllable of valuable or even earnest advice from my seniors. They have told me nothing, and probably cannot tell me anything to the purpose. Here is life, an experiment to a great extent untried by me; but it does not avail me that they have tried it. If I have any experience which I think valuable, I am sure to reflect that this my Mentors said nothing about.

One farmer says to me, "You cannot live on vegetable food soley, for it furnishes nothing to make bones with." And so he religiously devotes a part of his day to supplying his system with the raw material of bones; walking all the while he talks behind his oxen, which, with vegetable-made bones, jerk him and his lumbering plow along in spite of every obstacle.

....

The mass of men lead lives of quiet desperation. What is called resignation is confirmed desperation. From the desperate city you go to the desperate country, and have to console yourself with the bravery of minks and muskrats. A stereotyped but unconscious despair is concealed even under what are called the games and amusements of mankind. There is no play in them, for this comes after work. But it is a characteristic of wisdom not to do desperate things.

....

I went to the woods because I wished to live deliberately, to front only the essential facts of life, and see if I could not learn what it had to teach, and not, when I came to die, discover that I had not lived. I did not wish to live what was not life, living is so dear; nor did I wish to practise resignation, unless it was quite necessary. I wanted to live deep and suck out all the marrow of life, to live so sturdily and Spartan-like as to put to rout all that was not life, to cut a broad swath and shave close, to drive life into a corner, and reduce it to its lowest terms, and, if it proved to be mean, why then to get at the whole and genuine meanness of it, and publish its meanness to the world; or if it were sublime, to know it by experience, and be able to give a true account of it in my next excursion.

..................we live meanly, like ants; though the fable tells us that we were long ago changed into men; like pygmies we fight with cranes; it is error upon error, and clout upon clout, and our best virtue has for its occasion a superfluous and evitable wretchedness. Our life is frittered away by detail. An honest man has hardly need to count more than his ten fingers, or in extreme cases he may add his ten toes and lump the rest. Simplicity, simplicity, simplicity! I say, let your affairs be as two or three, and not a hundred or a thousand; instead of a million count half a dozen, and keep your accounts on your thumb-nail.

Henry David Thoreau, "Walden", 1854.

Workers

04 October 2009

Abe Stebbing
Oxbow Farm

My name is Abe Stebbing. I was born in Columbia, Missouri, March 4, 1981. I lived in Columbia, Missouri, until I was about eighteen, grew up playing soccer, playing the piano, hanging out with the old neighborhood kids. Then I went away to college for a year in Westminster, which is in Fulton, Missouri, about forty-five minutes away from Columbia. Played soccer there for a year, and then promptly dropped out of school, and I moved to Tennessee, North Carolina, was a trail guide and a river guide for a bit out there, on the Calais River on the Appalachian Trail. And then with a little pressure from my parents, I ended up going back to school in Columbia, Missouri, where my dad works at the museum at the University of Missouri. It's an art and archaeology museum, where he's a preparator, so he does a little bit of everything, installing the stuff, transporting it. So anyway, I started going there and just taking a couple of classes, looking for other schools to go to. I just kind of assumed I wouldn't like it. It was the school in the town I grew up in. But I ended up really liking it, and stayed there for a couple of years. Part of the deal with that was my folks would help me study abroad for a year, since I was going to school in my hometown, so I moved to Lithuania for about a year and studied there. I was an anthropology student, but they didn't have an anthropology program there, so luckily I met this professor who worked in the medical faculty there, but he taught a lot of forensic anthropology classes. He had pretty much no other English-speaking students, so it was just me and him. So I spent a lot of time playing with old bones in this guy's office. It was pretty fun, actually.

After I left Lithuania, I still had a semester of school left. I came back and finished up my last semester. And since then I've just been kind of bouncin' around. That was five years ago I graduated. And from there, let's see, I moved out to western Colorado, and kind of bounced between there and Utah, working wilderness therapy, and did that for about a year. Moved to the Northeast, moved to Massachusetts in the Berkshires and did trail work all over Massachusetts for just a season.

After that, hit the road, bounced around a little bit, and ended up out here, going to the Wilderness Awareness School. After not working for a few months, that's how I started looking for work, and I'd always been curious about organic farming. Growing up in Missouri, there's farmland everywhere. I was kind of surrounded with it, but didn't really know too much about it. And so just out of curiosity I contacted Luke and Adam down at Oxbow. Went out there, they needed help. I just fell in love with it more and more ever since I've been there.

I guess it all started when I was pretty young. My folks would always take me out into the woods, camping, various things like that—and also just growing up in Central Missouri, just surrounded by national forest. For a while we'd just go to the woods to escape any sort of authority and parents and go out and have a good time, and just get away for a while. Somewhere in there, I realized that's where I felt most comfortable and loved being out there. And so yeah, like I said, I've been doing trail work and river work. Pretty much all my jobs have been outside, and if they weren't I didn't really like them and I've kind of forgot about them. I've worked in restaurants and a bunch of other stuff, but it doesn't really register, didn't really think about it that much. And so actually one of my buddies that I had been camping with forever, he's the one that told me about Wilderness Awareness School, so he was kind of my partner in crime for a long time. So I started looking into that, and it's just an amazing place.

I have a kind of a love-hate relationship with wilderness therapy. Depending on the program, the one I worked for, I would not do it again. You take people out, mostly teenagers—I worked with adults a bit—but you don't really do that much. You kind of let the change in atmosphere and just getting them out of what they've been doing, because all of them come there with pretty serious drug addiction or they've committed crimes, they're doing this instead of going to jail. They don't want to be there at all. So it's like a waiting game. You just kind of wait it out. Some people like that, it's great for them, and it makes all the difference. And some people know how to bullshit and get out of there.

Wilderness Awareness School is kind of a complicated place to describe. A lot of people think it's like a wilderness survivalist school, which it's not. A lot of people think it's like a tracker's school, which it's not really. It's founded by trackers, but....I guess the main things they teach are ethnobotany, a lot of bird studies, bird language, and things on those lines. Basic generalist-naturalist studies, a lot of it specific to the Pacific Northwest. Then they have a really cool—they call it coyote mentoring. It's their mentoring model. That's another one of their big teachings. It's a lot about community building, too. And then of course there is the survivalist aspect to that as well, but it's pretty wide. It's a lot to jam into a year, it's a pretty intense year.

I think I wasn't really fascinated with farming when I started working at Oxbow. It was curiosity, and the kind of work that I thought I'd be doing resonated with me, being outside—you know, physical work. I love food, so that goes hand-in-hand with it. And yeah, I guess mostly curiosity. And all the stuff that everybody says about it being local and organic, and the importance of all that was definitely there for me, and it's there even more so now. But it's hard to really know much about it—at least for me—until I got directly involved. Because I'd talked to people about it, but I didn't know what it meant until I'd been doing it for the last couple of years. I like providing that opportunity, that possibility for people, through markets or CSA or delivering to restaurants even—or just talking about it with folks too.

I try to ask myself what I've learned every once in a while, and it's one of the things where I think down the road it'll become a little more clear. I mean, there's so many things: little things on how to grow food. That's something that I want to do for myself. I'm actually moving in about a month or so to Vermont, and my girlfriend and I have all sorts of experiments and plans for growing food, doing four seasons sort of things. I'm sure I'll take a lot of the stuff I learned from Oxbow there. I learned a lot about dealing with folks as far as like the markets go. It's kind of a little psychology experiment every market. You learn a lot about selling, marketing, how that works. It's amazing, the little changes you make at the market, and how it starts moving product.

There's just all sorts of little—like as far as placement goes, eye level, how much space it's taking up, how abundant it looks, all these different things seem to affect. I'll make one little change, like I'll take stuff out of a tote, or like raise it up a few inches or something. Like if I'm not selling something, and I start playing around and see what happens. And then without, like, a real surge in a crowd, sort of mysteriously it starts selling itself. So it's interesting.

What else have I learned? I think the classic work dynamic stuff, about not taking things personally, about it being a big crunch. In Oxbow, you probably noticed, there's a language barrier going on. It's really interesting to sort of navigate that. I mean, there's the ages, the language, the complicated family relationships, and the whole hierarchy. And so there's just learning how to sort of navigate through that, and remain happy and not take things too seriously and enjoy your work.

Luke and Adam are great bosses. They don't even really seem like bosses. Adam is an incredibly understanding guy. He is incredibly personable. He's really great at just taking care of his workers, knowing what they need. I've learned a lot from him, as far as like managing people. He definitely has his days where—I mean it's farm work, it gets crazy. But he'll remember something I did last season, and bring it up and talk about it. He just pays attention to his workers.

And Luke's great too. Luke seems more like kind of the Big Picture administrative sort of guy, you can tell. He's not quite as present with the workers as Adam is, but it seems like he's always got ideas goin'. And so they kind of like, it's just two very different sort of styles, and so I watch how they work and interact with each other and learn from them.

It's interesting, because at the Wilderness Awareness School, the idea that it's a survivalist school and it teaches you all about independence is there, but there's also the really strong community aspect to it. And I see that transfer really well over to the farm as well. Farming, a lot of the time, is about community and reaching out and meeting people and getting them your product and stuff. But at the same time, it's fiercely independent as well. Like Luke and Adam, everybody there, they're in a market and they've got to protect themselves and look out for themselves and survive. So there's that interesting balance in both places. They make time for themselves, and the Number One thing they're concerned about. I mean, their families, obviously, but also their workers and their farm. I mean, they spend sixty to eighty hours there a week, probably. And so they reach out to other folks, and they get it out there, but also they reel themselves in and keep things close and watch out for their farm. So it's an interesting balance. I've definitely noticed that similarity between Wilderness Awareness School and the farm.

Most of us speak pretty poor Spanish at the farm. But that's the language we mainly use to communicate because half the workers are from Oaxaca, and their family. And Spanish isn't *their* native language. I believe it's Zapotec. That's what they speak to each other, and so somehow it all works out. They know enough English, we know enough Spanish, and so we make it work somehow. It definitely breaks down from time to time. It causes irritation, but also causes a lot of entertainment.

The current group have been here for about eight years, to my knowledge—maybe longer. Not in this area. They've been up and down the West Coast. But they've been here, a couple of them for maybe three or four years, and then a couple just moved out here from I think Alabama actually. He moved out here with his family. I don't know what their plans are. I mean, they have some family back in Oaxaca that they think they plan on returning to, but when that is, I'm not sure. Maybe nine years, actually, they've been away from their families. Yolanda has worked, this is her third or fourth season. Her husband is working off and on, but he's here full-time now. He lost a job in Carnation. And then his brother and nephew just started this season. How long they're going to be here, I'm not sure, but I think they're all coming back next season. They're the field crew, pretty much, is how it's panning out.

I guess I'm the processing manager, is my official title. Early in the season I do seeding, I do field work, do a lot of weeding. And then as it gets busy, I slowly sort of funnel into delivery driving to restaurants and CSA, working a couple of markets a week, and then processing. All the stuff that comes in from the field needs to be processed in some way, cleaned, cut up, dunked in some water, power washed, and then it can go off to the food bank, a CSA, restaurants, one of four markets. So it's just kind of like a big game of Tetris. Definitely got better at multi-tasking since I've been there. I feel like it's kind of the central farm of the farm, like everyone goes out and does all these different things, and then there I am in the processing station. They come back, so I'm getting information—sometimes conflicting information from multiple people, throughout the morning. And so it's another sort of like psychology experiment: you get to know what people actually mean, what they're trying to say when they're talking, and get to know the different people in that sort of way. It's interesting. I definitely create a little more field work time. I think they're trying to get a more strict division of labor, slowly but surely, at Oxbow. Because last year it wasn't like this to the same degree. Towards the end of the year I was doing most of the processing, but it was kind of more split between Erin, who's an intern on the farm, myself, and a few workers too, so there was just more need for everybody to do a little bit of everything.

Part of my reason for coming to the farm is selfish, it's something I want to do, I want to learn about, and then do it for myself on this land I plan on having someday. Some of it is just because I feel like it's the right thing to do, because I can provide a good service for people. And again, I mean, that's selfish as well—that feels good to me. But there's definitely a political aspect to it. I think this is the way people should get their food, from local sources, from sources they can go and see and know what's going into their food and where it's coming from. I guess I'd say there's just a little bit of all those things. And still, I have some strong opinions, but a lot of it is just working itself out in my head, like this is pretty new to me, a couple of seasons doing it. So it's an ongoing interest.

Unfortunately I'm going to Vermont in probably mid November. So there's random.... We're going to be on forty acres in kind of an old house that's going to need some gettin' ready for the winter. My girlfriend Katie, who I think you met, she worked at the farm kind of off and on. She worked for the Wilderness Awareness School and the farm. So her folks live in Saratoga Springs, but they own this house and the forty acres that it sits on, and they plan on retiring there someday. Her dad is mid to late sixties, he's going to retire pretty soon, and he's really interested in growing his own food. And they've got a small orchard and some berries and things. And so kind of working with him, what kind of vision he wants for his retirement home. There's going to be a lot of planning. I started drawing up plans, working with the family. And then I also got ahold of Elliot Coleman's *"Four Season Harvest"* book, and it's been pretty inspiring. We want to set up some greenhouses and see if we can get fresh food year round. I have a few ideas. One is maybe to do just a small dozen-people CSA, because we have friends and family out there, and just kind of a small project. And there's also an interest in—while I really like farming, something is kind of missing for me. I like a little more change and a little more—not creativity, but a little more like building and change. So this is kind of a practice run for a possible future venture, and putting people's food into their own hands, installing gardens and orchards and food forests, sort of, in people's own back yards.

Like for example, my folks were out here visiting, and I took them out to the farm. They'd been in the car all day, and they were just beat and not that happy. My dad and my brother don't travel so well. We got to the farm, and we started harvesting stuff, and they just came alive, and they loved it. We've been in the rainforest and on the beach at La Push, and in the mountains. They loved it, but when I talk to them now, they talk about the farm. I think there's a real importance in putting food right at people's fingertips, and take it from their gardens to their kitchens. It's a really nourishing thing. So if I can start doing that for other people, I'd love to do it.

Like the difference between the Carnation markets and the Bellevue markets is astounding, the amount of knowledge that people come with at the Carnation market, like people have gardens and they know about Bellevue. People ask if I put dye on the purple. Just the wide variety of questions you get in Bellevue is pretty entertaining. People get dressed up. They've got like their farm clothes, which I think is just their clothes they go to market in, like their little bonnets and overalls they've just worn in the city. It's pretty entertaining. But hey, they're getting out there and they're going to the market, so it's great. But if those people could like have a garden, like a lot of the folks in Carnation seem to, that could be a great thing. So yeah, I figure starting with like friends and family. They're going to let me practice on their land and try to get a little....Yeah, Friends and Family. It's a safe place to start, right?

And, like I said, my parents and my brother loved the farm. And my dad's been talking about getting, you know, practicing permaculture in his back yard for years, and nothing's really happened. So I think that might be my next project, is go and work with him, because he's just a wealth of knowledge about stuff. He's not that old, but he has a hard time getting around and doing physical stuff all the time anymore. So I'd love to go help him get *that* started. We'll see if that's what I want to do for a while. That's sort of the first step.

I really think there are a lot of people my age who graduated who are making shifts like this. There seems to be sort of a split. There's a lot of folks, about half my friends have gone to law school after not knowing what they were going to do. And then some have moved to southern rural Missouri and bought up land, living with their brothers or their family or their girlfriend or whatever, they're trying to do a homesteading. I think there's a huge interest in—I'm twenty-eight, and I'd say there's a bit of interest among a lot of people around my age, in learning more about these things. A lot of them are just lost in our generation. The idea of keeping bees or farming, things on those lines, they're really romantic to my age group, I think, and a lot of us just don't know. Because I come from like a liberal small sort of college town, and a very academic city, and like, you're just kind of out of touch with all that stuff. So there's this romanticized idea of what it might be like. Which has got to be a big draw for a lot of people.

Sometimes working at the farm is really great. Then there's been certain experiences with—especially when you're dealing with customers. It's like, "All right, I'm doing the right thing." And then you can deal with the next customer who's just a total jerk to you. Or you could have a crazy day at work. I'm working like basically seven days a week now. And that gets pretty tiring, and your brain does a lot of funny things when it's tired, and you can convince yourself of a lot of different things. Then the fact that there's not a lot of money to be romantic *with*. Yeah, because I work a ton, and then it's like, "Really? This is all the money I got?" So you've got to have a good sense of humor about it.

Luke and Adam always kind of start at the beginning of the season talking about their philosophy, and then it's all kind of business from there on out. So I get sort of like hints of what got them into it, but I would be hard pressed to really speak for them and what their philosophy is. I think like they believe in the work, and they believe it's a noble pursuit, and they also just really like doing it for themselves. Luke says Sarah is the bread winner in his family.

I believe I might come back to the Northwest but it doesn't feel like home up here. I definitely miss the open hardwood forest. And it's beautiful. It's kind of seemed like an extended vacation, but the idea of being able to make anyplace you go, home, is also definitely appealing. I do like it out here, and I've met a lot of great folks. There's a huge community affiliated with the Wilderness Awareness School, like tons of people with tons of knowledge. I'm definitely going to miss that. And to be honest, there's still courses I want to take at the Wilderness Awareness School, which that—maybe come back here to farm and learn more. Who knows? I'm never going to make long-term plans.

Perhaps unsurprisingly, it is the very precarious nature of global/postmodern life that compels us to take our commitments lightly and to value our relationships less than we should. Movable capital demands a movable, and above all flexible, workforce. To get ahead in this world we must be ready to forsake any and all strategies/commitments to meet the new opportunities awaiting us. In this fluid context many of the bonds that tie us to community and place come to be treated like any consumable good—they can always be discarded if a new and potentially better "bond" comes along.

Clearly this trend must be resisted if we are to become attentive and affectionate caregivers of the places and communities we call home. It will not be overcome, however, as long as we remain wedded to the amibitions of our prevailing paradigm, ambitions that we know to be conducive to ill health, anxiety, stress, and fatigue. We need to see that the purveyors of this paradigm do not have our well being at heart, but instead have everything to gain (financially) by keeping us unhappy, dissatisfied and disengaged consumers. As we resist the ways of corporate and global ambition, we may yet come to see the grace and joy that accompany genuine efforts to make our living places an enduring and convivial home. We will discover that our lives are everywhere maintained and benefited by the countless contribution of traditions, communities, habitats and other organisms, and that we in turn have the potential to similarly benefit others.

To be an agrarian is to believe that we do not need the hypothetical (often false, and perpetually deferred) promises of a bright economic future to be happy and well. What we need—fertile land, drinkable water, solar energy, communal support and wisdom—we already have, or could have, if we turned our attention and energy to the protection and celebration of the sources of life.

Norman Wirzba, "Why Agrarianism Matters—Even to Urbanites", Introduction, "The Essential Agrarian Reader", 2003

22 September 2009

Emma Frantz
Growing Things Farm

My name is Emma Frantz and I'm twenty-two years old. I was born in the Central Valley in California, so I grew up in this agricultural area. Grandparents were cotton farmers, almond farmers. Grew up with all of that surrounding me. It was good, it was good. My parents were teachers, they did not farm. But when I was around seven, they packed up and moved my sister and I to Jamaica, so I spent four years there. Then we moved back to the Central Valley. And then I've been in San Diego, California, for the past five years, going to school, but I graduated in 2008. I did Third World Studies and Environmental Studies.

I read Michael Pollan's book, "*The Omnivore's Dilemma*", and then his other one, "*In Defense of Food*". And it was so inspiring, and it got me really, really interested in food, where it comes from, what we're eating, just our diets. It became one of my passions, just almost instantly. I read it and thought, "This is it, this is right, I need to look into this more and see if this is something I can get into in future years and find a job with this kind of stuff." So I thought that I should start where it all starts, in farming, and learn about that, and the land, and how to grow food. And I was also driven by this huge need for practical skills, because I felt like in college I just learned all these theories, I read all these papers, but I didn't learn how to do anything—especially provide for myself. I want to be able to provide, like sustain myself, if I have to, if I want to. So I got in touch with my cousin Shauna and I said, "Hey, let's work on a farm together!" And she said, "Oh, I live in Seattle, I want to do that." She found Growing Things with Michaele and she checked it out, she went and visited in the farm. "Hey, it sounds great, I'm doing this. You should do this too with me." So I said, "Yeah! Sure!" So I came to do this. It's been really great.

It's all, you know, life is just linked in these. There's so many influences and so many things. It started with getting interested in the environment. My dad has been a huge activist in the Central Valley, cleaning up the air. He's done a lot. It's been really inspiring to see him do that. And that's his passion—the environment, the air. He's really flourished doing that. You know, after sixty years of being a teacher—well, not sixty, I guess maybe forty or so—but he found this, and it's just his thing. So I thought, "Oh, that's really cool," started doing the Environmental Studies in San Diego. I really liked that, but it wasn't "**it**". I don't know, just things led to other things, and I just thought about what would be meaningful for my life. Farming has always been a big thing surrounding my life. But it's been the large-scale farming. But I just think that growing food sustainably, and providing that food for other people is one of the most important jobs a person can have.

My grandparents farm cotton, almonds. They've been doing that. My grandparents are very set in some of their ways. I haven't talked to them about organic farming. I haven't even talked to them about working here, and what they think of me working on an organic farm. I see them maybe twice a year. I'm sure we'll talk at Christmas time or so, but I haven't been that engaged in a dialogue with them about how they feel about what they do, and what I do.

A day at Michaele's can be long, or it can be shorter—it depends. A usual day will involve harvesting squash and getting a rash up and down our arms from the sap that comes off. It's interesting. So we get up, we take care of all the animals first: buckets of grain to the pigs, the turkeys, the meat chickens, and the laying hens. And if we have little baby chicks, we go take care of them too, make sure none of them have died in the night, because that happens pretty often. And then we harvest. We make sure everything has enough water. We weed. One of us will cook lunch for the others around noon. We feed the animals again, collect eggs. It's become a routine. We have our days where Monday is our day of rest, we have the day off. We kind of relax. And then Tuesday we start to harvest. Wednesday more harvesting because we work markets Thursday, Friday, Saturday, Sunday. So Tuesday and Wednesday, harvesting. Thursday morning, lots of harvesting. Friday, Saturday, and Sunday go by very fast. Because of markets, we're working from seven to eight, eight-thirty, if you go to a market. So that goes by fast, and then it all starts again after Monday. We get to rest. Markets are hard work. They're harder than working on the farm—for me, at least—because it takes a lot of loading and unloading heavy lugs of potatoes and squash, standing up all day, smiling all day. It's fine, it's great, I love that interaction with people: it's a good part of the week, as well as a hard part.

I like seeing the same people every week. You get your regulars, they come back, and every week they're friendlier, and you're friendlier, and you build more of this farm/customer relationship, and they find out more about your farm and the stuff you have, and it's good, it's really good, to see that happening, building up relationships with people.

What do I like best? Well, I thought I liked digging up potatoes best, after I did it once, but after today I don't know anymore! I spent a long time out there in the sun. So not potatoes, not potatoes. My favorite part so far? I don't know. That's really hard. Every part is a really good different experience. I'm a big fan of the chickens, I like collecting eggs a lot. Those chickens are funny to watch. It's not something you see in city life at all. So you come out here and you just see these little birds running around. They're pretty funny, I like 'em. The markets are really good, getting that experience of setting up on your own, and selling, and making decisions. It's been good to do that too.

It's funny, we were talking about how we've changed today and I think before I came to the farm I wasn't very good at doing problem solving, and like taking charge, just figuring out how to make things work. It just hadn't been something that was a big part of my life before. I would just say, "I can't figure out how to hook up this system. I'm just gonna not do it." But here, you know, Michaele has really pushed us to be that kind of person, to like take charge and just go and make decisions. We make a lot of wrong decisions, but it's all a learning process. So I think I'm better at that. And I definitely have a deeper understanding of what it takes to provide sustainable food, and to be organic. It takes a lot of hard work! A lot of bending over, down on your knees weeding. Yeah, just building up the land so it works, composting things. It's difficult.

I think this is a workable solution for providing food. But I think even more of a workable solution, not just having these organic farms that are providing for a lot of people, but everybody having a garden and providing for themselves. I know it's not possible for suburban areas—not suburban—urban areas. I meant more like apartments and like this packed city, city places, for them all to have gardens and to do that, there's just not space. But there could be space. There's so many parking lots, and I don't know.... Space could be provided for community gardens and for people to all work and then take home the food themselves. I think that's the workable situation.

I'm getting really interested in food security, so like a lot of low-income people don't have access to, or even the money to buy organic, or to grow organic, or even the education to start something like that. So I'm looking into working with youth gardens for lower-income students when I return to San Diego, and hopefully find a job in that area. That would be my goal. Yeah, to implement programs like that. I'd like to start programs, but do that with kids, teach them how to grow things, just so they know they *can*, so they have some sort of practical skills they can use if they need them. They can make money off of it, they can start gardens, they can go sell at farmers markets—just whatever happens, if they have that, they have the ability to grow food.

The most important thing I learned from Michaele......oh, there's so many things, so many things. I still have so many fears of....You know, before I came to the farm, I never would have picked up a chicken—too afraid, too afraid. But Michaele just makes us do things. She says, "Emma, go get the chicken and bring it over here. It has a hurt leg, go pick it up." She asks us to do it, you have to do it. You just do it, because she asked you to, and that's great. And she's a really wonderful person, and you don't want to not do it, because she's such a great person. And she's so capable that you want to be that capable. So you just do what needs to be done.

I think a lot of people are doing it. There's the 'WOOOF' program, the Worldwide Organization of Organic Farms or something like that. This isn't part of it, what I'm doing, but, I mean, people are traveling around, and like working on farms here and there. It's not internships, it's just like they stay two weeks, they stay two months, I don't know how long. And I think that's growing in popularity. I don't know why this is happening, if it's like a trend thing, or it's the popular thing to do, or if it's something that people are realizing is important. I know just like Michael Pollan's book was big. Lots of people read it, lots of my peers have read it, and that's where I got the idea to work on a farm, because he talked about it, he talked about people working on farms, students interning on farms. I just thought it sounded like a good plan. I didn't have a direction after I graduated, I didn't know what I wanted to do. Doing this was, I think, a good choice. I've read part of *Walden*—it's good—not the whole thing. It's funny how we think we have new ideas, but they're really old. Yeah, I definitely agree with that.

I'd like to work in farming first, and try and like gain some ground experience before I decide to commit three or four more years to a Master's or Ph.D. But I mean I hope so. Right now it's really my passion, so I hope that it remains so. I can at least get a grounding in the area.

Exactly what is it that is supposed be *sustained* in "sustainable" economic development? Two broad answers have been given:

The first states that *utility* or happiness should be sustained; that is, the utility of future generations is to be non-declining. People in the future should be at least as well off as those living in the present in terms of the levels of happiness they can experience.

The second states that physical *throughput*, the entropic physical flow from nature's sources through the economy and back to nature's sinks, should be sustained and non-declining. More exactly, the capacity of ecosystems to sustain energy/food flows over the long term is not to be run down.

These are two totally different concepts of sustainability. Utility is a basic concept in standard economics. Throughput is not, in spite of the efforts of Kenneth Boulding and Nicholas Georgescu-Roegen to introduce it. So it is not surprising that the utility definition has become dominant.

I adopt the throughput definition and reject the utility definition for two reasons. First, utility is nonmeasurable. Second, and more important, even if utility were measurable it is still not something we can bequeath to the future. Utility is an **experience**, not a **thing**. We cannot bequeath utility or happiness to future generations. We can leave them things, and to a lesser degree knowledge (provided that it is actively pursued and not simply passively received). Whether future generations will make themselves happy or miserable with these gifts is simply not under our control. To define sustainability as a non-declining intergenerational bequest of something that can neither be measured nor bequeathed strikes me as a nonstarter.

The throughput approach defines sustainability in terms of something much more measurable and transferable across generations—the capacity to generate an entropic throughput from and back to nature. Moreover this throughput is the metabolic flow by which we live and produce. The economy in its physical dimensions is made up of **things**—populations of human bodies, livestock, soils, plants, machines, buildings and artifacts. All these things are what physicists call "dissipative structures" that are maintained against the forces of entropy by a throughput from the environment. An animal can only maintain its life and organizational structure by means of a metabolic flow through a digestive tract that connects to the environment at both ends. So too with all dissipative structures and their aggregate, the human economy. All economies depend on what Wendell Berry has called the "Great Economy", the vast network of patterns and powers in terms of which all of life's necessities and values are parceled out and exchanged.

Bringing the concept of throughput into the foundations of economic theory does not reduce economics to physics, but it does force the recognition that "sustainable" cannot mean "forever", for as scientists tell us, the physical world is **temporally finite,** and will likely end in a big cooling or a big crunch. Sustainability is a way of asserting the value of longevity and intergenerational justice, while recognizing mortality and finitude. Sustainable development is not a religion, although some seem to treat it as such. Since large parts of the throughput are nonrenewable resources, the expected lifetime of our economy is much shorter than that of the universe. Sustainability in the sense of longevity requires increasing reliance on the renewable part of the throughput, and a willingness to share the nonrenewable part over many generations. Of course longevity is no good unless life is enjoyable, so we must give the utility definition its due in providing a necessary baseline condition.

Herman E. Daly, "Sustainable Economic Development", 2002

23 September 2009

Everett Patterson
Local Roots Farm

My name's Everett Patterson, I was born May 22, 1984, in New Orleans, Louisiana, and grew up in suburban New Orleans. My parents met in New Jersey in the seventies. My dad was a New Orleanian, going back in his family several generations. My mom was an Irish immigrant, who came over to be an au pair for some children. And they met in New Jersey where my dad was a janitor at the church that my mom was attending. So yeah, they had me and my sister in New Orleans, that's where we grew up. My dad was an English teacher and later assistant headmaster of the school where both my sister and I went from kindergarten all the way up through graduation.

No farmers in the family. I think my mother's father in Ireland grew up a farmer, so he was definitely a farmer. He became a doctor later on. So my mother's father's side of the family, yeah, was farming in Ireland, just a small farm. When I tell anyone on that side of the family that I'm farming, they're sort of like, "Oh, boring!" Well, you know, they're all in their nineties now, but in their memory of chickens and everything, I don't think they see the appeal the same way I do.

It wasn't even something I would have even thought about too seriously up until very shortly before I actually did it—maybe about a year or two before I did it. In high school it was sort of "get into college!" very academic focus. And then in college I studied medieval history and music theory and composition, neither of which had any bearing on farming. Well, there's some agriculture in medieval history, certainly. But not the practical angle. And as far as studying soil chemistry or anything like that, I haven't touched that.

Coming out of college a lot of people were kind of being funneled directly into these New York banking jobs, these high-paid sort of deceptively prestigious banking-type jobs, which I had no interest in, and had sort of an aversion to. And it was sort of I would like to, rather than moving around imaginary numbers for a living, I'd like to do something that has an actual tangible effect on the real world, whatever that is. Of course academia had blown out of the water whatever impression I had of what that was.

So I was working in cafés and that was probably where it started, being around food: being in cafés both in New York and in New Orleans, seeing, for instance, here we are selling strawberries imported from Mexico even though it's the middle of Louisiana strawberry season. I guess I got more interested, first, in just kind of the economic policy of it: sort of like I was in the newspaper, reading about corn subsidies, crop subsidies, just sort of the angle of food distribution and everything, how are we going to solve hunger, how are we going to solve farmers—keeping them in business—and all this, thinking about it more from the theoretical level. But like the more I thought about *that*, the more I realized I don't even know about—I don't have any dirt under my fingernails, I don't even know about how this stuff is really done. And so I guess I felt more and more, you know....part of the problem; the policy makers are detached from the material production of the food. So I thought whether I go on to study agricultural policy, for instance, or do anything at a more—I don't want to say higher level—but a more policy-driven level—I would like to first have the hands-on experience of just knowing what's involved in the raising of food. And the choice of going to a naturally grown farm, this type of farm that doesn't use pesticides and all that, was more because I knew it would be small and hands on, and a learning experience, than because of any sort of pre-existing allegiance to organic food. We never ate organic food growing up. The health aspects of it were sort of abstract to me, I didn't really care. I didn't pretend to understand the economics of it. But it was more I wanted an internship where I'd be able to actually do the stuff. As far as that's concerned, this has been very successful: I know a *thousand* times more about plants than I did coming in, given that I knew nothing coming in.

    The politics is just so damned complicated. Clearly—and I'm not badmouthing the farm here—but clearly we're not going to save the world by having a bunch of little farms in the Snoqualmie Valley that sell at farmers markets, vegetables of this quality for this price. We have six billion people to feed, basically. I'm open to industrialization, herbicides, pesticides. Part of me wants to just say, "Do whatever you have to do." Like, "We need to get this food made." At the same time, obviously there are these environmental ramifications, you know. I don't want to sacrifice the hunger of humanity sort of on the altar of environmentalism; say, "let's tear down the whole machine, let's destroy the system." Just Americans in particular have this amazing ingenuity of squeezing blood from a stone, in terms of getting crops out of American soil. I don't think we should discard that just because we've done it irresponsibly so far. For now, the organic food movement—and again, Local Roots is not organic—but for now the movement seems to still be confined to being sort of—I don't want to say a novelty item, because it's become a way of life for some people to go to the co-op and everything. But still, fringe, call it whatever you will, it hasn't, like, infiltrated society enough in a major way. It's still a subculture. And as long as it remains that, I'm not sure how much of a help it can be. For instance, at the farmers markets, I'm more satisfied, and I think the other interns feel the same way, to accept food stamps or WIC checks or whatever for food for a working family or whatever, then for somebody to be like, "Oh, you have exotic Italian heirloom vegetables!" I'm not particularly enthused about that angle. I'm not a gourmet or anything, and compared to a lot of the people at this farm, I have a less refined sense of taste or whatever. I'm not a "foodie," as they call them. I'm not in it for the gourmet aspect, although it is delicious. The stuff we eat on the farm is way better than what you'll get, standard-grown supermarket produce. In other words, at the farmers market I'm not as excited about the "we're providing super-quality stuff," as sort of like "it's local, you know the farmer," we're making it real, we're making it something more real and tangible than the Wal-Mart grocery situation—which again I'm not knocking, it's totally necessary. My family did, and still does all their produce shopping at Wal-Mart. When I go home to New Orleans, that's where we get our vegetables. And it'll be a little more difficult this year, because I've been spoiled by having all this great stuff at Local Roots.

    I would like to get into more reading on it in this coming month, when

I'm going to have less time to work. It's been a problem. The other interns are very diligent about doing outside reading on agriculture after work. To me, I'm sometimes a little burnt out at the end of a day of farming, to then sit down and read a book about farming. I usually tend to reach for the book that is as far removed from farming as I can. You know? But maybe once I have a lower work load.... It's weird, but there's these popular books about food now: Michael Pollan and all these guys. You know, these are like best sellers, so it shows that people are thinking about it. I'd like to just kind of catch up by reading those first. But then, I'm sure there's more in-depth.... I don't have a background in economics or anything, so I'm not sure what angle to approach that from. But no, as far as reading something that really shook me, the few sort of pop agricultural books that I have looked at, it's more like just kind of reading what you already thought. You read it and you're like, "Well, yeah, of course!"

Anyway, of course, it's all a jumble right now. I guess it was more a desire to sort of.... Not that I knew where I stood going in, and it was on some crusade for a certain type of farming, but I really kind of do want to figure out.... Like the one certainty is that this will be important in the years to come.

It's easy to get put off. You go to Whole Foods or whatever, and everything is so overpriced, and people are buying things for all these snobbish reasons. Of course I don't want to read too much—I don't know what's going on in their minds. But like you hate to see, it's like—we talked about this a lot on the farm—you know, people who shop at farmers markets or whatever for, quote, "the wrong reasons." On the one hand you could say it's good simply that they're doing it. Why does it matter why they're doing it? If they're doing it so they can brag to their friends that they shop at farmers markets, at least they're still shopping at farmers markets. On the other hand, there's a drive to sort of have an ideological, like, coherence to why you're doing what you're doing. Why *are* farmers markets better, really? I guess that's what I'm trying to figure out.

I left New York City two years ago, and if I go back there again, like, I'm no more qualified to any of the types of work that you can do in New York City, than when I left. I have this degree, I'm sure a lot of jobs are open for me. On the other hand, farming kind of spoils you: you get to work outdoors all day. I've had more than one person tell me it's hard to go back to other types of work after you've been able to work as a farmer. So it's vague. Maybe another internship. What I really want to do is work on this comic book. I'm doing this comic book. For a while, before I got the internship, I was progressing at a page every couple of days. Now it's crawled down to like maybe a page a month. And I'm just like.... I've got the script, and it's stretching on ahead of me, and it's never gonna get done at this rate. I want to do that. But no, it's something that in the long hours hoeing in the fields I have to mull over, "What am I gonna do after this?" And I'm not sure. I'm praying for guidance in that.

Of course the economy is looking bleaker these days. When I graduated in 2006, the job market was still pretty good, and so for me to say something like, "I don't want to take one of these high-salaried hoity-toity banking jobs," was a little easier to say. Even when I left last year my final café job in New Orleans, that was in September right as the recession was starting. And so there was still this lingering, "Uhhh, maybe this isn't such a good idea to give up a really high-paying job and go be a farmer." But talking short-term and long-term—and of course so much of the farming debate *is* about short-term benefits or long-term plans. Talking short-term/long-term, even just as a career move, like the demand for food is never going to go away. And I can get really good at doing some niche thing, or moving everybody's money around in funds and what not. A few things—food, shelter, clothing, education, whatever—the demand for them is never going to diminish, and so there is an *extreme* security. In that sense, it's the opposite of a risk. At times I'm sort of like, "Man, what am I doing?! Why am I still.... Why am I out here *farming*, of all things?!"

There is this romantic thing about being a farmer, too, right?—especially in the U.S. And when I was writing applications to farms, I was trying not to let that seep through too much, because I don't want to come off as like this college kid who read a little too much Thoreau or something, and wants to, like, go and be a farmer, and has no experience—which I just described exactly what I was. But I didn't want it to seem like a romantic thing. I tried to stress the pragmatic: oh, the problems facing the agricultural world today. But yeah, there was a huge wanting to be out there in the sun and with the dirt and the vegetables and everything, and loading up baskets full of vegetables and all that. The whole mythos around being a farmer. I guess you shouldn't be embarrassed to admit that that's part of why you're doing it. I'm not just being a Thoreau, like, this is not just part of some grand strategy. It's also enjoying the work in and of itself.

Who knows what could happen? But at Local Roots specifically, I don't know what's going to go on with them. Like I mentioned, this region has a lot of this type of farm, although they're in every state, it's happening everywhere. When I was looking around the websites, I was looking; Louisiana seemed to have just more of the mono-cropping and less of the internships I was.... Even mono-cropping, it's not that I'm down on it as a farming practice, but as a learning opportunity you would learn how to do *one* thing well. And Local Roots, we grow all kinds of stuff—barely enough stuff to sell. We diversify so much, some things we don't even grow enough of to sell, but just so you can have sort of your finger in everything.

It's problematic, and I don't think the answer is as simple as "organic local food at any cost." Because we have—you know, you're born into a society, and you have to make do with it. We can't erase everything and start anew. And I have a lot of grand narratives. I'm a Christian, and I'm kind of a socialist a lot of the time. And so a lot of my ideas *do* entail sort of like a thorough clean slate building up again from the new. And if I'm going to be a pragmatist, I really have to force myself to say, "No, Everett, this is not the time for revolution. This is the time for 'let us examine things and see how they really could work out together.'"

In our one-eyed focus on 'value added', we economists have neglected the correlative category, "that to which value is added," namely the throughput. "Value added" by labor and capital has to be added to *something*, and the quality and quantity of that something is important. There is a real and important sense in which the original contribution of nature is indeed a "pie", a pre-existing, systemic totality that we all share as an inheritance. It is not an aggregation of little tarts that we each baked ourselves. Rather it is the seed, soil, sunlight, and rain from which the wheat and apples grew that we then converted into tarts by our labor and capital. The claim for equal access to nature's bequest is not the invidious coveting of what our neighbor produced by her own labor and abstinence. The focus of our demands for income to redistribute to the poor, therefore, should be on the value of the contribution of nature, the original value of the throughput to which further value is added by labor and capital—or, if you like, the value of low entropy added by natural processes to neutral, random, elemental stuff. Failure to acknowledge this original value, as we now know, leads to its exploitation and destruction. Or, as Wendell Berry puts it, we increasingly see human economics succeeding by the invading and pillaging of the Great Economy.

Herman E. Daly, "Sustainable Economic Development", 2003

14 August 2009

Luke Yodel
Growing Things Farm

I'm Luke Yodel, I'm twenty-one, and I'm from Elkhart, Indiana. I'm an intern here at Growing Things Farm. I knew that for a while I've thought that farming was something that I'd really like, and something I could do as a possibility. You know, like, what am I going to do with my life? I don't know. One thing I could do is farm. That's always what I'd thought. But I'd never really.... I was attracted to it mentally, and so part of my goal for the summer was to see if I like it physically, and actually do it. And so then I was looking on the Internet for farm internships just for the summer, and found a database that was just full of them. So initially I was looking around Indiana, Illinois, Michigan, that area, and there are farms out there, organic small farms—not as many as out here. So I was doing that, and then I thought, "You know, I've been wanting to go to the West Coast for a while." And so I started just kind of on a whim, applied to a bunch in California and Oregon and Washington, just kind of at random, and ended up this was one that the schedule worked out. A lot of farms want the people to stay the whole season, but I was coming in June and leaving in August, which is kind of weird, and Michaele happened to be trying something new this year, so it worked out that I could come by.

I know part of it was I'm studying sociology, and part of it was the Sociology of Food course that I took. And the professor had done his specialization in food sociology, so this is kind of his field, and it was a real interesting class. I learned a lot about the systems of food and how we get food in America. That's part of what drove me to doing farming. And also, since then, and also through other, like sociology classes and stuff, I've been interested in living off the grid and living like not being dependent on the big structure or The Empire, as some call it. A guy out here that I met calls it The Empire—the United States Empire, because it's not a republic, he says, it's an empire. So I'm really intrigued about living very self-sustainably, and not being dependent on broader systems that I have no control over, and I don't really know what's going on. I think food is a really good way to start, because it's an essential part of life. It's very important.

As far as I know, all of my ancestors up until my parents' generation, on both sides, were farmers. I'm ethnically Mennonite, I would say, and grew up going to a Mennonite church, but haven't continued going. I wouldn't say that I'm religiously Mennonite, but I would say I'm ethnically Mennonite, and farming is a big part of that history. Basically Mennonites seem to have an identity that's different and it involves a lot of different things. Farming is one of them. They're always well-known as good farmers. Singing in four-part harmony is one of those things. I grew up always singing in four-part harmony in church, and it's just really interesting. And Mennonites also have this kind of ideology that involves a separation from the state, and I think that may be one place—kind of like Amish, but done in a different way, with most Mennonites. Some Mennonites can seem like Amish, like really conservative Mennonites that will only drive like black cars, and use less technology, and live really secluded. There's also a lot of Mennonites who are *very* active in peace and justice issues around the world and in our country and in politics; but still at the same time hold this identity that their identity is formed not by the broader political boundaries, but by the smaller community. And I like that about it. And so there's certain things I like, but I never was baptized. In the Mennonite religion you aren't baptized when you're a baby, you choose to be baptized, usually when you're an adolescent, sixteen, eighteen, something like that. So anyway, the farming, even though I know that farming isn't necessarily genetic, you know, like the ability to farm well. I guess some parts of it are, like a body that's sturdy, made for doing that kind of work—that makes sense. More it's my personal choices that I've made. But knowing that my ancestors were all farmers does encourage me, and I've always kind of felt like my body was made to farm, and I feel good when I'm doing physical labor, and it just feels really right to be working with the earth and pulling up these vegetables.

  I think it's been a very good experience, and very encouraging with the farming, because as I said, I'd always kind of thought of it as something I *could* do, wasn't really sure. But since being here, it's kind of like it's been answered, yes, I could do this; and yes, this is a good life; and yes, I feel great growing my own food. I don't really buy much other food besides what we eat on the farm—just some grains to make, I've started like making more of my own stuff, like I make granola now, and buy yogurt. Guess I could make that too. You know, just finding more and more ways of being a human, really. I feel like I'm more of a human here, and I'm engaging with my environment in a really cool way, which is something I really like, that I'm doing what I think humans *should* do, which is interacting with the earth and my environment in a creative way, too. I live in a tent, which is interesting. It's something I've kind of gotten over. I was nervous about it at first. It was like, "Geez, how am I going to live in a tent all summer? That's going to be weird." But I have an air mattress and a sleeping bag, and I found some bookshelves I put in there. You know? I've learned that you can survive in so many different environments, and I think that's a major part of being a human. Humans can live anywhere on the planet, and in space, for short periods of time. And that's one thing that I've always thought that sets humans apart from other animals. Other people would say a lot of other things that I don't agree with. I think that a lot of what we do is essentially the same thing that other animals are doing. But that we can live anywhere, I think that's based on our social ability. And from that, a lot of other things, like our ability to remember and write things down. Things like that.

  I've learned a lot about how food is made and processed and grown in big plants and then shipped around the country, distantly related to me. For example, on the farm this is stuff I grew and have been tending to over the months. Or if we didn't grow it, like these onions we didn't grow, but we traded with them at markets with other farms, with our produce. I didn't use any Federal Reserve notes to get this food, and I know that it was from this other farmer, and I know they grew it. But if I go to a supermarket and go to the frozen foods aisle and get some Hot Pockets, that's something I wouldn't have thought twice about maybe four years ago, but in the past couple of years, it's just become more and more evident to me that I don't like that, that food isn't good for me, and it doesn't make me feel good. And also, it's just very distantly made and produced and shipped around the country, and I just don't even know what it is, really. It doesn't seem like food to me anymore. Like the thought of going and eating that doesn't seem like eating food.

I would say community is a part of it, but I don't want to find a community and join it. I think that the community is made through—I think humans make community in everything they do. Being connected to one's food is very important in this community, because when you go to a supermarket and buy some Hot Pockets, you're connected to other people, but the act of creating food and then trading with it to someone else for other food or other goods, and we get like hummus or soap. Or not, I guess we make our own soap, we don't get soap. But we could conceivably trade for other things that we need, with our food that we've made. I really like how community is created through that action, and I think that the creation of community is something *very* human, but a lot of times in our society we're distanced from that, and we are not able to make that connection. I would blame a lot of the things that are wrong with our society on that idea—like being completely distanced, and like what's going on in the rest of the world to get the things that we have, like our clothes. Who knows how they're made? And who knows what's going on? And that's such a crucial part of being able to maintain the system, is us being ignorant and not knowing what's going on.

I think that my generation, in specific, things are changing. I mean, not everybody, of course. And I think other people would agree with me on a lot of that, but not think the solution is to go work on a farm. And that's reasonable. That's just kind of my reaction to it. But I can see how someone else would say, well, then I should be a nurse and I should heal people. Something like that, you know—it could be completely different. But my response has to do with food. I don't know, no matter what profession, I think that food would have to be a really important part of it, because that's how you exist.

I guess it's hard to say, because there's a lot of different people in my generation; a lot of different people in previous generations. I think that a lot of things were realized in the sixties and seventies, I think that was a changing time and place. And I've always kind of thought, "You know, man, I wish I was a part of *that*." But I think now that generation has taught *my* generation, and they've taught that from a young age, and there's a lot of things I think the generation before me learned throughout their lifetime, it's a different relationship to that idea, than my generation where it's more like just common knowledge. Kind of like one place we've seen this is in religion. And I think religion is becoming much less fundamental, like "I'm right and everybody else is wrong." But yeah, I remember growing up and thinking, "Well, if I was born anywhere else in the world, I wouldn't be Mennonite. I would be something else." And I couldn't say that Mennonites are right, because that's what I was born in, and that didn't make sense to me. And I think that a lot of people in our generation kind of take that kind of a laic approach to religion. Like everybody has their *own* religion, and that's okay, and it's a different path to the same thing. I heard something on NPR [National Public Radio]. They were talking about Coca-Cola using Woodstock as an advertising thing.

My dad was born in '51, my mom in '55. It's interesting, I mentioned that my parents' parents, my grandparents' generation, they were all farmers, but then on both sides, nobody in my parents' generation continued farming. Some of them have gardens—I think all of them probably have some form of garden, but not farming. It seemed like they were kind of distancing themselves from that life.

I think in our generation, that's also a common thing, a lot of people going to school and starting out with some idea of knowing what they want to do. For example, I didn't really know exactly what I wanted to do, but it was like, "I think I'll go for being a teacher, that sounds good," and then just kind of went with it, to go with something. I went with it for like two years, stayed with Education, and just like tried to take as many classes that were general education, that I'd have to take anyway, to like avoid actually being committed to it. Then when it came time that it was kind of like, "All right, I need to actually commit to this or not," I decided no, I just want to learn, I just want to study sociology and Spanish: sociology because I'm really interested in it, and Spanish because I'm also interested in language and I wanted to travel. So I was able to travel to Peru and Spain. So yeah, basically seek enlightenment through that system.

I've decided working toward a career is not interesting to me. I'm not interested in a specific career or something like that. From talking to people I respect, who are older, I've kind of gathered that a good approach would be to just kind of go with what I'm interested in, and go with what I'm good at, and just pursue those things, and it'll work out. And I feel really comfortable in most ways, that I can live and continue living a really good life without much money at all. If I can grow my own food, that's a very big part of that, and just be creative with life, and work with what I have, and work with what's around me. And other things will come, but I don't want my identity to be based on a career. I'm who I am, and I'm interacting with my environment. I mean, life can be simple, or life can be complicated, depending on how you look at it. I know life is complicated sometimes, but I prefer to say it's simple, when I can.

I don't know what I'll do after college. I would be content with finding some sort of job in the area, in Goshen. I go to school in Goshen, Indiana, which is a pretty small town. And I'm from Elkhart, which is like forty minutes away from that. So it's pretty close by home, and I've been kind of traveling around a lot recently, and that's actually made me *more* okay with going back home and living at home, because I think it's important to find a place, and find a place where you can be. Because I can exist—as I said, a human could exist anywhere. So I feel like the possibilities are endless, so it might be good to go with a place that makes sense, and that I know a lot of people. But I also like it out here. I've thought about coming back out to the Northwest and farming. I've also thought about doing WWOOF'ing (Worldwide Organization of Organic Farms), another, like, farm internship organization database thing, doing that in South America somewhere, because I know Spanish and I'd maybe like to go down there. But for now I'm feeling a little adventured-out. Like I kind of want to just go back to Goshen and be there for a year. That's why I said I'd be okay with just getting some kind of job. I really like landscaping or farming. Like there's farms in the area that I could work on. So just enough money to be able to pay rent. Actually, when I get back to Goshen, the first thing I'm gonna do is go to the farmers market and find a farm I can do some kind of volunteer CSA thing—at least until it all starts dropping off on the production. Because I can't stand the idea of not having a food supply. Like every time I leave the farm here, like if I go into Seattle to visit friends, I'm there for like a couple of hours, and I think about how nice it would be to be back on the farm. Even though when I'm here sometimes I feel bored and antsy, kind of want to get out and find some friends. And I do have friends here, but it's different. And they're all girls, too, so it's a little different friendship—more like sisters.

From what I've heard from the other women here, it seems like it's very empowering to women who are concerned about their identity being driven by gender roles and stuff like that: empowering to know that their bodies are useful. And as a man, I feel more like I was raised to know that I was supposed to do work. You know, just like the gender roles we were raised with involved that sort of thing.

But I think working on a farm can be empowering to anybody, not just women. I think it's empowering as a human to learn that you can actually do things, and you don't have to depend on a system to provide for you, while you go to a factory and do the same repetitive action over and over again, and just become a robot.....for The Empire.

For lunch today I'm making one of my favorite things I've been making a lot lately. It involves garbanzo beans and.... All you really need is like onions and garbanzo beans and oil and spices. But I put all sorts of other things in it too. I actually learned this in Spain. I lived with a host lady, and she taught me how to make this. Oh, the other important part is some dark leafy greens. It's a really good way to use dark leafy greens. So you basically just fry up onions and spices, and then put in garbanzo beans, fry those, and then put in kale or chard, something like that. Cooking has been one of my favorite things about this experience, because it's just so much fun to have fresh produce that you're turning into food. Like this is what I'm talking about, being a human. I'm adding my creativity and time and energy into something, and turning it into something useful for me and the people around me. And I love that. Other people here have a computer and spend a lot of time on it, but I didn't bring my computer, my laptop. There's actually wireless on the farm. I didn't expect that. So a lot of times they'll spend their time on the computer and just.... I don't know, I've been really glad to get away from that and not spend my down time on the computer or watching TV. More at school it's like the Internet, like just spend kind of like useless—it's kind of like useless time where I'm just not really doing anything much. I'm just kind of like on the Internet, looking at random shit. I feel like that part of my life has been eliminated in some ways here. And so what do I do otherwise to entertain myself? Well, I find it a lot easier to sit around and not really do much at all, just kind of like watch nature, and go hang out with the pigs, go hang out with the turkeys for a minute. There's stuff like the old house there, that's flood damaged, not useful anymore. So one day I just decided to power wash the porch, so we could hang out on the porch, because it was hot and there wasn't a good place to hang out. So I power washed it, cleaned it up, put up some decorations, and now it's a useful place to be, and it's fun. I love it. There's electricity there, ran some extension cords and power strips and stuff. It's just great to do stuff like that, versus—instead of participating in pre-packaged fun. That's how I think about it, just like fun that's packaged in order to *be* fun. I like to make fun with what's around me, and create it myself.

It is very interesting that we have to choose to.....survive. I don't know, it's interesting, I was taking a class—my school is Mennonite in background, so it was an Anabaptist history class, and part of that includes Amish and stuff like that. There was one, I think it was some interviews with an Amish preacher, just a bunch of different Amish preachers, and in the Amish community they don't do a lot of things that we consider part of our society. Like they don't use electricity, most of them. Like using a bike is debatable. And a lot of people would say it's a very restrictive lifestyle, and that they don't have the freedoms that people *should* have. But then the response from one of them was that really they're a lot freer than a lot of other Americans, because they don't *have* to make the choices of what to wear or what kind of car to get. Those kind of choices are a burden, is what he was implying—it's a burden to have that much choice. And I kind of relate to that. Going into a supermarket and trying to figure out what to buy, that's so overwhelming to me. I don't like it. I like having these ingredients that I can work with. I like the limitation. And I think out of limitation comes human ingenuity and creativity. And that's what we're supposed to—I feel like that's what I'm supposed to be doing, is dealing not with problems, but dealing with....adversity, in some ways. And we're not raised in a vacuum, there's all these stimuli that we have to react to. But it seems like in some ways in our society we're raised to *not* have to do anything, to be able to just work and then sit around. But I think that that's not how it should be, to be a healthy person. I think I feel very healthy on this farm, and I feel so great about my body and about my mind and what I'm doing. It's awesome. So we have to make a conscious choice to live how I think we should. That's interesting.

I think it'll be increasingly evident in the years that come as we are not able to be as dependent on fossil fuels, as that becomes more of a problem that needs to be dealt with. Or just out of necessity, not being able to ship food across the country. You know, people are going to have to get that food somehow, and I think becoming more local and more sustainable is a direction that, of necessity, we'll have to go; necessity and ideology will drive it—they kind of work together.

Economists have traditionally considered nature to be infinite relative to the economy, and consequently not scarce, and therefore properly priced at zero. But nature is scarce, and becoming more so every day as a result of throughput growth. Efficiency demands that nature's services be priced, as even Soviet central planners eventually discovered. But to whom should this price be paid? From the point of view of efficiency it does not matter who receives the price, as long as it is charged to current users (to expect future generations to absorb all these costs is to raise a host of complex moral questions). But from the point of view of equity it matters a great deal who recieves the price for nature's increasingly scarce services. Such payment is the ideal source of funds with which to fight poverty and finance public goods.

Reducing poverty is indeed the basic goal of development, as the World Bank now commendably proclaims. But it cannot be attained by *growth* for two reasons. First, because growth in GDP (Gross Domestic Profit) has begun to increase environmental and social costs faster than it increases production benefits. Such uneconomic growth makes us poorer, not richer. Second, because even truly economic growth cannot increase welfare once we are, at the margin, producing goods and services that satisfy mainly relative wants rather than absolute wants. If welfare is mainly a function of relative income, then aggregate growth is self-canceling in its effect on welfare. The obvious solution of restraining uneconomic growth for rich countries, so as to give opportunity for further economic growth, at least temporarily, in poor countries, is ruled out by the ideology of globalization, which can only advocate global growth. We need to promote national and international policies that charge adequately for resource rents, in order to limit the scale of the macroeconomy relative to the ecosystem and to provide a revenue for public purposes. These policies must be grounded in an economic theory that includes physical throughput among its most basic concepts. These efficient national policies need protection from the cost-externalizing, standards-lowering competition that is driving globalization. Protecting efficient national policies is not the same as protecting inefficient national industries.

Herman E. Daly, "Sustainable Economic Development", 2003

23 September 2009

My name is Rand Rasheed. I was born October 1986 in Iraq in the Kurdish region, in the city of Kabul, and grew up with Mom, Dad, three aunts, and four sisters all in one house. My dad worked for a number of different aid organizations: worked for MCR National as an interpreter and a translator; and he worked for a branch of UNICEF called OOFDA. I don't remember what the acronym stands for, but he was basically organizing groups of people to go into regions that had landmines that were placed in by Saddam. And he was helping clear out that area so they could go back and farm or live their lives.

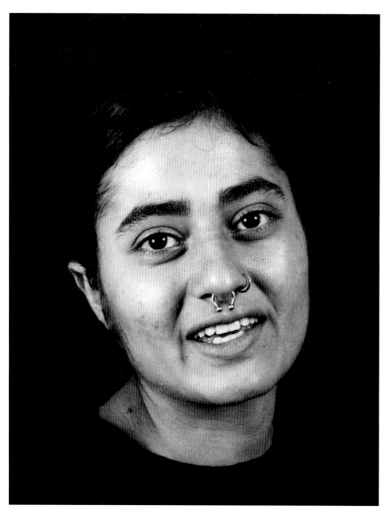

Rand Rasheed
Local Roots Farm

And in '97, there was a sort of threat that Saddam Hussein put out, saying that because the country was under sanction there weren't supposed to be any aid organizations and anybody who was involved should either flee or they're in big trouble. So my dad was given the opportunity of leaving with his family, so he decided that would be the safest option. So my nuclear family, my mom and four sisters, we came to the U.S. and have lived in the Seattle area since then.

I went to high school here, worked a number of minimum wage sort of jobs and what have you, and ended up at Local Roots through the food co-op that I was working at in Seattle. I was working at Madison Market. And I came out to volunteer a few times with a couple of coworkers, because of the work share that Local Roots and Madison Market have together. And I just totally felt like the farm was the place for me, and I really wanted to be on it. So I quit my job in February, and I started in April on the farm, and it's now the end of September, so five, six months. Six months, yeah. It's been *quite* a summer.

My dad actually is—or was, I guess—a green farmer, and his father before him, and his before him. So growing up, we would go—my dad has something like 200 acres in Iraq and he would grow barley and wheat and lots of grains and things. And there were some cows, and there was a family that lived on the farm that took care of the farm, so there's cows and a tiny acre of vegetables that grew. I remember really enjoying going out and playing in that. And then when we would harvest all the wheat, we would have some come to our house that we would clean out, or eat ourselves, or what have you. So yeah, going to the farm as a kid was definitely like a real special thing. My dad was very much devoted to continuing with the farm. They had drilled a well just a year or so before we left, and bought a tractor and stuff like that. So it's old family tradition, I guess. And he's *very* excited that I've grown interested in it.

I think a lot of political reasons brought me here, sort of economical-political reasons. Working at the food co-op I definitely became more aware of the food issues and all the politics with organics and conventional, and between big food companies and the tiny underdogs that are fighting through. I think there's just something young people like to do to try and save the world, and that's kind of, I think, what I'm....Yeah, save the world, sure. But I definitely saw Local Roots being just a brand new farm that had just started. This is their third season, and I am just very much attracted to like see how the process happened. I think I couldn't have come upon a better farm, because Siri, Jason, and Dan are all very involved in food politics, always learning new things about it. They're involved in committees and what have you, to try and organize—whether it's like defining agriculture with King County, or working with like the Harvest Coalition to try and organize the farms in the Valley, what have you. So it's been like a very good learning experience, I think, for me. Yeah, couldn't have picked a better farm.

It's great! They are all very intelligent people, and have a lot of knowledge to share. And they are constantly informing us. All of us on the farm are always learning something new from each other, and it's never a dull conversation. Well, there's once in a while a hot day when you're tired, and you realize you're telling the same story you have three times already. Yeah, it's been great, and again, because they're a new farm, they're easier to approach about ideas. I think whenever any of us has read some sort of technique or is slightly interested in something and we bring it up, there's always encouragement to continue with it. Dan is amazing to work with. Not only is he really warm-hearted and kind of a really accepting person of anybody he meets—he's friends with you the instant he meets you—but he's also *extremely* knowledgeable in farming and construction, any sort of hands-on sort of thing: anything from, like, "Where do I set up my tent?" "What should I do with *this* thing?" He totally is the person to go to. I really love seeing him first thing in the morning. Just a good sense of humor and just—it's lots of laughing during lunch.

Some of the ideas I have are that people won't find these small farms as unusual, hard to obtain sort of thing, and we'll hopefully encourage more people to do it. I think the more people produce food locally, and distribute locally, hopefully the more attainable it'll be monetarily and just socially. I overheard Everett talking about it and this is like an issue we *all* talk about on the farm. I think all of us have come from backgrounds that, you know, working class, and our parents couldn't afford this food growing up. And it's like we go to the farmers markets and we sell a bunch of turnips for three dollars. And you can't argue with a family that would go to McDonald's to get food. You could get three sandwiches for three dollars. So it's definitely been something that we've all had a really hard time with, just like knowing that the food we're selling is just like not going to be purchased by a great number of people, because of the price. And we also know that it's the healthiest stuff out there, and everybody should be able to have access to clean food. So hopefully in my little dream world, that this will continue to happen and to be supported so greatly that eventually maybe economically things will balance out, and the big guys that can afford to sell fifty cents for a bunch of turnips or radishes or whatever, will not be able to compete with that market, and I don't know, and living wages would have to be adjusted. It's a tough one. But that's kind of my idea. And then there's the whole idea of like any plot of land that is taken up by organic farming is like so-and-so percentage better for the world's environment, because a parking lot didn't go there, or a golf course didn't go there, what have you. So that's another thing, is making sure that land doesn't get taken over by strip malls. Yeah, that's kind of the idea: hopefully making healthy food available for more people.

Many cities now are converting parking lots and abandoned building sites for community gardens. I think it's called.... it's not part of Eat Your Lawn. I forget, it's like Pavement to something. There's a cute catchy name for it. There's like a church parking lot on 16th Avenue on Capitol Hill that they're turning into a pea patch. It's slowly happening. And I think urban farming is where it's at. For me, I see myself more doing that, then being hidden away in the woods. I kind of like the city. But making sure that kids know what their food looks like and how it's grown, and be able to have the choice of it. Also people.... I don't know if you're familiar with Yesler Terrace. It's in the Central District. You've seen their little pea patches and everything. That's affordable housing, and most of the people that live there are immigrants from all over the world who have gardening as a part of their daily life. And it's like a thing that you do at your home. I definitely wish for those people that need that in their life to have the opportunity to do it, even though they end up living in a tiny little apartment somewhere, that they have some sort of earth to turn.

When I grew up, my mom had a little vegetable garden, like a kitchen garden. And then we moved here and it's kind of an unusual thing. The same with hanging your clothes outside to dry. The apartment manager gives you a call when you do that. Yeah, I think there's definitely sort of a return to the way things used to be. I've noticed much more vegetable patches in the city, in the central districts especially. And like they just changed—there used to be a law, that little patch of grass between sidewalk and road was to remain lawn. But they've just banished that, and they're like, "Grow vegetables! Go for it!" So I think the city's also making an effort. Seattle's not the only one. It's all over the country. So that's kind of the world-saving thing.

I think it's the skill I really want to learn gardening, farming, what have you. And hopefully go into an existing program, or helping create one, that would do pretty much that—make people in the city grow their own food and be aware of how much work goes in. That's another thing, being aware of how much work goes into it. Like your garden, it just goes into bloom, and the next thing you know, there's weeds and vegetables, and you have to take care of both of them. I think if people know how much work it takes to grow a carrot, they would be much more appreciative of it when they're buying it or what have you. So yeah, organizing, definitely. I'm kind of the sort of person that's like, "Let's do it! Let's go!" I don't like to sit around and wait for somebody else to come up with the idea, or like come up with a way to do it.

What I might organize? I don't really know. Yes. I've thought about starting out sort of small. My friend is thinking about buying a house, and he's like, "I want you to plant up my garden." And I was like, "Oh yeah." And then I thought about it more, and that would be like something that I could do, is go into neighborhoods and help plant out pea patches, or people's back yards or whatever. I want to do that, at that scale, just to get a better idea of how all the organizing goes on a tiny little plot, and then hopefully go to something bigger. We have on the farm talked about just kind of trying to figure out how other farms are doing their business. You know, we're mostly a market farm. We do have a CSA, but there are like farms that do strictly work share CSA. You know, people come, put in all the work into the food. They take the food home with them, and then you have this like sort of really cool system where cash isn't involved. It's like very old-fashioned, just simple "work for your food" kind of thing. So that's something that I would love. I think if I were to ever have my own farm, it would be that sort of ideological magical place where you just come and help, and you take the food home with you instead of feeling like some sort of sell-out when you're selling vegetables to a restaurant that charges $120 a person, or something like that. You know? It's just like, "Oh! That's not my life! That's not my role! I don't want to see the world like that."

I honestly have thought about the price gap, but I haven't actually done the research of it. But I think living wage definitely has something to do with it. I think the prices of food.... Cost of living is getting higher. Living wage is just kind of always under it. And there's always the underprivileged that are just going to be under the bar always. But I think there are already a lot of programs. The farmers markets do accept food stamps. That's a really cool thing. They give like farmers market coupons through WIC. There's a seniors program that also does it. But I think for now.... We were talking about this the other day. We do have....something that happens at the end of the markets, we'll have food left over, we always do. Some of the farmers markets we do have people come and pick up donated foods, sometimes we don't. And the food does end up at the food bank, but a lot of people will pass it. They'd rather pick up a can of beans than a bunch of beets, just because it's like "that's something I have to work to prepare, this isn't." Or it could be that they don't know how to cook it, or they just have gotten really used to eating basic sort of junk food or whatever. But I think educating people, which was something I really liked when I was working at the co-op, is like educating people about the food they're eating, and what was important to eat, and how they should go about being healthier and getting whatever it is that they think they want out of feeling good. So I think education has to do with it. And I think if there's less competition in the market, then local food would cost less than buying from wholesale, far-away lands. So yeah, those are the two things, I think.

As for a brand new farm like Local Roots, I don't really know, I haven't talked to Siri or Jason about this much, but I don't know if they think it's like not attainable for them yet to attempt to do what Jubilee's doing, or that's not for them. I don't know exactly what their perspective on that is. Yeah, I don't know. But they definitely know that we feel like sell-outs when we're.... You know, it's just like all this sort of.... I'm *not* extremely happy about selling to places like that, that make food seem like this unattainable, expensive, sort of thing. "Well, I can't afford organic, and I can't...." You know.

I don't know where I'm going from here. I'll be staying—Tom and I are going to be staying a little past the other guys, so we'll probably be here until like December or so. And then, I don't know, I want to find another farm to work at, or intern or what have you, that is much more established, and possibly uses a technique that's different than this one, just to get a better idea of like what the options are. I read about them, but seeing them in function is totally different. I think so many people have so many different ways of doing everything that it's like you can *never* stop learning. So I'd like to do that—where, exactly, I don't know. I really like the Pacific Northwest and I'd like to stay here, but I think it would be a really cool challenge to just like push myself out there and go somewhere really weird. So I don't know, I've got 'til December to figure it out. But hopefully I'll do that, and then maybe in a year or two—in two years, hopefully—have my own farm or my own project or what have you. But I feel like whatever it is I'll be doing, it will definitely involve food.

Our love has become abstract, cut off from a deep (and practical) immersion in and commitment to place and community. What we fail to see, oftentimes, is how a ubiquitous consumer mentality directly contributes to this abstraction. Consumerism does not refer simply to the purchasing of many (often unnecessary) things. It is, rather, an approach to reality that fundamentally alters the ways we engage and relate to the world around us. As consumers our attention is focused primarily obtaining or anticipating (since the future is the primary temporal mode) for ourselves the commodities that will satisfy desires manufactured and induced by the market......A consumer mentality, in other words, contributes to our overall ignorance about the truth of reality, just as it works against a life of wisdom, because we now relate to the world more ephemerally as the scanners and purchasers of it.

Norman Wirzba, "Placing the Soul, An Agrarian Philosophical Principle", 2003

22 September 2009

Shauna Frantz
Growing Things Farm

My name is Shauna Frantz, and I'm twenty-five. I was born while my parents were abroad in Malawi in Africa. Then I moved to the Central Valley near Emma, which was a farming community. Our fathers are cousins, and so they have the same grandfather. So we have that same lineage of those large farmers with the almonds and cotton and alfalfa. And I have some uncles who are farmers, but my dad didn't want to take on the farming from his father, because he was more of a teacher, so he became a teacher. He doesn't teach actually, he then went overseas and decided he wanted to do computers. So now he builds training programs with computer technology.

My parents were overseas with the Mennonite Central Committee, which is a group. The Mennonites are pacifist people, and they were volunteering to sort of.... Well, my dad was teaching, and my mom, she's a nurse, so she was nursing. And he had a garden there, that they left too. But he is like a farmer in his heart, and he loves to compost. Emma and I, that's the heritage we share, is the Mennonite. My mother is not, though. She's some sort of something else, some American religion. When I moved here, I like wanted to get involved with the Mennonite Church, because I moved to Seattle for college. So I'm interested in that again.

I graduated from college here at U.W. in 2006. My degree was Apparel Design, and I graduated with it, knowing that I didn't want to use it in any professional way. I'm a kinetic learner. I like to be using my hands and my body. For two years after graduating from college, I was in this really amazing job, but it was a desk job. I just needed to like be more active and use my whole body and spirit, working towards something that was like immediately useful, and like satisfying, and clearly the good, right choice in my mind. So being on a farm and working to sustain, to build skills, to continue to sustain life in the future was really important, an important decision.

I think I've always romanticized farming, because of growing up, being on my relatives' farms. There's so much freedom in the farmland, and not being in the city, and just being able to run through the fields, or like just stand and be alone with growth and life. But I never really thought about it as something I wanted to do, because doing a mono-crop like they did, doesn't appeal to me at all. It doesn't seem as useful. I'd rather not participate in as much of the economic—you know, like this business industry part. Which is also why I wouldn't want to go in the fashion industry. I'd rather work more personal, like one on one. I really like to trade and barter. I wanted to work with animals and plants, and their relationship to each other is like really.... You know, it just seems so.... It's just so integrated. They support each other and we're here for each other.

In 2009 I got laid off, in January, at the start of this year, from my job, because of the economy, this wonderful recession or depression or whatever the situation is. Then I got really excited about taking that chance to move on my desire and need to learn more about growing things. So I went and found this farm with Michaele, aptly named Growing Things. She has animals and she has plants, and so it was just really perfect. At first she said that we'd be having sun showers, and we'd be staying in tents, and we'd be cooking outdoors. And I was really ready for that, I was really, really excited about just like getting rid of all, like, the urban shackles, and just like being really dependent, really feeling the dependence of the land and the weather and this Valley that's here. But then when we got there, there was places to sleep indoors with a heater, showers indoors, and there's a wonderful cooking range, so it wasn't quite as rustic as I was gearing up for. But it's been really good, it's been beautiful.

It feels so good to like every day, like, the only thing, rather than getting up and going to a job somewhere, your duty, like the business of yourself is to get up and take care of the land, and just like work and exert yourself towards growth and fertility, and wrestling with this Valley. Because of all the flooding, the farm is experiencing a difficult year, and we don't have as much bounty as Michaele's used to in her past. She's been farming here for a while. This is one of her worst years that she's encountered. While that's unfortunate, it's also, like, I would, selfishly, for myself, I'm really glad that this is the experience that I'm having here with her, because it's so difficult and it's so challenging, but she's persevering and she's like trying to get to know us well. You just see the real farmer in her, like the real human interacting with the land, and just like being really neat to give them this, or do this, or all these different—just to work with the land to try and make it as productive as possible. I'm trying to assess what actually happened with the flood, since there was a strong current that came through that farm area, like what happened to the soil, and just seeing the different parts of the acreage that are less productive than others, and how, like, oh, there's been some deposit here, or something was ripped out or something. So it's really interesting learning about just how.... And then additionally how all the farmers around affect the farm land, and the, like flea beetle problems or the slug problems that maybe came in from other farms, like either in the flood or just by proximity.

Michaele is so amazing. I feel like she's kind of just given this year kind of as a....just like....I mean, she's working toward it, but she has a really amazing attitude about it that's just kind of like, "Well, okay, I'll mow it down!" or "I'll wait and see," or "Let's use this ugly kale for grazing mix, rather than bunching it." She's really.... Yeah, it's great, because she has so much respect and reverence for the growing process and for the environment and what it needs and what it will do on its own. And so she treats it that way, respects it in that way, and hopes that the respect is returned.

I came here to make sure that my future experience with land is like, kind of, I mean, let me just shortly say, maybe not the way Michaele is a farmer. I'd like to do a farm.... I need it in my life, I'll just say that, but I don't want to be in charge of a whole lot of land and produce for a market and just be like that. And it's really idealistic of me, and I'm aware of this, but I'd rather work in a community on a farm, towards like working together where everybody has maybe a specialty that they work in, and there's more in the community and more, like, relationship sustaining, because.... Like it's a little bit isolating out where, like, the work that we're doing and

Michaele does, which is great and beautiful and a wonderful cycle to live, to like have the summer that's hectic and busy and full, but then it goes by, and then the winter people are more sociable because they have less work to do. And that rhythm is really beautiful. I think that I'd like to have more people involved all year round in my life. So either like in a rural environment, or an urban environment, I'd like to have *some* farming, but I wouldn't say I'd really be a farmer. But I'd need to have chickens. I know I need chickens. And I also like goats, but I haven't worked with them this summer, so that experience is to come.

I hadn't held a chicken before this year. And the other day while I was collecting eggs, I got one to sit on my shoulder and ride with me, which was one of the greatest moments of my animal history. But it's really hard to say what the greatest moment has been. It's really hard because it feels like it's all just been like one continuous moment, that's like maybe changing and morphing in like different colors and different textures, but it's all like one really important moment in my life.

It's going to take a lot of work to change the world. And it's important to recognize the chemicals that we're using and what we're doing to the land, and what we're doing to our bodies. And it's beautiful to see how to grow, like Michaele using weeds to act as her pest deterrent. It's just important. But I don't know whether the world can.... It's just organic farming, like especially in the grocery stores, it seems like with the standards being lowered, so it's more lucrative for the larger businesses and stuff, like. I'd say it's more important to buy locally, and buy like directly from the farmer. That's been so good for me, to, like, be more involved in the farmers markets and just to see directly how buying from the farmer helps the farmer go back to the land and make the land more useful and productive, therefore they can provide more for the customer. And I feel like there's so much lost in larger farm operations. So I don't know about organic, exactly, the whole movement, but like local, like buying and revering and respecting and honoring and thanking your local agricultural system, is really important.

I think when you cut off your connections to the important parts, like your food, when you don't have that connection, then it's easy to be disconnected from so much of life. I could see that, for sure. And then there's so many ways that we're disconnected from what we consume and what we have around us. That *is* what I like trying to do with my fashion, whatever, degree: I'm actually more interested in the textiles, and like gaining from the sheep, for example, or what it may be like taking that directly from the source and trying to cut out the middle process.

I'm dreaming about where to go from here, and I have some months to do that, to like sort of transition. The idea is to stay with some friends and family on their farms and get different perspectives of farms, and not be paying rent for a while—at least a few months, at least half a year of not paying rent—and just helping out in the same way, but not as intensely, because this has been like five months that I've been with Michaele, and I foresee like maybe one month here and a month there, but just like getting different perspectives on farming, and that tactile sort of life. And then I don't know what.

I would like it to be that we all need to turn towards like having more of a connection to the source, because it seems like it's confused intermediaries have kind of ruined things in terms of building a false wealth, and then not wanting to take responsibility for that falseness that they've built, and then also wanting to keep everybody believing in the falseness of it. And so I don't know if things will come to pass the way I'd like, but it'd be really fantastic if we could all just trade things. Michaele was telling us about this like really beautiful period of her life where they didn't really even use money at all because her family.... You're in Carnation, because like they painted the doctor's house and got credit there. Or like traded vegetables for a service. Or things like this where it's just no actual money was passing hands, and they were just relying on their skills and abilities and products of the community that they were in. That'd be really wonderful. And I hear of people in Los Angeles having community gardens or something, or whatever they were doing. And that's great. I don't know the bigger answer, because I am so—I am just too skeptical of organizations.

Michaele taught me so much. And when the work was too hard or whatever for my urban/suburban self, it was always amazing just to be like, "No, but this is Michaele's life. You think you can't work like twelve hours? You think you can't dig this mud? This has to be done, it just has to be done." And her perseverance and her, like….she has such a good attitude about it, even like the things that would seem objectively to be downers, she just works around it in her mind and comes up with a solution to it, rather than just being bogged down by them. That's been a really beautiful lesson to see and learn. She's just such a resource of information. I ask her way too many questions, and sometimes it's just sort of overwhelming. Everybody laughs and we stop because it was just too much. "Michaele, what is the turkey thinking right now? Why is it doing that?!" "It's just a turkey, Shauna, I don't know." But she's such a wealth. I think that people in the community recognize that too.

It would be great to come back here. But there's so much of the country in the world that I don't know anything about. But this Valley, in particular, since we're talking about this Valley, aren't we? This is really terrible, but I lived in Seattle for six years without knowing it existed. And when I came over the ridge and down Novelty Hill and opened into this amazing place…. I don't know, it's so beautiful. And I was reading in your book how you were like—people have amnesia about the floods and the rains, because when the sun comes out in this Valley it's like no other place. It's true, and Michaele's like, "It's my own piece of heaven." The view from the fields is amazing every day, every day. You can stop and take a stretch break and look up and, "How am I gifted with such an amazing experience, to be with this beautiful place?"

We can see how a consumer society and mentality contributes to abstraction if we compare it to the disciplines of production as they have been practiced in many traditional and indigenous cultures. To be a producer, an artisan for example, is to submit oneself to a socially/culturally defined discipline or craft that requires extensive training and patience. One must learn the art of design, which means that one must gain a sense for the deep reality of things, have a qualitative grasp of things as they naturally are. To know the nature of things means that one grasps their essential and manifold characteristics as they connect with the world of which they are a part. Building on Aristotle's famous account of how knowledge is achieved, we can say that someone who genuinely knows will be able to answer the following questions: What type of material will make the product good? What are a material's (and habitat's and community's) limiting conditions? What methods of production will yield the best (and the most sustainable and safe) results? To what end or purpose should products be made, and how well does this goal fit with broader social and ecological ends? What form or design will best promote quality, durability, beauty, functionality, i.e., excellence? To answer these questions is to enter practically into a complex, moral dimension that takes seriously the places we are in and the character of our dwelling within these places. They demand the sort of democratic and public conversation that has all but disappeared in our time……….True knowledge and understanding grow out of our productive engagement with the world, the engagement serving as the corrective and guide to our fanciful or flight-prone ways.

Norman Wirzba, "Placing the Soul", 2003

30 September 2009

Thomas Arnold
Local Roots Farm

My name is Thomas Arnold. I am twenty-three, born September 25, 1986. I was born in Virginia, and I lived there for two years, and then I moved to Seattle where I grew up and went to elementary school, high school, and then I went to the University of Miami for college. Studied political science and got a degree in political science, and a minor in business.

It was one of those things. I started taking political science and economics, and I figured if I was going to choose a field to go into, I needed to know what that field was about. The only way you could figure that out was by studying the general basics of everything: why the political systems work, what is the function of money.

Yeah. So that's sort of what I was thinking. I had a woman ask me what I was doing with my life last week, and I was like, "I'm working on a farm." And she was like, "So what are you going to do with your political science degree?" I was like, "What do you mean? What I'm doing with my life is political. That's what politics is, right?" So, I don't know, it was kind of funny. It was a funny thing to say, funny question to be asked, as if politics is outside of anything. Made me think about that. So I don't know, I kind of graduated and I wanted to get a job that I knew I could be outside, eat good food, be around people that were interesting, and I kind of lucked out being at Local Roots, so it worked out pretty well.

I liked a lot of the political philosophy behind farming. It's very interesting, the idea that you're sort of growing everything yourself; you're not sort of ... if you don't really particularly believe in the system, sending your money off to the system, and having that money going to the system, and then that system causes wars and economic turmoil for lots of people, and economic dominance, and economic openness, which leads to the destruction of other cultures and things like that. If we don't want to participate in it, then how do you get your money out? It's like stop buying things. And then how do you stop buying things? Grow your own food, you do things that are simple and practical and use your time very simply.

I've traveled a lot. Let's see, most recently I studied abroad in Ireland for a semester. And then that summer I went to Africa—my sister was in the Peace Corps. And I think the story that I was saying is one of the sort of reasons that kind of pushed me toward farming was that I was staying with some sort of subsistence farmers, and I kind of idealized their life. This guy was born basically with what we would consider nothing. He grew up in this little tiny village and he kind of fought his way through life, got a wife and a family and some land and built a house, and was soon kind of—he'd sort of made something of himself, and he could really say that "This is mine. I made this, I built this house, I tended these fields that fed my children," and all those things. I thought that was interesting.

This was in northern Congo, this little village called Nogbeni (sic), where my sister was stationed. So that was one thing. One of the biggest things that has sort of pushed me toward farming is that I had a landscaping company when I was in high school. Landscaping is very irrational, from an environmentalist's standpoint. You take the nutrients that the tree drops, and through evolution they know that they're going to suck up the leaves, and what we do is, we take the leaves and ship them off to be composted, and then we buy them back, and they drive them back over. It's so irrational, I couldn't deal with it—rather than just raking them to the pile. If you don't want to look at them, rake 'em in a pile somewhere in the corner, and then throw them back out once they've disintegrated. But we don't do that. So that had always bothered me. So I like the work of landscaping. It's fun, you get to design things. It's kind of an art. "Why is that plant there?" You're creating nature how you would like to see it, which is similar to farming, but farming is just for more of a human purpose, more for human purpose.

I like the idea of growing food, the idea that you can sort of create energy, that if you didn't use that land, it'd probably just be covered in blackberry bushes, and nothing would really be coming out of it. You can feed a lot of humans with very good healthy food. That's awesome. But then if you really want to take a look at the bigger picture, what are those people doing with *that* energy that you give them? So it's kind of hard, you know, because we feed generally the wealthy. The wealthy are the people who can afford our food—which is great. I mean, I don't mind feeding wealthy people. But at the same time, I think a lot of us come into it with a more, I don't know, like a.... You know, we sort of think of ourselves as kind of like, not the lower class, but we kind of relate to the working class. But we're not feeding the working class, we're feeding the rich—well, not always the rich, but generally—the people who have wealth enough to know about good food.

You can, like, start at the bottom of society and try and work with food banks—the economic bottom—I don't mean to say the actual bottom. You can donate the stuff left over to food banks. We do that at the end of markets and things like that. But at the same time, we still have to get money for things. If we send nutrients off somewhere, we're going to have to buy more nutrients to replace those in the soil. As a business, you can't just give things away. You can, a little bit. You can give over like your leftovers. To have a business, though, is just growing things for the food bank wouldn't really work. Well, it may work, but I don't know, you would need a subsidy or something like that. But I really like....they have a program at a lot of the farmers markets. It's like WIC checks. It means Women, Infants, and Children. They get these checks, these little two-dollar coupons. I'm not exactly sure how they get them. Probably some application to the government, or something like that. You have to spend them at farmers markets, which I think is a really cool program of sort of bringing sort of the lower class to the good food.

Urban gardens are great. You know, why should we grow our food so far away from where it's going to be consumed? I think it's a really good idea to have gardens in the city and stuff like that, if it's possible—especially when there's a recession and there's land that's being vacated. Normally people, there's not that many foreclosures and things like that, there's not that much free land. But at the same time, I mean, we've already sort of made the mistake of growing too fast. We made the mistake of making our cities too dense, and too spread out, and so we kind of have to work backwards, and how do we do that. Maybe urban gardens is part of the answer, but it needs to be many, many more other parts.

We have the issue in Carnation where horse farmers, or people who have like horse farms can also own the land, rather than farms for growing food. And I know that Jason and Siri are working through some programs that are trying to change the law so that some of the best agricultural land that we have close to Seattle, the Snoqualmie Valley, so why should it be used for horse farms? I mean, really, like what does a horse farm really offer to society? Very little. Okay, some people get to ride horses. That's great. But feeding people I think is more important. And to use great land that's really close for that, I think would be awesome. If there's more food being grown, the price goes down, more people get to eat healthy food. And then Safeways and things like that *have* to accept that food, because that's what's going to be.... And if it's cheaper, why would they not? The cost is so much cheaper, because there's so many less of those transportation costs and keeping things fresh. I mean, we can pick basil and corn and things like that, three hours before the market. You know, if you go to the supermarket, you get this little packet of basil for like five bucks. We can offer like a huge bunch of it, just picked, for three dollars. We can also do things a lot cheaper locally, which is interesting.

I took a class at the University of Miami. Our professor was Donna Shalala, who was the secretary of Health and Human Services under Clinton for eight years. And so she was sort of integral in the healthcare debate. They had a plan and it got basically shut down. There was the Harry and Louise commercial that came on television, and they basically shut the whole program down, saying that the government's going to run your healthcare and things like that. I took the class, and I was always trying to talk them into—we had a blog and stuff, and we'd go online and read blogs and go to chat rooms and stuff like, where we're talking to other people. And I kept wanting to bring up the relationship between healthcare and food, but it's really completely stayed out of that discussion.

I see preventative medicine as the most logical first step. I mean, I don't know, we're making ourselves sick. The reason we have the highest rates of obesity and diabetes.... If you look at the list of top causes of death: heart disease, stroke, cancer, diabetes, I think those are in the top five. And all of those are linked to the food you eat. And what insurance companies and the medical system do is, they expand the part of your life where you're dying. You start getting sick, you go to the doctor, he gives you medicine, and they try and extend that part of your life as long as possible. But it's in the best interest of the insurance companies and the medical system, for the most part, to push that age that you start getting sick lower and lower and lower, so you start taking medicines that start killing you when you're really young. You're taking all these things, when they're kind of pushing you to do it younger and younger. Their job, and their incentives, are to sort of expand the process where you're sick. And I think what we should really be focusing on is expanding the part where you're healthy: which is starting from when you're young, feeding you the right foods so you don't even have to go to the doctor, or if you go to the doctor it's just for a general checkup and to make sure everything's good, rather than going to the doctor to get your diabetes medication when you're thirteen years old. You know, you're not going to be able to be healthy mentally or physically, or really anything, if you start off like that, I think. I don't know, it's a hard thing to think about. I don't think there's any easy answer really, either. I mean, the problem is, I think, that no one's really looking out for that woman with three kids in the ghetto.

I think that's one of the reasons I was sort of drawn to sort of the food industry, and the organic. I'm also doing this sort of out of self-interest. I mean, I want to be in a job where I can move around a lot, and I get to eat healthy food all the time. And I'm around people who are also fairly healthy. If everyone around me was eating Doritos and ice cream and things like that, I'd probably be doing the same thing, just naturally. Normally, we're all hungry at the farm. If someone has a thing of ice cream, I'd eat it, because it's good. But it's like you can't just have it there, or you'll eat it, because the mind is tempted by those things—I think. I don't think there's particularly any easy answer to how to get poor people good food. The food is just going to get better. So it's like there's a spectrum of food and how good it is. I mean, the food that people are eating now, it's probably better than what people were eating in the 13th century, or what people even in the ghetto are eating. So the whole spectrum is what needs to move. The rich people can even get the *best* food, but we can improve the nutritional value of the food that they're even getting. And if we can move everybody forward, I think that's sort of the best idea. But I don't think it's that simple.

For next year, I was thinking about applying to some jobs in selling solar panels. Well, I guess I *am* going to. I'm like writing cover letters, and doing all the tedious job work. There are a lot of companies that are just installing solar panels on people's houses, on commercial buildings, and things like that. There's a lot of tax credits for it, up to $3,000 you get. So I was thinking about trying to do that. I'd like to learn more, like, technical skills. I think it would be a fun thing to learn and kind of get into all that. I like farming, but I also think that when you really think about the work that's done on the farm, the tractor does a lot of work. I mean, tilling a bed. I tend to think of myself as like pretty physically capable, but I couldn't get a bed to look as good as that in *days*, and the tractor can do it in seconds. So if we're really going to be looking forward to the future, we've got to figure out how to get energy, because the population is already really high. There's already suburbia. How can we make suburbia consume less? Well, start by putting some solar panels on the roofs. I don't know, I think there's a lot to think about: what's the energy payback for solar panels? I don't know. I don't really know exactly what it is. But if we're going to really compete globally, I think it really has to happen.

I have sort of a standing offer from Jason and Siri that I can stay on the farm for as long as I want, which is good, because I don't want to just sort of jump into the next job. One of my friends is a recruiter at a temp agency. He's sort of, "Oh, you could do this." I could be working for Starbuck's, getting complaint calls. No! No way! I'd rather do nothing than do that.

At Local Roots we try to keep the atmosphere pretty relaxed. Jason and Siri don't really like to be referred to as, like, "the boss," or anything like that. Of course a boss wouldn't want to do that. But it's fun. I've actually been really happy. They have a lot of energy, and they're like really excited about learning things, and they're always bringing out their i-phone and checking with the Wikipedia, whenever there's something that people don't really know. Which I like that, sort of push for knowledge, which is good. So I've been generally happy. It's inspiring, to be around people who are like always trying to learn stuff, because the people that I was in school with and stuff, weren't like *always* trying to learn stuff, and always curious. Curiosity's really nice.

Dan offers some different perspectives, I guess, because he's all about....he knows what he knows, and constantly learning and things like that. But that's not really his specific goal. His goal is to keep thing sustainable, and enjoy the process. He really enjoys just doing the everyday tasks. It's kind of different. I mean, when you're young, you kind of always have to think, "Oh! I can't wait to get this done! If I do this, then I'm only going to get this." And then once you get to that point, you're just waiting for something else to happen. You could always be thinking, kind of looking forward to the next thing. But if you do that progressively, then you're just sort of looking forward to your death. That's how I always think about it. If I'm always like, "Oh, if I just get this done...." Yeah, if I just get this one thing done, then I'll be in a good spot. Once I get that thing done, I'm not thinking about, "Oh, I'm good!" I'm thinking about the next thing. It's sort of like that progress that sort of leads to a lot of disappointment in people's lives. You're not enjoying the moment.

I was in India last summer, and I stayed.... There's this guru, I guess—you call him Guru Gi. His name's Shri-shri Ravi Shankar. I think it's an easy thing to sort of, I guess, preach. I wouldn't really use that term. But he always talks about living in the moment. That's what Dan sort of tries to do. He wants to live in the moment and be enjoying the process, which is kind of hard to do, I think, generally, for some people. I'll bet you some people don't get it, and some people get it earlier than others. I try to be like that. I don't know if I'm totally like that. One thing that I've sort of realized, doing farming, is I sort of like the building of things rather than.... I mean, I like tending the garden and doing stuff like that, but I prefer to do more like what Dan would refer to as corporeal work. It's putting something together, or sort of planning out a process. Like we need to build this tool shed: how do we do it, where do we start? And then sort of bit by bit putting together in your mind, and then physically doing it. I mean, I like doing that whole process. It's pretty satisfying. So that's one thing that's pushed me into the solar panel job, is that the process would be very similar. I don't know anything about electronics.

I've kind of felt, at least for myself, that I couldn't really do anything else until I learned how to live, basically. I have to like learn the basics myself, and at least have the knowledge. There's always all the talk about global warming and nuclear threat. And there's all these threats. If I didn't have the confidence that I could go out and live myself, those threats would really scare me. But since I think I can kind of take myself out of that, at least get rid of my own fear of anything like that, because I do at least have the confidence now that I could at least survive by myself. I know there'd be a lot of people coming out to rural areas. There's a whole thought process that goes on.

I just read a book, I think a month ago—I think I told you before—called "*American Empire*". It's by Andrew Basevitch. He's a *Washington Post* columnist sometimes. But his theory is that if you really look at our history, we act as an empire. We act sort of in the same mercantilist, sort of realist form, as anybody else. We're just sort of always trying to have our own personal lives be better. Each individually, we're all looking to improve our lives. And we all come together and we sort of create this United States. And some people are doing things for different reasons, and there's a whole lot of patterns and things like that. But when it comes to foreign policy, we are an empire. And until we embrace the fact that we are, everyone's going to be sort of confused about foreign policy. Like, "Why are we going to Iraq?" It doesn't make any sense, you know, until we come out and tell the truth about it. Then democracy can't really go on, until people know the *actual* truth. So I don't know, it's one of those things. It's like what can you do now? This situation already exists.

I don't really want to have to work in an office, and I don't really want to sit and do work that I don't really like to do. So it's sort of one of those things where for the rest of my life now, I at least will know. I mean, I can spend the time working in my garden, and then just subtract those hours from the work that I'm doing at work, at a normal job. Same with, like, I just started to try to learn how to work on my car. And if I learn how to change my own oil, change my filters and do things like that, then I can subtract the money that paid $30 an hour to, to a mechanic, and just pay myself that, metaphorically, or figuratively, I guess.

I don't really have a problem with money. I understand.... It's just where it goes. If you kind of follow where the dollars go, you put money in the bank, that money gets reinvested instantly in something, whether it be the U.S. government or some U.S. corporation, or really anything. So no matter where you have your money, it's always being invested. Say I don't like Ford, I have a problem with Ford, but I give my money to the Bank of America. I just invested in Ford. I just invested a little bit of my money in Ford. So do you take your money out and just keep it as cash? Or do you have to constantly be investing whatever you have in something that you believe in? Which I think is the best thing to do. Or even in yourself. I mean, there's so many investments you can make that are just yourself. Like for you buying a piano, or buying equipment, or buying a recorder. I mean, things like that. But I don't know. Or a place to live or something.

I think that, at least for me, it's very refreshing to know that I can live without having to go to stores. It's also very refreshing.... How will I say it so that it can be quoted, if needed? I guess I would say that farming is a very empowering thing to do. You are basically doing all of the work with your hands and the tractor. It's a very simple process, and you can see a business from manufacturing to market. It's just a very sort of microcosm of.... You could have learned to understand market economics and sort of general policies. For someone who graduated from college with no skills, and only skills in political science, which is something that's not really pursuable with my ideology, it's really sort of a relief to know that you can grow your own food relatively easily, and you can grow food for hundreds of people, on a small piece of land, if it's done correctly.

Farms, of course, are ultimately micro-ecosystems that exist within macro-ecosystems. As such, agriculture is an inevitable part of the larger dance of life—part of that complex, interdependent web of life that has evolved (and continues to evolve) over four billion years. We ignore that evolving complexity only at our peril.

The standard industrial answer to this cautionary tale is, of course, that we will always have the technological capability to restore any damage we may do to the ecosystem through our industrialized agriculture—especially with the newly discovered technological capacity of genetic engineering. We now seem to have convinced ourselves that we can redesign life to live better in a new biological order of our own making.

In *"The Future of Life"* E.O. Wilson gives the proper response to such misplaced optimism:

"Such is the extrapolation endpoint of techno-mania applied to the natural world. The compelling response, in my opinion, is that to travel even partway there would be a dangerous gamble, a single throw of the dice with the future of life on the table. To revive or synthesize the thousands of species needed—probably millions when the still largely unknown microorganisms have been catalogued—and put them together in functioning ecosystems is beyond even the theoretical imagination of existing science. Each species is adapted to particular physical and chemical environments within the habitat. Each species has evolved to fit together with certain other species in ways biologists are only beginning to understand."

Wilson, of course, is speaking here of whole ecosystems, not farms. But, again, farms are simply biotic communities that are integral to the ecosystem in which they exist. Consequently, anywhere agriculture is practiced, it must become part and parcel of the task of restoring the species diversity that is as essential to a healthy farm as it is to a healthy ecosystem.

Industrial agriculture with its specialization, centralization, and uniformity is simply another example of what Wilson calls "mistaken capital investment". We must now redesign agriculture so that it becomes an integral part of restoring the landscape's biodiversity.

Frederick Kirchenmann, "The Current State of Agriculture—Does It Have a Future?", 2003

25 September 2009

My name is Ryan Lichtenegger, I'm twenty-seven years old. My birthday is April 15, 1983. I was born in Minnesota, and lived there until I was fourteen years old. I grew up, I guess in the suburbs of Minneapolis, about thirty, forty minutes northwest of Minneapolis. It was out in the country, had dairy farms. I didn't grow up *on* a dairy farm, but we lived next to a dairy farm. My parents thought it was important that we had a place to run around and roam as children, and we did just that. I had one brother, who is five years younger than I am. When I was twelve, we moved right next to a dairy farm, just down the hill. And that's where I discovered I had an obsession with farms and tractors. I had been collecting toy tractors all of my life, for birthdays and Christmas, so I had a whole collection of small tractors—they're in boxes right now. But when I have a place of my own, they'll be on display. But I loved being on the farm and being around the cows and the tractors, and baling hay and all that. And then one day I wasn't down at the farm, and the farmer ended up passing away. His name was Bruce Crawford, and I remember to this day, he gave me a kohlrabi, and I had no idea what it was. And he had this old-timer knife that he had, and he cut a slice of it and it was the greatest thing I ever had. So to this day I love kohlrabi, because of him. He ended up dying because he fell out of his silo. One of the rungs on the silo ladder had broken off. I don't know how many feet, but a long ways. After that day, the farm didn't keep running. They sold the cows. His brother had lived there, and even his mom still lived there, who must have been close to a hundred years old. But ever since that day, they shut down. So that was my last day at the farm.

Ryan Lichtenegger
Jubilee Farm

And then I moved to Seattle with my parents when I was fourteen, in eighth grade, and grew up in Woodinville. Went to Woodinville High School, and took various jobs, a couple of restaurants, worked on a horse ranch up in there: Woods Creek Farm, it was called. Had thirty acres, and it had Warmblood draft horses, eighteen hands. It's a little big. I loved working on it, it was a good place. The people were okay.

I ended up going to college, and I couldn't keep that job because they wanted me for earlier hours, and that would cause me to sacrifice my school time. So I quit and went to school, studied digital art, got a four-year degree in digital art and animation. Tried to find a job after that, and couldn't find a steady job doing digital art. I worked for my dad's company, Light Sciences, doing some 3-D animations of medical devices and other type stuff, and that was kind of fun.

But I really liked being outside, and I discovered that after I graduated from school that I really loved being outside. I had landscaped through high school during summers for a number of years, and really liked landscaping a lot, so I went back and found a job with Signature Landscaping in Redmond, and landscaped for them for three years, and really enjoyed it. I loved the plants and the ground and working hard. That's probably what I've done most of my life, is worked hard and landscaped.

But then, I don't know what changed my mind, but I ended up thinking I needed to do something differently, because it just didn't feel quite right. So I started looking for different jobs. There was nothing really available, so I kind of stuck with the landscaping, and decided to buy a tractor. I was driving down Highway 2 one day with my dad. In Gold Bar I spotted a tractor on the side of the road, and I didn't know what kind it was, but there was a number and a price. So my dad was like, "You should drive back up there and check it out." So I did the next day, and I talked to this guy named Jim. He was an old fellow, and didn't know much about the tractor, but it was an Oliver tractor, and he didn't really know the year, but it was a '77 wide front. I didn't know what to look for in a tractor, I had no idea, but I just thought it was the coolest-looking tractor I've ever seen. It was painted like a clown: it had a red front and a yellow grill and green and red wheels. Just like, wow! And even though I grew up in the Midwest where Olivers were made, I'd never seen one. So once I picked up this tractor and brought it home—I was living in Duvall after school and everything—lived in Duvall for two years in a house with a buddy of mine—brought the tractor home, stuck it in the garage, and did as much research about Oliver tractors as I could.

While I was doing that, I joined—asked the librarian in Duvall if there were any tractor clubs or any sort of groups that collected antique machinery, and she gave me Brent Norlander's number, who lives in Duvall, and he was a member of Northwest Vintage Iron in Fall City. So I gave him a call and he said, "I'll pick you up. Give me your number." So he picked me up, brought me to the meeting, and I met a bunch of real nice people that I still hang out with, and go to meetings, and participate in the club. I learn a lot from the guys in the club—women too, a few of them. But now I had this tractor and I was part of this club. I was still lookin' for some sort of job, and I ended up leaving the landscaping company and moving antique furniture for Valley Furniture in Redmond. I didn't quite like that very much, so I needed to find something else.

It just so happened that the tractor club had their tractor show at Jubilee Farm. And I had never seen Jubilee Farm, knew nothing about it. I kind of explored the Snoqualmie Valley, and I knew it was beautiful and I liked it, but I didn't know the farms. So I ended up having the show at Jubilee Farm, and then met Erick Haakensen, and got to know him a little bit. He must have thought I was a good kid, because he asked me if I wanted to work for him full time that next year. So I told him, "I'll have to think about it."

And in the meantime, I worked at Jubilee Farm in the afternoons. After I got done at the furniture place, I'd go down to the farm at three, and work 'til six, sometimes later, through the late summer and fall. This was three years ago, 2006—the end part of 2006. At the end of that year, after doing the pumpkins and the harvesting and the whole deal that Jubilee has, I decided that I *would* work for Erick and Wendy at Jubilee. So I stuck through the furniture business through the winter—a really good winter job inside—and started in March at Jubilee Farm.

Right off the bat, I was just so excited. I loved it. I mean, I could keep my tractor at the farm. So I was still living in Duvall, and I drove my tractor from Duvall to Jubilee farm, which took about forty-five minutes, at 11 miles per hour. But I took the back road along the river, and it was really beautiful, and had my girlfriend follow me in her car with her flashers on. I felt like it was an incredible journey, I was on my tractor. But they let me keep my tractor at the farm, which was awesome.

From the day I started there, I got to know pretty much everyone in the Valley. Every other day, somebody would drive by, and I'd see their face and learn their names. Now I know a lot of people that live in the Valley, which I think is great, because I have a connection somewhere in life. I really loved working there. I started pruning trees, apple trees. Probably did that for like a whole month. All I could see in my sleep was branches. My hands were raw, but I loved it.

The spring was just brutal, because we planted everything by hand. We started everything in the greenhouse in little trays, and we had to transplant everything, except for beans and corn, and some other lettuces and stuff. But we still even planted lettuces by hand. To me, that just blew me away. I had no idea how much work went into vegetable farming. Coming from a dairy farm background, everything is done with machines. Like we baled hay with a baler, and raked hay, and *everything* was done with a tractor or bobcat or something. But we went out there and worked in the dirt, which I liked. For landscaping, I didn't mind getting dirty, or standing in rain. So I kind of had the best of both worlds. I got to play with toys and play in the dirt, just like when I was a little kid.

So now I've been at Jubilee, I guess this is my second full-time season, but the third year. Erick's kind of made me his left-hand man. Or right-hand guy? Is that what it's called? I've been there the longest so far. So he calls on me to do a lot of tasks that not everyone can do. A lot of times he'll say, "You're a really good worker, we're really happy to have you. You're very competent and doing just about everything we rely on you to do." So I feel pretty good working there, it's a good place. I've learned a lot about farming the last couple of years. I started leasing my own land from Ian McCray, who lives about three miles south of Jubilee. I have two acres that I fenced off from his cows last year, and took my Oliver down there, plowed two acres with it. The best view I could ever imagine, because you're looking right at Mount Si, just straight to the west, and it's huge. If I could own a farm, I think I would own a farm there, because it's beautiful. So I planted a cover crop last fall, and didn't quite know what I was going to do for this year, so I just kind of plugged away with the time I had and I ordered a bunch of seeds from Irish Eyes over in Ellensburg, and decided that I wanted to purchase things locally, being inspired by Erick and the local movement. So I try to buy everything as local as I can. From tractor parts to garlic seed whenever I can.

I started planting. I bought a grow lamp, and I rent a condo up on the Sammamish Plateau with my girlfriend, Kim. We've lived there for two years now. But I bought a grow lamp and started tomato seeds in February, inside. So in the evening my spare bedroom would just glow with this bright light, and so people come up to me and ask me what I'm doing. "Starting my farm seeds. Hey, c'mon!" So I had a bunch of tomatoes, probably about a hundred plants, and started everything inside, up until April. Then just started planting stuff outside. I plowed and disked. Had a little take-along disk that I snagged from Jubilee Farm. I can't find out whose it is, but nobody claims it, so I just said, "Well, I'll borrow it for a while." So that worked.

And then I bought a little greenhouse and started growing some food. And then I needed to do something with the food, so I started calling friends and said, "Hey, do you want to have a little CSA?" So I signed up like ten people that agreed that they wanted food, so I'd sell them a box of food every other week on Mondays. As the summer came on, I had a lot of extra food, so I decided to do a farmers market. Not this weekend, but next weekend is the last day for farmers market, and it's on Sunday. It's at Lake Forest Park. But it's a great market. I don't have a ton of produce to sell there every week, but I make enough money to pay for my seeds and my land lease. So it's really fun. I love the atmosphere at the farmers market. I never had really experienced farmers markets at all—coming from the Midwest, we don't have that kind of stuff over there when I was growing up. And organic farming was all new to me, and I loved it, and I really believe that it's the way to grow food. I *like* growing food, so to see people pick up your produce and pay for it, it's pretty satisfying. Hard work pays off—I've learned that. So I'm already thinking about next year, and ordered shallots and garlic. I'm planning on working for Jubilee next year.

I haven't decided if I'm going to be completely full-time or not. Erick knows I'm off to do my own thing someday, and it's just a matter of time. So my heart's really in farming now, and it's what I really love doing, and I think it's what I'm going to do for the rest of my life—really want to. I'm not sure exactly what I'm going to grow, but I like the CSA model, having a membership, and the one-on-one relationship with people. People and farmers should have a relationship like that. You should know where your food comes from, and should know how it's grown, how it's treated, how it's transported. So I will continue to collect tractors for the rest of my life, and now I just need to buy a barn and a house, or a barn and some land, or just some land so I can build a barn and a house—just somethin' so I can keep my stuff somewhere.

I had no concept of agri-business or mono-cultures or anything like that when I was growing up. That's just the way things were. Farmers grew corn, and I played in corn fields. And the farmer that I worked for, Bruce Crawford, I remember him planting a specific crop and watching it come up in the spring. And it turned out it was oats. And I thought, "Well, that's really neat, I've never seen oats before in my life. Right next to my house!" So they harvested the oats after they were ready, and then after the oats were cut down, something else started growing up. And I thought, "Gee, this is weird, what else is growing up?" It was bright green. It turned out to be alfalfa and clover. So he had planted two things at once as a crop rotation. I thought, "Wow! Farmers can do that? He can plant two things at once?!" So it was a really neat concept. And now, watching Erick do some stuff and plant cover crops and crop rotations, you really get a sense of taking care of the soil. And the more I read—and I was never a really big reader growing up—my dad always emphasized, "You need to read more. You need to read." And I think about that a lot, because I haven't been a reader. I've always been someone that holds things and touches things, and that's how I learn. I go out and I do things. So I don't really find time to read, but I've been making some more time to learn more about farming. That's my passion. So I read about agri-business and I watch the films about the corn farmers in Iowa. I really think it's terrible to have the mono-cultures on such great land. And I grew up in the land of black soil. And literally, the soil is *black*, so black. You can't find that color soil anywhere out here. So to me, now knowing how beneficial it is to have healthy soil, I really appreciate taking care of the soil. When I see just the one crop growing on that beautiful black dirt, it makes me sad inside, because you know that the corn is just sucking the nitrogen out, and replacing infertility with synthetic fertilizers. It's just a vicious cycle. So I hope someday that things will change again. I think that they're starting to. Going back to Madison, Wisconsin, to see my childhood buddy get married this last summer. And I didn't get to go into the town of Madison, but from what Erick told me, it's kind of the birthplace of organic farming, and farmers markets and stuff like that—and vegetables. But my girlfriend and her parents went into Madison and took some pictures, so that was really neat to see. But even just outside of Madison, you see thousands of acres of corn or soybeans, still just pluggin' away, plantin' the same things. The crazy thing that I noticed was here are all these beautiful farms, these gorgeous structures, these barns with the rockery around the base of 'em, and silos, immaculate lawns, well taken care of. But there's no machinery, there's no animals. What there are, they're just a few, and they're stuck in machinery sheds. But I scouted just about every barn I drove by to see if there were old tractors or implements sitting out, but there's nothin'. People live there, but they don't even take care of their own farms. There's bigger farms that take care of their farmland. It's sad, because all those farms are just empty now. There's so many, and so beautiful, and I would give anything to own a farm like that. I hope things change, I hope things go back to the way they were in the thirties or the early 1900s. Or, I don't know, back in the day before mono-culture and chemicals.

I recently went up to a little museum in Monroe, and I never knew it existed. And they have a bunch of antique tractors outside, and old horse-drawn implements. Everything's run on electric motors now, but a lot of hand-cranked stuff: the milk separators, and the grain grinders, the seed cleaners, and all this stuff. And I'm like, "Wow! Where *is* all this stuff?! I need this right now! I need these potato planters and potato diggers that were used fifty years ago, and now you can't find any of them anywhere." I was talking with the museum owner guy and I said, "Oh boy, if you ever run into anything extra, give me a call, because I would love to have something, a potato planter or a seeder or just something—something to pull behind a little tractor".

It's been interesting at Jubilee, it's been a lot of fun, I've definitely learned a lot. I guess my daily schedule is get up at 6:15 and eat breakfast. It's my favorite meal of the day, so I always eat a big breakfast. Then I get to work at eight, which I think is pretty late for farmers. I wouldn't mind working earlier and getting off earlier. We work from eight to noon, take a two-hour break, work from two to six, which is a little brutal in the middle of summer—during the hottest part of the day is at five o'clock or four o'clock, so we're working through the hottest part. So I have different thoughts on that. But the spectrum of work we do is very broad, especially when there are just two of us. Ian came on this year, so I work with him. We do farm-related stuff, and non-farm-related stuff. We moved the trailer this spring—moved the trailer, big trailer, up to the side of the hill. That was a huge project, and a lot of carpentry work was needed. So I did a lot of carpentry work for them. I do a lot of, I guess, orchard work, too—different kinds of farming, did a lot of pruning in spring. Every day is different, and that's one thing I like working there—you never know what you're going to do. I hear stories about some of the workers out at Circle Farm and how they do stuff on the job, and that's what they do for a year. If they're seeding, they seed. If they transplant, they transplant. That's what they do. But I do everything. In the winter, people are like, "Oh, are you only seasonal help?" and I go, "No, I'm full-time." They're like, "What do you do in the winter?" And I go, "Well, I fix tractors and mechanical stuff. I pack boxes for the winter CSA clients. I do deliveries. Any type of maintenance, equipment fixing, structural stuff, just about everything." That's what I think the job of a farmer is: you are skilled in a lot of things. You may not be an expert in everything, but you're a jack of all trades. And to me, I like that, because I'm a person that likes to know a little about a lot of things. I'm an observer as well, so I've been observing Erick and Wendy and how they work, how they run the farm, and how they treat people, and just everything. So I learn a lot by just watching.

I see a lot of things, and the first thing I see is great teamwork. Erick and Wendy have different roles on the farm, and they're able to handle so many different aspects. Wendy is really good with the cows and the orchard, and seeing smaller details. Whereas Erick, to me, seems like a Big Picture person. He really looks at the farm as a whole, and decides what needs to get done. To me, that's really important, as well as looking at the details. My kind of role, I think, that I've stepped into the last couple of years is looking at the details of things, and thinking ahead, really, whether it's "What do we do when a flood's coming?" and thinking, "Well, September's here, and October's here, and November's when it floods, so what do we need to do *now*, so we don't have to work that hard when it floods." And I've been thinking about that constantly the last couple of months. I've been watching Erick, the whole scheme of the farm and the way the fields are laid out, watching him rotate where the corn grows and where the beans grow. I don't exactly understand every detail about why he does what he does, but I'm getting the concept of him moving things around, and leaving part of the field fallow to recover, and running the cows over it. There's a lot.

    I really respect Erick and Wendy for the amount of knowledge they know. And Erick is just an incredibly smart guy, and his vocabulary and the way he talks is just incredible. And it makes me a little jealous, because it makes me want to read too, and find out what he knows. It's a little hard to communicate with them both, I think. They're great employers, and they're great people to work for, absolutely. But sometimes the communication lacks, so it's a little frustrating sometimes. But I have worked for some really shady people, so I can't complain. You know? Before I started, I asked a guy that worked at the farm, Randy—he was there with his family—I said, "I want an opinion of what it's like to work here before I decide to work here. What do you think about it?" He goes, "Well, after this year, I'm just gonna burn rubber outta this place." And I couldn't believe what he said, but I took his opinion to heart, and I decided to think about it. And I'm like, "This just doesn't seem right. Why would he say that?" Jubilee Farm wasn't the farm for him and his family. He was an older fellow, in his fifties, from Boeing. He decided he wanted to get into farming. They were, I guess, minimalistic and had different living styles or values or whatever than Erick and Wendy have, but to each their own. But he ended up burnin' rubber out of the place, and moved up to Skagit Valley and bought a farm. So good for him. But I decided to take his advice and not compare it to what *I* thought of Erick and Wendy, and I thought it would be a good opportunity, despite what he said. And I found out that it *is* great working for them, and the farm has been really good. I think they really need a person like me at the farm—somebody that knows some mechanics, somebody that knows carpentry work, even though I'm not a carpenter by *any* means. I can swing a hammer, I can learn as I go. But somebody is definitely needed at a farm full-time that has variety. I think they're great, they're great people, very friendly. Erick's really good with kids, and educating, and that is very obvious. That means he can talk to people and children. Sometimes when I'm working he has a group of college kids or high school students that he's talking to. I kind of want to stop and just listen, because a lot of the stuff he's telling them, he hasn't even told me. And I'm just like, "Oh! I just want to listen so I can learn some more stuff from him." But sometimes I can't, I've just got to keep workin'.

    It's a good farm. It's funny, there's so many farms in this Valley—organic farms, vegetable farms—and I've wanted to go to every single one of them and look at their stuff and how they work, but haven't had any time. I haven't even had time to go chat, except when I picked up vegetables from them in the winter. Even Erick says that too. He's like "Oh, I haven't had time...." He wants to come to *my* two acres to see what *I've* done, but he just can't break away from the farm. I'm like, "Come on down during lunchtime, and I'll just show you real quick, it doesn't have to be that long," but it just doesn't work. He can't, there's no break.

    One thing I *don't* like about farming is that my summers go by very fast. And as a person that loves the outdoors, I love to fish, backpack, hike, rock climb. And I got my girlfriend into rock climbing this last year, and she's just been all over my case to go rock climbing and go backpacking and stuff. I'd love to do that stuff, but this year's been really work concentrated, and getting my career developed. So I haven't had time to do that. I want to find a way to enjoy a little bit of both in my life. That's what I'm going to concentrate on.

The lessons we have learned from evolutionary biology, ecological economics, and the history of social movements suggest that the new industrialized food system......must, of necessity, be very short lived on any evolutionary timescale. Evolutionary biology reminds us that population explosions of any species inevitably transform it into a "plague species" that crashes in order to bring it back into ecological balance with the community of species on which it ultimately depends. Very large industrial farms, devoted to producing large quantities of a single species, fit the definition of a plague species exactly.

Ecological economics teaches us that human economies are ultimately subsystems of the natural economy. Natural ecosystems provide the natural resources that fuel human economies, and natural sinks recycle the waste generated by human economies. As these natural systems become degraded or overloaded, human economies begin to fail.

And the history of social movements teaches us that without a modicum of egalitarian rule, societies become destabilized. Such unreliable social environments are almost always costly to the entire biotic community. In today's political and social climate this could be an urgent matter. David Orr reminds us, for example, of some of the vulnerabilities and costs our industrial agriculture system may incur given our current social unrest. Orr suggests that, among other things, a centralized agriculture is not easily protected from terrorist attack.

> A society fed by a few megafarms is far more vulnerable to many kinds of disruption than one with many smaller and widely dispersed farms. One that relies on long-distance transport of essential materials must guard every supply line, but the military capability to do so becomes yet another source of vulnerability and ecological cost. In short, no society that relies on distant sources of food, energy, and materials or heroic feats of technology can be secured indefinitely........An ecological view of security would lead us to rebuild family farms, local enterprises, community prosperity, and regional economies, and to invest in regeneration of natural capital.

Finally, another discomforting analysis of our industrialized systems has been proposed by Charles Perrow in his enlightening book *"Normal Accidents"*. Perrow argues that as any system becomes increasingly complex and more tightly coupled, normal accidents, which inevitably take place in *any* system, become catastrophes. If Perrow is correct then we should expect an increase in food-related catastrophes in our highly complex, tightly coupled, industrial food system. (**Author's note: The bulk of supermarket produce travels at least 1500 miles from source to delivery point. A major interruption in fuel supply could vacate supermarket shelves of essential food products within 5 to 7 days**).

Frederick Kirschenmann, "The Current State of Agriculture—Does it Have a Future", 2003

Tendrils

15 December 2009

My name's Heidi Elizabeth Bohan. I was born December 28, 1954 in Troy, New York, and mostly raised—I was raised on the East Coast until I was about six, and we moved to California. And so I was part of that whole movement out to the California area, San Francisco Bay area. I was raised pretty upper class, but my dad had a high work ethic, and he bought us kids a peach ranch when I was twelve. I was the oldest of four, and we had twenty acres of peaches over in the San Joaquin Valley. I was a country club member and lived in the neighborhood that when I told my friends, they'd say, "Oh, you're rich!" But we had a peach ranch, and it was a three-hour drive or so over to the San Joaquin Valley, and we'd go over there and we'd thin and irrigate and spray and harvest. We lived in a tent, us kids had a tent out in the back, and my dad had a trailer. We'd go to restaurants where there were roaches and things like that. And we dealt with the heat, and we'd go swimming in the canal to cool down. So we kind of had that whole experience. So that's how I got started, I guess, with really an awareness of agriculture.

At the same time, I got into horses, so I also always felt that horses were a contributor, because no matter what class you are in, if you have horses, you're muckin' manure, girl or boy. And you're out there usin' a hammer to fix the fence.

So anyway, the peach ranch and the horses started leading me in this direction, and I became part of the whole hippie movement. I was a thirteen-year-old who ended up in a commune in northern California. I was oddly, the first person gardening in the commune that I lived at, which was Summerhill West, I started an organic garden, and I started poring through the "*Rodale Organic Gardening*" magazine. I did that garden myself. I was sixteen when I grew my first organic garden, and fenced it off. I was just trying to think about that the other day: how did

Heidi Bohan
Director,
Sno-Valley Tilth
Manager,
Carnation Farmers
Market,
Carnation, WA

I actually get goin' on that garden by myself? Because I don't remember anybody helping me with that. So that was pretty much what launched me into the food part of what I did. And we also had a milk cow—we had a little Jersey milk cow—and I raised chickens galore. I had hundreds and hundreds of chickens over the five-year period or more. And raised pigs. It was just part of the whole back-to-the-land movement. And let's see, "*Mother Earth News*" was another inspiration, so those two books were pretty big.

So anyway, that actually very deeply seated me in the awareness that we can't get too distanced from our food and our houses and our shelter. And I ended up living in a place that we called The Wilderness, that was actually seven miles from any road. We walked in or used horses. We built our houses from redwood trees that had been left from the logging, something like eighty years before. And we used all hand tools. We didn't use any chainsaws. We used all frozen mauls and wedges to split out these huge planks. And we used cedar bark and cooked over open fires, and just took the water right from the creek, dammed up the creek, and lived that way for about three years.

And then I worked a neighboring farm, which was the first legal commune in America, actually, called Church of the Golden Rule, Ridgewood Ranch, in Willets, Mendocino, California. And we grew fifteen-acre gardens there. There were about four of us that lived in The Wilderness, and we would walk or ride our horses over and grow out these gardens that are now being managed by John Jevins. I forget the name of that group now. But in any event, those lands are *still* being grown as organic grounds, those fifteen acres that we used to grow.

And from there, I moved to Montana. We decided we couldn't die in California, it wasn't hard enough. So we moved to Montana, and there you could die in an instant, if you do anything stupid there. And I think that really was part of the allure, is we really wanted to test our ability to survive really, and we started—me and my then husband, Greg, started a post and pole mill operation there. So that was actually using lodge pole pine, which grows in abundance there, and thinning, and making fence material and tree post material that's used around the country—I see it all over the place. So we ran that for a couple of years, and then I moved out here as a single mom.

Right away, when I moved out here from Montana, I moved in with my brother in the Rainier Valley. He had just bought a house there. And I looked on the maps, I pored on them through the maps, and I identified the Snoqualmie Valley, from the maps, as where I wanted to live. I came out here, and the first place I went to, the first place I drove to out here, was Tolt McDonald Park. And so me living now in the farmhouse right next to Tolt McDonald Park is an amazing full circle for me, and has a lot of sort of destiny attached to that. I'd always intended to move into Carnation. We'd actually looked at houses. But it took me years to actually end up out here. I ended up owning a house in Kirkland and living in Everett and a few other places before I ever really landed here.

I took my whole set of back-to-the-land skills and tried to work in nurseries here, but I just couldn't make a living and pay daycare on the salary they paid. So I ended up becoming a finish carpenter, and I did that for fifteen years, and sold that business and then got into education. I did that because all these employees that were coming to me in my woodworking business really didn't have the life skills to cope. It was very apparent to me that schools were not giving kids the education they needed in order to live in this world. They just didn't know how to interact, how to negotiate, how to be on time, how to fill out an application, how to problem solve. It was really amazing to me what the kids weren't getting. So I ended up developing a life skills program for a school for behavior disordered teens, that a friend of mine owned the school, and I offered to grow gardens first and then saw there was a whole bunch of other needs, and I started developing a curriculum that was integrated to academics, that was based on project-based, hands-on skills-building. So I had a life skills class, a shop class, a horticulture class, and a work program that I developed. And I integrated with all the academics, and I got a reputation around the area.

At that time it was new to integrate project-based learning with academics. This was very concrete, because in order for the kids that were in my shop class, for example, I let them build whatever they wanted, but they had to do a scale drawing first. And in order to do a scale drawing. Since most of the kids did not have the skills to do that, they had to work with their math teacher to come up with a scale drawing. And of course I helped them. And so we built things like speaker boxes and shelves to mount their stereo equipment in their bedroom, and little things like that. In any event, that was really exciting to me, to see how you could take something that was very real, and have it be of value to people that needed some direction.

I've been doing that ever since. I met Ralph Bennett, who's a Haida Native American, at that school. He's a carver and a storyteller, and he was preparing to move into the town I was living in, and move into a park as an artist in residence. I offered to help him in that effort. That's the Haida House Studio in Redmond. We ended up marrying, and I moved in as well, and so we've both lived at the Slough House Park in Redmond for four years, and developed a really intensive cultural education program with outreach to all the schools and the general public. We had just thousands of people coming through.

At that time I focused in on the local native people, because Ralph is Haida, who are from Alaska and the North so he really couldn't speak to the native people here. So I began to research the native people here, and discovered that they were the Duwamish and the Snoqualmie people (perhaps more so the Snoqualmie in the Sammamish Lake area, which is where we were). And then I began to apply my woodworking and horticulture skills and knowledge to the study of ethnobotany, and began to experiment with recreating artifacts and objects from using those skills, and in the process became known as an ethnobotanist. I'm still known as that today: I teach with the tribes and I teach at Northwest Indian College.

All of this was kind of concurrent with also working with restoration projects, native plant restoration projects in the area, and developing education materials that helped community stewardship, and people within the schools to interact with these projects, and make them real. So again, I was about getting people to connect with their food sources and their material resources, combined with the native plant restoration work, and the tribal ethnobotany work—all hands-on skills to empower people with this knowledge.

I have no academic training in this area, and yet the academics refer to me now. When I'm questioned on that subject—and I do have some people confront me on that, that I'm not an academically acknowledged ethnobotanist—after kind of telling them a little bit of my story, I've asked them straight up, "If I was a native person and I told you that, would you question my right to speak on this subject?" You couldn't! So through my marriage with Ralph and my acquaintance with his family and his guidance—he very much helped guide me in how I viewed what I was learning, and how I perceived. So I was very well coached. And Ralph was/is a native person who does not believe that the knowledge should be kept secret—except for, of course, the spiritual information. And I totally agree with that, and I honor that. But in terms of just the traditional knowledge itself, and the skills, that that should be passed on, and it doesn't need to just be kept with the tribes. Otherwise, it can be lost. And there is a role with white people helping to keep the knowledge alive.

So anyway, that's the skill base that I started really zeroing in on as a career and as an income for myself. But then just as a human being on this planet, I'm watching what's happening to where we're going. It's very evident that we have to deal with what's going to be happening in the future. I had the really great privilege of being able to spend about five days with David Holmgren, who's the co-originator of the permaculture movement, with Bill Morrison. Actually, David Holmgren is strongly associated with the coining of the word and the first early development of the concept. And so I got to spend time with him on one of his few visits to America, and I basically camped with him, with a bunch of people, for four days over in Twisp, and had his ear from the minute we were up in the morning drinking coffee, 'til goin' to bed at night around the fire. And so I really got that everything I'd been doin' in my life, all the skills, all the focus, was really around this notion, encapsulated in this notion of permaculture and sustainability and that work.

And just about that same time, I had been coming to the Carnation Farmers Market. I kept seeing the Sno-Valley Tilth Booth and picked up their flyer. I might have even joined at that point, because I knew they did the potlucks, and I kind of wanted to see what was goin' on. And while I was at the permaculture conferences and trainings, and you'd hear all this bad news, you can start to get a bit depressed and worried. Like, "How are we gonna pull this off?" And it can become overwhelming. And then I'd remember the Tilth. I'd think, "You know, those are people that are *doin'* it. They're actually in solution mode."

So I started attending my first Tilth meetings, and they needed some volunteerism. I just jumped to the forefront. To me, I could put in—because of the other work I was doing, I had freelance income coming in—I could put in four hours a week or so towards this, and not worry about the money part of it. So I ended up helping with making the booth at the farmers market more informational. So I went around and visited all the farmers, so this was really kind of a big moment for me. I was putting the e-mail out to ask if I could come visit people on the farm and take photographs, and in twenty-four hours I had ten farms scheduled and synchronized so that I could hit each one of them over a one-and-a-half-day period. It was amazing to me how fast they came on board, how efficient they were at it, and *effective!* I keep coming up with the word "effective" when I deal with the Tilth farmers.

So anyway, I went out to those farms, and I'd come out there with my little digital camera—not your big fancy camera like you have. I wish I'd had the fake fancy camera, because I think they were a little disappointed. But nonetheless they took me around, they treated me like I was actually a famous photographer or something, and gave me tours of the farm. Really, literally every one of them, would point to where the nearby river was, "There's the river, this is where it floods." It was always a big part of the discussion, is the river and the impact it had on their farm. And it was never in a negative way, it was more like "That's the reality of the life. It brings in the soil and it floods the land." So that's when I made the poster with the river down the center. I decided it had to be the river down the center, because that's what it was all about, was this water.

So anyway, I created that poster and I volunteered every market day I could that summer, and did education programs there; canning demos, and edible flower demos, and I did hand out literature and stuff like that. And I really loved it, I thought it was awesome. And that was the same year that I did fund myself to go to Tuscany, and I went to Tuscany in September of that year. My daughter and I planned that trip, and we ended up making farmers markets kind of the theme of the trip in Tuscany. So we made sure every town we visited, we went on the day that their farmers market was in place. And so I also got to see the farmers market in Salzburg. We flew into Munich and went to that market, and then visited farmers markets throughout Tuscany; and then came back completely inspired about a sustainable food system, because that's what you see and experience in Tuscany, and I didn't expect that. My daughter wanted me to go to Tuscany. She knew I'd love it. And I was very blown away by seeing an intact culture that was focused around its food; and its food was sustainable, they grew all of it, and still do today. And that's a pretty amazing model. So I came back totally inspired, recognized that the value here—we are actually, according to the permaculture models, we're a Mediterranean climate, and when you take a look at what we grow, it very much models what you can grow in Tuscany, which is a high elevation cold climate, and a lot of our foods. I still continue to be inspired by that as a model of where I'm trying to go with what I think I can bring to the table, along with I think I can bring to this whole effort the link between native, wild plants and their role today in the permaculture or the sustainability model. And that's in the form of hedgerows and wildcrafting.

And then that fall, the current market manager had an injury and she needed to have a guarantee that she'd have volunteers to help set up the market each week, and really we can't guarantee that. And so they asked me if I'd be interested in the manager position. So I asked, "Okay, what does that entail?" We figured out it would be no more than a day, maybe a day and a half a week. In the end, you could probably do that, but you wouldn't be trying very hard. And if you're going to really try, it's a lot more work than that. But I signed on and I've never regretted it because, again, to me it's such a part of the solution. I regret it on a hundred-degree day when I'm trying to set up the market and I'm about ready to swoon from the heat. I think it's the hardest job I've ever had, physically and even just orchestrating. I had a woodworking business that I had up to twenty employees, and I was managing a ton of money on short order. I did custom fireplace mantles. That was a very complex business, and I had wholesale and retail, and I had a store, and I had 1-800 numbers. It doesn't even compare to the complexity of managing a farmers market. I couldn't even figure out how to manage all the data coming my way. It's an amazing task. So I set up Access databases, just to track who's who, because you've got vendors, you've got customers, you've got people who want to help, you've got agencies that you've got to interact with. I mean, there's just a ton of stuff.

So anyway, I got that job that first year. I set up a really complex mind map for where I wanted to go with the market, and I could see where we could improve it, and we actually did see, I think, an 86% increase in sales that year, and people did attribute it to my efforts—even though I have to acknowledge, and I tell people, I think actually the market was maturing as well. I think it reached that point where we were getting there. And there were some tricks that I used that we definitely increased our attendance. And then with the guidance of the Tilth who manages the market, the Tilth board, they've just given me a ton of wisdom about "What am I really seeing? What am I really dealing with at the farmers market, from a farm-focused perspective?" And that's how the Carnation Farmers Market is run, is first and foremost this farmers market is for the farmers; it's second for the customers. And that's a really important distinction, because if it's first for the customers, you can compromise on who you have at the market, in order to satisfy your customers. So anyway, that's been a great guidance for me, and something I might think is a good solution, I bring it to the board of the Sno-Valley Tilth, and they'll explain to me why that might backfire, and not end up giving me the results I want to see. So I really feel like I've gotten a lot of excellent guidance from wise people.

When I was first getting to know these farmers through the Tilth meetings, and then going out to their farms, that's when I began to hear their stories. Like Scott and Amy to me is a prime example, and I use them over and over again, because they had made a decision at some point early in their marriage that they wanted to have an organic farm. I guess they went to a conference and they were inspired.

And they were both professionals: she was a teacher, with a degree; and he was an environmental specialist, I forget of what kind, working for an environmental company. And they both decided that in order to finance the farm, they needed to be firefighters. And I just *love* that! That people made that conscious decision to be firefighters in order to fulfill this dream of a farm. And they bought at the right time and they got that farm going, and I just think that people need to know that, so I'm really glad you're doing this book for that reason. It's not this old model we have of the farmer that's—I don't know what model that is anymore, I can't even remember what I used to think of as farmers, but it's not that anymore. We're really dealing with people that are having passion about what this is. They know the role they're playing in the society. I don't really have a desire to be a farmer. I know how much work that is, and it's enough for me to do a garden. But if I can help facilitate what they don't have time to do, in order to better accomplish what they're trying to accomplish, then I couldn't be happier. And so the farmers market, of course, is one avenue for that.

And then they asked me—I think it was a really smart move on their part initially—because they asked me at the end of the first market season if I would be interested in being the director of the Tilth. I was only getting a salary that paid for the eight months of market, and I think two months before market, to get going. And then for four months, there'd be no income. So in essence we just kept the income going for me to become director of the Tilth, and then we came up with an incremental pay increase over the years that would have me taking on more and more responsibility as the Tilth director.

And I have to say at first I thought it was almost comical to be called the Executive Director of the Sno-Valley Tilth. I just didn't see myself in that role. But now I'm really honored to have been brought into that role in that way.

When they hired me as director, I thought, "I don't really even know what the Sno-Valley Tilth.... I know what their mission statement is, but how does it work?" And so I did research, and the very first tilth meeting of any tilth organization ever was at Prag Tree Farms up in Arlington, and I happened to have been at that farm, so I know the location, it's still a community-owned farm. They definitely intended that tilths support organic farming and gardening, and that is the core of the mission of the tilth movement. And that did address some of the questions that I had as the Tilth director: "Who do we want as members of this organization, all farmers? Shall we try to be exclusive in any way?" Those were really questions that I had to struggle with. But I go back to that, we really are trying to support organic and sustainable farming for the future. That's what we're here to do.

So then *our* organization, the Sno-Valley Tilth itself, started more as a social connecting between the different farmers in the area. It was informally started now probably eleven years ago. Some of those members are still members. It was five years after they were meeting *in*formally that they got their nonprofit and became a chapter of the Tilth itself. And I actually forget the year on that. It was probably 2004 that they formalized as an organization and became a chapter of the Washington Tilth.

So when I went out to the farms and visited that one day and did the photography, I asked each of them why they were members of the Tilth, and each of them all answered that it was a way for them to network between each other. And they shared tools, like if somebody needed a certain kind of piece of equipment, they could ask to borrow it, and they did. And some, of course, had more equipment, like Full Circle Farms, and I just thought that was so great, that they would share their equipment and not think of each other as competitors at all. There's no sense of competition between the members, or even the farmers. I don't know all the farmers in the Valley, but there's such a sense of camaraderie in it, rather than competition.

The biggest project right now is still the Carnation Farmers Market, in terms of where it puts its most energy and resources. Its mission is to connect local produce with customers, so that's one of its best vehicles for that. But we have other projects now that I think are going to take us even further, and that includes some of the policy work we're doing, and the sustainable foods project for the Valley: how do we connect all the different pieces of what's going on in this Valley, and how to enhance them to make this work even better? So that's the commercial kitchen concepts, the value-added product, getting retail stores carrying these products, that kind of thing. So that's where I see us heading.

There is something that I tend to forget, and we need to not, is all our farming isn't just in the Valley, but we refer to it all the time as "the Valley," but there are quite a few farms that are up in the foothills that could be members as well. I need to start using the term "watershed" more—the Snoqualmie Valley Watershed. And the Sno-Valley Tilth includes Snohomish County's river as well, and that's in part because some of our original founding members are from down in that area as well. And there's been some debate whether we should *just* be Snoqualmie or not. And I still think we shouldn't limit who we are. I think that being part of a watershed is probably an appropriate approach.

But part of the reason we were discussing maybe just being Snoqualmie is because we primarily deal with King County Council. That's our Number One agency that seems to have the most influence on decisions out here in the APD (Agricultural Production District). So it's King County who designated the APD, and that was a good thing. Ron Sims had a big role in that. And the Snoqualmie Valley is unique in that not only is it protected in this APD, but it's protected by the flooding. It's a flood plain, so we're not likely to see a Wal-Mart moving in, in any near future, until that flooding is dealt with. So that in itself does protect us. And that is actually dealt with more at a federal level. So we're primarily dealing with King County Council. And then they have authorized a group, the King County Agricultural Commission, and that's made up of farmers from around the county that advise the council on policy. And one of our members is on that council or that commission, the Ag commission. And we have been able to make recommendations, and been *invited* to make recommendations to the Ag commission, and to our council member, Kathy Lambert, and to the council itself.

More locally, we deal with the Carnation City Council, because that's where our market is located, and that's been more related to these permanent market shelters that we're trying to set up.

The relationships with King County have been good; they're still good. The city council was not so good. That actually was very enlightening. It was enlightening to figure out, because it was such a surprise to see such a disconnect from the council to the part of the community, those represented by the farmers market, and to hear a mayor and council members actually say they didn't see the benefit of the market to the City of Carnation was a stunning revelation—but important, because it causes me to address that issue, and really get clear on what *is* the benefit of the market to the City of Carnation, for example. And I'm not sure of my information on this, but I'll go ahead and say it: that the reason they made that statement is when they first authorized a farmers market in Carnation, they did it on the basis where it would increase foot traffic in Carnation for their local businesses, and their local business would see an increase in income as a result of it. And so we've all sort of played along with that notion, that the farmers market's role is to increase foot traffic for the downtown area for local businesses. And we've all actually tried to come up with some data to support it, and most farmers markets around the country try to do the same thing, because most cities have that expectation. As a result of going through this process, which was a long and difficult one since last spring, and letters to the editor, and some pretty hurtful statements made, that kind of thing, I now no longer think that's the role of a farmers market in a city. I think it has that as an incidental side effect, and if that happens to be the case, that's the responsibility of the city and the businesses, to make best use of all these people that have come into town. If they want to draw them in, that's good. If they don't want to, that's fine. But our role is to bring farmers to customers and create that relationship. And that in itself is enough of a benefit where we don't have to make excuses for it any other way. We don't have to justify ourselves by dollars, how many dollars are we bringing to a city, because we bring a benefit that has another value to it, and it's not dollars. It has to do with health, it has to do with environment, it has to do with economics in terms of healthy economies that you can't necessarily, without great expense and trouble, come up with the data to prove those numbers. And people do it. Vicki Sontag's trying to do it through Ecopraxis, but it's very complex.

From my travel with my daughter that I mentioned, I decided to use the European farmers market as a model, actually the Salzburg market. The day of market in Salzburg is on Thursday morning and goes from 6 am 'til 11, and starts in the courtyard of the church in the downtown area. That's the base of it, but it stretches down side streets. It's an enormous market. And all the shops in the region shut down for market, because *they* want to go to market too. The employees and the owners of those shops don't want to be open, because they've got to go to market—rather than the notion that they're open to increase their business. I don't know if there's even a stall fee for the vendors. So you see people come, they park their cars, they had their little cars, they got out—and I saw this all through Italy—and they go into market, they have a definite shopping list, they're filling up their stuff, and they go home. There isn't entertainment. It's definitely a shopping experience. Not to say that we have to be that way here necessarily. I'm not saying businesses should shut down or anything around the market, because when I've said that, people are like, "Oh yeah, now you're gonna get goin' on *that*." I'm like, "No, that's not what I'm trying to say, but I'd like to put that viewpoint out there, that if we viewed our market in that way, we'd probably be closer to what our market should be judged as, that we're bringing food in from local farmers and producers *to you*. We're bringing them direct to you." But that's something you shut stores down for, and you don't go to work for, you make it happen.

I really see the Snoqualmie Valley Sustainable Foods Project as being something I'd really like to see. So with the end result that people can see that they can live....their food source can come from this area, but we've got to create systems to make that possible. It doesn't have to be just from this Valley, it can be Winthrop where we grow the grain. And we don't have the capacity, we don't have the volume of food production going on that would sustain us yet, but we need to create the systems for that eventuality. I'd like to see us start setting up the infrastructure, so as time goes on, and we will likely see the need to, we're able to be ready to do that. And a lot of that is around people's skills. So the people's skills in even being able to use and cook these foods is probably first and foremost. I think we have to get adaptable in making that possible in terms of ease of preparation. We have to have processing facilities so that people *could* have prepared lasagnas that are made from local product, that they can take home and thaw out and cook that evening after they've come home from work. We need that capacity. If we're going to really see it, we can't expect everybody to be able to cook raw foods every day at home and being all local. I just don't see that happening. But anyway, skills building around that, and then infrastructure support for that. So I guess that's where I'm going with this.

I personally moved into the house in Carnation there because I want to continue—I used to run a lot of public workshops with hand skills, around ethnobotany and traditional skills. Cindy Crepky and I have offered apprenticeship programs in the past so I will likely get into that again. And a lot of writing. And you know I've got the book that I published. I have a second book now that has been badly needed, that I've needed to do, is basically an ethnobotany revisited of this area. In the research for the first book, I kept finding myself going down paths that I couldn't go on, because it was getting me off course. But I found tons of really excellent data. Just in my work I've found there's just a ton of missing links in our ethnobotany story here. So I want to do a native plant uses book, ethnobotany revisited sort of concept. We don't have anything really along those lines here, so that's my next big project.

The Tilth has authorized me to try to get some assistance for the market, so it might be in the form of AmeriCorps volunteers, that kind of thing. I really need to get on the ball with that, because I can really use the help. And eventually we hope to have the finances, and I wouldn't mind even taking a cut in my pay in order to be able to afford an assistant to be able to manage the market just physically on site, that kind of thing. So those are goals.

We've got to get less reliant on oil and long-distance transportation. And we need to be looking at building our local food systems, and just what I spoke about earlier. And so these farmers that are growing, and doing it in a way that's healthy.... Well, there's the hidden piece. I work with the Snoqualmie Tribe and we're dealing with diabetes, and we're dealing with obesity, and we're dealing with this huge health problem in America, and it's around food. It's very clear food is at the core, I would say, of the bulk of our health problems. And so the solution in eating raw foods, not processed foods, that are grown organically, and with all their health benefits attached, I think has an immediate impact, that has an immediate need, we have an immediate urgency to deal with that. And we all know it, and we all know we need to eat more greens, we all know we need to eat more raw fruits and vegetables, and yet it's still difficult for people to do. So that's part of what this is all about. Then just the whole environmental impact that the kind of farming that we've been doing for so long just isn't working, it's causing too much damage, and probably irreversible damage, and that's the depressing part. So small family farms, and ethical treatment of animals, and all the issues that we hear about are related to these new but old farming practices.

So when I'm studying now about developing local food webs, and I'm reading a book right now—it's new—by Rob Hopkins—and he's talking about England and the developing of food networks there. And they're in as bad a state as we are, in terms of their infrastructures being broken down and building it back. But we're all doing it. We're all sort of worldwide being aware that we've got to get back to this. And I don't mean *all* of us, but a *lot* of us.

The people that show up at farmers markets, they know they're part of the solution. Whether that's *all* they do, or they do more, or they're growing some food in their back yard.... I see you have a nice garden right here. And I saw a bunch of nice gardens comin' up the road here. I was actually thinking, if this whole little community here could be assessed for their ability to produce their own food, it'd be interesting to do that as a little model. And actually, as I drove out here, I thought, I wonder if I could get a survey out there to find out how many people in this Valley—or this watershed—are growing their own gardens? And to what percentage do they think they're taking care of their vegetable needs for the year, or whatever.

Like, what kind of numbers could we pull? That's the kind of thing that I think is really interesting right now. What's our capacity to move away from what we believe is no longer going to be a successful system?—Which is large commercial agriculture. I just don't see that being successful in twenty years. I just can't see how it's gonna still be there.

Farm Journal

11 June 2009

Had a brief but profound conversation with Siri at Local Roots yesterday morning. The Carnation City Council has put the brakes on what appeared to be an accelerated plan to support the Carnation Farmers Market. We commiserated about the continuing confrontation between agrarian politics and the corporate-industrial paradigm. The latter, of course, is dominant and regards the agrarian resurgence in the Valley as, at best, quaint and nostalgic or, at worst, a hindrance to the rights of self-interest, unlimited growth and maximum profit. Specifically, although the Carnation Farmers Market is burgeoning and extremely successful as well as applauded by the general community, the Council decided that its economic value is relatively insignificant in terms of its benefit to local businesses. Their rancor is directed at the Sno-Valley Tilth whose organization is designed to support local organic farms, food production and distribution. Therefore, under the Tilth By-Laws, the hardware store, for example, can't be a vendor at the Market.

Recently, as part of the Parks Board Master Plan for City Development, the Farmers Market proposed an enlargement of the Market to build permanent vendor stalls and a commercial kitchen for processing of local food year round. At a public meeting, complaints from the community were raised over the use of the kitchen; complainers felt it should be available for social use by the general population. All the objections centered around the belief that although the Market and local food were "nice" they had minimal benefit for the majority of the community and, furthermore, city and state government should not use public monies to fund private enterprise but offer public facilities to serve "everyone".

One citizen made a pilgrimage to the State Legislature in Olympia to bend the ear of one of the two congressmen representing the District and persuaded him to vote to cancel the $162,000 grant the Legislature was about to award to the Market. The funds would be taken from the State's budget allotment for County Programs that would promote local job creation. One angry voice, shouting the threat of socialism, obliterated two years of effort by the Tilth and its Director, Heidi Bohan (also the Market Manager) to advance the resurgence of local food. The Mayor of Carnation was quoted in the local weekly newspaper saying that there is no real economic value in the Farmers Market for the City.

Meanwhile, I've been out every morning this week, walking the rows of kale, lettuce, radish, squash. Clear skies, fine morning mist in the air, "high-key" light and a resonant blend of warm sun—morning chill. The mixture of air, plants, the smell of the ground and the absence of technological din offer a key to one deep motivation for the appeal this work and life hold for the growers and interns alike. Only a techno-zombie would be unmoved by the pervasive serenity of the Valley and the profound Mantra of repetitive tasks—water each seedling as it enters the earth, move on...............talk is subdued, laughter easy, available, frequent.

The days are long now and as crops mature harvesting assumes a brisker pace; pick, load, haul to the washing station, prep, bag, box & label CSA deliveries, load into van, prep for Farmers Market, tally, keep moving—the pace is relentless............this will be a good year......if the weather cooperates.....need that balance of wet and dry.

Author's note: On 08 August 2010, after a large and often emotional outpouring of community support and testimony from local growers, the City Council, under the direction of its new Mayor, voted 4 to 1 to partner with the Sno-Valley Tilth to construct permanent market shelters in the commons, downtown Carnation. The community kitchen is still a dream but this was a significant change. The one dissenting vote, complete with Anglo-Saxon expletives, came from the former Mayor.

24 January 2010

I'm Bill Aal. It was a created name during the seventies. That's a whole story. I was born June 18, 1953. So my full name is William Hauptman Aal. I go by Bill. I was born in New York State and went back and forth between the city and the country a lot when I was a kid. I was born in Mt. Vernon, which is a suburb, and then my parents moved to the country. And when they got divorced, I moved back to the city by the time I was eight. "The city" meaning New York. Then, as soon as my mother could, she got us to the upstate area in Albany, and was close to the woods that she could find in a suburban community.

William Aal
Community Alliance
for Global Justice

So for me, going back and forth between city and country continued from the beginning. I went to University of Toronto to maybe escape the draft. When that didn't need to happen, I came back to the States and I ended up in Ithaca, New York, and was at Cornell, in the Ag school in the seventies and up through '80.

And so I've been pursuing, in my own life, this relationship between city and country, and between spirit and justice in the land. I have an undergraduate degree in microbiology from the Ag school at Cornell, and it's about microbial ecology. Never did anything with it, because people are more important to me than laboratories. And ever since I was thirteen, I've been pursuing a path around justice, and learned from an experience with a rabbi that I had when I was getting Bar Mitzvahed as a Jewish person. I was an atheist, my mother had been a communist when she was younger, and had this whole deal of not believing in God. And so I'd go to the rabbi and say, "I shouldn't be here because I don't believe in God." And he said, "Well, guess what, I don't either." And sure enough, he became a Unitarian minister. And so I asked him why he stayed there, and he said, "Because I could stand with my folks for justice." And he was one of the leaders in the anti-war movement in the sixties, in the mainstream anti-war movement, and in the struggle for black—Negro rights, as they called it back then. So it's been a long time sort of pursuing these intertwining pieces that led me to be working with Heather in the Community Alliance.

So from Ithaca, I was living in the countryside and going to school and learning about sustainable agriculture. I'd gone from being really involved in the anti-war movement in the late sixties and seventies, to burning out. So when I was in Ithaca, I was sort of going back to the land. That was my dream. I learned a lot about sustainable agriculture. We didn't call it that at the time, but that's what it was. I remember reading Wendell Berry's "*The Unsettling of America*", in the early seventies and late seventies and realizing that at a fundamental level our struggle was to reconnect to each other and to the land. And there was a relationship, as a nation, between our being forced off the land, whether it was from Europe or in this country into the cities, into these really inhumane relationships with each other. That led to the ability to destroy large numbers of people.

So we were part of the whole movement, and by the time the late seventies, early eighties were coming around, I realized I needed to be back in the city, because that's where fundamentally, while we could do the repairs on the land, the destruction was coming from the dynamics in the city. And so I moved to Seattle because it was more like a town back then, and less like a city than other places where I had some job offers doing computer stuff, and moved to the neighborhood I still live in on Capital Hill. This is all by means of saying that I ran into some people and became involved in a radical and political movement called the National Organization for an American Revolution, which was based in Detroit—an interesting place to be based—and was dedicated to looking at, as we used to say, the revolutionary leadership of people of color, and women, and working folks; and how those voices that had been locked out, both in this country and other places, were key to the solutions that we needed to find, and weren't the only voices, but they were the ones that had been locked out. And those voices, if they are included in, are thinking about how the world should be really changed in the way we look at solutions. So that led me to a lot of interesting places.

We were a very interesting group that allowed my now partner, Margo Adair, to be involved in leadership. She was a California hippie doing meditation work. And we had Detroit auto workers, and folks from the street, and all around, in the same organization. So it was a very rich environment exploring this connection between the land, between the kinds of relationships that needed to be rebuilt between people in different classes, and across the divides of color. And that organization lasted about ten years, and we still have relationships with each other. And it led me to be involved in the bio-regional movement, actually—interestingly enough, because that was about recreating culture and recreating this relationship between folks who'd been....alienated....I'll use that word advisedly....from each other and from the land, and to come back to it. And so for another ten years, more or less, I was involved in holding conferences and gatherings and reconnecting to country people. And through that, I started to realize one really key area that was scary to me, and to a lot of people, was around genetic engineering of food. As I go back and look at all my history, it all seems to lead to the same place.

I left microbiology partially because the first job I had was doing stuff around recombinant DNA in the seventies. And I realized the potential scariness of that, and I watched the scientists say, "Oh no, none of this will ever happen. It's very safe," blah, blah, blah. And I got freaked out about the scientific approach to the natural world. And so in the 1980s I was involved in Central America work, and I went to Nicaragua with the construction brigade. I went to Mozambique to work also in solidarity work. And during that time, I started to become acquainted with the issues around biotechnology, and in particular working with this guy Phil Bariano, who's still on the advisory board of the Community Alliance for Global Justice, and is a mentor to many of us in different ways around these issues of genetic engineering. My housemates and I made a video called "Risky Business", which is about agricultural biotech and the contradictions, as we used to say—the challenges of biotechnology. So through that period, we had a grass roots organization called Washington Biotechnology Action Council. It still exists in name. And we worked locally and globally trying to stop biotech, especially around agriculture, and to help wake people up to the dangers of it and to work on the policy levels and sort of in a similar way that we're working on all different levels in the food justice now, trying to figure out how to work out what were the underlying drivers behind this push towards biotechnology on the corporate side, on the scientific side. And knowing that there's so many people who resented this in our communities here and around the world, why was it still happening? So it was very much a movement against biotechnology. And in that context, as this was in the nineties, we started to realize the relationship to global trade and to things like NAFTA and the way that the international trade organizations and monetary organizations are pushing industrial models of not only agriculture, but of civilization, on the world.

And so in that period in the late nineties, as it was clear that there was a push towards what they called rationalizing the trade regimes, it was about creating free flow of money and ideas in one direction—well, free flow investment money in one direction, and free flow of a lot of other money back to the center from the peripheral countries. And because of all this mess, I'm involved in all these different places. I'm in the countryside hanging out with hippies and anti-forestry activists and the anti-free-trade people, and in all these different places, myself and my partner Margo started doing work with groups that were beginning to do creative organizing against large corporations. Anti-forestry issues, we held conferences on looking at the—or part of holding conferences on looking at the relationship between protecting the trees here and protecting the rainforests in Asia and Africa and Latin America.

And in this period, there were all these people who were making puppets and starting to have marches that were not just like anti, but beginning to say "What are we *for*?" And as that started to happen for me, I started to think, "Boy, I've been fighting against GMOs, and fighting against the corporations, and then fighting against a lot of different big entities for my whole life, and I need to start being about being *for* something," going back to that impulse that I had to become involved in revolutionary politics.

It was just around that time that people in the Washington Sustainable Food and Farming Network, a statewide policy organization, were looking for some expertise around genetically modified foods, because there was a fight around GMO wheat at the time. So in 1997, '98, I started to get involved. I got recruited to be first an expert, and then on the board—"expert" in quotes, of course—of this Washington Sustainable Food and Farming Network, which I was involved with for ten years. And what was really cool was I was in touch with folks not who were just fighting for the land, but about recreating a new relationship to the land. So going back to the bioregional stuff, and the Wendell Berry stuff and all that. For me it was just powerful to be hanging out with folks here in this Valley and over in eastern Washington and wherever who were saying, "We can recreate a food system that works for everybody." And it was so inspiring to be involved with people who are not just about vision, but about practical vision, about doing it.

I think one of the things is that it wasn't necessarily about planning. It was about, you know, in terms of the farmers it was about, "Yes, we have plans, and we have goals and stuff," but it wasn't about, like, *this* big. There were a few of the big thinkers in the world, and there's a few of us possy-wonks, right? We're thinkin' that way. But it's like, "I want to start to live in a different relationship with the land, and I want to produce food that is good for me and for the people who I sell it to, and I want to be able to get a good return—not in an economic sense, but on a full-life sense for the investment of work and time and energy I do. And I can't do it anymore. Like a friend of ours, Morris Robbinette, is a farmer over in Cheney, fourth-generation farmer, and he was doing it the traditional way—rancher—and he was going broke, and he was breaking his back, and his animals weren't happy, and at some point he just realized there's a different way to do it, and he starts to move toward holistic management and range-fed beef—not grain-fed beef, but free ranging beef. It changed his whole life, and he's able to make a living for his family, and so on. And so those kinds of examples led me to think, "How could we create policy changes?" And so we were involved with Pullman, with Washington State University, because we wrote letters that shamed them, basically, when they started to do safe food initiative in 1998. And it was food irradiation, it was GMOs, it was industrial agriculture. It wasn't anything about safe food. And so we pointed that out, and they got really upset and said, "What do you mean?" And we entered into negotiations with them. They wanted us to back off. And we said, "Well, we'll back off if you do these things." And some of those things came true. One of them is small animal mobile slaughtering units for the islands and for places on this side, so that small farmers could actually—and food producers—could raise animals and sell them. Go to the farmers markets these days and you see lots more of that. We said we want to see a center for sustaining agriculture and natural resources, not just on the books, but funded. And twelve years later, it's a fully-funded program, and Washington State has one of the first organic majors. And that was due to activism and engagement with an institution. So we've been meeting with WSU every quarter to see, first, if they were doing what they said they were going to do in this first letter of agreement, but then it became a very productive relationship. What I'm saying is, our advocacy group is able to meet with folks at WSU and engage with the institution and see change—incremental change, painfully slow, but actual change. You couldn't talk about organics at WSU back fifteen years ago. The researchers were doing integrated pest management, or they were doing alternative whatever, but they couldn't use the "O" word.

So anyway, the vision piece was so key in this practical thing. It's like, "What are we gonna do?" The kinds of things that we saw then I still think are true: to change our institutions like WSU and the other farming programs in the state to be able to actually support farmers where they want to go, not where the chemical corporations or the big trade organizations want to see farming go in this state. And it's a continual battle.

One of the things that the people in sustainable agriculture don't have as much is this international view of seeing how what we do here impacts the rest of the world, in as clear a way as I think the people in the global justice movement did. And I think one of the reasons, as we're sort of beginning to move into this connection with CHEJ, where I got re-involved with the community alliance through this…. I was involved in the WTO festivities, as I like to call them, where people came together to celebrate a different way of being, and different view of the world, as well as protest.

One of the things that the sustainable Ag folks didn't have, that the global justice movement had, was this understanding that there's structural reasons why farmers are pushed off the land: from the 1600s, if you want to go back—or further— in Europe, to the United States and to the rest of the world as it gets more and more sucked into this global madness. And I think that it was frustrating to me for people not to be able to see those connections. And so I think that the work on the farm bill, for example, in the last *two* cycles, didn't have the kind of focus that it does now, as we're moving into it, because there wasn't as much connection with the global justice movement.

So other things that we could be doing here, that I think need to be done on a policy level at the state level, is to make sure that farmers have a real reason to stay on the land, to make sure there's insurance programs, to make sure that there's education that is there for the kids, and to make sure that there's actual jobs that people can do beyond farming for big corporations. And I think there's a challenge to continue to get farmers and lifestyle activists and global justice activists together to rethink what the relationship is of our farming to the future of Washington State.

What's so inspiring about Erick and some of the other farmers here in Sno-Tilth is that they see that they could provide food for the city, for Seattle. And if people would only support them to do that, with policy changes and with actual dollars to buy food, and willingness to try to keep this land as productive land, that would be a huge thing. And so the farmers close in to Seattle, not just the ones over in eastern Washington or in the hills outside of Wenatchee who have been trying to do fruit farming in a sustainable way, and all that, I'm really inspired by the little bit that I've seen out here. And I know that one of our challenges in the city is to really hear farmers' stories in a way that's real and not romanticized, and to hear their desires for reconnecting to the city in terms of finding markets in Seattle from here.

The people who I know are small or medium-scale farmers, like Joe Hillsbury with Thundering Hooves, in terms of the meat market. And the fruit tree farmers, the ones who are trying to do the right thing are all pretty small scale, because the ones who have a lot of fruit to sell, they've got to throw their lots in with the global market, and there's just not enough capacity of people to eat that many apples or whatever. So the same people I made the "Risky Business" movie with, I helped make a movie called "Good Food," which was about trying to explore this very question. This question of scale is really a huge one. I wish I could point to some cases here. I think there's better case to be made in California where there's huger population densities for large-scale farming, or medium-scale farming to be really in relationship to the cities and to the population centers, than here.

So what's good for the land and what's good for farmers' pocketbooks may not be the same thing. And how do we navigate that in a way that still supports farmers? When I come around to what I hope for the Community Alliance for Global Justice is that we help city people realize that it's very complicated, and that there isn't one answer, and it has to be negotiated farmer to farmer, and city folks to farm folks, to say, "What do we think is best here?" And have that debate not as a debate about who's gonna win or lose, but what's best for the land and how do we make sure that farmers not make their own decisions only, but are able to have just livelihoods.

And the other thing about justice for me is that it's not justice for the humans, it's justice for the critters as well. And that's something that we don't talk about enough in CHEJ or in many of the sustainability conversations, it's sustaining the land, but sort of like for human use. Or sustaining the economy, or sustaining the culture, which I think are three aspects of sustainability, but it's not just sustaining the land, it is really about something bigger than that.

The thing about the Community Alliance that grabbed my attention—I was involved from the beginning in terms of helping to think about it on the advisory committee—but was the bold idea that there should be justice for people who are growing the food and who are eating the food here and abroad. And as we start to move from being just a fair trade and free trade organization, which is what our roots were, into thinking about strengthening local economies everywhere, what does that really mean? How do we actually support farming and farmers here, and farming and farmers in Africa, and for them to be able to not just self-determine, but on a community determination level, which is really the implication of self-determination. How do communities of people start to be able to thrive in their localities, and not be just sucked up into this globalized madness? So as we started to think about that, and to think about what a food justice project might look like, that informed people about the possibilities of growing food in the city, and hooking up with other people who are doing that, about what was going on in this Valley and the Green River and other places where they're still farming in King County and close by, that it's about changing the political will, if you will, of folks, so that they're not just thinking about their own, but as the farmers here are thinking about what's good for this region food-wise? And we'd love to support that in any way that we can—at least I hope so. On the one hand, doing the food justice work, and on the other hand beginning to look at the implications of what's going on in Africa, one more move of pushing people off the land, of trying to integrate them into the global system. So when we started to hear about what the Gates Foundation's plans were for Africa, or their hopes and dreams, it got really scary for us, because it was about making Africa even more enslaved to the global economic system. They talk about land mobility. And what's land mobility? It is the ability of farmers to sell their land and move into the city. And they sell their land so that there can be bigger farms. Just like in Washington State, people are forced into growing more and more acreage to survive. That was what the Gates plan is for Africa. And that to me is truly scary. I think if we started to make the connections for farmers here, to say, oh, the same dynamics are happening here as now they're just beginning—it's not just beginning, but a new phase is beginning, of pushing people off the land, and pushing them into finance capital, all the things that keep farmers from being able to really thrive here. We can start to see some solidarity. And for the folks who are in the global justice movement, for them to see what happened to farming here is a good key to looking at what is going to happen in Africa, and is happening in Asia and Latin America, they might get a different perspective.

Corporations promote biotech to make money, to control markets. And as Vanada Shiva and other activists around the world have told us, it's about control over very life itself. And so it's beyond just like "How much money can we make?" But actually control of the means of production, to use language from the old days. And to control not just the means of production, but the very way in which our lives are structured. And so the Monsantos, the Con-Agras, all the big corporations that are involved in food, they want to be able to lock it up from seed to table. And so to me that's a big piece. And they think it's the best way. It's not just that they want to make money, but they think it's the best way to do things. When we did a film on—my housemates did a film on military conversion. They went to McDonald Douglas and to people there who wanted to—the unions wanted, at the time when the military was crashing—that's no longer the case—the people in Milwaukee had an idea about reusing those factories for doing something different, and the unions proposed that to the management. They said, "Well, you can talk about wages and conditions, but *we* say what's going on about production. This is what we do, and we're never going to do community-oriented whatever." And I think it's the same thing here. You know, the big corporations—Monsanto thinks of itself as a sustainability group. And that's not just green washing, they actually believe it. It's scary.

It's about control over life itself. That's what I would say. I think that the corporations see that as a way—these big corporations see that as a way to make lots of money and to be able to be in business for a long, long time, because people need to eat. And if they control what we eat from the conception of the seed to the seed, all the way to the table, all this small farming is like scary; it doesn't fit within the paradigm of industrial agriculture. And they even say that about climate change now. It's like, "Okay, climate change means Africans can't feed themselves except in big farms. And so everybody has to leave the farm and leave it to us," meaning our way of doing things, "and you all move to the cities." It's like taking people away from the land, which is about resilience, it's not about efficiency, it's about being able to provide for yourselves and for your communities through thin times and thick good harvests and bad harvests, than to, "Okay, you can't do anything. We're going to move you into a place and you're going to be dependent on our processed food, to be able to get your food." So I think that's really what's ultimately at stake. It's like, "We can do it better. We should do it better. And we're going to make a lot of money off of you at the same time." There's people who are trying to do the right thing within each of these big corporations. They get in for all the right reasons in their minds about trying to feed the world, even do ecologically appropriate things, reduce pesticides, but they're part of a huge system that is geared to go against their better instincts. And so then you get sucked in and there you are.

When I talk to farmers about why would they want to—they're independent folks, most farmers I know—they don't like to be controlled by anybody, right? And I point out to them that if they go down the GMO road, they're going to be like the contract farmers in Kentucky or down south around chickens in Alabama, where you don't get to control anything, except how long you work. They're like, "Oh yeah...." But then they still think that they're being given choice about seed and whatever. But everything we've seen around the way that the GMO wheat and soy and now alfalfa potentially is going, is you don't get to control the conditions of how you grow things at all. You sign away your rights to determine how you're going to grow things. And so that's why I wonder why the big farmers actually sign up. For a moment they were saying, "Oh shit, we don't want to do that," but then they get sucked back in. And then they get more sucked into debt, and they think they're going to save money like that, and it's true.

I'm really hopeful, because of what I see here, the people still continue to struggle to try to grow food, even though it's discouraging. And I'm hopeful when I go to the farmers markets and see the thousands of people that are showing up to the farmers markets and the kids. I'm hopeful, I'm involved in the transition initiatives. I'm a trainer and I go around the country talking to people about building resilience. And I can see people are like.... It's not just that they see their personal lives as being in danger, but they see the whole planet. And more and more people who are conservatives and who are mainstream, as well as folks that have been doing this for a long time are saying, "We need to do things differently." And so in Oklahoma City; and in Houston; and in Athens, Ohio; lots of different places I've been where folks are not like the groovy San Francisco/Seattle/whatever are saying, "We know what we're doing is not going to save us or the planet, and we want to build more resilient communities." And so that's what gives me hope. And what gives me hope is to see 400-500 people show up at our dinners at CAGJ's dinners and our teach-ins. It's not just one-shot deals, and what's hopeful is to see things like Clean Greens springing up, and the tremendous response. Those are things that give me hope. And I could go and tell the things that don't, but coming out here and seeing that they're still green, this close to Seattle, gives me hope.

The Green Revolution package was built on the displacement of genetic diversity at two levels. First, mixtures and rotation of diverse crops like wheat, maize, millets, legumes, and oilseeds were replaced by large acreage monocultures of wheat and rice. Second, the introduced wheat and rice varieties came from a very narrow genetic base, compared to the high genetic variability in the populations of traditional wheat and rice plants. When these high-yield seeds replace native seed systems, species diversity and resilience are lost irreversibly. The destruction of diversity and creation of uniformity simultaneously entail ecological instability and vulnerability.

Vandana Shiva, "Globalization and The War Against Farmers and The Land", 2003

Industrial agriculture is also translating into economic warfare against the poor. Hunger has grown in the Third World in direct proportion to the spread of industrial agriculture and the globalization of trade in staple foods. This is no accident. Industrial agriculture is an efficient system for robbing farmers of wealth and pushing them into debt and dispossession. The costly seeds, chemicals, and machinery that replaced the farm's internal resources were originally supported through subsidies. Today, they are obtained by borrowing from the same agents who sell the pesticides and seeds. A new phenomenon of corporate feudalism is emerging, as global seed and agrichemical corporations combine with the local feudal power of landlords and moneylenders to trap innocent peasants into unpayable debt. More than twenty thousand Indian peasants have committed suicide since the seed and agriculture sector was opened up to global corporations. Of late, some farmers have sold their kidneys in order to clear their outstanding debts with the pawnbrokers.

Over the past few decades, costly pesticide use has increased there by 6000 percent............All manner of false claims made by the seed corporations (**Monsanto, in particular; Author's note**) to entice and entrap farmers. While the rhetoric of the "Green Revolution" and genetic engineering is the removal of hunger, the reality is that high-cost, high external input agriculture creates hunger by leaving nothing in rural households. Peasants must sell all they produce in order to pay back debts. That is why the producers of food are going hungry themselves. And 65 million tons of grain rot in storage because people have been robbed of their entitlements and purchasing power to access the food they have produced.

....

It is the trading giants like Pepsi and Cargill who have benefited from the redirection of food subsidies benefiting the poor. Pepsi Foods, a Pepsi subsidiary involved in contract farming, exported one hundred thousand tonnes of rice from India in 2002 for a profit of 12.2 million rupees while people in India faced starvation. Meanwhile Cargill exported tonnes of wheat in 2001 and planned to procure much more during the 2002 harvest. Trade liberalization is a recipe for starving the poor to feed the corporations. While the World Bank and International Monetary Fund remove subsidies from food for the poor, they encourage subsidies to grain giants like Cargill and Pepsi for exporting grain.

....

Perhaps one of the most fallacious myths propagated by Green Revolution proponents is the assertion that high-yield varieties have reduced the acreage cultivated, therefore preserving millions of acres of biodiversity. India's experience tells us that instead of more land being released for conservation, by destroying the diversity and multiple uses of land, the industrial breeding system actually increases pressure on the land: each acre of monoculture provides a single output, forcing the displaced outputs to be grown on additional acres...............The combination of industrial plant breeding and industrial animal breeding *increases the pressure on* land use by a factor of 400 percent while separately increasing output of grain and milk by only a factor of 20 percent. The extra resources used by industrial systems—either by the Green Revolution or the new biotechnologies—could have gone to feed people. Resources wasted amount to the creation of hunger. By being resource wasteful through intensive external inputs, the new biotechnologies create food insecurity and starvation.

What does all this evidence mean in terms of "feeding the world"? It becomes clear that industrial breeding has actually reduced food security by destroying small farms and the small farmers' capacity to produce diverse outputs of nutritious crops. Both from the point of view of food productivity and food entitlements, industrial agriculture is deficient as compared to diversity-based internal input systems. Protecting small farms that conserve biodiversity is thus a food security imperative.

The ***monoculture of mind*** is the disease that blocks the creation of abundance on our small farms.

Vandana Shiva, "Globalization and The War Against Farmers and The Land", 2003

24 January 2010

I'm Heather Day. I was born September 1, 1969 in Pullman, Washington, and I've lived in Seattle for ten years and a lot of my life. I was born in Pullman because my dad was a professor at the time, of sociology, at Washington State University, but we moved when I was a kid, to Bellevue. My folks chose Bellevue over Seattle because the school levy passed every year. I grew up with a single mom. My parents divorced when I was six. She was very active in the Unitarian Church. She was president of the church for a long time, and I definitely got a lot of my sort of, I don't know, ideas about community involvement, from her; a famous story is my first word was "strike!" And the reason is that my parents were carrying me on their back in a march in Pullman during the lettuce boycott, the migrant farm workers struggle. And I came home, and the whole march was over, "Strike! Strike!" And I came home and did that in my chair.

It was interesting because it was the sixties, and my dad was a professor of sociology, and there was a lot going on at that time. One of the huge influences was that our church was a sanctuary for Central American refugees, as part of the sanctuary movement. And so, I mean, I was very politicized as a kid, and was terrified when Reagan was elected, and thought there was going to be a nuclear war. I mean, I was very, like, tuned-into stuff like that, I cared about politics, cared about the Central American problems, but I really didn't know much about activism. There was a lot of activism going on around me, but at that time I just didn't know how to get plugged into that. Bellevue wasn't a hotbed of activism necessarily—at least in my world. But I went to Evergreen State College, and had a brother who went there and studied performing arts. He's sort of my closest sibling, so that had a big influence on me. And I ended up just loving it, and loving its social justice orientation. And I was able to live in France for a couple of years, which you wouldn't be able to do as a college student—most people wouldn't, anyway—and was there during the first Gulf War, and it was really interesting to see the media portrayal, just how different it was from the U.S. But really, I sort of found what I was looking for in my last year of college and didn't want to finish. But in terms of like getting the Big Picture analysis, like political economy and really studying social change movements and the history of that, that sort of like gave me the push to get involved in activism. So at the time the biggest thing going on in the world in my view was the North American Free Trade Agreement was being negotiated. And my education had just given me a frame for understanding why that was important. So I got involved in this great grass roots statewide network called

Heather Day
Director,
Community Alliance
for Global Justice

the NAFTA Justice Committee, which taught me some, like, grass roots organizing skills, and it was fun. You know, it was big issues, like lots of community education and trying to engage people in street theater. It was like statewide coalition politics that were interesting. So that kind of was my first really in-depth, sort of all-out—all my extra time was spent doing that. And that just really shaped me. In a lot of ways that's still why I'm doing what I'm doing. I'm still very much involved in activism.

That was, what, early nineties? You know, the World Bank and the National Monetary Fund, like their intervention in the global south was in its first decade, and that critique was mounting, what a failure that was. And so NAFTA was bringing it home, it was like the U.S. trying to have an influence in our region, on another scale. And I would think we didn't even understand how problematic it was at the time, and just how radical of a departure it really was from, like, traditional trade relationships.

I guess from there, another really big influence in terms of how I think about the world is I ended up getting involved in SISPIS, in the committee on solidarity with El Salvador, which is probably out of my growing up in the sanctuary movement. It spoke to me, although I didn't know a ton about Central America. SISPIS has really been a home to me ever since. I got involved in the mid-nineties, and I was a staff organizer for several years in Seattle and other places. So that was the first time I traveled to the global south, and I went to El Salvador three times, and just really learned about globalization and neo-liberalism from people, their perspective, and just saw, especially in El Salvador, that had just been crushed by civil war—I mean, like environmentally devastated and population decimated, and to see that they're still struggling on this really difficult level economically because of the continuing U.S. intervention there. But at the same time, this insanely ambitious vision and really like capable of fighting back on an amazing scale for considering what they've been through. Just incredibly inspiring. I just learned a lot about how to organize through SISPIS, because I really trained activists. So got involved in that, got my first job doing activism, which is a huge privilege and unusual, and also really hard because it was very little money, but it was worth it. And then my last year—this was in '99, and I was just moving back to Seattle, and found out about the World Trade Organization coming to Seattle. Through SISPIS, got involved in that organizing, which is what led to what we're doing today. So the Community Alliance for Global Justice, where I'm the director now, was formed by folks who were involved in the organizing in 1999 and wanted to see trade justice organizing continue in our area. It's important to acknowledge the work that a lot of people are already doing, including SISPIS and other groups—but wanted to create a membership-based, multi-issue, multi-sector group to work on trade justice issues. There's so much momentum coming out of '99, even though we're fried and exhausted and burnt out in some ways. You know, there's still like this really inspiring organizing, for example, on a neighborhood level—you know, people organized by neighborhood to mobilize for the march and for the week of action. So it was clear, there's like all these people who've been educated about globalization issues that we thought we could tap into and mobilize and continue that work.

One of the largest movements today is for food sovereignty, and that really comes out of the experience of farmers of the global south, not having any say over the direction that agriculture has gone in their countries because of intervention by the World Bank and World Trade Organization rules about agriculture that have forced small-scale farmers to convert to large-scale farming and mono-cropping and use of chemical fertilizers, and sort of the whole industrial model of agriculture, geared towards export, that has pushed millions and millions of people off their land, and made them into displaced, homeless, migrating farmers in a lot of cases. And that's just one example of how this global trade regime or whatever, globalization, has displaced people and taken democracy and the decision-making power away from people. So from a really Big Picture perspective, it's a concern with the U.S. and Europe imposing a sort of neo-colonialist or imperialist regime on the world. The people are forced to go through economic transformation that they didn't really choose, in order to meet the needs of corporations in the north, ultimately, is really what it's about. The issues are with democracy and lack of self-determination and loss of sovereignty, all of which has resulted in greater poverty and displacement of people.

One of the impacts has been that whatever stability there *could* have been has been dismantled. And I don't think it's like there was a time when agriculture was ever particularly stable or easy for people, right? Like it's always been a really difficult way to make a living, but at least some of the programs that were in place to help stabilize prices and markets have been dismantled to make it easier for corporations in the north to continue to produce below the cost of production, and then dump their goods on the south. And then, another huge casualty is the loss of soil, the loss of healthy earth to produce in. And just like through green evolution, the introduction of like chemical fertilizers and supposedly higher yielding yields and all that kind of stuff that happened in some parts of the world, and it's being pushed again in Africa right now. You know, it's depleted the soil, which is a huge.... I mean, it's possible to regain, but it's a *huge* loss for the ecosystems and just sort of general balance of things in the world. So I think that's important to understand, that like the tragedy of NAFTA is not just that a million people were displaced from their farms and can't grow all these varieties of corn that will be lost forever. People have lost their whole livelihood, their culture, their way of connecting to one another. It's really a tragedy.

The food justice movement is a wonderful place to be because people are so interested in community and like connecting and caring for one another. But it's really about like connecting to one another again, and finding community, and knowing who grows your food. I think it's a very healing movement, in a lot of ways, which is why I think it's growing.

I think where Community Alliance for Global Justice has played the strongest role is in community education and empowerment of people just to feel like they can participate in something larger. Like there's a lot of really important ways that people are learning the skills, and relearning how to grow food and understanding the importance of buying from local farmers at the farmers market. There's a lot of support and energy around that, and I think the CAGJ brings sort of a bigger perspective *why* it's important, and helps people feel empowered to participate in the political process, to talk about the U.S. role in—like the government's role in making decisions about our food system. So we're helping people find their voice in our democratic system locally, but also recognizing that the U.S. plays a huge role in undermining the ability of small farmers to survive all around the world, and that we can do something about that too, by fighting for a better farm bill, or fighting against the so-called trade agreements. So really trying to find a way for people to participate in organizing locally. So mostly what we're doing now is bringing people out to the farms and actually doing monthly visits to different food and farm sites where people can get to know—like you were talking about, get to know their local farmer and actually see what people are trying to accomplish—fishermen, and all different players in our food economy. Kind of build a sense of community through that. And another thing we're bringing to the local food movement is just the real focus on social justice in the food system. We just published "Our Food, Our Right: Recipes for Food Justice." I should have brought you a copy! I'll send you one. It's a guide to food justice, so just helping people understand all the different ways of understanding what food justice means.

Most importantly it's about self-determination. It's about having a say in the decisions that affect you in the food system. So from a local level it's about ensuring that people who want to farm have access to farmland, and dealing with all the layers of obstacles that there are to that. The fact that, you know, people really want locally grown food, but there's a huge waiting list of people who don't have access to land. So that's one of the issues. One of the main things that we're focused on, or interested in working on, is access and ensuring that everyone has access to locally grown healthy food, and it's affordable, and geographically accessible, that there aren't food deserts in our communities where people don't have access to any food.

I think CAGJ today, up to this point, has been involved in community education about that, but I think some of the most successful programs are the farm-to-school programs. And I've heard there's a new farm-to-hospital campaign. So trying to help create those networks where farmers can provide their food to kids and to some of the people who need it most. And beyond that, I think there's a need to work on a huge structural level. Like the farm bill has the potential. It'll take us a long time, I think, to wrest the farm bill away from corporate control. But we're starting now to work on the farm bill, and the next one is in three years, and CAGJ is starting to talk about it and trying to network and find, really wanting to build a movement nationally. It's happening, and it's really exciting. It's the first time ever that people besides farmers have seen the farm bill as impacting them.

We also focus on the role of immigrants in the food economy, so just trying to foreground and understand the role of immigrants, and educate about that: educate ourselves and others, including farm workers. They're sort of the backbone of our economy but are invisible to many people. So we've done a lot of research in trying to understand where we can plug in and support those, organizing around food rights issues. Yeah, and supporting small farmers is another part of food justice, and the idea of food sovereignty, which comes out of the global south and out of Via Compasina, which is an international network of millions of small farms. It's inspiring to us. That's where, like, one focus on the role of women in the food economy—something that they really are highlighting for our work internationally and locally. I think that's something we want to start focusing on more. But also the whole idea of democratizing the food system, kind of at the root of food justice.

I think another exciting development that I think is another way that we've been trying to plug into finding the places where we can make changes: the food policy councils, and we've been participating somewhat in the Acting Food Policy Council, which is kind of a Puget Sound level council that hasn't quite been established. And then now there's a new bill for our Washington Food Policy Council. So I think we have to look at all those levels as spaces where, like, regional and statewide and national, like we have to have strategies at all those levels. There certainly are strategies in place, and I think the issue around access to land is one of the main issues people are concerned with. There's grant funding for addressing the issue of food deserts, and just complete lack of access to any fresh produce in some neighborhoods. I've been trying to increase access through supporting produce being introduced into corner stores, like neighborhood corner stores. I know that's one project that will be a focus. I mean, the food policy councils, they're really just beginning. Like we participated in a national conference of food policy councils and learned that there's a hundred of them or more in the country now, and they're just sort of this thing that is really new, and still pretty unstable, and there's not a lot of funding. It's sort of hard to see how to sustain them right now, but there's clearly like this real driving need to have food policy that's integrated on all these different levels. So it just seems like a space that has a ton of potential, and that's worth supporting and raising people's awareness about the importance of it. Like we have to get funding for them and support them in the legislature and not just, like, approval, but actually funding for them.

We're a space for people to get the information and tools they need to be active and involved in these issues, both locally and thinking about it on a global scale. So we're not a social service organization like a lot of groups are that are directly involved in food procurement. For example, like we're here to get people involved and feel like they can participate on all these different levels. So we're still looking for the best opportunities for change, so trying to figure that out. A lot of what we do is thinking about internationally, the impact of our choices here. Like the Gates Foundation is based in Seattle and is a transnational corporation that's based in Seattle, and they're having a huge impact on agriculture in Africa. It's not just something that's over there. It affects us in King County.

That's why I'm going to Kenya, to meet with small farmers there, and to understand the struggles they're facing. They're violently against Monsanto, and we're violently against Monsanto. They're not just violently against Monsanto, but they're violently against the Gates Foundation facilitating corporations like Monsanto developing their agricultural system in Africa. We have to get involved, we have to do something about that. So that's another thing that the Community Alliance for Global Justice is doing, is trying to understand how we can support sustainable agriculture around the world, both by countering the Gates Foundation and by countering just U.S. policy in general, through the farm belt, through the trade agreements, etc.

I think the food justice movement is just beginning and is really exciting. I mean I think it's really providing people with hope, and like a sense that we *can* make a difference. I think for a long time people have been aware and trying to find ways to make a difference, or like supporting fair trade has been something that we can do to try to provide sustainable livelihoods for farmers who grow our coffee and our necessities like chocolate around the world, right? For people who have been struggling against trade agreements and trying to have an impact on globalization, the food justice movement is a positive alternative. People are seeing that they can make a difference in their everyday lives, and it's really powerful. Our organization's really grown. So it's clear to us that it's just really compelling and important work. I have a lot of hope for what we can accomplish. I think we're changing the terms of the debate pretty rapidly, we could see it happening. But, you know, we're up against the most powerful corporations in the world. Ultimately that's what we're dealing with here, so that's hard. Hard to see how we can break their power. But it's possible. Like when the World Trade Organization came to town, and those protests were so successful because everybody had something to protest against. I mean, it has an impact on all aspects of our lives. And it's the same thing with corporate power. Everyone can mobilize against corporate power all over the world—except for the very rich, who are benefiting.

It's funny, I sort of have my doom days. I think there's a pocket of hopeful people that don't understand reality or something. I don't know, I think it's hard to feel hopeful in the U.S., particularly. I've been privileged enough to travel, especially in Latin America, where social movements are incredibly powerful, and they've been able to elect the first indigenous leader of Bolivia, for example. We really feel their sense of momentum, and I just try to stay connected to that larger sense, and just remember that the U.S. is a particular beast where it's really hard to feel like you're part of something, that we'll actually change things. But I don't know. I think of, like, people in El Salvador who continue to have hope even though they've been through unimaginable misery, and they still are organizing and being strategic and having hope. You know, if we don't have hope, then what's the point? There's no point in doing this work, if you don't have hope that you actually can change anything. It's funny, though, as you get older, too, I'm feeling my age. Being forty, I don't know, I can just relate to people being like, "Well, it'll be up to the younger people." But even the election of Obama, I mean of course it hasn't been the sea change that anybody hoped for, and I certainly didn't think that it was going to transform the U.S. by any means, but you know, it was just proof that people are hungry, hungry, hungry for change. And the right thing can mobilize people.

"The yield of the soil depends less on its richness than on the degree of freedom enjoyed by those who till it."
Montesquieu

A farm is true to its essential nature, in the best sense of the word, if it is conceived as a kind of individual entity in itself—a self contained individuality. Whatever you need for agricultural production, you should try to possess it within the farm itself (including in the "farm", needless to say, the due amount of cattle). Properly speaking, any manures or the like which you bring into the farm from outside should be regarded rather as a remedy for a sick farm. That is the ideal. A thoroughly healthy farm should be able to produce within itself all that it needs.

You will recognize the justice of this statement if you consider the Earth on the one hand, from which our farm springs forth, and on the other hand, that which works down into our Earth from the Universe beyond. Nowadays, people are wont to speak very abstractly of the influences which work on to the Earth from the surrounding Universe. They are aware, no doubt, that the Sun's light and warmth, and all the meteorological processes connected with it, are in a way related to the form and development of the vegetation that covers the soil. But present-day ideas can give no real information as to the exact relationships, because they do not penetrate to the realities involved. Let us today choose this one: let us consider, to begin with, the soil of the Earth which is the foundation of all agriculture.

The surface of the Earth is generally regarded as mere mineral matter—including some organic elements, at most, inasmuch as there is formation of humus, or manure is added. In reality, however, the earthly soil *as such* not only contains a certain *life*—a vegetative nature of its own—but an effective *astral principle* as well; a fact which is not only not taken into account today but is not even admitted nowadays......Here we are coming to a realm of knowledge, immensely significant for practical life, which is not even thought of in our time.

Rudolf Steiner, "Agriculture Course—the Birth of the Biodynamic Method", Lecture Two, 1924

Author's note: Rooted in Homeopathy, Biodynamics, as part of Rudolf Steiner's (1861-1925) philosophy, "Anthroposophia", is historically part of a wider philosophical, spiritual and religious reaction to the social degradation of industrialization and the absolute devastation Europe suffered during WWI. With Steiner, the sickness he and others perceived in society was evident in industrialized agriculture which negated folklore, astrology and necromancy as critical aspects of more traditional medical practice (the use of herbs and alchemic formulations) and agricultural practice guided by the stars and phases of the moon. Steiner's ideas enjoyed renewed support via the "Whole Earth" movement in the 1960s and 70s and his influence remains strong amid the current agrarian resurgence. Several farms built upon Steiner's "Biodynamic" principles operate in Washington State and offer training programs in his methods.

18 December 2009

I'm Barry Lia, born March 31, 1953, Oceanside, California, Camp Pendleton Naval Base. My family spent two years in Alaska when I was about one and a half to three and a half. Moved down to California. We had two record snows, though my dad was from Minnesota, where his little tiny hometown is my vicarious hometown and heritage. It's one of those "Lake Wobegone" places. But he hit two record snows in Alaska and decided California was the place to be. So we moved eventually to Sacramento. I grew up, elementary school and high school in Sacramento. About every summer we would travel to Colorado where my grandfather and grandmother lived, and ride horses. My grandfather had a livery stable, and we'd ride out. It was on the edge of town, we could ride out the country roads, or sneak over to the fairgrounds and ride around the track, and had all kinds of fun.

Barry Lia, Ph.D.
Sustainable Farming Advocacy

One year I remember Grandpa and my uncle raised some cattle, we did some branding, shot at gophers, did those sorts of things. If we didn't go to Colorado, we'd go all the way back to Minnesota to the hometown. And my dad's cousin was still farming before he retired. He's passed on now. That was really a deep experience. One summer coming back, I insisted on planting corn in a little patch by the fireplace around our suburban home in South Sacramento. It was pretty much a suburban life otherwise.

Then I went to UC-Davis for college. That's the agriculture college, the old farm school, for the UC-California system, though I didn't study agriculture. I was just studying general biology, and very attuned to ecological relationships and such. Studied a lot of marine biology. And then around about....that was 1974, I think it was, a couple fellows came—young folks, students—from UC-Santa Cruz, who had been working there at the garden that was established by Alan Chadwick. And this was a biodynamic garden that he was setting up. And he set this up on the worst soil he could find on the Santa Cruz Campus, to prove that the techniques were effective. So he had quite a cadre of students and enthusiasts, who followed, and they came to speak at Davis, at the Ag school, and they were talking about sustainable agriculture. When I heard them—I've still got the notes—I didn't write down who they were, but they made a big impression. And what they said about this biodynamic agriculture really struck me as the way to go: the ecological approach it took, and what not. So I carried that interest for many years, digging up holes in the lawn where I was renting here, or renting there, in student days. And then graduate school, even, I was doing the same thing.

I had approached both a soil scientist and a brain scientist when I decided it was time I was going to go on to graduate school. And I had been doing work in laboratories, cutting tissue and staining tissue, so the brain scientist thought I was worth something, and the soil scientist didn't have much interest in me, so I got a call from the brain scientist. I ended up in neurobiology. But all this time I was still gardening, and even in my student rentals, digging up spaces to grow things, and continued studying and reading about this biodynamic work, taking workshops and whatnot through the years.

Then I married my wife, Janet. We met at a lutefisk dinner—I'm of Norwegian background—and she was teaching Norwegian at this Sons of Norway lodge. I'd gone with my mother and a friend of hers to this lutefisk dinner—rare opportunity to get a chance to eat it. So there she was. Janet stood up to announce the classes she was teaching in Norwegian. She had her hair in braids, and she had on one of those folk costumes, you know, Norwegian folk costume, and it accentuated her features. So anyway, I asked her about classes afterwards. I thought I would start taking classes to learn to speak better than I had learned through my family, which had pretty much only passed down the cuss words. So we got talking, and I said, "Well, how'd you learn Norwegian?" She said, "Well, I was on a farm in Norway." I said, "Oh! What were you doing there?" She said, "I was an apprentice." "What kind of farm?" I said. And she said, "Oh, an organic farm." And I said, "Oh, what kind?" "Oh you wouldn't know," she said. So I pressed her further, and she said, "Biodynamic farm." And I said, "Oh yeah, like going over to Rudolf Steiner College here," which was in Fair Oaks nearby. "Yeah, yeah!" So then we got to know each other, and eventually we were married, in large part because of that interest in this biodynamic agriculture.

So I went on, grad school, post doc work, came up here to do post-doctoral work at University of Washington. We would give occasional introductory workshops in biodynamics. People who heard about us then might be in King County Extension, or at the Waldorf School, or various places. And at our home, of course, we gardened. It's grown into a little urban homestead now, with a few hens and I think this year the front lawn is going to disappear—either some sort of grain for chickens, or wheat, we're not sure. My daughters think these Nigerian goats are really cute, and we may finally get some goats around the house. But for that, we'll have to team up with neighbors to do the extra milking chores. So that hasn't happened yet.

So we've developed quite a little urban homestead, like many people are doing, and it must have been about six years ago, in 2003, through a friend of mine who's a researcher out at WSU in Pullman, who did research on biodynamic compost, and the effect of the biodynamic preparations *in* the compost, I got to meet a fellow up on Lopez Island, at S&S Homestead Farm; S&S stands for Henning Schemsdorf and Elizabeth Simpson, his wife. They had been up there for years.

He was a professor at the University of Washington, in Scandinavian folklore, speaks Norwegian. That's one plus. But he had, every summer, raised all the food he could, up in an orchard/garden on the island on a property, expanded that property over the years. In 1994, I think it was, he retired up there to farm full time. So I met him then about that time, 2003. In 2004 he organized a workshop, which we have then subsequently handled these workshops annually since then.

There was a fellow that I had known of up there, who unfortunately passed away shortly after the workshop. He had a brain tumor. It was incredible; I was looking forward to meeting him again. He had been down in the Seattle area. And so we had some mutual acquaintances, and this acquaintance that we knew had been coming to Henning to gather the intestines from slaughtered cows, and the big membrane that covers the rumen of the cow. Those are used in making the biodynamic preparations. And he had been coming for a couple of years to Henning during slaughter time, and finally Henning asked him, "What do you get these for? Why do you want these parts? You usually don't make sausage with cow intestines." So then this fellow says to Henning, "Well, they're for the biodynamic preparations. Don't you make them?" And Henning said, "What?!" And he said, "Well, Henning, you *must* make them. You're the only biodynamic farmer on the island I know." And what he meant was, that Henning had a farm that was by and large self-sufficient. His inputs were raised *on* the farm, and he capitalized his own farm, as we like to say—self-capitalizing. So the livestock were fed on grass, and grain was raised on the farm, what little grain they got went to the chickens and the pigs. And things were proportioned to be self-sufficient: don't raise more cattle than the grass and the land can handle. Those are fundamental aspects of biodynamic agriculture. The first principle might be what's called the farm individuality, or sometimes farm organism. So that that farm has its own character, its own self-reliance, animals are apportioned to the fodder; the manure is apportioned to the other crops, while other crops are apportioned to the manure and the fertility that can be raised through the compost. That's a fundamental practice of a biodynamic farm.

So essentially Henning had all of this going, all of the aspects of biodynamics, out of his cultural tradition from Germany. He had come over when he was seventeen years old, after living through the bombing of Dresden and such. So he was a very self-reliant man in the first place, but carried from his farming heritage what he felt should be done. What inspired him was coming here at the age of seventeen, given a job by a German-American who offered him entry to the country, a job working in a meat-packing house. And that experience convinced him that he would never be part of that... he had to raise his own food, best he could. So that's why he went out and bought land, and that was his life path.

So now we've come up in my life to 2003 or so, and meeting Henning and Elizabeth, and traveling up there to plan workshops and to work on the farm, once or twice a month—at least twice a month, on average, over the years—so quite a serious commitment. Both of us helping him to learn this biodynamic agriculture, and to learn from him, his handling of livestock and handling the farm organism. So over the years we've built up this teaching and workshops and they're building on each other. We always include artistic activities, and the notion that farmers need to be perceptive, and there's no better way to develop that than through artistic activities.

Over the years, my wife Janet's interest has moved from farming, which she trained in, in Sweden and Norway, to artistic work, visual arts, which she trained in when she came back to the States. So we recruit *her* to lead courses in artwork, artistic activities, during these workshops, which incorporate the themes that *she* understands from biodynamics into the activities that we do in the workshop.

Last year, 2008, we were awarded a small grant from the Bio-Ag program. That's WSU's program, biologically intensive and organic agriculture in their CSANR, the Center for Sustaining Agricultural and Natural Resources. So the Bio-Ag grant funded students who attended our course here at Roger Thorson's Carnation Tree Farm, in the loft there, and we had our main lecture courses there plus some afternoon activities we did at Jubilee Farm in the middle of winter. At that course for the last meeting, we all carpooled up to Lopez Island and gathered at the farm there, so that they could see that farm and have that experience.

We're hoping this winter to give similar courses in Pierce County, San Juan County and maybe give some workshops down toward the Vancouver area, maybe even an introductory workshop out in Spokane—all in the works.

Meanwhile, I think it was 1999, the year of the WTO in Seattle, I spent time in my own training development with a group called The Wannabe Farmers. They were based in Seattle, and they were leasing a small plot of land out at Jubilee Farm—Erick and Wendy Haakensen's place. And just working with shovels, by hand, that scale yet—gardening scale, you might say. The idea was to raise crops and bring them to the farmers market and get the experience of selling at a farmers market, and practicing and learning and working their way toward being farmers. The success of the group was its failure, because several of the key people ended up going off to farm on their own, and the group sort of dissolved and disbanded that year. But I had great experience then, hauling about 300 pounds of Walla Walla onions in my little Chevy Nova, out to one of the farmers markets in West Seattle.

But I got to know Erick from that experience—met him anyway. That year he had a couple other people—Kelly and Carrie—who were running the CSA. I remember I got in as an NGO delegate at the WTO for the Western Sustainable Agricultural Working Group. And the first day, the demonstrators locked arms blocking the door and I couldn't get in. I was in my suit and tie, expecting to try change from the inside at this conference, and couldn't get in, so I wandered a little bit through the streets, and there's Carrie and Kelly carrying a big banner, "Farmers Unite!" or some sort of thing, you know. So I joined them. There I'm in my coat and tie, and I'm marchin' with them as well. I've never seen a picture of that, but I hope somewhere in the archives of the Battle of Seattle, that's one of the pictures. Ironic.

So then it must have been, I don't know, two or three years ago, Erick had gone to ACRES conferences back in the Midwest, from ACRES USA, and heard about biodynamic farming, got all excited, and began working his way towards it himself. And so I found out about that, I forget exactly how we got together, and I started sort of alternating between Lopez Island and working out at Jubilee. I have Fridays off in my work schedule, and so Fridays are kind of my farm days, and I spend them either up there or down here. So then I've been helping Erick as well, making preparations, the biodynamic preparations, and applying them, and doing this and that sort of work on Jubilee as well as Lopez Island. I guess that kind of brings us up to the present on what I've been doing.

The biodynamic movement started in 1924 in late June, as a course, eight lectures, given by Rudolf Steiner to farmers in Europe. It was held on what would be a fairly large sugar beet estate, raising sugar beets for commercial production—not a small little homestead. Then those lectures were the foundation for an experimental circle of people, of farmers and some researchers. That included Dr. Aaron Freid Pfifer, who came to the States and visited in the thirties, and returned to stay permanently in about 1940. His was more of a research background, scientific background. He went on to develop microbial compost starters for municipal composting programs in the fifties in Oakland and other cities. We keep learning and starting the same solutions again and again through the years. But that experimental circle went on about into the sixties, and it was held pretty tight and close. You sort of had to be in the circle to get the mimeographed sheets that were the agriculture course. So it wasn't published really publicly. But then in the sixties it was. It's been now widely available, freely available. There are folks back in Virginia who sell the biodynamic preparations, they make them in large quantities, and they're available for anyone across the States. There are other sources in European countries. And there is a biodynamic association in the States, just now trying to build itself up and become more influential. The first principle of Biodynamics, I think I've already said then, would be the farm individuality.

The next idea would be a phrase that Steiner used: substances carry forces. Forces is a difficult word for me in that regard, because we think of physics. I'd like to say relationships or powers or find some other way to phrase it. It's a view that is definitely non-materialistic, non-mechanistic. Steiner's anthroposophy in many ways is an answer to the materialistic view of the world, which tends to lead us to nihilism and a loss of moral relations to the world—not in a sentimental way, or in a church/religion way—but more of relations where you feel a deep connection to your being in the world, and your interdependence with the world—that your food isn't just something that comes in a bag and you pay for, and that's the only relation, as deep as it goes. So in the Ag course, if you ever read it, when he speaks of carbon or nitrogen or oxygen, it's not chemistry. He speaks of the relations they carry, or the powers that they represent: oxygen carrying life. It's what energizes us, carries the hydrogen that goes into the carbohydrates that we get our calories from. When he speaks of carbon, he speaks of it as carrying form, as a form-carrier, because it is largely those carbon chains that make up the structures of us; nitrogen giving sensitivity. That's what gives us the proteins and the ability to mobile and sensitive and such. So that would be then the farm individuality, substances carry forces or relationships, and then probably the third thing that stands unique would be the biodynamic preparations.

So I'm a fully-trained scientist, published scientific papers, I even have a paper in "*Science*" magazine. I continually read the scientific literature on soil biology, plant morphology, various things. And there's an expression that I found in a book by David Korton, the book called "*When Corporations Ruled the World*". In the first edition of that book, in the epilog, he has a phrase that puts it very well: that this scientific materialism is an "exceptionally partial view of reality." So I'm getting to my point about the biodynamic preparations, and the word I like is lore, L-O-R-E. We work with a lore, given to us largely by Steiner. And these preparations, you take, for example, chamomile blossoms, dry them. You gather the cow intestine, and you stuff the blossoms, moistened, into this intestine like a sausage. You bury it in the ground over the winter, and it goes through a fermentation process, a transformation. You take it out in the spring, and that substance that you have looks kind of dark and humus-y. That is one of the compost preparations. That material goes into the compost. Now we speak of it not just as having chemical analysis and what it is, but we use that preparation and speak of it as "harmonizing" the compost, along with the several other herbs that are similarly fermented or transformed. And so that harmonizes the compost. It helps to regulate the compost, so that the nitrogen is preserved in the decomposition and the building up of the compost material, building up of the humus. And there's less gassing-off, so there's other health-giving properties that go on.

Now this may be working through different microbes, growth factors they release, there's so many things, possible explanations, scientifically, for what might go into it. Lyn Carpenter Boggs, my friend out at WSU, did her dissertation on the effects of the compost preparations on compost. And so she did several replications, but took dairy manure from the WSU dairy farm, mixed it well, made two identical piles, poked holes in both of them, put preparations into the holes of *one* pile, not the other, for comparison, and then studied various things, enzyme activity, temperature, this and that—and found significant differences in the biodynamic compost pile. Now, that then was put out on soil, and within one year only of application, there weren't any measures that she could show were different from the other soil that had received the other compost pile. But that might be expected. You're only making so many measures, and we don't know that they're the *right* measures and such. But when people study these farms over time, they find that these preparations work in the soil. There's generally more earthworms, there's better tilth in the soil, and these sort of qualitative differences, though the nitrogen levels and such, as you measure, might be the same as any other field. But the quality of the produce, we feel, is higher. And I'll describe an experiment that was done up at Lopez Island in a moment.

But the notion then of this lore—there's a knowledge or a wisdom or a lore that's used in Biodynamics that may not have scientific backing or understanding. But it works. And that's what we go by. And even in science, I think, too, we do science to learn and to certify what works, to have certainty.

Now, in biodynamic work, based on this lore, many, many of us feel we get an experience of certainty about it, and the benefits it has. It's not far from traditional farming, basically like was done in Europe: crop rotation, all the basics you can find in, say, the biodynamic farming practices textbook. There's a book from Europe, Soufer and Westinghausen, that's like a college textbook on agronomy and animal husbandry the biodynamic way. And it's largely, like in traditional farming, plus the addition of these preparations, this lore, and this different world view on how you're working with nature on an ecological basis rather than a material basis where you would be computing NPK and such and such. So we rely a lot—maybe the fourth principle would be relying on biology. It is **bio**dynamics. So more and more when I look through the literature on the relations of root exlodates from a plant out into the soil to feed and culture and cultivate the microbes that live around the roots, attract them, enhance them, and *their* services back to the root, or their services releasing phosphorus from the parent material of the soil, or.... There's just a complex web. I mean, we speak now of the soil food web, but it's just so amazingly complex, and more and more is being discovered, so that in a way you start to say to yourself that relying on that lore may be a little bit safer and a little bit more secure than sort of a hit and miss, only going by scientific findings in books. So that might be the fourth attitude in this anti-materialistic view, relying on this lore, that relies largely on the biology that's there. And we can really appreciate that. The more you study the biology, the natural history of soil and plants and animals, the more you can see it as the way to go.

So for example, when Henning and I took a master goat class, offered by the WSU Extension together, we had hoped to get the natural history of the goat—you know, its evolution and how it lives in the wild, and how we domesticated it and such. But what you get is largely feeding, according to sort of chemical nutrition, and diseases. You hear very little about the natural history of the goat itself. So we'd lean more toward the natural history than toward the other aspects.

Context is a very big word in what we call Goethian science; Johann Wolfgang von Goethe, known for "Faust". He was a wonderful naturalist, *wonderful* naturalist, absolutely. And his way of science was different—it was a more synthetic and holistic approach, trusting human perception, to be able to be trained to perceive nature in a deeper way. So Steiner himself began his career as a scholar editing Goethe's scientific writings. It was very influential on him, so that his thinking carried on this holistic approach, and encouraged him to sort of apply the same approach to what you might call the spiritual or psychological or 'soul life' of man as well. Craig Holdridge in the Nature Institute is largely exploring this Goethian science and writing in that frame of thought, critiquing genetics, critiquing various aspects, evolution and such, trying to develop a language that would be precise about relationships—rather than substance.

When I spoke at the biodynamic field day at Jubilee Farm, I put up a little chart, and I had sort of the evolution of human consciousness from sort of hunter-gatherer age, through agricultural cultivation, to sort of markets and crafts and guilds, and on into the industrial age. And in the industrial age we had sort of focused purely on substance and had lost sort of relation that earlier people had lived in, relation to nature. Now we're trying to find a lore that brings us closer to that relation again through biodynamics. We're doing this now intentionally and consciously, whereas before we were forced from necessity to be in relation with nature. We have to find it now, we have to deliberately make it and work with it. So context is a big part of that. And certainty, of course that's the big drive for science. So people are constantly asking what scientific validation do you have of biodynamics.

I'll just describe an experiment that was done the last few years up at S&S Homestead Farm. Henning's soils up on the island are former forest soils. They've been grass pasture for a number of years since settlers came. But they tend to be more acidic. So he had a pH of about 6 on his pasture. And of course you can apply lime, that'll bring your pH up. And when you bring the pH up, 6.4-6.6 or so, you'll start to get greater nutrient availability and improve the quality of the pasture. So he got to wondering if these biodynamic field sprays might improve the situation on their own. So Henning and Lyn Carpenter Boggs and Jennifer Reeve, a researcher who's now at University of Utah, designed an experiment where they had random block design out in the pasture, strips about twenty feet wide, twelve of them or so, into different treatments: a control treatment where nothing was done, a lime treatment where it was treated with the amount of lime that agricultural extension agents would recommend to bring up the pH, and then other strips that were treated with Aaron Freid Pfifer's formulation of a biodynamic field spray that includes the preparations and other agents. So this was done over a two-year period, and the soil was analyzed, and the forage that grew from the soil. The control strip stayed at pH 6, where it was before. The lime strip, like it should, came up to pH 6.4, or .6 even, 6.6, I'm sorry. The biodynamic strip, given just the biodynamic field spray, changed. Its pH changed to 6.4, almost as much as the lime. And that's done just by the biology.

Lyn repeated a phrase she had given me earlier, "everything is everywhere". All the microbes are out there—the environment selects. So what conditions, what context those organisms are in determines what will happen. Just like a cheese, if you get the right temperature and the right amount of salt you get one cheese. A little warmer and a different amount of salt, you get a different cheese. So out in this field they've done something like making cheese. We've stirred the soil life in that strip that it has harmonized itself, brought its pH up, and actually the forage taken from that strip had more crude protein, better quality, than either of the other two strips, even though the pH wasn't as high as in the lime conditioned. But 6.4 is enough to make nutrients available, as conventionally understood. I like to think that it's not only making those nutrients available pH-wise but it's this biological activity that goes on helps to release phosphorus, which is really the main limiting mineral, from the soil, make it available. That's kind of shown in other studies as well. So there's a validation. Really, can't argue, it's got scientific certainty, it's laid out with random block design, the lime hasn't gone over into the control strip. I mean, there's one control strip that's covered with lime on both sides. It's not just leaching across or doing anything that way. So it's a pretty strong argument, besides other studies. The research that's been done tends to be not published in peer-reviewed journals, and that discounts it.

The resistance from the scientific community comes because biodynamics has this anthroposophical background—Steiner's intention was to bring the spirit in man to the spirit in nature, and the world. So speaking of that way, for a scientist, is generally just not done. I mean, I'm an oddball myself then. I feel comfortable with my feet on both sides of the fence, the fence isn't too high.

Wolf Storl wrote a wonderful introduction to biodynamics called "*Culture and Horticulture*". He goes through some of the evolution of consciousness and history of agriculture. He describes how he was rather skeptical when he first came, as an anthropologist, to study a village taking care of handicapped people in Switzerland. They were farming biodynamically, and he was really curious. If there was an aphid infestation on some crop, he'd ask the farmer, "What are you going to do? How are you going to handle this? Shall I go get the spray?" You know, the pesticide. And the farmer said, "No, no, no." The farmer's looking—and I forget the exact story—but he's looking up at the gutters surrounding this plot, this garden area. He was looking for the context for the conditions that were leading to this infestation, to handle those. Or how could he strengthen the plants? What had he done cultivation-wise? Looking at all the relations, rather than, "Let's get a substance we can pour on it and hammer these guys."

At the field day, there was a fellow here from Zambia. He was on a fellowship, and returned shortly after he'd been here for four months. He came up to me afterwards and said, "I've been here for four months, and I finally found what I came for." I think in the feeling that, yes, biodynamics would save the soils, this would restore or rebuild or enhance the soils.... Like many ecological, organic systems or ways of thinking, soil is key, the humus is the human. I mentioned Chadwick. He took the worst patch of soil on a hillside he could at Santa Cruz to demonstrate the power of this way of working to amend the soil and bring it back to life.

Our house, when we first moved in, in 1991, the people before us were weed 'n' feeders, and there was what used to be a flower bed had not a weed in it. And we filled in what was kind of a swimming pool in the back yard, since we had very young children and the walls of it were cracking, and it wasn't going to be a pool. We had it filled in with Cedar Grove topsoil and compost, figuring that was the best we could do locally. And it's been now eighteen years, and it was very sandy topsoil I'll have to say. But it's only now that earthworms are really coming into that soil, after all these years of our biodynamic treatment even. I mean, it's been productive, we've grown crops—that's not the point. But this kind of life that can come to it does take time. And the question will be, "How much time to we have?" The question will be, "Will we do the labor?" Because it's not something *to* be mechanized. So the farm isn't viewed as a production machine. It isn't viewed as something we put in on this end, and we take something out on that end. So on any farm there's a process of composting and fertility management that's quite labor intensive. So we're gonna need a lot of farmers in the future, if we must go this way. And many signs say we're going to, as oil peaks, that this is the way we'll be going. So I have faith that it *is* the only way that we'll really restore and retain soil. The industrial practices just don't promise that, and have not shown that they can do that.

I think it was Marcy Stillman, on KUOW Radio, misspoke one day. I think they were talking about the green revolution in Africa, the Gates Foundation and Rockefeller Foundation, Ford Foundation, whoever they are, funded a program. And she misspoke and said "green revelation", instead of "revolution." But I think that's what we need, we need a green revelation—a revelation about the soil, it's the soil life, how to feed that soil life, how to put it to work. It is a living thing that requires tending. It *can* be mechanized to a degree. In Australia they spray the biodynamic field sprays out of helicopters and airplane, you know, because there are broad stretches of rangeland there. But there are numbers of stories where people have restored land, and I think this is a proven way to do it. I like to call it the proven biotechnology, true biotechnology.

I was just thinking, today, as I was looking at *Mother Jones* magazine. It had a column on the right-hand side of one page about what the $14 trillion of the bailout for the banks could do. Sometimes you're faced with these things that just like, "Oh my goodness!" I guess what that represents to me, like another film I just saw, "Why We Fight", on Eisenhower warning us of the industrial-military complex—and you might add agro in there too. So how do we change, or how do we grow out of this. I put most of my faith in local action. I think that the only way to fix the economy is to do without it, and to begin to make our own local economies, our own self-reliance, in a way extending this notion of a farm individuality to a community individuality that's self-reliant, self-sufficient. And there's lots of literature on this now, and it's a movement that's growing stronger and stronger. And I think that, I *hope* that the biodynamic movement can serve and help foster that development. A lot more people are recognizing that you *have to* pay more and buy less, and foster this kind of resurgence that's happening from grass roots.

I love that word, *terroir*, that we start to see our food as having *terroir*. Now, I think we can have that sense, not just in a snob sense. I mean, we're not all Robert Parkers, and fine nose and what not. But for me, it's also just having food that *does* taste like it's from somewhere. You know, one thing that struck me.... Well, a *big* thing that strikes me up at S&S Homestead, there I'm more like family, and I can sit down at the meals. And when you have fresh raw milk, where you can smell the animal, that to me is really important. When you swallow that milk—I was pointing this out to some students that were visiting afterwards—afterwards you can smell kind of in the back of your throat. You can start to pay attention, you can start to appreciate that there's something finer there. The meat that we get from up there is the only beef I eat. I'm fanatically scared of mad cow disease, I suppose more than is necessary. And again, you can smell the animal, even, after you've cooked it. So to have that sense of *terroir*, that's not a snobby sense, but a sense of connection, a sense of reality, that's so valuable.

Erick and Wendy and I were speaking to a group of people—you know, we were talking about biodynamics—she said kind of accidentally, "I wouldn't trade this for anything." Maybe talking about the hardships or this or that. "I wouldn't trade it for anything." And it struck me—as nonfarmer yet—we've all traded it for something else. Here is primary reality and primary life, primary production, the basis of the economy, and we've lost the connection to the humus. We've lost our humor and gotten all serious about these other activities and games. It's just out of perspective, when you have $14 trillion and defense account and everything else that goes on. That again, it's being aware, not just of tasting things that have *terroir*, that have reality in local, but also in our economy, to remember what we've traded for in our activities, for our food, and that there is a relation there.

About the same time I met Henning, I was studying with an economics group, I ran across this idea--the notion, ekonomia. And this is something I brought up in the farm field day as well—ekonomia and prematistika. I think I pronounced them *fairly* well. They're terms from Aristotle. And the first one, ekonomia, *ekos*, is the household or the homestead, the holding. Ekonomia was the natural exchange among farmers in Greece at the egalitarian time of Greece, when everybody had about the same holding, the citizens, the *daimos*. Everyone had about equal power, representation, you went to the town courtyard and held up your hand to vote, you know. That was a certain period in Greece when the aristocracies had collapsed, and things were pretty egalitarian. That was true democracy. Then that situation of natural exchange among people changed as powers grew in Athens or in different places, and trade became a big thing—trade among nations and here and there—and people then could, as Aristotle put it, "buy coin". Chrematistica, *chrema* means "coin", so it was this financial system that built up, and along with it came these power relations that destroyed democracy in Athens and in Greece, ultimately, and it's what we're seeing today. We see these banks running chrematistic bubbles, and there's no natural relations among them. For Aristotle, ekonomia or natural relations of exchange—could be money, you could use coin, but it had a natural relationship. Chrematistica is *unnatural* relations. To Aristotle, it was like incest, breeding these coins on coins.

So that might be another, I think, aspect of biodynamics, this ekonomik aspect, and a social aspect. The farm that raised sugar from the sugar beets where the course was held, raised that sugar for industries that were trying to set up a different kind of economic relationship that was sometimes called associative economy, where all the stakeholders, consumers and producers, get together to determine what should be produced and how we will pay for it and honor it. That requires a different kind of working. We're not there. But that picture of local economy, which is getting stronger and stronger, that stands behind biodynamic work as well. In fact, the first food certification label was, I believe, back in the 1920s, started by the biodynamic farmers, the Demeter Certification. And I know for sure that the first two CSAs in this country were biodynamic and brought biodynamic folks on their impulse. So we've had quite an influence, though hardly anybody knows about us. That CSA has become more of a subscription farming model, where you subscribe for the year. Originally it was where they, in an associative economic relationship that customers—not consumers—the *customers*, the people, got together and bought land, held the land together, managed it together with the farmer, directing the farmer, and under the farmer's guidance, to raise and produce the crops that they shared among themselves. So that's the kind of ekonomik relation that biodynamics would hope to move to.

In 1986, in western Massachusetts, Robyn Van En founded the first community supported agriculture (CSA) project in the United States at her Indian Line Farm. In a CSA, consumers guarantee the yearly production costs of the farmer through a shareholder fee. Working in collaboration with shareholders, the farmer determines an annual operating budget. Ideally, the budget is then divided by the number of shareholders to determine the cost per share. CSA members pay in advance so that funds are available to the farmer during the growing season. In return they receive a weekly share of the harvest and the security of a local source of organically raised vegetables. Because of Van En's initiative there are now over one thousand CSA farms around the country. Yet the question remains.........How can young farmers gain affordable access to land in the first place? Again, Indian Line Farm provides a model.

When Van En's farm came up for sale, the sale price was too high for entering farmers. The rising cost of the land put the price out of reach, a typical problem in regions close to urban areas or deemed valuable for vacation homes. The market value of the land reflects the demand for house sites rather than the social benefit of maintaining a local farm. If the citizens of the southern Berkshires wanted Indian Line to remain an active farm producing vegetables for local sale, they would have to partner with the famer to purchase the farm.

The community, working through the Community Land Trust in the Southern Berkshires and The Berkshire Taconic Landscape Program of The Nature Conservancy, made a one-time donation to purchase the land. The Community Land Trust holds title to the land, and The Nature Conservancy holds a conservation restriction. This arrangement enabled two young farmers to purchase the buildings and enter into a ninety-nine year lease on the land, the use of which is determined by a detailed land use plan: the buildings are to remain occupied by those leasing the land; the land must be farmed; at resale the buildings must remain affordable to the next farmer; the farmer is to employ organic practices and meet the conditions of a land-use plan developed to respect the specific ecology of the site.

Susan Witt, "New Agrarians", 2003

6 January 2010

I'm Don Stuart. My birth date is July 13, 1943. I was born at Swedish Hospital in Seattle, and have lived here all my life. I have a sister, so there were just the two kids. Both my parents worked: my dad was in the outboard boat and motor business for many years and my mom worked in a bindery. We lived in west Seattle. And then about the time I was going into high school—say, '60, '59—I guess I was *in* high school at the time—we moved to Bainbridge Island. Actually, it would have been about the time I was a sophomore in high school we moved to Bainbridge, and then I graduated from Bainbridge High School.

About the time I was entering college my dad bought a commercial fishing boat. I should say he bought a boat but completely tore it apart and rebuilt it, and went commercial fishing in Alaska, salmon trolling in Alaska. That's how I worked my way through college was on my dad's boat in Alaska in the summertime.

I went to Washington State University for two years and UW for two years, and then UW Law School, graduated in 1968 from UW Law School. Went in the Navy, was Navy Judge Advocate General Corps, stationed at actually right here locally, in Whidbey Island and then Seattle, two years each. So that makes it 1972 when I got out of JAG. And then I joined a small law firm, doing trial practice, and became a partner. I was with that law firm for about six years. That was the time period during which we had the sailboat at Fremont. We had a little Alden yawl, a very nice 39-foot Alden yawl, which I loved.

Don Stuart
Pacific NW Director
American Farmland Trust

About '85 or so, I went back to practicing law part-time. I practiced full-time in the wintertime, so I'd come back from fishing in the winter and go practicing law. Fishing had its difficulties, and plus, it was very physically challenging. I had tendonitis and all kinds of issues. I remember all during those years I would come back in the fall and I'd think, "Thank God I'm not a commercial fisherman, thank God I'm a lawyer and I can go back and practice law. That's something I know how to do, I can do that." And then about springtime, I'd say, "Oh, thank God I'm not a lawyer. Thank God I'm really a commercial fisherman and I can go fishing." And that was essentially—maybe that's due a little bit to my inherent optimism, but that was essentially how I worked my way through. And finally at some point I sort of realized that neither of these things was much really to my liking.

It probably would have been about 1990, both my wife and I wanted to do something different. I had decided that the most logical thing was nonprofit work, and I had decided that as a lawyer and a commercial fisherman, I was in a great position to work for a nonprofit representing the commercial fishing industry. I mean, I just sort of thought that out in advance. And I came back from fishing the final year and here was a job for executive director for a trade association representing Washington-based commercial salmon fishermen, called Salmon For Washington. They needed an executive director, it was sort of a start-up organization, involved a lot of lobbying in Olympia, and basically putting together a good strong political advocacy program for the commercial salmon fishermen. So I applied for the job. I think I was the only applicant. But I managed to get the job and worked for them for about six years, so from about 1990 to '96.

In '95, the sport fishermen brought a statewide ballot initiative that would have essentially eliminated commercial fishing completely, and it was really motivated, essentially, by their desire to catch more fish, and to do that, somebody else had to catch fewer. So nobody really wanted to get together at the time and try to solve the problem with the loss of habitat and the fish resource disappearing. It was all about catching more of what there was to catch. So I would say that was one of the major frustrations with that six years, was the fact that we basically fought with each other while we watched the resource disappear. You could watch it happen.

I won't go into detail, but the structure of the political system, and the way it works for nonprofits and for trade associations and trade organizations, the way the political system works, it does not position them in any way, shape, or form, so that they can take proactive environmental stands. It just plain doesn't. It's one of the things that gave me some insight, really, now, into how the Farm Bureau approaches its work. As frustrating sometimes as they can be, I have a certain sympathy for the position that they're in. They have to represent the industry, and they have to represent them based on things that are imminent. And so they're worrying about whether they're going to stay in business tomorrow, and they can't really be thinking about whether there's gonna be farming twenty, thirty, or fifty years from now. That's in their spare time, and that's definitely not at the top of their agenda, and it *can't* be, it really can't be, and the political system *prevents* it from being.

And then I went to work for the Washington Association of Conservation Districts. I just basically applied and took the job. That was in '97, early '97. And they were for the first time looking for an executive director, and going to have a full-time lobbyist. They had been doing everything with volunteers. And actually, doing, I would say, an amazing job with volunteers. There's some really rather remarkable people in that organization. But anyway, I worked for them as their executive director, kind of helped them, I think—I hope helped them—pull together an organization over that three-year period from '97 to 2000. And then in 2000, the American Farmland Trust position came up, and I applied and managed to get the job.

I had spent six years working on natural resource issues for the fishermen, and actually they're pretty similar: fishermen and farmers see the world in a remarkably similar way. But until I worked for the conservation districts, I really didn't have much connection with agriculture. And so I guess you could say—I kid them, saying that they polluted my mind. But I do think about the world, and the world of agriculture, along the same general lines as the conservation districts do. Really, the districts are the world, kind of a self-contained world in and of themselves. It's a whole philosophy of how this should work, obviously based on the benefits of conservation incentives versus regulation; based upon private land ownership, and with a very deep respect for property rights. And yet, that does not prevent them in any way, shape, or form, from being really strong advocates for conservation, and they work well with landowners, and they get a lot done, I think—more some places than others, but they get a lot of good stuff done. And that all wraps itself into a whole sort of philosophy. It *is* a community. It's a very remarkable community. And it's of a size that's manageable. The conventions, probably 300 people come to the convention, probably 600-700 conservation district supervisors and personnel and staff personnel around the state.

Our mission is to stop the loss of farmland, and to try to get the farmland that is saved, to try to help farmers make their land and their farming practices more environmentally friendly. I would say it's ostensibly an environmental organization, obviously. But it's just evident that we can't get the job done without the farmers.

There's really two approaches to a lot of problems and this is one of those examples. You can go about a problem, you can try to move the mountain one shovelful at a time, or you can try to move the whole mountain. And obviously trying to move the whole mountain is a lot harder, but maybe if you work at it hard enough, you might move the whole mountain *just a little bit*. I'm kind of gettin' too old to have the patience for the one shovelful at a time. I see a lot of environmental groups that are really very satisfied with one step at a time, and I very much respect that. But getting policy in place, getting changes in the system, that will change the way that farmers, or the vast majority of farmers go about doing business is way, way preferable. But you're never gonna do that if you focus on two or three farmers at a time. You've got to move the whole industry, and to move an industry, the industry has to want to be moved. That's just the way it is. So we try very hard to work with the entire Ag industry, and encourage all of those niches and bits and pieces of this puzzle, all of which fit together in the bigger kind of picture, to try to get systemic change—that will actually make this industry more sustainable. And when I say sustainable I mean to include economically sustainable in that equation.

We've done integrated pest management work, to try to educate farmers on IPM on the environmental side. We have done a lot of work to try to get purchase of development rights programs in place, both at the county and at the state level, with some success. Just as an example, in terms of the land protection side, when I first came on board in 2000, the farmers were very, very alien to the idea of purchase and development rights, to the idea of conservation easements of *any* kind. At the time, there was a national organization that was proselytizing against any kind of conservation easements, and raising hell about it all over the country. And they proselytized to the landowner community heavily. So I just decided that the starting point had to be to convince the agriculture industry that this was *good* for them, as opposed to the other way around.

Purchasing development rights means basically paying a farmer/landowner the difference between the agriculture value and the market value of his land. And in exchange, the landowner provides an agricultural easement, which is like any other conservation easement, except an agricultural conservation easement is one where the conservation value being protected, as opposed to wildlife or trees or habitat, the conservation value being protected is agriculture. And so a simple agricultural conservation easement simply says you define what the piece of property is that you want to affect—the landowner doesn't have to do this to *all* the land, they can pick whatever portion they want to use—and basically the easements are very flexible so that the landowner and the buyer can write into the easement whatever they agree to, whatever they want, and the essence of any conservation easement is kind of don't develop. And usually for environmental conservation easements, it's try to preserve the land for some environmental conservation use. In this case, that's Ag.

So the easement usually has two fairly straightforward objectives: don't develop this piece of land in ways that are inconsistent with agriculture. And secondly, don't subdivide it further than it's already subdivided, or further than whatever you've agreed to in the easement. Those two things.... You can add other stuff. You can go into all kinds of detail: "Well, I want to protect this particular strip down here, because it's a beautiful riparian area and I love the animals and fish, etc.," or "I want to protect this wood lot, and we're going to selectively harvest it." You can spell all that out, if you want to. But the simple, cleanest version is just don't develop and don't subdivide. And the thing that's nice about that is it requires very little monitoring. If you develop something on the property inconsistent with an easement, typically you're going to know that by driving by. And you'll also probably have to apply for a permit to do it anyway, and so you're gonna pick it up; similarly, if you subdivide. Again, you have to do that, it's public, it's in the public arena. There's not a lot of controlling, outside controlling going on. The landowner pretty much owns the property outright, and do what they want. So it's really kind of a nice type of easement.

With the purchase and development rights program, basically you've got a market value for a piece of land. Let's say you've got a hundred acres, and that hundred acres is worth, for agriculture, say $2,000 an acre. So it's a $200,000 piece of property for agriculture. That is to say that if that land was under an easement, and its only real use was Ag use, what would it be worth? Well, it's worth what a farm business can afford to pay for it, and still remain in business, and still be able to cover the carrying cost. At $200,000 it's worth, maybe, say, at 6 percent interest, let's say $12,000 a year carrying cost. That's the alternative use investment of that money. So really, when you say that 100 acres is worth $200,000 to a farmer, what you're really saying is that that land is capable of producing enough revenue that it can cover the costs of production, provide a little profit, and cover a $12,000 annual investment carrying cost, and still keep that farmer in profit. That's essentially the message. So that's its Ag value. That's kind of what we define as Ag value. It's whatever it's worth *to* a farmer for a long-term sustainable farm business.

Of course we know that a hundred acres in most places in the country, in most places in Washington, and certainly any place in this part of the world, is worth a *lot* more than $200,000, and so let's say, just speculatively, that this hundred acres is really worth a million, so the difference is $800,000. So to purchase the development rights, such as the Washington Wildlife and Recreation Program, or the Federal Farm and Ranch Lands Protection Program, those programs would cover that $800,000. They would pay the farmer $800,000, usually in cash, although you can make different arrangements, but usually we're talkin' cash, and that in exchange.... So the farmer enters the transaction with a million-dollar piece of real estate, gets $800,000, provides an easement, and by putting that easement on the property, the value of the land is reduced, of course, to $200,000. So it's been devalued, it's only worth $200,000, that's all it's ever gonna sell for now with this easement on it. But the farmer has the $800,000. So the farmer comes out of the transaction in a cash position, in a total sort of value position, hopefully the same as they went in, and obviously the $800,000 is their money, they can spend it, they can go to Reno, they can invest it in the stock market, they can buy more land, pay off debt, whatever they want.

These programs around the country have been immensely, immensely popular. The ratings of the programs amongst farmers in those states that have them, are like anywhere from 92 to 96 percent range. It's like after the fact, come back ten years later and ask the farmers.... It's just like an amazingly high.... They love the programs, because they are ultimately very respectful of property rights. It allows the farmer to extract that excess dollar value out of the land, the farmer can retire, the farmer can use that money to equalize an estate plan, so if you've got three or four kids and only one wants to farm, you can work it out. Lots of advantages. Lots and lots of advantages. And you can do it charitably as well, although we don't usually focus on that, we try to focus on the creation program.

So from about 2000 to about, I'd say, 2004, I managed to get some grant funding to basically do my own effort at proselytizing, and I was all over the state—all over the region, actually—but all over Washington, trying to.... I've really focused on Ag, and I very much focused on the Farm Bureau, because the Farm Bureau is the political behemoth in the Ag industry, and very much so in Washington. And the Farm Bureau had policy that was in opposition to conservation easements generally. That's the core of the Ag landowner community, and if you're gonna influence the Washington State Legislature, you just have to be there. I made presentations to farm bureaus at local counties. I would typically call up the local president and I'd tell him who I was and tell him, "Look, I'd really appreciate the chance to get together. What I'd like to do is I'll buy you breakfast, I'll buy you lunch, coffee, I'll come to your house, whatever. You just state the time, I'll be there. And just give me an hour or so of your time, to explain how this works, and why I think it's good for Ag, and...." More or less the explanation that I just gave you, is the heart of what I told these guys. And then if they like it, if they think it makes sense, "Then what I would really appreciate you doing my next request would be to let me come to your monthly Farm Bureau meeting, County Farm Bureau meeting, and let me talk to you about these things, and talk to them, and answer their questions." And I would do that. Sometimes I did that first, sometimes I went and talked to the president first. And then usually at those meetings I would offer them some language for a resolution. The Farm Bureau is a very grassroots organization, and they take stuff from the bottom, up. So I offered resolutions, and I got several county Farm Bureaus interested enough that they supported this idea at the state convention.

In '95, Mike Ryerd who is the lobbyist for the Washington Wildlife and Recreation Coalition and a few others at the Washington Wildlife and Recreation Coalition, really wanted to put a farmland program in the WWRP. If you experience, if you see, first hand, what happens to them every year when they go to advocate for WWRP at the state legislature, you'll understand why the rural conservative legislators really resist. There's a very strong tendency and belief that the government should not own more land, that the government should own less land. The less land government owns, the better off we are. And having the government own interest in land and buy land is just seen as a bad thing generally. That land should be in private ownership. That's a very strong, strong feeling, and that just is absolutely countered by WWRP. So you get a very strong push-back from the conservative rural legislators on the WWRP appropriation every year, and their reasoning was, that if they had a really good farmland preservation program that was built right into WWRP, that that would help to enlist some support from rural conservative farmers. And I think that's good logic. I think it's gonna take time. I don't think it's quite worked that way yet. I do think that there's definitely increasing support for these programs statewide.

So anyway, in '94, the Farm Bureau opposed a piece of legislation to create a farmland program. I think it was actually at the late fall 1994 convention that these resolutions came to the fore in the Farm Bureau, and they changed their position. And one can always take credit for things that you're not entitled to so I hesitate to take credit for that, but I guess in my own mind I think I had some influence on that. I certainly hope I did. In any case, it was a great outcome, and the Farm Bureau took a much more progressive position, I think an *excellent* position, after that. There were some things they wanted to see, and there were concerns they had. And they wanted this land to remain in private ownership, which I wholeheartedly agree with. They had some stipulations, but in the end they were willing to support the program. So in '95, WWRP offered these amendments again, and it passed.

And so in '95 we ended up starting a Washington State Farmland Preservation Program, but not a lot of money. I think it's ranged between maybe 4½ million dollars to maybe 8 or 9 million dollars for the biennium, for the farmland side of things. But it's a great program, it's evolving, it's doing a lot of good, and it allows us to match the federal Farm and Ranch Lands Protection Program. And then it provides a great additional incentive for locals, county-level programs. So just kind of the way I think about this is if you take that money, the federal Farm and Ranch Lands Protection Program money, there's probably at least 2 to 4 million dollars that can and sometimes does come into the state of Washington from that source. You've got anywhere from, say, 5 to 10 million dollars that can flow in here through this WWRP Farmland Program. We only have, at this point, half a dozen counties that have a farmland protection program, and I'm not just sure what that adds up to. One of the better programs is Gadget, which puts about $500,000 or so each year. If we had, say, even ten counties, but put $500,000 each, annually, into a program, that'd be 5 million dollars going into farmland protection. These tend to be the more urban counties—the rural ones just can't afford it. So that's a source of money. Then you've also got transfer development rights programs that help to contribute to some extent. They usually don't amount to much, but there's work goin' on for that. And *that* can contribute a piece of the money, especially for farms that are closest to the urban center, where the people are most familiar with the farm, that are paying the money to protect it, because the money's coming from an urban area to usually a nearby rural area. That's *that* money. That's money that I think could work for Snohomish Valley, for example—transfer development rights money—*if* we can get the bugs worked out and get this done. So I feel that's one of the hopes, but those are usually more expensive properties, because they're closer to the urban center. So that's a good use for that transfer development rights money.

Transfer development rights is a great theory that doesn't always work out in practice. But there's a lot of effort going on to create them. Essentially the idea is that there are places that could stand more development, most ideally in an urban area, and that they're places that we'd really like to protect and have *less* development. And we're not able to do that with growth management, so we basically set up receiving and sending zones, and we pick areas to receive development rights, that we are willing to accept more development, and basically in exchange for that increased intensity of construction and development—it can be population, it can be density, but it can also be other amenities—we ask the developer to make a contribution to Transfer Development Rights Fund, and then that money goes out into the nearby rural area and purchases. The notion is that having nearby rural lands, like from my perspective, Snoqualmie Valley, a gem by all measures of the Seattle area—by having that, you've really enhanced the life in Seattle, you've enhanced the quality of life. So it's a quality-of-life addition to the nearby urban center. And actually, King County has had a TDR program that's worked pretty well, mostly focused on timber, but with some Ag over the years. And right now there's an effort going on to do this in the four counties: King, Pierce, Snohomish, and Kitsap.

But the essence of it, that was kind of the first very focused farmland protection piece. If you have purchase and development rights programs, the public pays, and it pays heavily, I might add, to protect this land and keep it in agriculture. But you don't take any steps at all to make sure that it's managed in a way that is publicly environmentally responsible, you're just never gonna get there. You're never gonna continue to have the public support for the program. Ultimately you'll poison the program with problems and issues that arise on land that's protected, and why'd we protect this land when the owner doesn't seem to have any respect for the public's interest, and etc. All that can come up immediately.

I became really interested in our incentives system, our conservation incentives system, and in about '97 convinced the Puget Sound Action Team to fund an effort to analyze and to try to reform or find ways to reform and improve our incentives system. Really, there are really just two ways of getting environmental improvements on private lands, and one involves regulation: you tell the farmer what to do, and if they don't do it, you put 'em in jail or fine 'em or somethin', right? And the other is incentives. You basically offer them a financial incentive, pay for the cost of the work and hopefully offer them something that is an inducement to do it. We don't, as a society, draw the line between those two very well.

Obviously, a landowner as a member of society has an obligation or responsibility to a certain level of performance. You can't just ignore everybody else's interests and willy-nilly just pollute the heck out of your property, and who cares about my neighbors and the people downstream. That's just not responsible. And we all know that there's a certain level of conduct that is inherently socially necessary for just kind of a baseline level of social responsibility. But there's also a lot more in addition to that, that landowners can do to contribute to the social well-being. And we don't generally have a theory about where to draw the line between when you tell 'em to do it, and when you ask 'em to do it. Everybody approaches that problem differently. We just don't think it through—and there are some things you *could* think about in making a judgment like that. But we don't do that. Instead, it all becomes political. If we have enough money for incentives, then great, the farmer gets incentives. If there's no money for incentives, then maybe the farmer doesn't do it, or the landowner doesn't do it, and then everybody gets mad at 'em, and then first thing you know, there's a big push, "These people should do more!" and you've got regulation in place. It's all political. It's very rough justice, I guess you could say. And it's particularly of a concern for farmers, because farms are businesses, if you use incentives. If you don't use incentives, everything's done with regulation, and you basically require the farmer to carry the burden or responsibility. That's gonna increase cost of business, and you're very likely gonna drive this person off the land.

Remember that a lot of these farmers own land. In the state of Washington, roughly 75 percent of our active farmland, of the fifteen or so million acres that we have in this state, roughly 75 percent, about 11.3 million, have a market value that's higher than its Ag value. And when that's the case, and you're the owner of that piece of land, there's a point in time when you start to think, "Well what the heck am I doin' *this* for?! It doesn't make sense." Might be you borrowed the money and bought the land yesterday, but it also might be you inherited it from your great-great-grandfather. That doesn't matter, really, in a way. It's about what it's worth, and it's about the alternative use value of the money you've got invested there. And there's a point at which you just get frustrated and say, "I can't do this anymore."

As long as 75 percent of our Ag land has a market value that's higher than its Ag value, we know what the future holds. We know for sure that as these landowners either get tired of doin' this and get frustrated as they retire, as they die and their children take over, as they ultimately sell because they have to sell, as that happens in the years to come, we know that those properties that have a market value higher than their Ag value will sell to someone who's not going to use it for agriculture. They're going to use it for some more intensive—I might add less environmentally friendly—land use. So if we know that.... I mean, that's what we face. That's the magnitude of the problem we face. It's structural, it's built into the system. That's why I think the future, without help from the public with TDR programs, and with environmental stuff, the future actually, I think, looks rather bleak. That's why we need to help our farmers stay on the land, and to help them deal with these environmental challenges, because they are the place, they're the last place, where there are actually possibilities for getting environmental gains.

Think about this—the Northwest is expected to double in population by about mid century here, and to grow by a factor of anywhere between three and seven times by the end of the century. So we're looking at massive growth. If you think about it, Washington has a population of 6 million now; picture the state with 30 million people, say five times what it has now. I guess I have to be somewhat pleased that I'm gettin' older and I won't see that. But it's a future that doesn't look at all pleasing to me. Those people, that growth, has environmental impacts. So the environmental problem is not going to go away, it's going to get worse. We're going to have greater environmental problems in the years to come. There absolutely can be no doubt about that. As the population increases and the impacts on the environment increases, it's just plain absolutely gonna happen. And we still face the question of how are we going to address those increases.

It's very costly to use incentives, so the easy solution is always to find somebody to pay for it themselves, and to actually go out and regulate. That's absolutely the easiest first step, first choice solution that's likely to appear. And then add to that the fact that most of these people are going to be urban. And from the Ag perspective, the urban centers are where all those crazy liberals live. I mean, you know, it's really the urban folks that kind of will vote for any tax and are perfectly happy to accept regulation and to regulate other people. All those urban liberals, how are they going to react to Ag? So just as kind of a fundamental political equation, you look down the road, and you know darned well that if we're constrained and feeling pressure from environmental concerns and issues now, it's not going to get better. It just plain is not going to get better.

The small organic farms really are keeping farmers on the land and land in agriculture, and contributing good environmental value to the society. These are farms, they're businesses, and their profitability is what determines whether they stay on the land. If the land value goes way up, beyond what a farm business can afford to pay, that has an impact on profitability. Lots of them don't necessarily factor that into their thinking all the time. But in the longer run, they ultimately all do. And so you gotta get the land costs down to what a farm business can afford to pay. Or I should say differently, you've got to remove the differential between the Ag value and the market value. You've got to somehow....those have to be the same.

One way is, of course, to bring the land value down. And you can bring the land value down with purchase and development rights programs like WWRP— King County had such a program. You can bring it down with zoning. You could come out here in perfect theory and say, "Well, you guys that have 5-acre zoning, sorry, you're now 20s. And you guys that have 20-acre zoning, you're 35s. And all this Ag zone land that we have at 35"—I think King County is 35, so I forget, 35 or 40—"Well, we're gonna make those 200." Right? You could zone it. And when I say "could", I think the possibility of that happening is close to zero.

The better alternative to me is purchasing development rights. So that's bringing the land value down. But you can also bring the Ag value up. You can make the farm more profitable. That is always the first thing that every farmer is going to tell you, "Well, yeah, yeah, you don't have to do that. Just make me profitable enough and I'll be all right, and I'll be able to afford this land, we won't have this problem." Right? That's a good Adam Smith economics solution, except that agriculture is a land intensive business. I don't think the farmers that we're dealing with really want to move into downtown Seattle and have some kind of high-rise greenhouse. They want to be farmers. We're talking about an open, attractive, agricultural valley with working lands and a mix of uses and all that. That's land extensive. That means, ask yourself, you take a square foot of soil, and you plant a plant on it. And then you wait six months and then put a lot of money into that. But just think about it from the land perspective. You do all this, and then you wait six months, and then you harvest a crop, and the crop you harvest, you sell for pennies. You know, the profit on that square foot of land is literally pennies. And then, you know, probably the other six months, it's got a cover crop in it, so that might be all you earn off that piece of land for a whole year. Compare that to what a Wal-Mart can do with a square foot of, say, shelf space, or parking lot; or pretty much any other more intensive land use. What is that square foot worth to almost anybody else? It's *way* more, *way* more than the pennies a farmer can earn on it. So *my* feeling about it is that the world would have to be very seriously in trouble, the planet would have to be essentially starving, and approaching Easter Island before food or agricultural production achieves a price that would allow that piece of property to be worth enough to compete with the Wal-Mart and the residential housing. So given that, it's a little bit like parks: if you don't set parks aside and buy them with public money, you don't have parks.

I'm very pessimistic. Pessimistic isn't the right term. I have very deep concerns. I think this: that if we don't do something—I'm not necessarily talking now about any specific, like global warming, but if we don't do something about this land value differential problem that we have, if we don't do something dramatic, or *start* doing something that will *become* dramatic over a period of years—it doesn't have to all happen tomorrow—we could start chipping away at it. We've taken some first steps with creation of the WWRP program. And we can add to it—pieces here, pieces there. It isn't impossible. But just in terms of dollar value, I think we have to do something, make a start at building a vision of the future, that over, say, the next thirty years, will take a significant piece out of this problem. If we don't do that, I think we *are* in trouble. There's lots of land in the Midwest that actually can produce agricultural products, and so I think we're in trouble there too, but we're *very* specifically in trouble in coastal states like ours, and *very horrifically* specifically in trouble in places like King County, like Central Puget Sound.

Carnation and this Snoqualmie Valley, this is like a little gem. And the only thing that protects it at the moment, frankly, is flooding. That's the only reason, the fact that it floods. If it didn't flood, if they really did decide to build a dam upriver, suddenly all that land would acquire a value that would be way in excess of their Ag value. All those farms? Bang! They'd be gone! Maybe not overnight, but *they…. would….be….gone!* You could sit down and you could say, "This is history." You could look at it and say, "This is history."

Forgive me if I wander back into the environmental side of this, but I do believe that that's part of the solution. I think there are several solutions: the political activism; I think that the direct market agriculture that's conducted by all the small farmers getting that kind of public contact and public sort of beginnings, nurturing of public understanding of agriculture—all that is just hugely valuable, because we really have to convince those urban areas about these issues. And I think that will help. I think having the WWRP type programs, and making those programs, that helps. Having good, effective farm advocacy helps. But I'm also becoming…. And I do believe that we could assemble enough purchase and development rights money to make a significant dent in this. I'm convinced if we had, say, $60 million a biennium to spend on purchase and development rights throughout the state of Washington, it would be amazing. With the other money that it could get from the feds and from local communities and etc., contributions by farmers, contributions from environmental foundations, all of it added up and brought together—TDR programs, all of that—if we had, say, 100, 120, 150 million dollars to spend per biennium, that's what, $60 million to $75 million? That's only $750 million. That's a small fraction of what we spent for Boeing, and this would be money that would *stay* in the community, that in fact would stay here because it *couldn't* go away, would actually be invested in keeping these farms in farming. It would be a wonderful boost to the Ag community, but a huge boost to the serious intentions of local economies. So I think it could be done with TDR.

While I don't want to use the word "pessimistic", I have deep concerns, but I also have hope, because I think it's quite doable. It's quite within the realm of reason to hope that we could accomplish this, just with TDR. *But* I also think we've got to solve the environmental problem. And I think that agriculture can address that. And that really is where this work with the incentives programs, making them more specific, what more effective has led me, over the last couple of years, what happened with that incentives study was at the end of it we had a whole series of recommendations. One of those was the creation of ecosystem services markets that agriculture could supply ecosystem services to a growing society. If you think about all those people that are coming, and about all those environmental impacts that we're facing, we have to mitigate and offset for those, right? Some of those markets are global, so people put exhaust and pollutants into the air, that's a global problem. Anybody, worldwide, can address that problem with offsets. And I think having an ecosystem market for carbon offsets could be a *huge* benefit to Ag. If this climate bill passes, the price of these carbon offsets is likely to go considerably higher, and it could easily become a significant source of revenue for farmers. There's all kinds of things that farmers can do: reducing nitrogen in the soil, reducing nitrous oxide emissions from the soil. Just on an on, a whole host of ways farmers can address that problem. That's one. That's one opportunity.

Another opportunity is water quality trading. We have this whole NRCS field office technical guide with all these practices. There's hundreds of them, and the vast majority of them are actually water quality practices, and farmers are really good at improving water quality. In fact, the well-managed farm doesn't need to pollute at all and can still remain very profitable using good NRCS practices.

We do a lot of the mitigation, we do wetland mitigation, we do habitat mitigation. There are *lots* of ways that farmers can provide the values that wetlands provide, without necessarily impairing their farm operation. So you've got a transportation project, a highway goin' through, or you've got a shopping mall or some development project that's going to have an impact on wildlife, you can put an easement. This project is a part of its mitigation requirements, permit requirements. We go out, find farmers nearby in the community, and can pay to keep those farmers in agriculture: basically purchase an easement on the property, a farm agricultural easement, and perhaps pay them some sum of money to implement practices or to be friendly to the wildlife that is being destroyed over here by the shopping center. That's stuff that's going on all over the country. It's stuff that has happened and is happening here in the Northwest. Those are all examples. Flood mitigation is another example where you keep farmers in agriculture, so that somebody else somewhere, maybe downstream, can continue to proceed and build a shopping center that local communities so badly want.

If we're going to grow, if we know we're gonna grow dramatically, and if we know that that growth is going to have environmental impacts and we're going to be looking for places to get environmental lift, and we know that our farms are the places where that environmental lift is possible, you sure can't get it in the city. And if you're going to go out on the public lands, the public lands are already more or less managed for natural environmental value. So it isn't the public lands, it's really our farm and forest lands. And of the two of those, the farms are probably the greatest opportunity. It's an opportunity to get environmental gains that can make up for the environmental losses that we know are happening and are going to continue to happen as our society grows. This is the *cheapest* way for society to go. Otherwise, they're building a hundred-million-dollar plan, or the big expensive smokestack scrubbers, or they're doing some kind of horrendously expensive mitigation to make up for.... Or they may not even be able to *build* the shopping center or the highway or whatever. Those would be *massive* social costs that would potentially stymie our economic prosperity—something which not many people are all that thrilled about.

So here's an alternative, here is a way less expensive way of reaching environmental sustainability, of making up for the environmental damage that we do as a society as we grow, and at the same time the farmer stays in traditional agriculture, we do not change that, minor compromises. Here's a way that this becomes a significant supplement to their income, provides society with an inexpensive way to address environmental challenges, and here's what happens, you can envision this kind of future—and suddenly our farmers, and I might add, *local* farmers, become a lynch pin, critically necessary piece of the puzzle, if society is going to grow. Suddenly losing our farms puts us in a position where our society can't prosper. Saving our farms is the way we solve our environmental problems, as opposed to now, where many people in society who don't really understand Ag tend to think, "Oh, get rid of those farms! They're bad actors and polluters," and this and that. There's a lot of bad press and bad attitude toward agriculture out there. Here's a way to transform all that, and to transform agriculture from a position where we're struggling all the time to fight just to stay alive. Instead, we put ourselves in a position where we're sort of a prime....I guess you could say the "love child" of the broader society, become a lynch pin, necessary piece of the sort of prosperous future we all hope for ourselves.

One of the things about using the environmental offset mitigation sort of scenario as a way to get agriculture some money is that it helps them to protect agricultural lands and keep them in agriculture, not in development. And they're all local. With wetlands, with wildlife habitat, lots of farms have places that our wet and unproductive soils could easily be serving as wetlands, or farmers could use practices that provide wetland functions and that add up to mitigation for wetland loss in those circumstances where an actual wetland is not absolutely critical, we could find ways to do that. I just know we can. And with wildlife habitat, obviously it's going to be a segment of habitat, it's always going to be local. If you damage something here and you have to replace it somewhere else, you're going to need to replace it somewhere in the same watershed, in the same habitat segment, in the same area. So what that means then is that this is another really, really good reason why these local farmers in the Carnation Valley, in the Snoqualmie Valley, for example, are needed by the city of Seattle and local urban communities, because they're not only providing this wonderful access to local fresh food, the food security and safety, but also, at the same time, people then begin to get it, that these people are also providing a *massively* critical environmental service—another reason why food and why farms need to be local.

I especially think it's important for places like these, because these are the farms that are the first to go. They're also the farms that are the most expensive to protect, the ones we're losing first, and the ones that are most challenging. But this problem is not limited to King County, it's all over the state of Washington, all over the Pacific Northwest. The reason you have to deal with the problem here is that if you set up a statewide purchase and development rights program, and all the money, you find that 100-acre parcel, and you spend five or ten million dollars protecting 100 acres, how do you justify that to a legislator from Okanogan or Yakima? They just see that as absurd. What?! Why, we could have protected *thousands* of acres with that money?! What kind of sense does *that* make?! And so the political equation for purchase and development rights is tenuous. It has to be something that is worthwhile, valuable, and useful for rural communities. At the same time, we have to address these problems in the urban edge—we have to do both. And one of the things that's nice about the ecosystem services markets, or what we've kind of tended to call conservation markets, is that they allow us to tap into that urban wealth, to address some of the more expensive pieces of the problem, leaving us with some wherewithal and possibilities for also dealing with it in the areas in eastern Washington and the more rural areas that face this problem in spades.

It fits in so beautifully with the sort of resurgence of rural agricultural economies. It would supplement those economies. It would help to link those farmers to their consumers and customers. It probably encourages organic agriculture. And I don't think you have to be organic to be environmentally responsible, by any means, but certainly can't hurt. In many ways it's very good. So that's where we are now.

The fact is, any, *any* Washington farmer is probably environmentally way more responsible than wherever else people are going to get that beet. I mean, really, anywhere else on the planet. We are *the* most environmentally responsible, by far. Perhaps we've got some stiff competition from Europe, and absolutely in the urban surround areas. Not only are they protecting the land by buying those beets at the Farmers Market, they're also encouraging environmental responsibility and helping that farmer contribute to environmental quality in this region. One of the ways that farmers become more intensive in their land use is by selling direct. And frankly, it's *the* technique that they have. There really isn't much else, outside of maybe greenhouses. You know what I mean? There isn't much else that they can do. And that can be very effective. But even so, I fear that it's not, in itself, enough. It's one of those things that can bring *up* the profitability of Ag, and the Ag value of that land, boost that Ag value up closer to its market value. I still fear.... I still just look at this, and the more I look at it, the more I just become convinced that you're never gonna get there with that alone. I honestly believe we tend to kind of try to fool ourselves. I honestly believe that most people that buy fresh and organic foods do so because they think they are more healthy for them, that they're more healthful. They don't buy locally, I think. I say that—this is a horrible generalization—but I think probably the majority are not buying locally, and not going to the farmers market, because they think that they're doing something that's environmentally good—and they are. That's something we need to *really* build upon, very much to build upon, to build that into the market understanding of this.

29 December 2009

I'm Doug Hanson—Douglas Hanson at work and Doug Hanson to my friends. I'm fifty-two years old as of this recording, and I was born in Pennsylvania in 1957, and then moved to the Northwest, to Seattle, in 1960 when I was three years old. I've lived all around the greater Seattle area since then, and moved to Duvall in 1998, so about twelve and a half years ago, and we've made our home in Duvall, want to stay in the Valley, and very much love this way of life and the area that we've chosen.

I grew up in Seattle until I was in third grade. We lived in north Seattle, in the Shoreline area. Then my parents moved to Bellevue and I attended middle school and high school in Bellevue. Really, I think I'm a child of the East Side. After high school I went to the University of Washington. I got a B.A. in speech communication at the University of Washington in 1981, and chose to still live on the East Side. My wife and I were living in Maltby for a few years before moving to Duvall. I think just really liked the rural life but also closeness to the city aspect that the life in the Valley here gives us.

I work for a company right now that is a manufacturer of organic products, an organic dairy manufacturer, and the brand name is Organic Valley. Most people will probably recognize that, not the business name, which is CROPP Cooperative—stands for Cooperative Regions of Organic Producer Pools, meaning owned by farmers around the country, maybe 1,400 farmers around the country. We make organic dairy products and organic meat products under various brand names. I've had my whole career in food, really. My first real job was working in a grocery store, cleaning the meat department, of all things—maybe part of the reason I'm a fish-a-terian now.

Douglas Hanson
National Sales Manager,
CROPP Cooperative
Organic Prairie
Duvall, WA

I do eat fish. Growing up in the Northwest I've not given up fish. But I don't eat any poultry or any meat, and I haven't for about twenty years or so. But having started in high school, cleaning the meat department in a grocery store, and then becoming a box boy and a checker and a stocker, and really working my way through college in grocery stores, started my career in food. And so I've really been involved in food in one way or another since about 1973.

When I graduated from University of Washington, I got a real job, and I was selling food. And it made sense that I would move away from working in the grocery store, to working for a company that sold food, and back then, it was about 1981 until 1989 or so, I worked for traditional grocery companies. I was a broker, I represented many companies, they were sort of your standard companies in grocery today: Pillsbury Company, Green Giant, Hunt's, other brand names that people would recognize. That's what we call regular grocery, or conventional grocery nowadays. Those were good jobs for me. I sold the military, I traveled all around the Northwest and I sold to military bases to their grocery store, called the commissary store. Big business, important business, worthwhile business for me, but during that roughly eight or nine years my wife and I were saving a lot of money, as much money as we could—it wasn't much, but it was a lot for us—knowing that we would end up traveling as much as we could around the world. And so those jobs for me were a beginning of a career in food, but also a means to an end. And the end for me was to do some traveling and really see the world.

I guess maybe the important thing is, that when all that travel was done and I came back and resumed a career, I stayed in food, because I knew food and had grown up with that industry all of my working life, but then took a turn and entered the natural and organic industry as a sales manager. And that was important, because it was relatively young industry at that time. Natural and organic products were not widely available. Grocery stores like Safeway or Fred Meyer in this area didn't carry any. Most of those products were sold in small health food stores. But it was a very interesting business: interesting because the products were more healthy, not contaminated, the way I see it, with pesticides or herbicides. And it fit my frame of mind at the time. Having traveled the world changed my political views, and views on business. And so it was a way for me to continue a career in the food industry, while at the same time satisfying myself by being somewhat on the periphery of regular business, real business. Natural and organic products were not part of the mainstream at the time, and I liked that. I liked that point of view, I liked being somewhat of an outsider or different.

Through the eighties when my wife and I were saving money to do this travel, nobody really knew that we were going to do that—nobody in industry, nobody in business, nobody at my jobs and at work knew that I was saving money and would one day leave my job and travel. I knew that I would. Me and my wife were probably the only ones that knew that. My parents went along with the idea. They didn't probably believe that we ever would. Our families, brothers and sisters, never really thought that we would do this—which made it more important to do, because we didn't want to be saying that we were going to do this, and then end up not doing it.

And then the day came that we had reached whatever financial goal we set to figure we had enough money to survive for a while, we put our house up for sale, and we sold our cars, and we sold most of what we owned, and stored the little bit that was left in my wife's mother's spare bedroom. And we bought good backpacks and good raincoats and good sweaters, and we traveled around the world. And it was not completely unplanned. It was planned in terms of weather, to be in the Southern Hemisphere of the world during the winter up here and summer down there, and to be in the Northern Hemisphere during the summer up here. But as far as what we were going to do and what we were going to see, there were really very few set ideas about what the whole goal was going to be.

I went into the travel with probably one point of view, and came out the other side with another point of view. I think that I became a much more compassionate person by traveling. We saw a lot of poverty. Heck, we were *living* in poverty. This was not vacation, it was hard work to travel. It was hard not knowing exactly where we were going to stay each night or when we were going to eat or where we were going to go to the bathroom or brush our teeth, let alone being with one other person twenty-four hours a day, seven days a week, fifty-two weeks a year, for two and a half years we traveled.

So my view changed and I became more compassionate, more understanding of other people, much more liberal in my views. And those views have stayed with me since then, and will, I know, through the rest of my life. That probably is the most enduring change for me, and I'm most satisfied with that. When it comes to how that relates to food, and my career and my involvement with food, again I think that the travel helped me express my difference, how I am different compared to other people in sort of regular society. And then coming back and becoming involved with the natural and organic industry I think expressed that difference.

My own family, my brothers and sister and my parents, really probably couldn't define what organic products are, to this day, and I've been in the industry for twenty years. The difference is that people who know about and eat or grow or are some way involved with organic food, have a much deeper knowledge about where their food comes from, why it's important to know where your food comes from, how it's grown, what goes into it, if it's in meat; and the food's relationship with our own bodies. Most people don't think about that. Most people buy food at the grocery store, have no idea where it comes from, how it was grown, where it was grown, other than for it to be available to them in abundant supply at the lowest possible price. And that's absurd, in my view. It is approaching one of the most important aspects of every human's life—that is, nutrition and food to sustain our life—with an absolute hands-off and uninterested point of view. And it's hard for me to understand how an average American or a person around the world can really go through their entire life without thinking more deeply about the food they put in their body, two, three, four, ten times a day, depending on the person.

Politically I'm aware—more aware, I think, certainly than the average American, than most Americans. I follow politics, it's a hobby of mine. I'm about as liberal as one can be. I don't look liberal. I've had people say that they suspect I am almost on the religious right because of the fact that I keep my hair short and so forth. But that should be a lesson to us all, I suppose, not to judge people in *any* way, let alone by the way they look. I enjoy being a liberal because I think I envision it in terms of a freedom that maybe most people don't think about. I view my liberal politics as being against the norm, allowing people to do what they want to do, without interference. And yet at the same time there is a compassion to the liberal point of view that means we all have to be part of a greater society and a community, and that we have to look out for one another and help one another, and strive for the greater good. And I firmly believe that that is the case. It's not easy to pigeon hole somebody into one particular point of view. That's not to say that we should not rely on ourselves. And it's not to say that each of us doesn't have an obligation to contribute to society, be it through taxes or whatever, to support what needs to be done for the greater society, but at the same time, we must maintain our own individuality and our own individual freedom, and so those two points of view, I think, could be viewed as in conflict with one another. And I don't live that conflict, I think that they can live in harmony with one another.

When it comes to religious points of view, I respect other people's positions and whatever they choose to believe. I've often described myself as an antagonostic. That's a half antagonist and a half agnostic. And the antagonist part of me has a difficult time accepting the established religions and their need for conformity of ideas and their control, really, I believe, over people's lives—often through guilt and a belief that isn't.... Well, it's just belief. And there's nothing wrong with belief—or faith, I guess, as people call it. I don't find fault with people for that, if that's what they choose. I just don't choose that for myself. I guess I feel more grounded in reality. The real problem I have is when I am open minded to other people believing what *they* want to believe, and yet they're not as open minded about me believing what I want to believe. And there's an irony in there that is difficult to accept and difficult to explain to people when they don't allow me to be something that they are not, which is a true believer.

So that's the antagonist part of me. The agnostic part of me just.... Agnosticism is a fence sitter. It's an uncertainty. It's not the same as atheism, which is a disbelief, but it's certainly not the other side of the coin, which is full belief. I think that as humans we're incapable of knowing what occurs after death, how the universe was created, if there's a Creator. At this point in our human development, anybody who says they know for a certainty anything about that big topic is nuts. They don't *know*. Nobody knows. And so again, agnosticism is not *dis*belief, it's just there's no way *to* believe, to know, to know for a certainty. So I'm an antagonostic.

I guess looking at my own life—and I will say what I said before—it's not often that a person looks in depth at their own life. Sometimes we're too busy to take the time to really do that. In describing my political views, in describing my religious views like I've just done, I think it goes hand in hand with my entry into the natural and organic food industry. It's on the periphery of mainstream in many ways. It's a niche market. And I'll expand on that in just a second, because it didn't *used* to be a niche market, it used to be that organic was the only thing there was, because there wasn't fertilizer and pesticides and growth hormones and other things. It used to be that people grew food naturally, and processed it very little, and consumed it, mostly what they grew themselves or what their neighbors grew. I guess the natural and organic industry tries in a way to get back to that same kind of root base of how food is produced. And yet that is on the periphery in today's society. And so being on the periphery sort of reflects my political view, my religious view, my place in life really. It's trying not to be just a cog in a societal machine, and instead I'm a little bit on the outside. But then coming to where I am with you today, I bring a much different point of view than maybe other people that you've spoken with. I'm not a farmer, I grow a garden and enjoy that. I'm a member of a CSA and eat local food and seasonal food as much as I can—I'm not perfect. But I come to the food industry from a little bit of a different perspective than others that are sharing their experiences with you, because I sell food, and I have worked with distributors with food, I'm on the business side of food, not on the growing side of food. I'm proud of that. It's certainly a necessity. The thing I'm most proud about, I guess, is that I am on the business and selling side of *good* food, of organic food, as much local, and certainly as organic as can be.

Organic Valley is a brand name. The company I work for is Crop Cooperative. And it's owned by farmers. There are about 1,400 farmers that own the business, and yet we're a business. We have a board of directors, the CEO—we call him our C-EI-EI-O. He reports to the board, he's got a management team, VPs, and chief operating officers, and chief financial officer, and so on. It's a regular business. It's about a $520 million company this year in 2009. So it's big for the industry, and successful, and growing, and important, because it is recognized in the organic industry as being not only a producer of high-quality product, but a respected company in terms of maintaining its commitment to strong organic rules, strong organic standards, to uphold the integrity of the organic seal that is published by the government. And I guess setting the bar high for organic production. It permeates through the entire company, from the owners, the farmers, and the way they treat their animals and their pastures, and the feed that goes into the growing of the animals, all the way through to the processing plants that we work with and the organic standards that they must maintain to process the product organically; to packaging and making sure that there isn't excess packaging or unrecyclable packaging whenever possible.

Really the commitment to the organic ideal, and the organic ideal is a commitment to renewable energy, a commitment to the clean environment, to humane animal treatment, to no use of pesticides and herbicides and artificial growth hormones in products. That organic ideal, that sort of permeates from top to bottom through the company and through all of the steps necessary to take a product such as milk from the grass on the pasture, through the animal that's eating it, to the milking and the storage of the raw milk, to the processing of the raw milk into pasteurized milk, into a carton, and transported through the distribution system to the store shelf to the consumer's table. We call it "farm to fork" in many ways.

So we try to maintain the highest standard that we can, and that's not meant to be a sales pitch, it's meant to, I guess, satisfy or help people understand that there is truly a strong regulatory body out there, and a strong commitment on the part of most organic producers and companies to maintain that ideal, to strive for the cleanliness in the product that the organic seal represents.

We don't regulate ourselves as a company. We are third-party certified. That means that there's an outside agency that visits our farms, visits our processing plants, visits our records on every level. From the farm, the farmer must keep records of all feed that is purchased, that goes into the feeding of the animals. It must have a farm management document on hand and up to date, that talks about the seed that goes into the growing of the pasture. Pasture's not just regular grass like you'd have on your front lawn. Good pasture is made up of, well, what most people would call weeds: grasses and weeds and other things that animals, cows, eat to have a complete nutrition. All of those, all seed, all aspects of the management of the farm must be documented and then certified by this outside agency.

There are many that are approved by the government. The one that Organic Valley Crop Cooperative uses is Oregon Tilth. Oregon Tilth is the first organic certifying agency in the country, established, I don't know when—in the seventies I believe. They're certified themselves now by the government. The government does have to, under the organic rules, it's called the USDA organic seal, which is governed by the NOP, which is the National Organic Program under the USDA, Department of Agriculture. That agency must certify the certifiers, and then the certifiers certify the companies, the farmers, the products, and we're not allowed to put the Oregon Tilth seal—logo or their words—on our products without meeting their standards. Nor are we allowed to put the USDA organic seal on our products without meeting the standards set by the USDA. And the seal—without going into all the detail about what the seal encompasses, there are certain levels of the use of the word "organic," legally, in food production.

In a nutshell, there's 100 percent organic, which means 100 percent organic. There are no parts of the product that are not organic: the feed that goes into the animal, the seed or any kind of manure that goes onto a field, that becomes 100 percent organic. There's a 95 percent to 100 percent organic called "organic" as opposed to "100 percent organic." That is what our products are. That allows for minute amounts of ingredients such as sea salt or vitamin D in milk, which is not an organic product, to be included in the product, often, like vitamin D in milk, regulated by the government. It must be added, and still have those products called organic.

The next level is a much lower level of organic. It's from 70 percent organic product to 95 percent. Those products are not allowed to use the USDA seal—that is, the USDA organic seal—on their products. They can have on the front of their package terminology that says "made with organic grain", or "made with organic oats," or something along that line. And they can have up to three organic ingredients in the ingredients statement on the side of the panel, where the ingredients are listed.

But they're not considered to be complete organic products, because they have a good portion of the ingredients that go into the product as not organic.

Then, below 70 percent is, I believe, you're not allowed to even mention the word organic on the front of the panel, although you may include ingredients on the side panel under the ingredient panel that may have an organic sugar or some other ingredient that might be organic, but it doesn't reach the level of 70 percent of the ingredients or more.

This brings us to the whole topic of integrity in the system, integrity of the farmer, and the trust level that the consumer puts into the products that they buy. If you're shopping at a farmers market, often those products will not be wrapped with an organic label. They won't have an organic bag holding them together, or a bag that says organic. Instead, you're really relying on the farmer to explain the method they use in growing fertilizer, which most often, in the case of organic growing, should be a manure of some kind, a manure from animals that haven't been eating on pasture grasses that have been sprayed with pesticides and herbicides, or chemical fertilizers, and so you're trusting really that the farmer is doing the right thing by getting to know that farmer. And by spending time on the farm talking with the farmer, with others who have known the farmer for a long time, that's really the best way, I think. In my own experience, I'm a member of a CSA here in the Valley, have been for ten plus years. My kids have celebrated birthday parties, running through the hay maze built by good old Farmer Erick, and we love it. We know what our farmer does, what methods our farmer uses. We completely support those methods, and trust him. I hate even to use the word "trust", because it implies that you could be fooled. When you know the farmer, you don't have that worry. And so I don't have the worry about that. And I think that's one of the most satisfying aspects of becoming a member of a local CSA or getting to know your farmer at a local farmers market is not having that worry; having that innate trust, really, through relationship and through community, not through regulation.

This is the reason why a USDA organic seal is an important part of our life. And what it represents is a certain amount of regulation and certification and procedure, really, that is strictly followed and monitored, in place of the relationship. It becomes the relationship, really, for the average consumer. And I'm not talking the average consumer who buys at a local farmers market. I'm talking about the consumer who buys at their local grocery store, one of the grocery stores that has 2,000 stores around the country. And the average consumer doesn't know where the product comes from in that store. They certainly don't know the farmers that grew the product, so they have to rely on other things, and those others things are the USDA seal and what it represents. That's a good thing. Without that seal, there wouldn't be a way to identify those products. I think there would be a far greater amount of fraud in the industry, and I think right now there's very little. I can't say none, because there's always room for that, but very little fraud or unethical behavior. And I think the government brings that sense of trust to a product that carries the USDA organic seal, and that's a good thing for the consumer. A consumer that shops at the local grocery store has to have a way to buy good product—"good" meaning clean product, organic product—and have a certain level of trust and understanding that that product has met the standards necessary to be called organic. I think that's a good thing. Not every consumer is looking for organic product, but a lot of consumers are, and I think it's an industry that will continue to grow. I think that it will grow for many reasons: I think as people become more educated about the food they eat, and especially as they have kids, and I think that new moms are the most concerned, and sometimes the most informed about the food they buy, they're certainly looking for organic product, and they need to have *a* level of trust in the product that they're buying, whether that level of trust is from the government through the seal, or through their local farmer, depending on their own shopping habits.

The idealist in me would like to think that we'll go more and more toward knowing your farmer. But the fact is, is that when we have 8 or 10 or 12 million people living in cities like Los Angeles and New York and Chicago and others, all of those people aren't going to get to know their farmer. So the reality is, for the vast majority of people, that's not going to happen. That doesn't mean that vast majority of people don't have access to organic food, because they do if they choose to. They can buy organic food at their grocery store. The Safeways of the world carry organic lettuce and organic broccoli and organic apples, *and* those consumers have power to influence what those stores carry, by requesting it. I think that it's sad that the average consumer really doesn't know the power they have. They have the power to direct what a big, big company will do, by simply asking for it. The power of the consumer is far greater than the power of the salesperson, because the consumer pulls the produce through, and the salesperson pushes the product through, and they're two different points of view. Having said that, I think that the local farmers market, the local farm, the local CSA is here to stay. I think it's going to become bigger, although on the big scale of things, it's still a small part of food distribution in the country, and probably will remain so, realistically. But it won't go away. I think that as time goes on—and I mean five years from now, and ten, and twenty, and fifty years from now—what's unfortunate, I think, is that we're going to see more and more negative results of the way the vast majority of our food is being grown and consumed. We're going to see.... Heck, I was reading an article today about antibiotics in meat. One of the reasons I don't eat meat from long ago, although if I was to eat meat, I would certainly eat organic meat for many reasons, humane animal treatment for one, but antibiotics and growth hormones certainly also.

I think that the negative results, the depletion of the water table, the pollution of the water table through pesticides and herbicides, the strains of diseases that are antibiotic resistant because of overuse, extreme use, of antibiotics in virtually all animals grown for human consumption, with the exception of the relative few that are grown organically, all of those things I think we're probably at the very tip of the iceberg in terms of negative effects. And I think that those negatives effects are going to multiply probably exponentially as time goes on. We're going to see a little bit here and there. Then five years later, there's going to be a body of evidence. And then ten years and twenty years later, there's going to be a *massive* body of evidence. The real question in my mind is whether or not, as a society, we will be able to overcome the forces of industry that are intent on suppressing that kind of negative information from the public. That comes full circle back to my political views. I think it's unfortunate that our politics today are dominated by money, and that money is the root of all evil, as they say, and it is certainly true in politics. We see that in almost every piece of legislation these days, where it is crafted not for the benefit of the consumer or the public, but rather for the benefit of the corporation. That's not to say that corporations are bad, or that business is bad. Heck, I *work* for a business, and it's a good thing, and I've got a good job, and I enjoy what I'm doing, and I hope to keep it and retire at this job. But there are corporations out there: name dropping, the Monsantos of the world, that are intent on controlling 100 percent of the seed in the world. And if you don't use Monsanto seed, you are taken to court and prosecuted and you go to jail! And that's GMO seed; it's certainly not organic seed. It's the Archer Daniels Midlands that have a *huge* investment in high-fructose corn syrup. And if you look at almost any ingredient in any grocery store on any package, one of the first ingredients is high-fructose corn syrup, which harms society in many ways, let alone the obesity problem, but all the way down to the soil. High-fructose corn syrup means growing millions and millions of acres of nothing but corn, and spraying those fields with pesticides and herbicides which harm the water table and deprive the land of biodiversity and any life, really, whatsoever, with the exception of that corn. Those fields have no bugs in them, no good bugs in them, nothing! They're dead! With the exception of the corn that's growing by the use of fertilizer. Those things are very negative impacts on society, and those industries that control those aspects of the food in our society have a very big investment in keeping all of that knowledge from the greater society. So I think that it's an uphill struggle. I think that each of us can do our part. In many ways it's a small part, but it's our choice. And I've said to many consumers walking the grocery store aisles as I do my job, just to vote with their dollar. And really, I think to a large degree, without walking in the streets in protest, that's the best thing that the consumer can do as an individual, is to vote with the dollar. And what that means is, choose to spend your dollar wisely. Choose where you're going to spend your dollar, whether that be on organic clothing, whether that be on organic produce, or organic milk, or whatever the product is, by becoming knowledgeable and educated about how you're spending your dollar, you are choosing to support those things that are important to you, as opposed to blindly spending a dollar and having it go, even without your knowledge, to a place that may end up harming you in the long run. If you don't educate as a consumer, if one doesn't educate themselves about where that dollar goes, they may be spending that dollar and having it go to a very, very large, multi-national corporation that is either raping the land or polluting the water or controlling the seed and preventing diversity in the worldwide food supply. And so the way I look at it is, as an individual I choose to vote with my dollar. If there were ten individuals like me, it would have a bigger impact. And if there were a hundred or a thousand or a million or 300 million, like in the United States, it would have a huge impact, and we all have to take that first step on a very long journey. And that first step is changing the way we as individuals purchase products, and hope to convince others to do the same.

  I am hopeful. It all comes full circle to my religious views. You know, my view of life is that we are here for a very relatively short period of time, and that when we're gone, we're gone. And when I'm gone, the next day everybody else is still gonna get up and go to work, and they may have remembrance of me in one way or another, I hope, and I hope positively. And so the greatest impact that I can have in life, not knowing if there is anything beyond my life, is to have a positive influence on the people around me, and the land, and my choices throughout my life—especially with my own family and my kids—helping to educate them to do the right things and relating to food, to eat properly and to get to know their farmer like I've gotten to know mine. I guess I have an overall optimistic view of life and society in general, but there are very strong forces out there against the need for knowledge in our society about good clean food. The way to do it is through grassroots and the individual effort and then in a small way through companies like the one I work for in trying to educate a larger community, a larger community of buyers at grocery store level, of consumers through literature that we provide at stores, and farm tours that we take people on—little things, really—little things that we hope spread.

  You know, it's not that I'm not hopeful, because I am. It would be sad to go through life unhopeful and as a pessimist, and I don't do that and I don't want to do that. But as a realist, and as a realist coming from a different point of view, from a business point of view, having experienced firsthand many of the barriers that I've talked about here, even simple barriers like getting a grocery chain to pick up a very high-quality and desirable product that we might come out with. It's difficult for the simple reason that a conventional grocery company pays more money to the grocer, to put their product on the shelf, and I can't afford to do that, because we're a relatively small business, all things considered. So I know there are barriers out there. I think we just need to continue to try to work through them, and we'll do that.

USDA—Regulations for Labeling and Market Information for "Organic" Products, Organic Food Production Act, amended, 2005

The ACT provides that a person may sell or label an agricultural product as organically produced only if the product has been produced and handled in accordance with provisions of the ACT and these regulations. This subpart sets forth labeling requirements for organic agricultural products and products with organic ingredients based on their percentage of organic composition.........Four categories of organic content are established: 100 percent organic; 95 percent or more organic; 70 to 95 percent organic; and less than 70 percent organic.

100 Percent Organic: For labeling and market information purposes, this regulation allows a "100 percent organic" label on: (1) agricultural products that are composed of a single ingredient such as raw, organically produced fruits and vegetables and (2) products composed of two or more organically produced ingredients, provided that the individual ingredients are, themselves, wholly organic and produced without any nonorganic ingredients or additives. Only processing aids which are, themselves, organically produced, may be used in the production of products labeled "100 percent organic".

Organic: Products labeled or represented as "organic" must contain, by weight (excluding water and salt), at least 95 percent organically produced raw or processed agricultural product......Up to 5 percent of the ingredients may be nonagricultural substances (consistent with the National List) and, if not commercially available in organic form, nonorganic agricultural products and ingredients in minor amounts (hereinafter referred to as minor ingredients—spices, flavors, colorings, oils, vitamins, minerals, accessory nutrients, incidental food additives). The nonorganic ingredients must not be produced using excluded methods, sewage sludge, or ionizing radiation.

Made with Organic Ingredients: Multi-ingredient products containing by weight or fluid volume (excluding water and salt) between 75 and 95 percent organic agricultural ingredients may be labeled or represented as "made with organic (specified ingredients or food groups)". By "specified", we mean the named of the agricultural product(s) or food group(s) forming the organic ingredient(s). Up to three organically produced ingredients or food groups may be named in the phrase. The following food groups may be labled as organically produced: beans, fish, fruits, grains, herbs, meats, nuts, oils, poultry, seeds, spices, sweeteners, and vegetables. In addition, processed milk products (butter, cheese, yogurt, milk, sour creams, etc.) also may be identified as a "milk products" group.

Product With Less Than 70 Percent Organic Ingredients: These are multi-ingredient products with less than 70 percent organic ingredients (by weight or fluid volume, excluding water and salt). Nonorganic ingredients may be produced, handled and assembled without regard to these regulations (using prohibited substances and prohibited production and handling practices). Products that fail to meet the requirements for one labeling category may be eligible for a lower labeling category. For example, if a product contains wholly organic ingredients but the product formulation requires a processing aid or less than 5 percent of a minor ingredient that does exist in organic form, the product cannot be labeled "100 percent organic" and must be labeled as "organic". If a multi-ingredient product is 95 percent or more organic but contains a prohibited substance in the remaining 5 percent, the product cannot be labeled as "organic", because of the presence of the prohibited substance, but may be labeled as a "made with...." product. Further, a handler who produces a "100 percent organic" product but chooses not to be certified under this program may only display the organic percentage on the information panel and label the ingredients as "organic" on the ingredient statement.

National Organic Food Production Act, 1990, amended, 2005

4 February 2010

Judy Neldham
Owner
Grange Cafe'
Duvall, WA

I'm Judy Neldham, born July 17, 1953 in Stockton, California. I grew up in a suburb of San Francisco called Moraga, and so I lived a pretty suburban lifestyle growing up. My dad worked in San Francisco, he was a salesman. My mom was a stay-at-home mom for most of her life. She went back and completed her degree at UC-Berkeley later on. I attended the same university as my brother, University of California at Davis. Graduated with a degree in human development, with the idea that I'd become a teacher, which I did not do. I also studied communications at San Francisco State University for a year, and then just ended up working in various jobs, particularly in sales jobs. I married a baker, so ended up both of us selling bakery equipment, and one thing led to another, and we ended up starting our own retail bakery. My husband's family has owned a retail bakery in Oakland, California, for three generations. It's just about ready, unfortunately, to probably close, though. The business was opened in 1929, and this might be its last year, actually. It's still run by my husband's cousin.

So we ended up moving up here for work, selling bakery equipment in Washington. We both lived in Bellevue for twenty years, raised four kids, and then moved out to Duvall just about three years ago to start the Grange Café and to be closer to my brother, Luke, and Sarah and Pearl. So that's where we got where we are.

My mom was a great gardener always when we were kids, so I grew up with the idea of having a garden always in your back yard. But it was really through my relationship with my brother that I began to understand the differences between local organic agriculture and industrial agriculture. I felt like I was pretty typical of an American mom as recently as five years ago, not really understanding food additives and the dangers of different ingredients in processed foods. And my brother was sort of quietly bonking me over the head, trying to get me to become more aware. We were on a budget, like a lot of people are, and not really thinking about the fact that food could be unsafe. And I think a lot of Americans tend to believe that if it's government regulated that that means somehow that it's safe and clean. Probably four years ago, when we decided that we were going to go into starting this restaurant, I had really started to examine a lot of the issues that my brother was bringing up with me. I started to do more reading. And then I went to Quillisascut, which is a farm in Rice, Washington, that does a farm education program. Well, my brother actually bought that for me for my birthday.

It was a good thing. So I took my daughter with me, and we went there for a week. It was designed for culinary professionals mostly, and since we were beginning the restaurant, Luke thought that would be a great experience for me. And it turned out to be probably the most transforming experience that I'd had to that point in my life. We were on a farm, a working farm with goats. So Day One we wake up at 6 a.m. and they've recently slaughtered a lamb, and we went through the whole process of quote unquote, "humane slaughter". But just looking at an animal, we went through the breakdown process in the kitchen. We really lived farm life. So we worked in the garden, we baked bread, we did a number of field trips to local orchards and other farms in the Valley. We planned meals every day together, ate at a communal table at night, and then after dinner talked about food politics; particularly geared towards Washington. So we talked a lot about apples and the history of apples and what happened with apples in the state. I can't even explain what it was. A lot of people go there and say the same thing, that you go there with one idea, but that five or six days spent really experiencing organic life, tending to the compost pile every day, and getting the eggs and making cheese and making bread—it just renewed.... Renewed is the wrong word, because at that point I wasn't as committed. But it really committed me to local agriculture. I think it was just like the light bulb went off. And so for me, I came back with a clarity about what my brother was talking about—finally. So that was a great moment.

It's called Quillisascut Farm School, but it's a working farm, so they do a variety of different programs: some for nonprofessionals, students, teachers. They probably have ten classes a year, I imagine. The culinary instructor there is also an instructor in Seattle—Central Culinary—but she's published a handbook called "*The Sustainable Kitchen*". Oh, that was another part of it that was really enlightening, was water and learning about water use. When you end up coming into a restaurant like I did, that's probably one of the main areas where you see tremendous waste, is washing dishes. I learned a lot about how to be more effective at controlling water and using water properly. But anyway, when we came back, we opened the restaurant, and I think at that moment I felt that everyone had an awareness, like me, of the importance of local food, the importance of organic food, and the problems with our industrial agriculture system. And I quickly learned that that was not true. And so we've struggled to do our restaurant, to try to stay as true to our local theme as we possibly can.

I think price is one of the major obstacles for the local food and organic food movement. It's a little more expensive, it's harder to do, and yet food too has been turned into such a commodity that everybody relates to.... Food, they think, has to be cheap. They look at the $1 hamburger, the $5 sub that's twenty-four inches long. Everything is geared to that low price point. Food isn't a nutrient, it is a commodity. I'm a member of the Chamber of Commerce in Duvall, and so one of my lines now for people is, "When you look at a dollar hamburger, ask yourself the question why does it cost a dollar? And do you want to eat a $1 hamburger?" Because I think most people don't really think about what they eat, surprisingly, even though it becomes a part of them. They think a lot more about buying a television set, or the shoes on their feet. And they'll invest in those things, but investing in their food is not high on the list of, I would say, average Americans right now. The cheap food is. And our cheap food being subsidized by the U.S. government, factory farms, and people don't understand what the cost of that food is, or the cost to our water or our air, our economy, in the long term. So slowly, slowly, slowly, we worked to create a menu.

We worked to work the cost out of it, in order to make us more accessible.

We want people to be able—everyone really—to be able to come into the Grange and talk to us about what we do. And yet we don't want to come off like zealots either, or that somehow what we're doing is better than what everybody else is doing—although we do think it is. All those things. In certain communities there's still a fear of the unknown and organic, sort of hippie.... I even had one woman come in and say, "This isn't that *organic* food is it?" We really discovered there's a lack of information, a lack of good information, about food—because our government wants it that way, I think. They prevent a lot of information from coming to consumers, and that's a real problem, because Europeans know what GMO products are, and have the choice whether or not to buy them or not. Here the only way you can talk about GMO is if you don't have it, and you have to disclaim it. So we do everything sort of opposite to what's reasonable. So it ups the bar for people who are doing organics and local food. But because it becomes such a meaningful part of your life, I've accepted that, and I'm just willing to accept the pace that this is going. Besides the restaurant, I'm working with other groups, where I spend a lot of time with people that are more like me. I get satisfaction from doing the restaurant, but it's hard, at the same time. I think a lot of people who are involved would tell you that. The most common complaint is, "Why are you so expensive?" And I'll say, "Well, we have pasture finished beef in this hamburger. We made the bun ourselves, with organic flour. We made the aioli ourselves. The potatoes on that plate came from Full Circle Farm." I mean, it's a completely 100 percent handcrafted hamburger with organic, organic, organic. And that resonates with some people, and not as much with others. And that's kind of sad, because if it's all.... It's hard to be all about price. We feel we have a great relationship with our community, and know our farmers, and we want people to feel the same kind of satisfaction that *we* feel, being involved with all these people. So it's just a work in progress.

I'm not sure if there is one strategy—but mostly to be low key about it, and not be too hard core, and try not to act like I know something that you don't know. But to just guide people toward reading for themselves, and self discovery. Now there's a lot more, I think, in the mainstream media. Like *Time* magazine recently wrote a cover piece about the *real* cost of cheap food. There are a lot of social networking sites that people go on, and they review restaurants. And restaurant owners hate them because people hide anonymously and take really cheap shots at people who are working really hard. And so one fellow recently *really* came out after us. But one of the consistent things in all of his reviews was, "It's a nice place, too expensive, too expensive." So you can contact people like that directly. So I contacted him and I sent him a link to "The Real Cost of Cheap Food." Didn't say anything other than, "You might want to read this." Our goal is for people to understand that food is about health, and food is a nutrient, it's not a commodity. That shift in consciousness has not taken place yet. And our whole healthcare system is in chaos because of the fact that either through willful ignorance—I don't know if it's willful ignorance—it's ignorance—that we're poisoning ourselves and we're killing ourselves, and we're creating all of this manmade illness through our food supply, which is costing the economy hundreds of millions of dollars. And although corporatism or corporate capitalism is one of the problems, the other problem is Americans not eating properly, not getting outside, not eating fresh food. So we're to blame somewhat too, for health issues.

Will Allen said, "We all have food in common. Everybody eats." And so his approach with his organization is soft sell. It's quietly, unaggressively, trying to get that message out. And so I think that the approach we've tried to take is just keep repeating what we're doing, and little by little, people seem interested, to talk to them more about it, to direct them to other sources where they can read more about it, to become involved. We've started a slow food group in the Snoqualmie Valley. It's great! It's not very big. I mean, there's kind of a small group of people that come. But some of our events have been pretty big. So Labor Day we probably had sixty people.

Slow food is the opposite of fast food. But the organization was started, I think, more than twenty or thirty years ago in Italy by.... I can't remember his name, but he was fighting against McDonald's Corporation opening a McDonald's on the Spanish Steps in Rome. And my daughter actually was in school in Rome through the University of Washington, and so that was my first introduction to slow food, because the students there, architecture students were designing slow food eateries in the United States when they came back. And so when I came back from being there—this is maybe six years ago—my brother Luke gave me the book "*Slow Food*". Very boring, but I got all the way through it. Just basically the organization supports people eating at home, or dining home, but dining slowly with friends, incorporating the mealtime into social life, and looking at where you grow your food. There are multiple areas that slow food is concentrating on: reviving old food traditions, and heirloom products, heirloom vegetables and meats. They've developed the arc of taste to kind of reintroduce younger people to older foods that they may have not seen before, but that their grandparents might know about. Basically we just get together and we do potlucks. We cook from our garden when we can, and talk about what we like to eat. It's just food 'n' fun, more than anything. Not *too* hard core.

Duvall is extremely eclectic, and we see ourselves.... We have this great building, the grange, which of course is in the original grange hall, which was a farm organization. So we have this wonderful heritage already built into the walls of our building. And we have this great building, which for whatever reason—and it demonstrates itself to me every day—that makes people happy. People come in there, even people that are kind of stiff and uptight, and they sit in The Grange for a while, and they relax. They just enjoy themselves more. I have a perfect example: I had a guy there today who's had numerous business meetings that he's booked with me, and he's kind of a certain type guy. He works for the pharmaceutical industry. At first he wasn't very friendly to me, and kind of little by little he's warmer and warmer. And today he left like he was a good friend of mine.

So I feel like we've got this great building, we're doing a lot of things besides our restaurant which is sort of the focus. But we've got community theater going on upstairs. We have community dances. We had our first square dance in December. We've got art, Celtic music every week. We're not getting the community in through maybe the food right away. We're getting them through music, through art, performance. During the art walk we had *really* outstanding performance artists. So I think over time.... These are all integral parts of getting everybody in Duvall—and we won't get everybody. We won't get everybody. There's Microsoft people, there's artists and hippies and off-the-gridders, and kind of rednecks, and everybody. So I think there's some parts of our neighborhood that have suspicion about us. But if we get 'em in, that suspicion kind of goes away. And I think that's our goal, is to open our place up enough, that enough people come in and have the community experience at The Grange, through either food or music or lecture or canning or whatever it is, and eventually that will bring them to the local food community. The whole local experience is what we're trying to be about. It started with just food, and then it's gone way beyond that.

Charlie's Produce is the largest produce supplier in this area, and they're actually dedicating themselves to local farming a lot more than they used to be, because we've been customers of Charlie's for years over in Seattle. They couldn't really tell you where things came from. So when we started asking, they wouldn't know. I mean, your tomatoes one week, you're getting tomatoes, could be from Mexico, they could be from California, they could be from *Holland*, believe it or not, we found out one time. So Charlie's has started to listen to their customers and they're becoming more actively involved. I'm not necessarily a free-market capitalist, but there are certain things that are market driven, and the more people that want to know where their food is from, even places in big companies like QFC, will start responding to that. And of course PCC does an outstanding job. My concern, and I don't want to be *so* negative, but is that people use that to attract people in, rather than legitimately supporting it. And they're the really legitimate supporters of local, like PCC. I don't want to classify and call something legitimate and illegitimate, but you've got Whole Foods, who's come in, with sort of a less sincere approach, but still overall.... I guess you make choices in this, because if somebody's supporting organic, even though you consider it kind of insincere, it's probably not wise to make a value judgment about it, but just be happy that people are getting organic food—it doesn't really matter *why*—but that they are.

Here we have cities in decay. We've got an economy that's floundering. But we could *re*create, in our cities, urban areas, our own local food supply, and people could be employed *and* healthy. And out of kind of the ashes of all these ruined manufacturing facilities that have gone over to China, we could rebuild something more significant.

It's great to be a part of your community and meet your farmer, and support somebody in your own community, and that dollar is probably going to come back and be spent at the local market, and everyone's going to start exchanging dollars and you'll get more value for those dollars. But also, it could be one of the tools to rebuild our economy. And right now we have this massively inefficient and ineffective industrial agriculture system, which really hasn't achieved any of the goals it set out to do. Instead, it's robbed the soil of all of its nutrients. It has to be subsidized to stay in existence. And fresh food is not getting back to people the way it should be. I don't know if I believe exactly that all things happen for a reason, but the economic downturn, and some of the things that are happening, may actually enable local agriculture to develop at a faster pace.

What is it that prevents somebody maybe, would be my question. What is it about organic? I think a lot of times it's price. Okay, well is food important to you? There are a lot of people that don't really understand that a constant diet of Big Macs can kill you. Once people start making connections, maybe through becoming ill themselves, or through the government finally—the national health system does decide that there's money in prevention—the government would get involved on a larger scale. But I don't see that as happening any time. I think this has all got to be really grassroots, because the money in America is keeping people sick, I think. I mean, it's heartless to say that, but it's in treating people who are ill, and not keeping them healthy. So if you grow your own food—or you grow your own pot for whatever ailments.... I mean, I just think there's a lot of things that are going on in the United States that are counterproductive to people's health and well being, because they're not profitable to the powers that control our government right now. That's the way I look at it. So we've got a real political problem in the U.S. that has stood in the way of information. It's been a huge barrier for people to understand. It's like high fructose corn syrup. You can still call a product natural that has a very unnatural sugar in it. So what's the definition of natural then? It's meaningless.

If Wal-Mart's able to supply organic milk, it's not organic milk anymore, because there just isn't the kind of quantity yet of true organic milk product that's being produced in the United States to supply Wal-Mart. So there has to be something behind that. And that's the battle, is the corporate giant trying to take advantage of this movement to manipulate people, to sell them something that isn't true, get more money for it, and rip them off so to speak—for lack of a better word. I think American consumers are getting ripped off daily with organic labels, because lobbyists are able to do anything they want. I mean, it *seems* like that now, even with Obama. As frightening as that is. It just doesn't seem like *anything's* changed.

I have optimism about the future when I go to events like I went to last night. And then sometimes I have—it's sort of like side by side. In fact, I made a joke to my husband last night when we were in this—it was probably hundreds of people sitting in this auditorium, and I said, "We're probably all the people that will be in prison together if there's this right-wing takeover of America." You can take that part out. At some point we'd probably be the food terrorists. We would become the food terrorists in this country, because you can make everything—what's white is black, and with the right kind of warped message machine you can make anybody the bad guy. And so suddenly organic growers could become bad for America or something, instead of good.

It's *completely* backwards, the people's understanding—or people like that. That's core ignorance about our food supply. It's funny, they fear government, they don't want government telling them what to do, but then they believe the government's actually going to care about food safety. I think we're kind of headed for this major collapse in America, and so it's probably having local food supplies, and strong local communities would be the one way to survive all that. Because I just don't see how it can keep going the way it is. I'm very political. I'm less so probably today than I was a year ago, because I feel sort of disappointed at a core level in government, and democrats, and what is a democrat? What's a Republican? What's the difference? So I just assumed, sort of like I did with—digressing here—with local foods and doing the restaurant—that once we opened the doors, it would just sort of be this easy transition into everybody getting it. I have the same thoughts about, "Oh, now that Obama's elected, and the majority in both houses, everything's gonna be great!" And here we are....

I think at this point, is the country so controlled by corporate interests that change has now become impossible. And there's that appearance right now that that's the case. And that people can spend billions of dollars to maintain the status quo, and to *keep* information away from people. And so from a survival standpoint, I think being a locavore is a good thing—a locavore—that's kind of a buzz word. But if you did live in a community, you might not be able to make your own shoes, you'd just have to wear your shoes longer. But you could make your own clothes probably, and feed yourself. And we could do a lot to generate our own energy. And people in Washington could help the resources to be much more self-sufficient than a lot of other parts of the country.

I came from an open-minded place to begin with. I was always a liberal—not that I understand exactly what that means right now. So I've kind of gone through life with my eyes open, waiting to learn new things, and wanting to learn new things. So I think change is possible. With people like me, this whole thing is becoming important again. It's so funny, we're not going forward, we're going backward, to try to recover our lives again. This is like with the way my mom grew up. You save everything, you recycle everything. I grew up with rubber band balls and drawers full of plastic bags that you reuse until they fall apart. Hanging the laundry out. Everyone had a clothesline. I'm old enough to have been raised by a Depression-era parent who.... I grew up with seasonal food. My uncle was an orchardist. He had Bartlett pears mostly. I remember knowing exactly when apricots were in season in California; when we knocked the walnuts; when we knocked the almonds. We had a lot of agricultural experiences, even as city kids. I always canned with my mom. So there was then kind of the generation after mine, I think a lot of that through the industrialization or the sort of rapid industrialization of the food supply has kind of taken a lot of that out. And people moving more into cities, and not growing gardens. And now it's coming back more, which is good. And so now you look at your grandmother and think, "Wow, look at all the things she knows! She can sew!" My mom can do anything. And that's because she learned how to bake from scratch. She doesn't grind her own flour or anything, but I'm sure if I said, "Let's try it!" she'd say, "Sure! Let's do it! I can do that!"

So I'm entering this new time with a sense of some excitement because I am more involved. Well, I'm actually *deeply* involved in local food. And it's kind of a race for time, sometimes I think, and I hope that we can get there fast enough, before the collapse. And my brother, for a young guy he's pretty wise, because he says, "Just do what you can do, and be satisfied with that. I'm here as a farmer...." He doesn't watch the news too much—kind of peripherally. He votes, he knows what's going on, but he's not like looking at the Internet every day. If you spend too much time fretting, it's just counterproductive.

At the Grange we have a chalkboard up. It shows our farms on our menu. We let people know what we're buying. When we get something new in, we do like to tell people about it. So just word of mouth education. And we'll continue to do that. We're doing more community food activities, too, through the restaurant. And that, I think, is bringing more focus on what The Grange is about, but basically, too, what local food, and supporting local food is about. And that's where Slow Food and our meetings, we do most of our meetings at The Grange, our potlucks and the bigger events, at The Grange. I'm seeing the restaurant as just a part of everything we're doing, rather than the focus now—although it's important and it's helping to pay our bills. But now I see that as just one of the spokes in our wheel, that we're building lots of spokes, because our goal is really to engage our community. And through that process, part of that will become food and local food, as we draw together more and more as a community, through all the social activities everyone loves. Because everyone *does* love music, I think, and they do love good food, but they love art. I think that's what's really great, too, about Duvall and Carnation out here. We have a high appreciation for the arts. And people like community. I think we're lucky in that sense. We're very close, becoming closer all the time. I feel like I know way more people now, that I've met in the last two years, than in the last twenty-one that I spent in Bellevue. And that's great, because that's really the connections we're making through our restaurant, and through what we're trying to do with food, are the most lasting kind.

We have a standard menu, and then we have specials all the time. So right now it's not as great, because it's winter, and the only thing, we're getting intermittent raising greens, hardy greens are still growing, lots of potatoes, carrots, parsnips, beets. In Washington a lot of varieties of potatoes grow. So there's lots of choices with potatoes. And I'm not as versed in this as my brother would be. It'll still be months and months and months before we start coming into things like the sprouted broccoli. I don't remember all the things that come in first, but then salad greens will start coming in again. But now, after three years of doing this, I know, "Oh, my brother's going to have the purple sprouted broccoli, and it's so gorgeous, and it's so delicious!" And we just have it for a few weeks time. And then we're gonna have a certain green bean. And that experience in this restaurant is what I remember as a kid, being excited about food, because of the absence of it, and then the reappearance of it. At The Grange—rather than keeping the same things on the menu all the time, some things will appear at our restaurant in May, and something new in June, and something new in July. And then for people who are becoming more involved in that, like we are, it's an exciting time. So through our menu, we're introducing people to the seasons and what is growing here in *this* state. We do have a shorter growing season, and we fudge a little on what local is. We're still getting lemons and oranges from California, and some things like that. But basically letting people know about the bounty of our area and what grows here. I think a lot of people don't really realize that farmers are growing food that's actually in our restaurant. Like you can just drive down the road and watch these people.

I've worked with kids a little bit. We've done some projects with an elementary school teacher who did a student garden. They had their own harvest in their classroom garden. I met them at Oxbow Farm, and one of the guys there let them harvest raspberries and carrots, and then we came back to the restaurant, and our chef at that time did a cooking demonstration. We talked about all the things that we had, all the things from their garden, and then the things from Oxbow, and we put it all together and made this delicious salad. And these little five- and six-year-olds ate it all! They were so excited. I think that was so memorable, because little kids *love* to garden, and they love to dig carrots up, they love to pick raspberries. And to be able to keep that excitement about food through life, it's a tough challenge. But restaurants like ours, that's hopefully one of our goals, is to make people engaged in their food supply too, and excited by it, and excited by the fresh taste and the beautiful colors. I mean, just the idea of having a dairy now again in Duvall, we may be able to make cheese from cows that are just a mile down the road. And for me that's one of the really exciting parts of the restaurant, is little by little be able to introduce maybe more and more products as they become available.

Nowhere is the debate over the appropriate application of technology more polarized than in the field of biotechnology. Downplaying notions of population control and land reform, industry advocates push the idea that genetic engineering will solve world hunger. Despite altruistic rhetoric, genetic engineering companies design sterile crops to ensure that farmers—large agribusiness and subsistence farmers alike—must keep on buying their proprietary seeds. There was a time when prudent farmers kept their best seed stock for next year's crop. Now they get fined for doing so.

Despite the dramatically increased yields promised by industry, a study by the former director of the National Academy of Science's Board on Agriculture found that genetically modified soybean seeds produced smaller harvests than natural seeds when he analyzed more than eight thousand field trials. A USDA study found no overall reduction in pesticide use associated with genetically engineered crops, even though increased pest resistance is touted as a major advantage of crop engineering. Whereas the promise of greatly increased crop yields from genetic engineering has proven illusive, some fear that genetically modified genes that convey sterility could cross to nonproprietary crops, with catastrophic results.

Given the significant real and potential drawbacks of bioengineering and agrochemistry, alternative approaches deserve a closer look. Over the long run, intensive organic farming and other nonconventional methods may prove our best hope for maintaining food production in the face of population growth and continuing loss of agricultural land. In principle, intensive organic methods could even replace fertilizer-intensive agriculture once cheap fossil fuels are history.

....

Whatever we call it, today's organic farming combines conservation-minded methods with technology but does not use synthetic pesticides and fertilizers. Instead, organic farming relies on enhancing and building soil fertility by growing diversified crops, adding animal manure and green compost, and using natural pest control and crop rotation. Still, for a farm to survive in a market economy it must be profitable.

Long-term studies show that organic farming increases both energy efficiency and economic returns. Increasingly, the question appears not whether we can afford to go organic. Over the long term we simply can't afford not to, despite what agribusiness interests will argue. We can greatly improve conventional farming practices from both environmental and economic perspectives by adopting elements of organic technologies. Oddly, our government subsidizes conventional farming practices, whereas the market places a premium on organic produce. A number of recent studies report that organic farming methods not only retain soil fertility in the long term, but can prove cost effective in the short term.

....

As much as climate change, the demand for food will be a major driver of global environmental change throughout the coming decades. Over the past century, the effects of long-term soil erosion were masked by bringing new land under cultivation and developing fertilizers, pesticides, and crop varieties that compensate for declining soil productivity. However, the greatest benefits of such technological advances accrue in applications to deep, organic-rich topsoil. Agrotech fixes become progressively more difficult to maintain as soil thins because crop yields decline exponentially with soil loss. Coupled with the inevitable end of fossil-fuel-derived fertilizers, the ongoing loss of cropland and soil poses the problem of feeding a growing population from a shrinking land base. Whereas the effects of soil erosion can be temporarily offset with fertilizers and in some cases irrigation, the long-term productivity of the land cannot be maintained in the face of reduced soil organic matter, depleted soil biota, and thinning soil that so far have characterized industrial agriculture.

Many factors may contribute to ending a civilization, but an adequate supply of fertile soil is necessary to sustain one. Using up the soil and moving on to new land will not be a viable option for future generations. Will modern soil conservation efforts prove too little and too late, like those of ancient societies? Or will we relearn how to preserve agricultural soils as we use them even more intensively? Extending the life span of our civilization will require reshaping agriculture to respect the soil not as an input to an industrial process, but as the living foundation for material wealth. As odd as it may sound, civilization's survival depends on treating the soil as an investment, as a valuable inheritance rather than a commodity—as something other than dirt.

David R. Montgomery, "Dirt—The Erosion of Civilizations", University of California Press, 2007

21 December 2009

I'm David Montgomery, born in 1961, from Stanford, California originally, grew up there, and ended up gradually working my way up the West Coast, and now teach at the University of Washington, where I teach geomorphology in the Department of Earth and Space Sciences.

I was always fascinated with maps, since I was a kid; just sort of topography and land forms, navigating, hiking, that kind of stuff always interested me. But I was never actually exposed to any geology until I got to college. So I think I'd sort of had a topophilia from a young age, just very intrigued by topography, thought it was beautiful, loved to be outside, loved to hike. And quite literally maps, I think, are probably the thing that seduced me into being a geomorphologist. That, and then once I was exposed to geology and geomorphology in college, sort of solidified it. But in high school I was very interested in biology, because of the influence of a particular high school teacher who just got me absolutely fascinated with the world of organisms and how plants work. But once I got to college and realized that the biology program at Stanford was all about training pre-meds, I got completely turned off and discouraged and took a geology class and went, "Wow!" and headed off into geology.

How did I get into geomorphology from there? I think it was my junior year, maybe my senior year of college, I took an introductory geomorphology class, and it was fascinating. The ability to read topography, go outside and sort of look at land forms, look around the world and try to start piecing together the recent geologic history of what literally shaped the world around us, that really seduced me, I got very interested in it. And then once I finished college, as a geology major, I was wondering, "Okay, well what do I do now?!" And I got a job essentially working as a geologist for environmental consulting companies around the San Francisco Bay area. And what most of their business back in the early eighties involved was mapping areas where people were thinking of developing, and so you'd identify where are the faults, where are the landslides, what are sort of the constraints that people would be wise to recognize and deal with in that kind of work? And then also I did some work in zohydrogeology contaminants in the Santa Clara Valley. It's clean-up work on some of the big early industrial sites there. And just really had the chance to drill a lot of holes, dig a lot of trenches into hillsides all around northern California. And the patterns you see, they're interesting. What causes landslides? How they worked, how to interpret what you see, and connect sort of the geology,

David Montgomery
Professor
Geomorphology,
Department of Earth
and Space Sciences
University of Washington,
Seattle

the soils, and the way the water moved often through the landscape. It really started to fascinate me, and I decided to go back to grad school after a few years of that. And I was fortunate enough to be admitted to a program that had one of the best geomorphologists running it, and I got trained up pretty well.

What I started working on for my thesis in geomorphology is the problem where do stream channels begin? If you stand in a river and you walk up, and if you keep walking, just uphill in a river, eventually you're going to come to a mountaintop, right? What's the things that actually control where the transition from going from you're in a stream, you're in a river channel, until one, you're on a hillside? Where does that transition actually occur? I spent about five years working on that problem, walking lots of streams, mapping where those points are, and developing physics-based models to try and predict where they would be once you understood what the processes were that governed that handoff from hill slope to river channel.

So I spent years working on that, and then got a job working at the University of Washington, focused on the problems of how people change streams and rivers, and how that then influences salmon. So the way land use influences downstream things—and in particular salmon, because back in the early nineties, sort of interest in salmon conservation was what was driving a lot of applied geomorphology in the Pacific Northwest. Because people don't tend to care all that much, usually, about soil, dirt, rocks, and water for their own sake. Perhaps we should! But the problem of how people influence land, influenced things we really care about in rivers and streams, and things we like to eat and get out of them, was a source of a lot of research interest and funding. So I worked on trying to understand the dynamics in nature of stream channels and rivers in the Pacific Northwest; and how land use changes influences the movement of water and sediment and wood, and how that in turn influences the creation of habitat, which influences the abundance of salmon. I did a lot of work focusing on the connection between those, but also worked on other things like sediment transport after the eruption of large volcanic eruptions like at Mount Pinatubo.

What happens when a river's overloaded with sediment? How does it process it? As we saw at Mount St. Helen's as well. Or the problem of sediment transfer from the Andes to the Amazon. Half the sediment coming out the Andes never makes it out the mouth of the Amazon, so where does it go, where does it pile up? And the evolution of topography, what sculpts mountain hillsides? What limits the height to which mountains can rise? How do glaciers sort of trim off mountains and keep them only so big? The Cascades turn out to be a great example of that. So I've worked all over the world, from the tropics to the Himalayas to the Tibetan Plateau, and the Pacific Northwest, which is a *playground* for geomorphologists. Lots of active processes shaping the world: there's volcanoes, rivers, glaciers. The Northwest kind of has it all, in a small area. So for someone who works on the kinds of things that I do and tries to understand the forces shaping topography, it's a really nice place to be.

My book, "*Dirt*", started back when I was an undergrad. I read a book called "*Topsoil and Civilization*", which was written in the 1950s, and made a lot of the same points that I make in "*Dirt*" in terms of the importance of soil conservation. It's an issue that has cycled in and out of public awareness, by maybe fifty years or so, for the last couple hundred years. I read that book as an undergrad, was fascinated by it. It literally changed the way I look at the land. It gave me a fundamental appreciation for how important soils are to human societies. And I carried that around with me for twenty-five years. After "*King of Fish*", my first book, did well enough that I was thinking, "Okay, well, what am I gonna do for a second book?", I thought, "Okay, well why don't I update the argument about what is the importance of soils for human societies?", because it seemed like the issue had fallen off of sort of the public radar, and yet if you look at the problems facing humanity in the 21st century, the problem of soil conservation—and I would argue soil *restoration*—are two of the biggest issues facing us, but they're slow-fuse issues, they're ones that never quite seem to become the crisis du jour, because they happen so slowly that they're pretty easy to ignore year by year.

When I had first suggested the idea of writing *"Dirt"* to the publisher, the first response I got was, "You're gonna write a book about *dirt?!* You're crazy. Who's gonna want to read that? What are you talkin' about?!" But by the time *"King of Fish"* had done well, and people were like, "Okay, maybe this guy actually *can* make an interesting story out of dirt," and the interest in farming, and the interest in how we treat the land, and how that then in turn sets how long the land can support people, I think the time was ripe for people sort of *thinking* about the connections. And so when it came time to write that, and I proposed it to a publisher, it was found to have some strong interest.

If you look at soils the way a geologist does, and that's the sort of perspective that I come from, there's something.... They're created, they're destroyed, they're stored. I mean, you can view soil as a system, as much as an object. And when you look at a soil in a landscape, you're looking at a snapshot in time, the way a geologist sees it. So where'd it come from, where's it going to, how long will it be there? Those are the kind of questions that a geologist will bring to the table on it. Most people sort of view soils as something that doesn't change; topography is just part of the world. And there were arguments for *centuries* about whether the world was created with the topography it has today, because it forms so slowly that you don't really sort of think about it as a dynamic system, because over the course of our lifetimes, we just get to see a little tiny bit of the change. So it's like very few people view soils like they view their bank account.

I mean, you look at your bank account, you know you've got income, you know you've got expenses, and you know that if you spend money faster than you're making it, eventually your savings are going to be depleted. Well, soils are no different, it's the same kind of thing, except the income is essentially how fast that rocks break down and weather to form new soils and mix with living and dead stuff, biologic matter—because soils are sort of the interface between geology and biology. And they're also lost, they're eroded. If the pace at which they're eroded is balanced by the pace at which cells are made, you can essentially build and maintain a soil of some thickness on a hillside. But if they're eroded faster than they're replenished, eventually soils will thin, eventually their fertility will decline. And if you *make* soils faster than your erode them, you can *build* soils. So soils are a dynamic system, but most people don't view it that way, because they tend to change naturally fairly slowly.

In a natural system, it can take 500 to 1,000 years to make an inch of soil. People can make soil much faster with investments of labor and energy and organic matter, but nature does it very slowly. And so I became very interested in the problem of, if you view farming as an experiment, if you will, the way people change what's happening on the surface of the earth, you change the vegetation and start growing things for food, what happens in terms of the ability of the soil to maintain that activity over the long run? And turns out you can think about it in terms of two ways: one is physically maintaining the soil itself as a physical body; and if erosion happens faster than you're creating new soil, eventually you run out of it. And what's that time scale, how long does that take? This was something I was very interested in looking at. The other way to look at it is how long can you maintain soil fertility? And so when you think about sort of maintaining agricultural productivity, over the long run we've got to do both. We've got to maintain the soil itself, and we've got to maintain its fertility. You can think of them as sort of different tracks that are important to align and get both of them right. Because if we have farming practices that maintain soil fertility but end up losing the soil, we haven't gotten anywhere. And if we maintain the soil but lose its fertility, we haven't gotten anywhere over the long run.

So I started looking at the problem of agriculture and how to maintain it through the lens of those two aspects of the soils. And it turns out that the history of humanity viewed that way is a very interesting one, where the same tale essentially gets told and retold, society after society, because the changes happen slowly enough that people have not always learned the lessons. And it turns out that the way that people treat land, in the end really does, I would argue, set the time scale over which the land can sustain people. And if we expect the land to be able to take care of *us*, we've got to take care of the land. It really is that simple.

I think a big part is an issue of time scale. If somebody dropped a bomb in your neighborhood, that after it went off it took 200 years for the ripple to move through your neighborhood, you might ignore it, because you wouldn't notice it. It wouldn't be happening on a time scale that would be of immediate interest to you, whereas like a real bomb in real time, oh yeah, you'd duck and cover, hide—it's an immediate and obvious threat. I think that we have a very hard time as a species of recognizing the sort of slow, long-term threats, the systematic ones that play out little by little, but that have a direction to it that add up to big change, given enough time. And that's where I think that thinking like a geologist can help us *recognize* those problems, but we're almost hard wired as a species to sort of be in reactive mode, to deal with the crisis of the moment. And I think that was actually one of the things that made us very successful as organisms a long time ago. But ironically the ability to sort of respond quickly in the here and now—our short attention spans, which I'm guilty as anyone of having—really compromise our ability to understand, let alone act on the long sort of slow-burning problems and crises. And the problem of soil erosion and soil conservation is the poster child for the kind of long-term slow issues that we kind of know are gonna add up and hurt us in the long run, but is it gonna do it this year? You know, it's hard to motivate people about saving the soil when it's being eroded at a pace that globally averages out on the order of a millimeter a year. You know, your fingernails grow faster than that. And so how big a crisis is it? Well, it's a *huge* crisis if you look over the next hundred years. But if you look at the problem of securing food for *this* year, or in any given year, it may not rise to the top of the lists that trouble farmers or that compromise their ability to feed us all. And we grow enough food in the world today to feed everybody on the planet. The real question in terms of conserving soils is whether we'll be able to do that in a hundred years. And there's lots of opinions about where the tipping point might be. But if you think like a geologist and look out a hundred, two hundred years, there's really no doubt that we've gotta get it right this time. Or we're not gonna be able to feed everybody down the road.

I mean, the human population is rising, it's projected to go above 9 billion sometime mid-century. And whether it'll keep going or level off or come back down, and in what manner, it may do any of those things. It really is an open issue that's going to play out depending on sort of the socio, economic, and cultural evolution of humanity, and part of that can be managed quite consciously of what we want to set up in terms of the regulations, rules, sideboards, values that society is trying to offer, promote, and implement. And if you look at the amount of farmland that's available to feed a person today, globally, and you project out fifty years, even if we conserve all the farmland we have, if you double the human population, and take it up by 50 percent, go from 6 billion to 9 billion, if we don't make new farmland—and we're farming about everywhere on the planet that we could farm in a sustainable fashion over the long run as it is—although we're not farming them sustainably. But there's not whole new continents left to discover and turn into the next breadbasket of the world.

And so if the human population goes up by 50 percent....and we're already at about the limit of being able to produce enough food to feed everybody if we distribute it equitably, well, how are we gonna jack up the food production of that other 50 percent to cover the people who haven't been born yet? It's a real conundrum, and if you couple that with the problem that farming practices today, conventional farming practices today, degrade the soil, and that we're losing farmland at....at *any* rate would be an alarming pace, if you look forward fifty to a hundred years, because we're gonna need every scrap of fertile productive land that we can get to feed people down the road. But still, that's decades away. You know, there's the potential for it to play out, sort of the longest slow-running train wreck in human history, where you can see it coming. We've got the advantage of hindsight this time. But if you look fifty, a hundred years down the road, we're gonna need every scrap of farmland that we've got, in as fertile a condition as possible, to be able to feed the world.

The troubling thing about modern conventional agriculture in *my* mind is that we've gone through this exercise in the last century of essentially going from relying on native soil fertility, to relying on fertilizers that we add to soils, that essentially support large harvests. And there's a whole history of that, and motivation for it, but if you've looked at the way that we grow food today, and think about how we're gonna do it in a post-petroleum world.... We use an awful lot of fossil fuel to generate the energy that we use to crack the nitrogen that we use to make the nitrogen-based fertilizers that we use as a *substitute* for what used to be native soil fertility. What are we gonna do once energy becomes expensive enough that it would be very difficult to maintain that? And if somebody invents a radically clean, cheap, free source of energy, all kinds of problems are gonna be solved, potentially including this one. But if that's not the case, does it really make sense to essentially be relying on fossil fuels to produce fertilizers to grow our food in the future, when if we are to restore the world's soils, and actually try to rebuild the native soil fertility that can produce comparable crops, to conventional farming, we'd be in a much better position, a much more resilient position as a species and as a civilization, if we are to actually embrace the idea that we would try to grow our food based on a more ecologically grounded model. The problem, though, is that, of course, is called alternative agriculture these days—instead of conventional agriculture—which it used to be! And by that, I don't mean sort of going back to the Middle Ages to grow food, but relying on native soil fertility we can actually, using modern technology and modern understanding of soil ecology, grow comparable harvests of crops, using intensive organic methods as we can, using sort of intensive chemically-based agriculture. And that, I think, is the big challenge facing humanity in terms of how we farm, is trying to decide which of these paths we're going to go down, because fifty years, a hundred years out, it's really gonna matter, in terms of which one we're going be able to actually sustain.

The First World Conference on Climate Change was not exactly a resounding success, was it? It seemed like a terribly sad endorsement of business as usual at a time when we really need to reconsider and rethink some of the fundamental ways that we are living and acting on the planet. We've got a few decades to get it right.

The most frustrating thing about it is that many of the conventional arguments that are offered for *not* changing are pretty widely viewed within the communities that sort of know a lot about them, as sort of sham arguments: the idea that we don't really need to worry about human-induced climate change due to fossil fuels, sort of the "climate denier" argument. There's very few, if any, sort of credible scientists who really buy into that. It's quite transparently a political argument that's being made to obfuscate and delay doing things that actually *are* in our collective interest. The argument that reshaping the economy to sort of wean ourselves off of fossil fuels and onto newer energy sources, if you look at an economy and how to actually keep it healthy, the idea of infinite growth is an oxymoron. I mean, that's a recipe for having petri dish economics in which basically we consume everything on the planet and then we're done. That's not a very bright future to offer our descendants. But the idea of one that's based on change and turnover, more ecologically-based *idea* of economics, is one where you would view the opportunity to retool whole sectors of the economy and go from fossil fuel based to clean energy based, that's an economic opportunity. There'll be winners and losers in a game that's involved with change, but that's inherent to the idea of keeping it dynamic and viable. You've got to grow *new* businesses that will replace old ones, much in the way cars replaced horses and there were winners and losers in the early 20th century because of that. We need to do the same thing, again. And I simply don't understand the argument about how the economic cost of reducing our reliance on fossil fuels would be an economic disaster. To me it seems like the biggest economic opportunity we've seen in the last fifty years, because it would require redoing everything, and that means jobs! That means selling stuff and buying stuff! It means an economy! I just don't get that one.

And finally, the third sort of big misconception is that organic agriculture can't feed the world. I mean, if you look at the sort of crop yields you can get using intensive organic agriculture, it can compete with, or outcompete conventional agriculture. And there's tradeoffs, and some certain soils, some place, some crops, it might be a little less, might be a little more, but the idea that we can't feed the world with organic agriculture, which is the first thing you sort of hear agribusiness apologists essentially argue, has been shown to be essentially wrong in study after study after study, particularly if you're thinking about sustaining it over the long run, because organic agriculture is resilient. Fossil-fuel-based agriculture, viewed through the lens of decades to centuries out, is not resilient. And so how do you want to define our ability to feed the world? is an interesting question.

So those three big issues, I think, are ones that it's distressing to see the level of spin that's actually applied to them, when the choices we face in all three arenas are pretty clear when you view it fifty years out. And if you reverse engineer the kind of world....if you think about the kind of world you'd want to have, fifty, a hundred years out, and then trying to analyze what it would take to actually get there, it provides some pretty clear policy suggestions that are not the things that were adopted at the meeting.

I think it absolutely *is* a problem we could solve if we put our minds to it. The problem is that I think we like to argue too much, in terms of if you get a whole group of scientists saying, "Look, you put carbon dioxide into the atmosphere that you've taken from below the ground, it changes the carbon cycle on the planet, and one of the consequences of that is that the world will function more like a greenhouse and it'll get hotter." At that level, there's no argument! There's no argument to be had! The argument thing comes in, in terms of, "Well, what's that gonna mean in terms of what we need to do?" And at that point, different interests will get involved, and people are very good at arguing, and scientists are *experts* at it. It's what we're trained to do.

In some arenas, argumentation is a very constructive tool, because it can help you hone ideas, it can help you discover things. Argument is at the heart of science. But it's also at the heart of politics, and that's where it can—it doesn't always actually act as a force that sort of advances the interests of humanity, because it can be employed for those who quite simply don't want to *see* change, because they're doing quite well right now, thank you very much, as it is. You can't expect the oil companies to be supporting solar energy with all their heart and might and lucre.

I've given some talks out at farms and have been contacted by people who are very interested in the issue of organic farming and local food. The work that I did in putting together the book, "*Dirt*", and looking at the role of soil and its importance in the rise, course, and decline of human societies, I think really helps provide a philosophical foundation for why we need to go organic. And we really *do* need to take care of the soil that feeds us if we want to keep doing that indefinitely into the future, and that *is* the definition of sustainability. Then we really need to take care of it, because it is a system that can be squandered. It can be a system that can be invested in. It's a system that can be restored. I think that the sort of work in synthesizing the experience through history and the argument for why this is not just a crazy radical thing to do, but it's actually *essential* for humanity to do over the next century, is sort of where it lies.

I went to New Zealand a few weeks ago to give a series of talks for the New Zealand Organic Agriculture Association. I was really quite happy to hear some organic farmers there say, "Your book essentially provides the foundation, the reasons for why we do what we're doing—we just didn't realize it." I think a lot of people, and people who get into organic agriculture in particular—organic gardening *or* organic farming—realize that the soil's alive, it's a system, and it's the best avenue towards healthy, productive crops or a garden, is a healthy productive soil. The soil is one of the systems where its productivity really does come from the ground up, if you pardon the pun, where investing in soil life is the way to actually invest in a system that is disease resistant, is resilient, can continually produce abundant crops, with crop rotations and the appropriate kind of attention to maintaining the productivity of the soil. But the key really is a living, healthy soil.

This is the antithesis of the model that is now called conventional agriculture, in which the soil is treated effectively as a substrate to hold the plants up as we add the food that the plants need to grow. Well, plants don't *just* need nitrogen, phosphorus, and potassium. They need other elements from the soil as well, and those get depleted over the long run if we're not sort of promoting the ability of soil microorganisms and microrhizoli fungi to break down rocks and create essentially—bring new nutrients *into* the pool. This is not to downplay the importance of nitrogen, but there's a lot of other nutrients plants need as well. And the basic philosophy of treating soils as a substrate that we add stuff to, it's kind of large-scale hydroponics, but we're doing it outside and in the real dirt. Same kind of idea: you're adding the things that it takes to grow the plants, adding nutrients. That's not a terribly efficient way to deal with it, unless you've got an abundant, huge, cheap supply of energy, which we've had for the last century, in the form of fossil fuels. That era's coming to a close—at least has every indication of coming to a close.

But people are creative; we're a pretty ingenious species. Somebody might figure out a cheap, magic source of energy, and if so, hey, great, gimme some! But that may not happen. And if we treat soils as a living system that we can invest in to promote the activity and cycling, and that instead of viewing soils as a subject to *add* stuff to, we view soils as essentially a biological engine for producing new growth. Well, how do you feed that engine? You feed it by restoring life to the soil. You feed it by promoting the cycling, the turnover. You do it by promoting *life*.

And if there's one thing that I think this planet as a whole illustrates most eloquently, is that life supports life. I mean, there's the whole problem of nature tooth and claw. Things do eat each other. We eat plants, we eat other animals, but that process, that turnover, the cycling of things is essentially what gives rise to new life. And I think we'd be foolish as a species to miss that lesson in terms of our own sustenance. We really *should*, I think, go back to...we should reinvest in life to be able to support our *own* lives, as we become, as we are, the dominant life form on the planet. And I think as a species we're still struggling with that. We're still struggling with our relationship to nature, with our relationship to the *land*, with our relationship to the world and the universe. But if you think about which one of those we really need to get right, it's our relationship to the land, because *it* really is what sustains us. Half of humanity now lives in cities, so the real danger is if we become completely disconnected from the land, we might—that's not a recipe for making good decisions about sustaining civilization in the long run.

There's only a 40-day supply of food on the planet at any one time, and in most big cities, we have maybe a week's supply of food in town. And I'm probably being generous there. We're far closer to the edge than anyone *ever* wants to admit, because we rely on things, the continual recreation and flow and movement of goods—and food in particular—to actually keep us going. *And* the risk of that being a giant musical chairs game that stops all at once is admittedly really, really low, but the reality is, is that that *is* how we're living—sort of hand-to-mouth on the planet, as a species. And it's something that, given that, we should be *deeply* concerned with the resilience of our food supply, because we can't afford to have the music stop.

I've gotten very interested, in the course of writing "*Dirt*", in terms of issues of local food. My wife and I are working now on collaborating on a book about global soil restoration. And it's going to be part memoir about how she essentially restored our north Seattle yard and turned it into a very productive organic garden. And literally, as I was writing "*Dirt*", she was restoring the yard around me. And it kind of took me a while to figure out that, "Oh, wait a minute! She's showing me that we really can reverse this, and the beauty of the argument for soil restoration is that it can be done a lot faster than soil degradation is usually played out." I mean, it takes decades to centuries, usually, to sort of ruin agricultural land, but we can actually restore it pretty darned fast. It just takes changing the way we do things, paying attention to organic matter, cycling, paying attention to the life in the soil.

There's been some pretty degraded bits of land in both urban environments and on farms, that have been turned around in a decade. And to a geologist, a decade is like an instant (snaps fingers). That something could happen that fast and be that effective is....I'm tempted to call it a miracle, but it's not, it's just that's the way the world works, it can be done. And that's what gives me some hope for the idea that we could actually solve the problem of protecting the soil *this* time around, because there's a road map, we can see how to do it. Whether we'll do it, of course, is the big question.

Farm Journal

23 April 2010

Yesterday was the 40th Anniversary of Earth Day. I am, fortunately, old enough to remember and to have witnessed and participated in some of the efforts which have indeed changed American awareness of environment and its peril at our hands. I have also witnessed the steady swing of the political pendulum as it oscillates in response to the various economic and social pressures which have defined each of those ensuing decades since April, 1970 and their respective stances regarding government regulations of private behaviors in environmental practice. Much has improved (the Clean Air Act, wetland preserves, old growth timber protections, endangered species acts, etc.) but the deep, systemic problems remain unaddressed in any meaningful ways; population growth, depletion of renewable resources (water, soil and rainforests) as well as alternatives to non-renewables (oil and coal depletion and the resulting energy crisis) and by no means last or least, global warming and climate change. Denial remains as the presiding response despite political lip service paid during election years. We still appear to be losing our race with the environmental changes we have to a large extent precipitated. The long and short term future challenge will involve adaptation to the changes we cannot significantly correct and stabilization of those still within our control.

The recent International Summit on climate change demonstrated how difficult, if not impossible, a unified global response will be, and such a response is at this juncture probably the only sure and effective one we could make. All of the systemic corrections required cannot be achieved by one nation alone. Globalization of virtually all economic processes has finally preempted any nationalistic control; the boundaries between any one nation and the next are now so porous that the concepts of "nationhood" and "national interest" are absurd anachronisms. Whether we like it or not, we are indeed citizens of the world.

---

1. *The Great Ball on Which We Live*

The world is our home. It is also the home of many, many other children, some of whom live in far away lands. They are our world brothers and sisters......

2. *Food, Shelter, and Clothing*

What must any part of the world have in order to be a good home for man? What does every person need in order to live in comfort? Let us imagine that we are far out in the fields. The air is bitter cold and the wind is blowing. Snow is falling, and by and by it will turn into sleet and rain. We are almost naked. We have had nothing to eat and are suffering from hunger as well as cold. Suddenly the Queen of the Fairies floats down and offers us three wishes.

What shall we choose?
'I shall wish for food, because I am hungry,' says Peter.
'I shall choose clothes to keep out the cold,' says John.
'And I shall ask for a house to shelter me from the wind, the snow, and the rain,' says little Nell with a shiver.

Now everyone needs food, clothing, and shelter. The lives of most men on the earth are spent getting these things. In our travels we shall wish to learn what our world brothers and sisters eat, and where their food comes from. We shall wish to see the houses they dwell in and how they are built. We shall wish also to know what clothing they use to protect themselves from the heat and cold.

These are the opening sentences of "Around the World With the Children", by F.B. Carpenter, a third-grade geography textbook found by James Agee in the bedroom of the ten-year-old daughter of an Alabama Tenant farmer in 1936. The excerpt was reprinted as a "Preamble" in Agee's book, "Let us Now Praise Famous Men", which, in collaboration with the photographer, Walker Evans, is considered a masterpiece of Great Depression documentary work.

Epilogue
Somewhere Northeast of Eden
A Personal History

Since the bulk of the material in this book is presented in the form of oral history it seems only fair that I offer one of my own; that is, one side of my life story as it pertains to the central topic here—food—its sources, politics, ethics and its value. Most of all, it is my contribution to the embedded question in every story and answered by each story teller here, i.e.; "What should I eat?" And, after that; "Where does it come from, what's in it, is it good for me, and, how will I know?"

Equally vital is the odd presupposition that these are, in fact, necessary questions because, apparently, we do not, in any trustworthy way, know the answers. Our food industry is in question and our distance from those who produce, package and distribute our food is beyond easy access or conception. We are left to the assurances of the USDA, FDA and the supermarket.

In the course of working on this project, I have come to believe that eating, the act of putting the food in my mouth, is a political act; political in the sense that my act of eating speaks directly about my relationship to my community and ultimately has impact upon its future. Therefore, I now find it bizarre that most of my fellow citizens have no idea, not only as to the origin of the foods we eat, but also have no knowledge, in any meaningful way, about the people who produce it; what their lives are like, how they manage to make a living, what they think about food, and agriculture, or if they too are uncertain about their food. Moreover, when most Americans put that morsel of whatever in their mouths they have no sense of the massive web of human connections and interactions that brought it there nor do they consider any of those things at all before, during, or after dinner.

Finally, after this two-year journey into agriculture, I find the persistence of this ignorance in our society to be, at the very least, absurd, if not obscene; all the more so because it has become the accepted state of consciousness. Fear of poison only reinforces our preference to be dependent on corporate and government authority to guarantee our safety. We willingly abdicate our food responsibility and expect the FDA and the supermarket to act in our behalf. For most of us, "knowing" a farmer is at the outer limits of conception and/or capability. At best it is, like eating itself, a scheduling problem. And, all of the above exists within a society with access to an abundance of food unheard of in the history of the world.

Here then, is my personal history of eating; my journey from ignorance to the utter pleasure and joy of "knowing"—not only the names of those who grow the food I eat but who they are, where they live and what their farms have done for me.

....

My name is Jerry Mader. I was born in Great Falls, Montana on August 28, 1944.

In the fall of 1950, I entered 1st grade at Franklin Elementary School in that city and, the next spring, I received my First Communion at St. Joseph's Catholic Church six blocks from Franklin. Both buildings date from 1910 and both my parents went to school and church there. My father was born in 1902, my mother in 1905. The house I was born into and lived in until I graduated from Great Falls High School was located one block west of Franklin. Both my parents grew up in houses built by my grandfather one block west of there and next door to each other.

They, like me, walked to school every day and my father did so, my mother said, at a respectable distance behind her lest anyone see them walking together. Eventually, as the 'boy and girl next door', they walked together, became sweethearts and got married in 1924 in St. Joseph's Church. The next year they had a child, a girl, and the three of them lived through the 'Roaring Twenties' and the 'Great Depression' in a tiny house just three lots east on the same side of the street as the houses they'd grown up in. When I unexpectedly appeared in 1944, they had just moved into a new two-bedroom house across the alley. Eighteen years later, in the spring of my freshman year at college, my father died in the kitchen of that house; most of his 61 years lived within one square mile of neighborhood.

In my neighborhood on the Westside of Great Falls in 1950, there were no supermarkets. They began to appear around 1955 or so, one at a time and with mixed initial response. Instead, within the square mile of neighborhood there were three markets; two of a size large enough to supply us with the necessities for a healthy, by 1950s standards, diet.

My parents shopped at "Upp's Market" located six blocks from our house. It was owned and managed by Mr. Uppinghouse (I never knew his given name). My parents had credit at Upp's Market. Their budget only allowed so much a month for food and so Mr. Uppinghouse carried a running balance (no interest charged) which, when my railroad-man father got some overtime, they managed to pay off. It was a common arrangement then; all the families on the Westside were working class, all on budgets, all had a running grocery bill.

"Old Man Uppinghouse", as he was affectionately called, knew each family, their children, all by name, their current activities, and, most often, their more distant relatives, grandparents, etc., plus their family history in the neighborhood. Most of those families had lived there since the neighborhood was platted in the 1890s by the founding father of Great Falls, Paris Gibson. He had designed the city as a "New Minneapolis" on the wager that the Great Northern R.R. would run its main line there, at the famous Great Falls of the Missouri where Lewis and Clark had portaged around in the summer of 1805 on their way to the Pacific; still hopeful at that point for a NW Passage. Gibson's dream, like that of the explorers, was only partially realized.

The other store, "Noble's Mercantile", had more history as the first market on the Westside built near the railroad yards to supply workers' families during the first blush of immigrant occupation in the neighborhood. These were Polish and Russian workers, recruited by the railroad who found not the Main Line but a spur of the Great Northern built to serve the Anaconda Smelter and the Sand Coulee coal mines. James Hill ran the Main Line to the North, the Marias Pass an easier route over the continental divide.

Noble's Mercantile contained a Post Office, a dry goods section including shoes as well as a large supply of food staples, canned goods and meat. Built in 1900, its outer walls had already started to sag when I was a child and my mother told me stories about the landless Indians who came down from the plains and sat on the Mercantile porch in the afternoon when she was a girl and how "Old Man Noble" always put a few sacks of groceries by the front door for them when he closed up for the night.

We bought groceries on payday; every two weeks and that, apart from the occasional need for salt, butter and other minor items, was the extent of our shopping. On the corner of Central Avenue and 9th street, one block north and east of my house, was Dixon's Store whose limited food stock took care of emergencies and kept the neighborhood children supplied with penny candy.

One of the most notable aspects of community organization from my childhood was the fact that we walked; we walked to Upp's Market, we walked to church (eight blocks), I walked to school until I was forced to take the bus to high school, as we did to go into town. The bus stop was across the street from Dixon's. We did not own a car.

What did we eat?

My mother baked six loaves of bread once a week. On 'baking day', pies, apple cake and cookies might also appear and for Sunday dinner, a pineapple upside down cake was an infrequent treat. Beyond these, in keeping with neighborhood demographics, the fare was ethnic; in our case, from my mother's tradition, German peasant food—lots of pork, beef, both with gravy, potatoes and root vegetables. She also favored German cabbage stews, sauerkraut and potroast. In the winter, fresh produce was scarce, so we ate a variety of canned vegetables, fruits, some pickles my mother canned and as garnish for my peanut butter sandwiches, chokecherry jelly which my mother canned every fall; enough for most of the year.

Picking chokecherries was an annual late summer event which I often shared with my mother, grandmother and great-aunt Mary when they made the pilgrimage to the banks of Wolf Creek where, for two or three days, they gathered the hard, blood-red, bitter little fruit until many bags were filled and my mother calculated she had enough to keep her mashing and boiling and seeding for a week.

My father worked on the Great Northern Railroad beginning in 1918 when he was sixteen years old and ending when he died in 1963, aged 61; a forty-five year career. For thirty of those years he worked in the freight house loading and unloading all manner of products including food. His first-hand experience, therefore, gave my mother a sense of what was well-packaged and shipped and what was downright unsanitary.

Our meat and poultry came from Montana stockmen who maintained small feed lots and several butchers in Great Falls had their own ranches to stock their independent markets. Chicken came from similar sources (mega chicken ranches were not yet the norm) and was expensive; a Sundays only treat. All of it, of course, traveled from the freight house to Upp's Market to us. For Thanksgiving and Christmas, my father bought our turkey and Christmas goose from the Hutterites who had their community (like those of the Amish) 100 miles north of Great Falls near the town of Havre. The Hutterites liked my Dad and one family in particular appeared each holiday eve at 4 pm and waited for him at the loading dock to hand him a fresh free-range bird. When he got home, my mother critiqued the purchase and then, after supper, I watched as she carefully pulled and singed the remaining pin feathers, filling the kitchen with the unforgettable aroma of burnt flesh and sulphur. Next morning their roasting aroma greeted me and no meals have captured their magic since.

Every summer my mother planted a garden as she had her entire adult life. Her father was an avid gardener who studied the work of Luther Burbank and had a reputation as the most celebrated tomato grower in a neighborhood where backyard gardens were status symbols and horticultural war zones. Indeed, when my mother married and moved away from home (two lots away) and planted her garden, he is reported to have slipped in at dawn one morning to steal her largest heirloom tomato and haul it off to work where he claimed it as his own!

The harvest from our garden when I was growing up was enough to keep us in fresh vegetables well into the fall and canned goods until after Christmas. I loved helping her plant and it was an annual joy for me to pull the first fledgling carrots and munch them, right there in the garden, garnished with more than a little dirt. Each year was sweet as the last with other favorites being kohlrabi, potatoes, beets, sweet corn, cucumber salad (soaked in vinegar with sweet onions) peas, cabbage and rhubarb.

    We did not eat outside family traditions; no Italian, no Polish, no Russian, nor anything highly spiced. Mexican food was unknown to me. Even though some of those groups were citizens of the neighborhood, ethnic boundaries were not crossed at the dinner table and, unfortunately, ethnic slurs abounded when those foods were mentioned with the traditional labels applied; Dago, Wop, Polack. I would have to wait until I arrived at the University in Missoula to move beyond the culinary segregation of the neighborhood and discover the taste of the world.

    In summary, I learned to eat what I ate from my parents and family tradition as did everyone else in the neighborhood. We ate what we ate because that's what "our people" always ate and, outside the diet of "our people" other foods were suspect, although the specificity of that suspicion was never defined.

    The boundaries of ethnicity were real enough but loose and as my parent's generation gave way to their children's "Baby-boomer" generation the lines steadily blurred and at last dissolved into the general culture of the car, the suburb, the supermarket, TV dinners and 'Fast Food'. I remember the confusion and look of horror in my parent's eyes as they viewed the sacrilege of the first "open seven days a week" Albertson's Supermarket on the Westside. And, it is astonishing to me now how rapidly it all changed.

    By the time I entered high school in 1958, Great Falls had its own urban strip, 10th Avenue South; five miles of pavement lined with motels, car dealerships, discount clothing stores, shopping centers with supermarkets, malls and of course, McDonald's and the 15-cent hamburger; sometimes ten for a dollar. When I began my final year at the University of Montana at Missoula in 1966, Noble's Mercantile was closing and Upp's Market was a convenience store like 7-11. Dixon's store was no more and the tiny little neighborhood store on the way to St. Joseph's Church had been replaced with a duplex.

    In the spring of 1968 I was a new homeowner with a family and the stuttering beginnings of an artistic career and I found myself planting my first garden since childhood. I'm not sure what prompted the move: having a house and a yard—a yard which seemed incomplete without a vegetable garden and a deep unconscious awakening to my family history and that Westside neighborhood clotted with backyard gardens; gardens my childhood friends and I would, on certain wild summer nights, plan and execute commando raids upon carrot and radish rows, berry patches and apple trees. The stolen fruit tasted all the sweeter for being stolen and I did, unlike my fellow thieves, eat it. But there was another force which had insinuated itself into my consciousness—the appearance of the first "Whole Earth Catalogue" with 'flower-power', the "Summer of Love" and 'access to tools' sprawling over every page.

    Rejection of the "Establishment" had turned the Berkeley crowd, organized by Stewart Brand, Gary Snyder, and Stephen Gaskin, among a host of others, back to the land. And, by reaching back into farming and rejecting established, industrialized everything, they began the "Organic" movement. The social sickness they perceived, exemplified by University and public school education, corrupt, corporate controlled politics and the 'Immoral Vietnam War', was to be cured by healthy, home-grown food, herbal medicine, 'off-the-grid' housing and energy, poetry, music and communal living.

    One of my responses to it all was to grow vegetables and sell some (beautiful leaf lettuce that made my mother proud) at the first Street Market in Missoula, Montana; a town, which by 1970 was being rapidly invaded by California hippies in pursuit of open space and land for communal living and organic farming. Two natural food restaurants appeared as well as several 'organic food' stores with whole grains and sprouts galore. One in particular, "Freddy's Feed and Read," a book store and organic food co-op was right next door to my house. Freddy's carried all the current "healthy" food products, cookbooks and shelves full of Marxist, Maoist, Whole Earth literature as seen in the Catalogue along with visionaries like Buckminster Fuller, E.F. Schumacher, Fukuoka and Gregory Bateson whose books soon found home in my library. Of course, the latest issues of the 'Whole Earth Catalogue' were there and gone in minutes.

Freddy's soon became a neighborhood meeting place, occasional music performance venue, poetry reading theater and informal discussion room where food and the politics of food were among the hot topics. Given the store's proximity to the University of Montana campus (one block away) participants in all activities were never in short supply. And, I was a participant as well, wasting many an afternoon in hot debate with my Maoist friends over their hopes for a communist resurgence in America. When I left Missoula and Montana in 1977, Freddy's was still going strong.

Two years previous to my exodus to Seattle, I had flirted with actually buying a farm, had one selected and even put earnest money down. Fortunately or not, the deal fell through and, in part, pushed my deeper need for a more expansive space for my career into being. In the ensuing decades, my gardening was sporadic and eventually non-existent. Cooking, and cooking with natural ingredients became a new passion but even there, I was hardly the purist who had been an early organic avatar (of sorts) in Missoula. Nonetheless, healthy food, farming and all the attendant social issues remained at the periphery of consciousness and when my wife and I finally moved from Seattle to Carnation in 2004, with the purchase of one-half acre of land and questionable buildings, the garden returned and, somehow, with it my reintroduction to the organic, agrarian resurgence in the Snoqualmie Valley and now—this book.

....

I began this personal history of eating with the hope of discovering why I eat what I eat and, perhaps in turn, discover hints as to the answer for all of us. Clearly, the answer(s) is (are) complex and hardly what most people would guess.

Food choices, good or bad, seem to bear little relation to 'free will'; choice in the end, really not choosing. As my personal history demonstrated for me, my parents and our community told me what to eat, what was good, healthy and socially acceptable. And with those messages came the equally profound and unconscious messages about what "not" to eat. These were entirely about social distinction, ethnicity, religion and race. The health of Chinese or Italian food was suspect, not by way of direct experience (apart from anecdotes about gastric distress from spicy Italian food or the claim that Chinese food doesn't fill you up and you're hungry again in an hour) but simply because the food was not "our food", not from "our people". Case in point: as a Catholic, I was denied meat on Friday in remembrance of Christ's suffering on the Cross while those heathen Protestants in the neighborhood had steak. Finally, I would argue that humans, in whatever social arrangement, including an ethnically and racially tolerant one, eat as their particular group dictates; sometimes with difficult or disastrous consequences.

When Lewis and Clark arrived at Ft. Clatsop on the Oregon coast after their long river trek in search of a NW Passage, they faced a food crisis during that long wet coastal winter of 1806; game was scarce and what little they captured was lean, low fat elk and venison. The local natives, the Clatsop, offered quantities of fat, protein rich smoked salmon; food that would have luxuriously sustained them for the winter. To a man, the explorers refused to eat the fish. Their mistrust of the

Clatsop and their view of them as 'uncivilized savages' coupled to the bright red appearance of the smoked fish were barriers they could not cross and it cost them calories and comfort; they were hungry most of the time. Not unlike those Norse colonists who came to Greenland a thousand years before, who also refused, in the face of starvation, the offerings of fresh fish from the Eskimos because they were "Skralings" (inferior beings, not humans). Lewis and Clark were bound by the rubric of behavior dictated by their white, Anglo Saxon Protestant heritage and were willing to starve rather than eat the food of the "other".

In America in the year 2010, ethnic tradition as a primary driver for social choice has all but disappeared. In its place we have Political Correctness and legally enforced 'tolerance' for all the "others"; racial, ethnic and socio/sexual and, the resultant heresy and stigma of reverting to traditional stereotype. Overarching these, however, we have Advertising coupled with the American Medical Association and its battery of scientific tests and data, psychological and physical, all aimed at defining and protecting our "health"; nutrition is an ever shifting rubric within the fabric as it struggles for primacy as a cause of all our ills. Our food 'choice' now is based on what science tells us is 'good' and what advertisers want to sell us as being scientifically essential for a good, healthy diet. The food industry is the prime mover in this equation and is, like all corporate structures, driven by the bottom line and consumer wants and needs (which the industry created), i.e., convenience, and affordability with maximum profit.

My personal eating history, in its own peculiar way, is a chronicle of that cultural shift. My childhood and coming of age witnessed the rapid change from home-made, home-cooked, locally produced food products and family dinners to factory processed and produced food/dinner products sourced from factory farms to be consumed at the convenience of individuals; the family sit down evening meal is an anomalous rather than a normal experience. The bulk of the current population has become a non-organization of individual consumers who buy and consume in relative isolation. Around them are a smaller percentage of purposefully organized subgroups whose various ideological credos attempt to 're-traditionalize' food consumption as communal experience with 'healthy', unprocessed, 'natural/organic', non-factory produced food products as the emblems of well-being, environmental conscience, and political correctness.

Surrounding us all are the urban poor, living at the margins in vast urban deserts where fast food restaurants and small convenience stores are often the only sources of food. Their "choices" are really only one choice—processed food. Beyond choosing between a 'Happy Meal' or the McNugget Combo, the "Omnivore's Dilemma" does not exist for the urban poor.

I would argue, finally, that "choosing" for humans is less free than we pretend. As I've tried to sketch here, our choices are determined by our economic status and the various judgments of our peers, our families and our ethnic heritage, religious traditions, scientific and socio/political authorities. Our innate prefference for fat and sweet foods (perhaps salty) and the elemental demands of metabolism notwithstanding, each of us looks to the behaviors of others before we look to ourselves when we choose what to eat. The success of the advertising industry depends on social proof. Being in the 'right' club is more potent than being "right" and alone in your choice. As the old adage states; "standing up when others sit" remains our greatest challenge. "Health" is rarely the root cause and, ironically, one needs to be in reasonably good health to even consider the problem at all. A starving person in Bangladesh does not care if his food is "organic" or not. As one of my humanities teachers in college declared, "It's damned hard to think on an empty stomach." With that caveat, the peculiar, if not absurd, irony is that we in America, awash as we are in an abundance of inexpensive food, cannot decide what we should safely eat and books like "The Omnivore's Dilemma" are 'Best Sellers.'

....

As I hope my personal eating history has shown, I have been not that much different from my peers in my multifaceted dilemma about food and what to eat. Producing this book has, however, given me something I did not have when I began. And that 'something' has to do with the political epiphany I noted in the preface to this personal history. Indeed, it has been sharpened over the course of tracing my dietary chronicle here.

To reiterate, I have come to understand that no matter what I choose to put in my mouth at dinner tonight, that gesture, eating that particular food, is a political act. By eating this potato or this chicken breast, beef steak, fish or bread I have allied myself with a whole network of people whose livelihood depends on food production—a specific type of food production. And, for each item on my plate, there are hundreds of lives involved in the existence of that bit of protein or vegetable matter. More importantly, if I proceed as I have throughout my eating history, I will take that food and never know a single one of those people.

I don't know them and would have to travel many miles to find them. But I do know where they work if they are in the current dominant meat processing/packing industry. There are forty such plants in Washington State alone. I also know where the animals are raised but again would need to travel a great distance; feed lots in eastern Washington or in states farther east all the way to the mid-west. Indeed, all the meat and poultry I've purchased from the major supermarket chains comes from factory farms.

In each of these food factories, thousands of animals are confined in small spaces, wallow in their own excrement, are fed a variety of antibiotics and growth hormones and feed which is not their natural diet. Cattle are fed corn for 120 days which fattens them to the desired weight and will also kill them if they eat it longer than that. Cows are ruminators—grass is their diet. After those 120 days, they go to the packers where the assembly-line process kills and butchers 400 cows per hour (some places more).

The people who work in the packing plants are 90% migrant workers (most illegal) the remaining 10% of the staff are Anglo managers. On average, the workers earn less than minimum wage and suffer on-the-job health and personal injury risks like no other workers in America. Most of them are illiterate and do not speak English. One in three of them is injured or killed on the job; wielding sharp knives making the same cuts all day with the line moving at speeds with which they can barely keep pace. Most will be forced out within a year due to injuries. If you are injured, your limited insurance can take months to respond to your claim. If your injuries prevent work, you lose your job. There are no unions.

I know these things only from reading. I have never been to a meat packing facility and, from what I've read, it would be difficult if not impossible to get an unguarded tour. So, no, I don't know what those workers' lives are like—I can only guess. I know also from reading that feed lot operators and poultry ranchers are subject to the mandates and demands of the packers who buy their meat and birds. If they fail to comply, the packers go elsewhere to buy. Free range chicken and grass fed beef are out of the question. If they want to stay in business, they do what they're told. I can also only imagine what their lives are like.

None of these scenarios are anything I would tolerate; at least I think so, from my position of "full stomach" and social status which puts me at an enormous distance from those whose economic situation is so desperate that they must risk losing limbs and/or their lives to earn enough in a strange country to feed their families; knowing, that even this much, with all the risk, is more than they can hope to make at home in Mexico or Central America.

This is vicarious knowledge for me and most of us. We have to think hard as we stroll through the aisles at Safeway to get any sense of those sources from the beautifully packaged mountains of food that invite us at every turn. There is no stink from the packing plant, no fetid excremental tang in the air as we pass the meat counter, no blood, no scarred workers, many without fingers struggling against the relentless procession of carcasses and body parts, no walking through a chicken farm with thousands of birds, ankle deep in chicken shit, stepping on rotting carcasses to find that nice plump roaster for Sunday dinner.

It is hard to imagine and for most of us, somehow irrelevant. The overwhelming convenience of the supermarket and our complete acculturation into the system over the last 50 years has made even amnesia as an excuse irrelevant. One cannot long for that which does not exist in memory at all and you cannot know what you've never known. Most of our children believe food comes from the store, wrapped in plastic and bought, as mom says, at bargain prices. Most have never seen a chicken or a cow. Most of us, like them, have never tasted a fresh egg.

But for me now, after two years on this project, sharing the lives and eating the meat and produce from these Snoqualmie Valley farmers, knowing where my food comes from and, most of all, who grew it, has become a behavioral imperative and, therefore, a real choice. I not only can but must choose what I eat. Now, when I sit down to eat my evening meal, I am given more than flavor and nutrition. I know with each morsel I chew that Scott and Amy Turner raised this cow on the grass in their field, that this cow had a stress free existence (I saw Scott scratch her forehead like a puppy) and that Scott and Amy suffered the remorse of killing her even though the "kill" was correctly and humanely done. When I chew the meat, I know that I metaphorically consume a profound aspect of the Turner's lives, their celebration of life and living things and their ultimate respect for the animal they've chosen to sacrifice for my well-being. They are willing to make that sacrifice and endure its consequences knowing it is an absolute necessity for living. We all live at the expense of someone or something other than ourselves. Each of us—no matter how isolated we become from the reality of existence and death will ultimately have to make that sacrifice. As my railroad-man father told me as I was about to leave home for college, "There is a price for everything and you will pay it—especially for the good things."

Scott and Amy Turner are real people; actual living persons who have made enormous sacrifices to keep their commitment to farming. Every time I eat the food they produce, I see their faces, I hear their voices, I smell the air and feel the atmosphere at Blue Dog Farm. Each morning I place a cup of their blueberries atop my granola and taste again the earth, the distinctive flavor their soil has given those berries; a flavor not to be found anywhere else on earth.

And so it is with each of the farmers I've presented in this book. Each one now gives me food and with it come those deep connections to their lives and the soil: Luke, Sarah, Adam, Erick, Wendy, Jason, Siri, Dan, Dave, Laura, Michaele, Susan, George, Lena, Claire—all of them now part and parcel of my existence. I know now that I will never live in any other way. I will not eat without my farmers' work gracing my table. To do otherwise would be an act of betrayal whose price I cannot afford to pay.

And yet, there remains a consequence even for the decision to look to my local farmers. Those immigrant workers are still there, trapped in the employ of meat packers, large scale vegetable farmers, and chicken processors. My loyalty to "my farmers" serves them and me well but what of those factory workers I still cannot see? Unless the source of their assembly-line nightmare is fundamentally changed, those unknown workers, trapped by ignorance and poverty, will remain where they are. My turning away from the food they produce will scarcely be noticed. And, despite my choice, indeed, as consequence of that choice, I remain connected to them. They live in my state. They are my neighbors. Therefore, I still live at their expense. I still buy some vegetable products from supermarkets and many other food products derivative of meat byproducts as well as eat at restaurants whose food sources are unknown even to them (although each day I get closer to being completely local) and, politically, I do little to relieve their plight. The powerlessness I feel with that realization is but marginally abated by what I've discovered and the personal changes I've made over the course of producing this book.

However, I am not alone in my attempt; others have chosen the alternative and more do so every day. It is my hope, therefore, that this book and the voices presented here will contribute to that momentum. There is a number, unknown to me, whose arrival will deny the profitability of Tyson Meats and all the rest; i.e. the number of consumers who turn to local sources for food. Tyson is not, after all, in the business of fair labor practice or healthy food production despite their claims to the contrary. They are in the business of making ever increasing profit margins at ever diminishing costs to the Company. At some point, if enough consumers abdicate, they will be forced to change or go out of business. And with their demise, my deepest hope cries out, so also will die the mythology that we cannot feed our hungry planet with any method other than factory farming guided by corporate oligarchy. The farmers in this book, through their behavior, their service to the soil, and their products prove otherwise.

May they be heard!

Hunger's Timeline

- 1974—500 million hungry people in the developing world. The World Food Conference pledges to eradicate child hunger in 10 years.

- 1996—830 million hungry people. The World Food Summit pledges to reduce the number of hungry people by half by 2015.

  —12% of the U.S. population is hungry. U.S. Farm Bill increases food nutrition programs (Food Stamps, Women, Infants and Children in Need) and food banks augment donations of government surplus with locally and industry donated food.

- 2000 Millennium Summit—World Leaders pledge to reduce extreme poverty and hunger by half by 2015.

- 2002—850 million hungry people. The World Food Summit + 5 admits to poor progress on the Millennium Development Goals.

- 2009—1 billion hungry people. The FAO High-Level Conference on World Food Security announces that instead of reducing the ranks of the hungry to 400 million, hunger has increased. The World Bank recalculates its projections for extreme poverty upwards from 1 billion to 1.4 billion. Over 3 billion people live on about $2—$5 a day. (These projections were made before the financial crisis engulfed the world, driving down income and ushering in the global recession.)

  —12% of the U.S. population is still hungry. Despite $60 billion yearly in government food nutrition programs and the explosion of over 50,000 food banks and food pantries across the nation, one in six children in the U.S. go hungry each month and 35 million people cannot ensure minimum daily caloric requirements.

The Monopolies Controlling our Food Systems

- 83.5% of all of the beef packing in the United States is in the hands of four firms: Tyson, Cargill, Swift & Co., and National Beef Packing Co.

- Five firms (Wal-Mart, Kroger, Albertson's, Safeway and Ahold) control 48% of U.S. food retailing.

- Smithfield, Tyson, Swift & Co., and Cargill pack 66% of all pork in the U.S.

- 71% of all soybean crushing is done by three firms—ADM, Bunge, and Cargill.

- Just two firms, DuPont and Monsanto, control nearly 60% of the United States corn seed market.

- Monsanto and DuPont together control 65% of the maize seed market and 44% of the soy market.

Free market dogma states that market competition will lead to overall efficiency and therefore lower prices for consumers. In fact, what the numbers indicate is that the increase in market concentration has led to extreme volatility. Unless we want the world food system to end up like the world financial system, these monopolies must be dismantled.

Eric Holt-Gimenez and Raj Patel, "Food Rebellions—Crisis and the Hunger for Justice", 2009

Farm Journal

26 January 2010

Michaele Blakely just left my studio—good portrait session—excellent interview. And, as it so often happens, she said something valuable which didn't get recorded. We were talking about change and how to best implement the kind of change in consciousness we both see as necessary if small farms are going to have a future and, indeed, if we as humans are going to have a future worth occupying. Then she told this story which I begged for permission to use; I know I can't give it her poetry but I can't not include it in whatever it is that my imagined book will be.

When Mt. St. Helen's erupted in May of 1980, Michaele was living in Portland, Oregon in a predominately African-American neighborhood; in fact, she was the only white woman on the block. It had been somewhat difficult living in that neighborhood and she hadn't yet really felt welcome. She remembered the unbelievable stillness after the blast and the eerie midday darkness. After spending three days indoors waiting for the air to clear of ash, she couldn't bear confinement anymore and went outside.

She entered a world completely gray; gray street, gray trees, gray cars, gray houses. The streets were empty. Her house, once brightly painted, looked sad and drab. She couldn't bear to look at it or her yard. She went to the side of the house, got the hose and began to wash the blanket of ash off the sidewalk. It looked so much better. She decided to hose off the shrubs and the car. And then she washed the façade of her house; and then the rest of the front walk to the edges of her property lines, and the street.

The next day, she went out again and saw her neighbor across the street washing her house and yard. Soon, others joined in and more and more until the entire neighborhood was washed clean. A few days later, after people on the streets all around hers had begun to wash their homes, newspaper reporters and photographers and the Television News cameras and reporters showed up and took interviews; they made the evening news and the Sunday paper.

When neighborhood clean-up gained momentum and spread through the city, Michaele told her husband government was going to get into it and it wouldn't be good. Sure enough, new ordinances were adopted with restrictions on ash disposal and dispersal complete with a permit process and fees. Even so, Michaele found herself with new friends in the neighborhood and the general acceptance she'd not had before.

I told her one of my favorite edicts from a psychiatrist friend: "Most people want a change but to get it they need to have a task; just one—one that they can accomplish." The world needs a house-cleaning; politics and doomsday notwithstanding, change may, in the end, only happen one sidewalk at a time.

Flood 2009—view north, toward Duvall, WA from bridge at Novelty Hill

The Snoqualmie Valley Preservation Alliance (SVPA) filed a federal court lawsuit against the U.S. Army Corps of Engineers (Corps) to challenge the Corps' decision approving Puget Sound Energy's (PSE) renovations of the Snoqualmie Falls Hydroelectric Project. The approved work includes lowering the diversion dam and widening the river. The lawsuit was filed in July 2010 against the Corps, and PSE joined the lawsuit on the side of the Corps in August 2010.

The SVPA is a nonprofit organization committed to the safety of residents and businesses impacted by flooding and to the preservation of rural life in the Snoqualmie River Valley. The SVPA members represent farming, recreation, business and citizens living within the Snoqualmie Valley.

The SPVA lawsuit challenges permit authorization by the U.S. Army Corps of Engineers for the PSE Snoqualmie Falls Hydroelectric Plant upgrades project. In authorizing the PSE project the Corps did not take into account the cumulative impact of the project downstream from the Snoqualmie Falls.

Since 2000, major upstream projects with downstream flood impact have included the Snoqualmie "205 Project" completed in 2005 (a $4.6 milllion flood reduction project for the City of Snoqualmie) **Author's note: The City of Snoqualmie is located above the Falls and the town of Fall City, see map.**

The 205 Project widened the Snoqualmie River above the Snoqualmie Falls with the removal of about 50,000 cubic yards of dirt and rock from the right and left riverbanks. The Corps estimated minimal impact downstream based on studies done during the 1980s and 1990s.

Three of the largest floods on record in the lower valley have been in the last four years (as of July, 2010). The fourth was the 1990 flood. The 2006 and 2009 floods both set new records. **Author's note: On March 31, 2011, the court ruled in favor of the Army Corps of Engineers. SVPA will regroup and appeal.**

> Since the first womb spat forth a baby's corpse,
> The mother's cry has fumed about the winds;
> O tidal winds, cast up her cry for me
> That I may drown, let loose her flood of tears.
>
> It was a haggard night the first flesh died,
> And shafted hawks came snarling down the sky;
> A mouse it was played with an ivory tooth,
> And ravens fed confection to their young.
>
> Palm of the earth, O sprinkle on my head
> That dust you hold, O strew that little left;
> Let what remains of that first miracle
> Be sour in my hair. That I may learn
> The mortal miracle, let that first dust
> Tell me of him who feeds the raging birds.
>   Dylan Thomas, "The Woman Speaks"

> I read somewhere of a shepherd who, when asked why he made, from within fairy rings, ritual observances to the moon to protect his flocks, replied: 'I'd be a damn' fool if I didn't!' These poems, with all their crudities, doubts, and confusions, are written for the love of Man and in praise of God, and I'd be a damn' fool if they weren't.
>   Dylan Thomas, prefatory note to his "Collected Poems", 1953

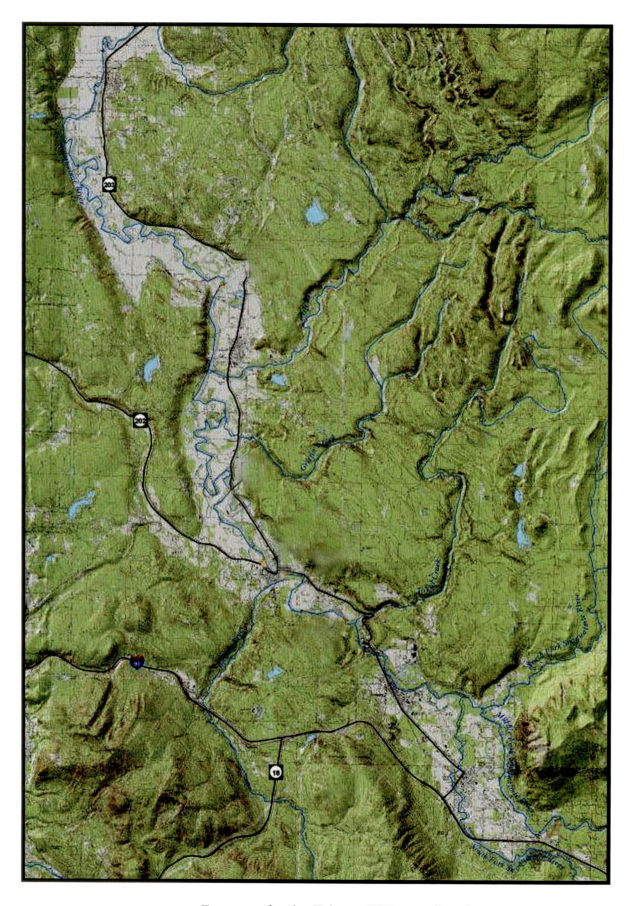

Snoqualmie River Watershed

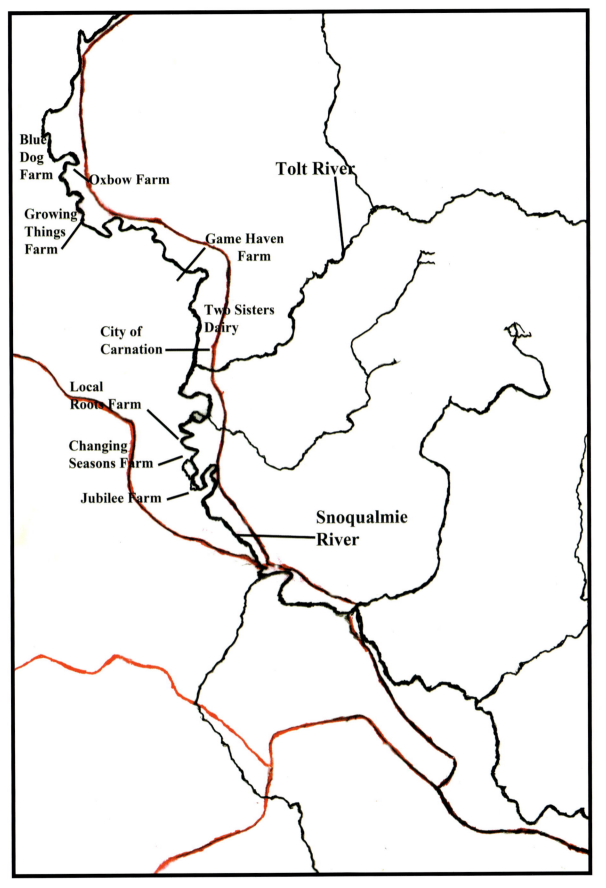

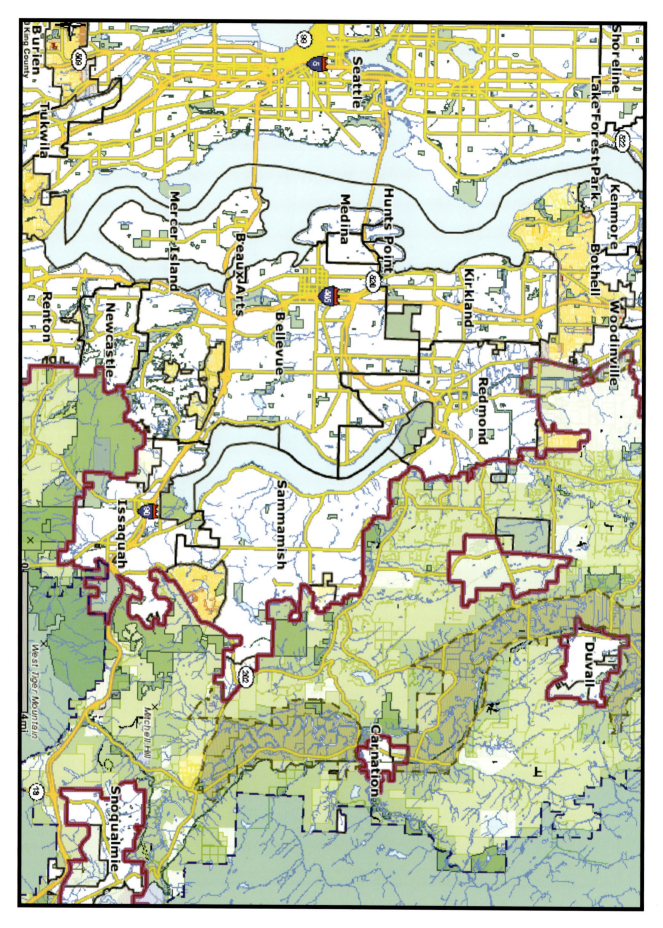

Greater Seattle Area & Snoqualmie River Watershed

Bibliography

This list contains the books I read during my work on this project including those quoted in the text. I found some via the bibliographies they contain and others at the suggestion of my literate farmers; their favorites, often. The classic literary and poetry sources are from my personal library. This list is by no means comprehensive and I suggest the reader take these and follow where their inclinations lead. The growth in interest in organic farming, land reform and food is producing a wealth of good scholarship and writing on issues that will determine our future in the 21st Century.

Ausubel, Kenny, "Seeds of Change," 1994, Harper Collins Publishers.
Berry, Wendell, "The Unsettling of America," 1977, Sierra Club Books.
Bowden, Charles, "Blood Orchid—An Unnatural History of America," 2002, North Point Press.
Brown, Lester, "Plan B-4.0," 2009, W.W. Norton & Company.
Carson, Ann, "Nox", New Directions Publishing Corporation, NY, NY, 2010
Cummings, E.E., "The Complete Poems: 1904–1962", George J. Firmage, ed., Liveright Publishing Corporation, 1991.
Cummings, E.E., "i—six nonlectures", Harvard University Press, 1953.
Daly, Herman E., "Beyond Growth," 1996, Beacon Press.
Faris, Stephan, "Forecast," 2009, Henry Holt and Company.
Fukuoka, Masanobu, "The One Straw Revolution," 1978, Rodale Press.
Georgescu-Roegen, Nicholas, "The Entropy Law and the Economic Process," 1971, 1999, Harvard University Press.
Gore, Al, "Our Choice," 2009, Rodale, Inc.
Heinberg, Richard, "Fifty Million Farmers," 2006, E.F. Schumacher Society.
Heinberg, Richard, "The Party's Over," 2003, New Society Publishers.
Holt-Gimenez, Eric and Patel, Raj, "Food Rebellions!—Crisis and the Hunger for Justice," 2009, First Food Books and Grassroots International.
Jackson, Tim, "Prosperity Without Growth—Economics for a Finite Planet," 2010, Earthscan.
Klett, Manfred, "Principles of Biodynamic Spray and Compost Preparations," 2009, Floris Books.
Korten, David C., "When Corporations Rule The World," 2001, Kumarian Press, Inc.
Montgomery, David R., "Dirt—The Erosion of Civilizations," 2007, University of California Press, Berkeley and Los Angeles.
Montgomery, David R., Bolton, Susan, Booth, Derek B. and Wall, Leslie, editors, "Restoration of Puget Sound Rivers," 2008, University of Washington Press.
Patel, Raj, "Stuffed and Starved," May, 2009, Melville House Publishing.
Pollan, Michael, "The Omnivore's Dilemma," 2006, The Penguin Press.
Rosset, Peter, Patel, Raj, and Courville, Michael, editors, "Promised Land—Competing Visions of Agrarian Reform," 2006, First Food Books.
Schlosser, Eric, "Fast Food Nation," 2001, Houghton Mifflin Company.
Steiner, Rudolf, "Agriculture Course—1924," 2004, Rudolf Steiner Press.
Thomas, Dylan, "The Collected Poems", New Directions Publishing Corporation, NY, NY, 1952.
Thomas, Dylan, "The Poems of Dylan Thomas", New Directions Publishing Corporation, NY, NY, 1953.
Wirzba, Norman, editor, "The Essential Agrarian Reader," 2003, University Press of Kentucky.
Yeats, W.B., "The Collected Poems", Richard J. Finneran, ed., Scribner Paperback Poetry, Simon & Schuster, Inc., NY, NY, 1996.

Sno-Valley Tilth Member Growers—Carnation, Washington

Blue Dog Farm
425-844-2842
www.bluedogfarm.com

Carnation Tree Farm
425-333-4510
www.carnationtreefarm.com

Changing Seasons Farm
425-333-4199

Dog Mountain Farm
425-333-0833
www.dogmountainfarm.com

Full Circle Farm
425-333-4677
www.fullcirclefarm.com

Game Haven Farm
425-333-4313

Growing Things Farm
425-788-0480
www.growingthingsfarm.com

Jubilee Biodynamic Farm
425-222-4558
www.jubileefarm.org

Local Roots Farm
206-679-9512
www.localrootsfarm.com

Marigold and Mint
206-419-1222
www.marigoldandmint.com

Misty Mountain Honey
425-333-6439

Oxbow Learning Center & Organic Farm
425-788-1134
www.oxbowfarm.org

Summer-Run Farm
www.farmgirlcsa.com

Tolt River Farm
425-333-6886
www.toltriverfarm.com

Washington Tilth Association Chapters

Everett Tilth
PO Box 1401
Everett, WA 98206
www.tiltheverett.org

Seattle Tilth Association
4649 Sunnyside Ave N
Seattle, WA 98103
206-633-0451
www.seattletilth.org

South Whidbey Tilth Assn.
2812 Thompson Road (office)
PO Box 252
Langley, WA 98160
www.southwhidbeytilth.org

Sno-Valley Tilth
PO Box 48
Carnation, WA 98014-0048
www.snovalleytilth.org

Spokane Tilth
W. 35 Main
Spokane, WA 99210
office@spokanetilth.org

Tilth on the Willapa
PO Box 41
Nacotta, WA 98637

Tilth Producers of Washington
PO Box 85056
Seattle, WA 98145
www.tilthproducers.org

Vashon Island Growers Assn. (VIGA)
PO Box 2894
Vashon, WA 98070
sfjunebug@Yahoo.com

Washington State Farmers Market Association
c/o Cascade Harvest Coalition 4649
Sunnyside Avenue North, Room 123
Seattle, WA 98103
425-610-9487
info@wafarmersmarkets.com

Postscript
Sunset in the Garden

Farm Journal—April 12, 2011

    Three floods this winter; the last at the end of March; none were catastrophic; each was five feet above flood stage, enough to make all the farms into lakes. The last one took a chunk of Jubilee Farm in its wake. Many farms had seed in the ground, some had starts; all gone. Erick says he won't break ground 'til after April 1 from now on; that means no more spring crops; fall crops are pretty much a hopeless proposition anymore; the rains come too early. To top it all off, the court ruled in favor of the Army Corps of Engineers in the suit brought by the SVPA (see p. 341 above) to curtail their amendments to Snoqualmie Falls and force impact studies. Clearly, the Valley as an agricultural asset is not within land use consideration for the County; the developers hold sway. Erick and the others wonder how long they can continue within longer rainy seasons and more frequent, destructive floods. Without significant change, farming in the Valley might well be history within five to ten years. At the present general level of informed awareness about food sources, it is doubtful the farmers and their farms will be remembered; their idyllic stories recorded in this book might survive in a library or two but beyond that, they won't be missed. In twenty years, they might well be just another Heritage Artifact struggling for survival in a Historical Museum.

    Uranium-235 has a half-life of 704 million years; Strontium-90 (a product of nuclear fission), 28 years. One wonders what the half-life of ignorance is. In the case of Galileo, 326 years and depleted; for Darwin it is 150 years and counting (Darwin still losing to the Bible).

    On the Galapagos Islands, Darwin's famous finches love the pollen which collects in the cup at the base of the pistil inside the cactus flower. It is a significant food source, often the only one. It also presents an access problem. The flower's stigmas (surrounding the pistil) are 25 millimeters long whereas the distance from the tip of the finch's beak to its eye is 21 millimeters. Without intervention, the stigma will poke the finch in the eye when it tries to get pollen. The flowers typically open between 9 and 11 am. Then the finch comes and carefully holds the stigma aside with its foot while it has breakfast. However, some finches arrive early, before dawn when the cactus flowers are folded shut. These early birds pry open the petals and attempt feeding before anyone else gets there. The stigmas invariably poke them in the eye. The greedy finches snip the stigmas, feed, and thereby beat their competitors in the game of survival. They also render their food source impotent, like the farmer who eats his seed potatoes. On average, this presents only a small problem since cheaters are few in number. However, if there are more than two seasons of severe draught on the Galapagos, the effects from cheaters would increase as flowers failed to reproduce putting the entire finch population at risk; three or more years would render them extinct. The stigma snippers would, in effect, have promoted species collapse to get just a little more pollen than their fellows can get. Further, the snippers pay no immediate cost for cheating and so Darwin's process of selection (which favors individual success) actually supports the behavior. Generally, in Natural Selection what's good for the individual is good for the group. But when the good of the individual clashes with the good of the group it is still the individual who profits even if it brings the downfall of the entire species. The cactus finches could easily cheat themselves off the planet.

    As my still hopeful book goes to press, the struggle in the Snoqualmie Watershed between individual "rights" (property and commercial) and the "common good" remains. It is, as it always has been, a Faustian bargain for all parties concerned.

Addendum

Time passes, things change and true to the adage, so do they go in the Valley. As this book goes to press, Jason, Siri and Dan have decided to end their partnership. Local Roots will now be the sole operation of Jason Salvo and Siri Erickson-Brown (and, although he doesn't know it yet, their newly arrived farming partner, son Felix). Jason and Siri are purchasing 40 acres north of Carnation near the Novelty Hill bridge; the dream of owning a farm coming true sooner than they imagined. Dan Beyers will continue to pursue his farming vision on his land at the former Local Roots location.

Jerry Mader has been a professional artist working as a classical musician/composer, writer and photographer since 1967. He studied music, music composition, humanities and philosophy at the University of Montana from 1962-1967. His principal music composition teacher was Eugene Weigel. From 1969 to 1971 he studied photography with Lee Nye at the University of Montana, Missoula. In 1976 he studied with the American composer, Michael Colgrass (Pulitzer Prize—1978). In 1983 he received a Bachelor of Arts Degree in General Studies from Antioch University.

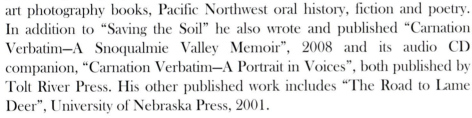

He moved to the Seattle area in 1978 where he pursued his musical career, receiving commissions from the NW Chamber Orchestra, the Cascade Symphony and the Musica Viva Chamber Players. He taught music composition and theory at the Cornish School for the Arts and Music and Humanities at the Northwest School in Seattle. His photographs have been exhibited throughout the NW, recently at the Richard Hugo House, Seattle—a combined reading/photography exhibit of "The Road to Lame Deer", 2006.

In 2007 he founded Tolt River Press, a publishing company dedicated to publishing fine-art photography books, Pacific Northwest oral history, fiction and poetry. In addition to "Saving the Soil" he also wrote and published "Carnation Verbatim—A Snoqualmie Valley Memoir", 2008 and its audio CD companion, "Carnation Verbatim—A Portrait in Voices", both published by Tolt River Press. His other published work includes "The Road to Lame Deer", University of Nebraska Press, 2001.

Jerry Mader currently lives in Carnation, WA where he continues to write, compose music, make photographs and design books.

More copies of "Saving the Soil" can be purchased directly from Tolt River Press at: www.toltriverpress.com or by writing to:
Tolt River Press,
PO Box 1075, Carnation, WA 98014
Email: maderphoto@msn.com